Change!

COMBINING
ANALYTIC APPROACHES
WITH STREET WISDOM

Change!

COMBINING
ANALYTIC APPROACHES
WITH STREET WISDOM

edited by
Gabriele Bammer

Australian
National
University

PRESS

Published by ANU Press
The Australian National University
Acton ACT 2601, Australia
Email: anupress@anu.edu.au
This title is also available online at http://press.anu.edu.au

---

National Library of Australia Cataloguing-in-Publication entry

Title: Change! : Combining analytic approaches with street wisdom
                 / Gabriele Bammer.

ISBN: 9781925022643 (paperback) 9781925022650 (ebook)

Subjects: Change.
                 Social change.
                 Change (Psychology).

Other Creators/Contributors:
                 Bammer, Gabriele, editor.

Dewey Number: 303.4

Cover design and layout by ANU Press

Contents

Part 3 Synthesis

For Warren Bond, and Norbert and Maria Bammer

Acknowledgements

The change project was supported and funded by the Australian Research Council Centre of Excellence in Policing and Security. It was one of the contributions of the Integration and Implementation program, led by Gabriele Bammer.

Particular thanks also go to:

- Bernadette Hince, who copyedited all of the chapters.
- Jessica Ford who helped organise the symposium and Peter Deane who oversaw the audiotaping of the proceedings.
- Alison Ritter, Peter Deane and Caryn Anderson, who informed the shape of this project through a series of discussions in 2008–9.
- Lorena Kanellopoulos, Emily Tinker, Eleanor Garran and Teresa Prowse (cover design) from ANU Press.

The symposium participants.

Front row (left to right): Jim Butler, Christine Nixon, Gabriele Bammer, Kate Carnell, Beverley Raphael. Middle row (left to right): Sarah Pearson, Simon Chapman, Mark Stafford Smith, Robyn Gillies, Bernadette Hince, Lindell Bromham, Ian MacLeod. Back row (left to right): Michael Wesley, John Reid, Grant Wardlaw, Craig Browne, Paul Griffiths, Peter McDonald. Missing: Dee Madigan, Francesca Merlan.

Source: Stuart Hay, 2013.

Change!

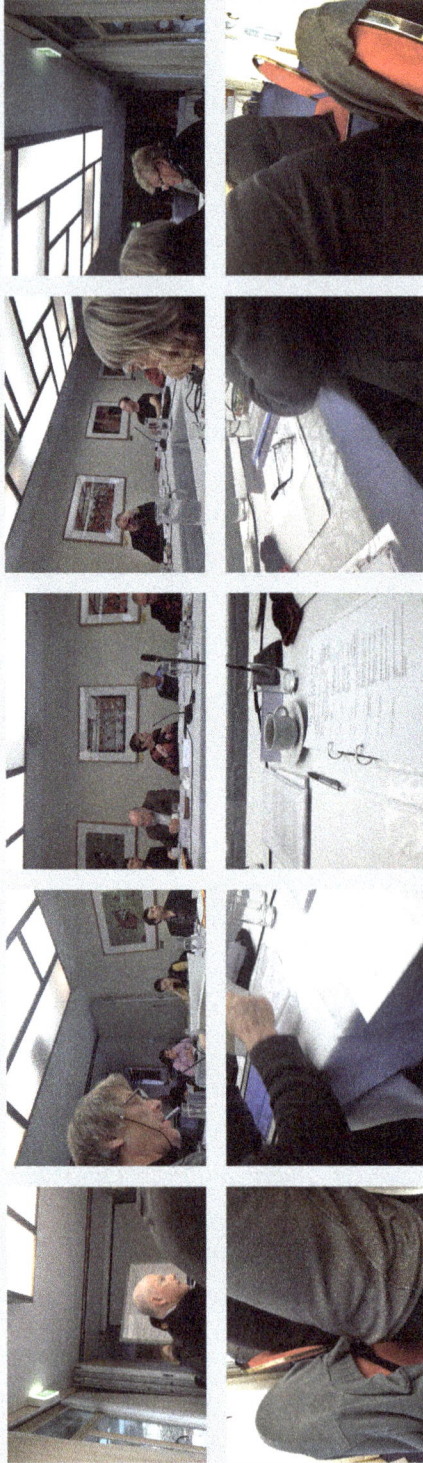

The change symposium.
Source: John Reid, 2013.

Part 1
Introduction

1. An Approach to Understanding Change

Gabriele Bammer

Change happens all the time, so why is driving particular change generally so hard? Why are the outcomes often unpredictable? Are some types of change easier to achieve than others? Are some techniques for achieving change more effective than others? How can change that is already in train be stopped or deflected?

Knowledge about change is fragmented and there is nowhere in the academic or practice worlds that provides comprehensive answers to these and other questions. Every discipline and practice area has only a partial view and there is not even a map of those different perspectives. Further, it is no one's business to pull together the range of diverse understandings. Until now, no organised area of enquiry has set itself the task of developing a comprehensive approach to change.

The purpose of this book is to begin that task by gathering a variety of viewpoints from the academic and practice worlds. Eighteen perspectives are presented here to demonstrate that developing a better understanding of change, and more effective approaches to dealing with it, requires grappling with the complexity of change. Contributors have expertise in advertising, anthropology, art, demography, economics, education, evolutionary biology, global environmental change, industrial innovation, international relations, materials conservation, media advocacy, organisational change, philosophy, politics, psychiatry, security-based intelligence and sociology. (Of course there are many more viewpoints on change that are relevant—child development, ageing, neuroscience, history, psychology, chemistry, defence, international development, to mention just a few.)

The approach used in this book is multidisciplinary. Every contributor tackled the topic of change as they saw fit. There was no attempt to start with a shared framework or a common specific aspect of change. A multidisciplinary approach allows the richness of different perspectives to be demonstrated. The challenge comes in developing syntheses from the contributions, as it is not certain what the points of intersection will be, or even if there will be any. A multidisciplinary approach is therefore most useful when it is not clear what the focus of a project should be or when fresh thinking on a topic is required.

A case study of multidisciplinary synthesis is presented as the concluding chapter to the book. It explores how research impact can be improved by better understanding change, using the perspectives in the book to provide fresh thinking. In that chapter the challenges of synthesising multidisciplinary contributions are also discussed in more detail.

The remainder of this chapter describes the process used to produce the book, particularly the criteria for choosing participants and how they were invited to interact. The organisation of the chapters is also presented, along with a summary of each.

The 'intelligent lay reader' is the target audience. You do not need specialist knowledge, but you may need to look up specific terms or allusions to particular events. Rather than try to clarify everything that may not be widely understood, the aim has been to a) add enough identifying material to make such terms easily searchable and b) make sure that important meaning is not lost if such terms are skipped over. The book is deliberately not uniformly easy to read—some of the ideas are simply harder to grapple with than others. But all the chapters are worth the effort.

How contributors were chosen

I chose the contributors using the following criteria:

- final number of around 20
- diverse range of areas, but attention to policing and security
- covering both the academic and practice worlds
- as far as possible did not know each other or at least did not know each other well
- senior
- had not participated in a similar previous project (on multidisciplinary approaches to uncertainty)
- gender balance
- resident in Australia.

Twenty is a manageable number of contributors in several respects. It allows for a diversity of perspectives and a few drop-outs do not have a major impact (there were two drop-outs in this project, leaving 18 final participants). As described below, contributors were brought together in a two-day symposium and this number gives everyone a reasonable opportunity to speak and to interact.[1] This number provides enough material for a relatively large book. Twenty does place obvious limitations on coverage of the topic, as well as on some aspects of the mix of participants, as will be discussed below. Nevertheless there are still enough contributions to allow a synthesis to be developed.

I chose areas that were as different as possible, rather than ones that were more closely aligned. For example, while there would be valuable perspectives from each of psychology, advertising, counselling, psychiatry, life-coaching and so on, I chose only two of these (advertising and psychiatry), so that other, quite different, perspectives could also be included. Apart from the considerations about policing and security discussed next, the choices were idiosyncratic— what I thought would be relevant and of interest—rather than following some pattern.

I did boost representation from policing and security, inviting contributions from four people in that field—former Victorian police commissioner Christine Nixon, criminologist and intelligence expert Grant Wardlaw, and international relations and security expert Michael Wesley, plus one other who had to drop out. The project was conducted under the auspices of, and funded by, the Australian Research Council Centre of Excellence in Policing and Security,[2] which was keenly interested in research impact. It made sense to draw on policing and security expertise and to compare and contrast that with expertise from other areas.

The decision to cover both the academic and practice worlds—combining 'analytic approaches with street wisdom' (Ravetz 2008, xvi)—was deliberate, as I would argue that both are needed to develop a better appreciation of change. The practitioners were leaders from different walks of life, with considerable experience to contribute. Indeed, some of the participants have held positions in both the academic and practice worlds during their careers.

I tried to go beyond people I knew or even knew of in issuing the invitations. Of the 18 participants, I knew 12 personally. I only knew of one of the other six (Dee Madigan), having seen her on television. Lindell Bromham, Craig Browne, Ian MacLeod and Francesca Merlan were referrals from other people in their fields. Robyn Gillies was found from a search on the internet of the highest ranking education departments in Australian universities. Of course, several other people were approached who were not available or interested. Another determinant of setting the number of participants at 20 was practical—I simply ran out of time to keep approaching potential participants,

---

1   Two of the participants were not able to attend the symposium, but still made written contributions.
2   This Centre of Excellence operated from 2007 to 2014; for more information see www.ceps.edu.au.

especially finding suitable people I did not already know. I also attempted to ensure that the participants did not know each other, or at least did not know each other well. In addition, of those I knew, none were close collaborators of mine. I had not previously worked with eight, I had worked with three others more than 20 years before, and there was only one with whom I had consistently crossed paths for a long time and we had not actually worked together.

The rationale behind this selection process was to give the project freshness and edge. The idea was to invite people who enjoyed being out of their comfort zone, but also to try to ensure that everyone had similar levels of discomfort. I did not want anyone to feel isolated, either because there were cliques of people who knew each other or because there was an overemphasis on particular approaches. Consequently, I also aimed to have clusters of different kinds of participants. This involved ensuring not just that there was a cluster of practitioners, but also that there were academic clusters from science, the social sciences, and humanities and the arts. I wanted coverage of not only policing and security, but also clusters interested in the environment and in health. The clusters are described in Table 1. Finally, exclusion of participants from an earlier and similar project on uncertainty (Bammer and Smithson 2008; Bammer and the Goolabri group 2007) was primarily about ensuring similar levels of discomfort by avoiding the inclusion of participants who had a better idea of what to expect.

A key ingredient, given this mix of participants, was that everyone was senior and expert in their area. This was the foundation for building trust in the group. Trust is often dependent on the fact that participants know each other and have previously worked together successfully, but I had engineered this out as far as possible, so another basis for trust was needed. The process which is described below was designed to allow participants to rapidly figure out that they were in a group who 'knew their stuff' and that they could rely on each other's expertise, even though they could not necessarily judge it themselves. Choosing people who were senior was not just about their higher levels of expertise, but also because they were less likely to feel they were in competition with other participants. Those who are still establishing their careers often feel they have to prove themselves against the others in a project and this can block their ability to take a genuine interest in what the others have to contribute.

I aimed for gender balance in the group, but not for cultural diversity. Indeed I opted for homogeneity, concentrating on Western culture. This is not to denigrate the contributions of other cultures to understanding change. On the contrary, in the larger scheme of more comprehensively understanding change, inclusion of a wide range of cultural perspectives is essential. But in this initial project, and with a group size of around 20, I was wary of tokenism and of isolating those asked to represent a particular cultural viewpoint.

Restricting participation to those resident in Australia was partly about the expense of including international participants and partly about avoiding the dynamics that the inclusion of international participants often sets up, especially when there is only a small number in the group. One dynamic is that the international participants can dominate discussion, especially if they are from more powerful countries. A contrasting dynamic comes when participants are from less powerful countries; in such cases they are often marginalised. A final reason was that we had plenty of talented people close at hand.

How the book was developed

Invitees were asked to write a paper on 'how [their discipline or practice area] thinks about change', with the intention that these papers would become book chapters.[3] They were asked to be descriptive and to communicate what is known (rather than write a speculative essay). Those writing perspectives from particular disciplines were invited to cover one or more of the particular ways their discipline thinks about and deals with change. Those contributing practice perspectives were encouraged to reflect on lessons from their experience in bringing about and/or dealing with change. The boundaries between these two types of contributions were not sharply drawn. For many of the practitioners, I had to reinforce the message that they were invited to write a chapter based on their experience, not an academic paper.[4]

While these were the terms in which the invitations were couched, the intent was to encourage a group of smart senior people to write chapters on aspects of change that they had direct experience with—either as the focus of their academic work, or in the practice of their employment, or both—and to see what that uncovered.

The second part of the invitation was to discuss each other's contributions at a two-day symposium. Instead of presenting their own work, everyone was assigned two chapters and was asked to describe them to the whole group, as well as to comment on them in light of their own chapter. I aimed to apportion the chapters so that at least one was likely to be outside the reader's comfort zone and the allocations are shown in Table 1.[5] One stated objective of this exercise was that it would allow each author to see how well two 'intelligent lay people'

---

3   The chapters were given more evocative titles after they were submitted and edited.
4   My basic message was 'If I had wanted an academic paper, I would have asked an academic'.
5   Four participants had not submitted their chapters at the time assignments were allocated. Three of these late chapters were divided among the four authors for comments. The fourth chapter was not produced before the symposium and the perspective was presented at the symposium. Because this chapter was not available to comment on, two of the late chapters received three sets of comments. Francesca Merlan and Dee Madigan

had understood their contributions, which could guide any post-symposium revisions. The process also aimed to be an efficient way of sharing the information produced, getting everyone up to speed and initiating engagement between the participants. By and large, participants summarised the gist of each other's chapters very well. With the author in the room, questions could be answered, misperceptions clarified and missed points added—but mostly this was not necessary.

The symposium was structured to ensure everyone had the same amount of time to present their two assigned chapters and enough time and flexibility was also provided to allow free-ranging discussion after each report, including giving right of reply to the authors when their work was presented. The proceedings were audio-recorded and transcribed. After the symposium, participants were given a copy of the transcript relevant to their chapter and the opportunity to revise the chapter.

Table 1 Participants and their topics, the clusters they represented and their assigned chapters.

Participant	Topic (and clusters)	Assignment: read and presented on chapters by (see footnote 5 for more detail)
Lindell Bromham	evolutionary biology (science)	Peter McDonald (demography) and John Reid (art)
Craig Browne	sociology (social science)	Sarah Pearson (industrial innovation) and Grant Wardlaw (security-based intelligence)
Jim Butler	economics (social science, health)	Paul Griffiths (philosophy) and Mark Stafford Smith (global environmental change)
Kate Carnell	politics (practice)	Robyn Gillies (education) and Michael Wesley (international relations)
Simon Chapman	media advocacy (practice, social science, health)	Ian MacLeod (materials conservation), Grant Wardlaw (security-based intelligence) and Dee Madigan (advertising)
Robyn Gillies	education (social science)	Christine Nixon (organisational change) and Francesca Merlan (anthropology)
Paul Griffiths	philosophy (humanities and the arts)	Mark Stafford Smith (global environmental change) and Beverley Raphael (psychiatry)

were not able to attend the symposium. Francesca produced comments on her assigned chapters, which I presented. Dee opted not to comment on other chapters, but welcomed comments on hers. Two participants were therefore assigned her chapter as a third paper to read.

Participant	Topic (and clusters)	Assignment: read and presented on chapters by (see footnote 5 for more detail)
Ian MacLeod	materials conservation (practice, science)	Robyn Gillies (education), Kate Carnell (politics) and Dee Madigan (advertising)
Dee Madigan	advertising (practice)	n/a
Peter McDonald	demography (social science)	Lindell Bromham (evolutionary biology) and John Reid (art)
Francesca Merlan	anthropology (social science)	Lindell Bromham (evolutionary biology) and Christine Nixon (organisational change)
Christine Nixon	organisational change (practice, policing and security)	Simon Chapman (media advocacy) and Peter McDonald (demography)
Sarah Pearson	industrial innovation (practice)	Craig Browne (sociology) and Ian MacLeod (materials conservation)
Beverley Raphael	psychiatry (science, practice, health)	Mark Stafford Smith (global environmental change) and Paul Griffiths (philosophy)
John Reid	art (humanities and the arts, environment)	Sarah Pearson (industrial innovation) and Michael Wesley (international relations)
Mark Stafford Smith	global environmental change (science, environment)	Paul Griffiths (philosophy) and Beverley Raphael (psychiatry)
Grant Wardlaw	security-based intelligence (social science, practice, policing and security)	Simon Chapman (media advocacy) and Francesca Merlan (anthropology)
Michael Wesley	international relations (social science, practice, policing and security)	Craig Browne (sociology) and Kate Carnell (politics)

How the book is organised

Six chapters describe how academic disciplines think about change (those by Bromham, Browne, Butler, McDonald, Merlan, Wesley). Two are based on the author's experiences in bringing about change (those by Carnell, Nixon). The 10 remaining chapters (those by Chapman, Gillies, Griffiths, Madigan, MacLeod, Pearson, Raphael, Reid, Stafford Smith, Wardlaw) take a more eclectic approach—some describe the author's activities in making change happen but also add an appraisal of the field or results from a research study, some focus on a particular topic in their field, some describe several topics in their field. The strong point of the chapters is their diversity, hence rather than grouping them into the three categories, discipline-based, practice-based and eclectic chapters are mixed but follow a loose narrative thread.

The opening chapter is by former Chief Minister of the Australian Capital Territory Kate Carnell, and describes her key learnings about change during her years in politics. Although making improvements is a prime motivation for people to enter politics, it is sobering to experience how hard this is. Among the challenges of making change happen in government, she discusses managing risk averseness by public servants and others, the art of negotiation and compromise, and key ingredients for some of her major policy successes, concluding with how the accumulation of policy failures, even when they are greatly outnumbered by successes, leads to change fatigue.

The next two chapters discuss change focusing on two of the most critical challenges faced by societies and the politicians who lead them: respectively, global environmental change and war.

Scientist Mark Stafford Smith offers fresh thinking on responding to key environmental challenges, particularly global climate change, which is uniquely characterised by certainty about the long-term direction of change coupled with uncertainty about the detail, much of which comes from not knowing what actions humanity will take. He works through difficulties for individuals and organisations in understanding and responding effectively, highlighting the value of 'requisite complexity'—using cheaper simple actions when these are sufficient, and more expensive complex approaches only when they are essential. Importantly, he suggests that considering climate change in the day-to-day decisions of policymakers and other societal actors, where relevant, can provide a way through the paralysis that can come from confronting this issue.

War between nation states, and how explanations by the discipline of international relations are influenced by ideas about change, provides the focus for the chapter by scholar and practitioner Michael Wesley. He describes three competing schools of thought, each of which has considerable evidence to support it and none of which is easy to discredit. Teleology provides an optimistic view, seeing the world on a solid trajectory to becoming more peaceful, based on the power of rational thought and behaviour. Cyclicality argues that the constant pressures for change on internal and external state relationships result in a perpetual cycle alternating between relative peace and widespread war. Episodism focuses on the complexity and unpredictability of changes in relationships between nation states, as well as conditions that result in inertia and inability to respond flexibly when new conditions for war arise.

The next chapter describes the broader perspective of one of the disciplines that international relations draws on, namely sociology, where change is a central consideration. Sociologist Craig Browne provides a masterful overview of major themes and debates about change in the discipline, both historical and current. Just two are considered here. First is the 'double character' of society as made up of the actions of individuals and the extent to which individual actions are constrained by what society 'allows'. Different ways of approaching this relationship between 'social action' and 'social structure' characterise many of the major streams of sociology. This interaction also explains significant differences in the ability of various groups within society to control and modify their lives and also the difficulties of making change happen. Second is work on social movements, some of which are directly concerned with the promotion of change and others with resistance to change, especially by mobilising resources and citizen participation to challenge state power.

Another discipline, psychology, underpins the work of the advertising industry, where changing consumer behaviour is the core business. Dee Madigan draws on her own experience as an advertising 'creative' to describe some of the simple, yet powerful, messages the industry employs to exploit basic human needs, especially for security, love and belonging. She also describes techniques, especially the use of images, for circumventing rational thought, as thinking is not only ineffective in getting consumers to purchase a product, but is actually counterproductive. More sophisticated messaging and ways of manipulating the mind have developed in parallel with new media, progressing from newspapers to radio to television, to, now, the internet. The internet has also given greater power to consumers to 'talk back' and provides a potential lever to enhance corporate social responsibility. In particular, the role of corporations and the advertising industry in promoting obesity and other social harms remains a topic for lively debate.

Banning advertising of cigarettes and other forms of smoking has been an important part of the strategy for controlling availability and use of tobacco products. Simon Chapman provides insights into how the most recent advertising ban—the introduction of plain packaging—was achieved, especially the role of media advocacy. He demonstrates not only the need to exploit opportunities for change when they arise, but also how a media profile can assist in preparing fertile ground. As well as being a successful public health campaigner, Simon is a researcher and the second part of his chapter reports on a study of the use of advocacy through the media by other public health academics who are considered to be influential. Like Simon, these researchers rate the media as 'peerless' in its power to influence, and they also provide lessons on managing simplification, framing, having an opinion and being available.

The next chapter takes a different tack, presenting many of the conundrums in dealing with change. Grant Wardlaw describes the difficulties of understanding, directing and assessing change in the high-pressure, rapidly evolving world of intelligence for national security, where he has worked in both practice and academic capacities. He highlights the challenges in grasping a) what change is necessary, b) how, and how much, the intelligence world has actually changed and c) whether change has been effective. He also demonstrates how general understandings about change management, as well as resistance to change, are complicated by the specifics of context. Although his own position is that both fundamental change and the capacity for continuous adaptation are required to address transnational threats from 'targets' who are small, constantly changing and have 'no permanent addresses', he also presents other competing views.

Continuous adaptation is a hallmark of evolutionary biology, with the inevitability of change in the genetic make-up of all living creatures and in their environments described by biologist Lindell Bromham. Her chapter begins with the 'breathtakingly simple' mechanisms of evolution: mutation, natural selection and substitution, and divergence. Knowledge of these evolutionary principles is essential for humans to begin to understand and manage our own interactions with the changing biological world. But considerable caution is required because the outcomes of evolution are often 'devilishly complex'. Using extinction as an example, Lindell demonstrates how relevant data can be interpreted in multiple ways, which are open to modification as the discipline of evolutionary biology itself changes in the face of new ideas, analyses and findings.

The discipline of demography focuses on human population change on a shorter (non-evolutionary) time scale. Demographers study life transitions ranging from the fundamentals of birth, death and migration, through to changes in, for example, occupation, disease status and area of residence. These changes are a consequence of human decisions, which in turn are shaped by what society makes possible. As researcher Peter McDonald lays out, demography is about not only how and why populations change, but also the consequences of change, especially repercussions for public policy. Regardless of whether the demographic changes are relatively stable (such as population ageing) or more fluid (such as distribution of occupations), they have many influences, including on consumer behaviour, voting patterns and preferred leisure activities. Public policy responses can be through mitigation (i.e. influencing the determinants, for example restricting migration or encouraging the use of birth control) or adaptation (i.e. dealing with the consequences, for example building more aged care facilities). However, Peter demonstrates that demographic forecasting is very inaccurate, which poses problems for developing policy responses.

Philosopher Paul Griffiths return us to the gene, but explores a different facet of change: conceptual evolution and how it assists scientific development. He illustrates his argument with two different—and concurrently used—meanings of the concept 'gene', showing how each allows valuable scientific work to progress. Indeed he posits that 'stretching and warping' constructs to fill 'epistemic niches' resulting from different scientific requirements is a functional part of the scientific process. Attempting to impose definitions and to stifle this process is counterproductive. He goes on to posit that concepts, such as 'innate', which have entrenched vernacular meanings that conflate different scientific constructs, hamper scientific investigations by obstructing the evolution of new conceptions which could serve specific scientific purposes.

Conceptual evolution in the understanding of mental illness is one theme in psychiatrist Beverley Raphael's chapter. Over time there have been changes in the distinction between normal and pathological grief, for example. Determining when grief and other human attributes like violence, fear and forgetfulness are disorders or just part of life is an ongoing challenge. The chapter provides a broad overview of mental illness from the perspective of evolution in definition, diagnosis and prevalence, as well as models and systems of care and treatment, and describes how these are influenced by various changes in society, culture and the environment. Three other drivers of change are also highlighted: 1) scientific research, including the promise resulting from advances in neuroscience and genomics; 2) technology, which has provided access to information and treatment, as well as producing new problems of its own; and 3) the advocacy of those affected by mental illness and their carers.

In contrast to the sweeping overview of changes in mental illness and psychiatry, the chapter on education by researcher Robyn Gillies analyses contemporary changes and what they mean for Australia. She employs three ways of examining change. First, she reviews negative unintended consequences, based on the case of the widespread introduction of standardised national and international assessments. Second, she explores how negative impacts can be anticipated based on lessons from past changes. The example used is current and past curriculum changes in Australia. Third, she describes how ingredients for successful interventions can be extracted from exemplar overseas cases. Here she draws on lessons from the introduction of education reform agendas in Canada, Finland, Singapore and Hong Kong.

The analysis of changes in education is from an academic perspective. Much can also be learnt from the inside story of introducing change as a leader and manager, which is provided in the next two chapters by Christine Nixon and Ian MacLeod.

Reflecting on 40 years in policing, which was capped by reaching the highest position as Chief Commissioner, Christine Nixon distils 10 lessons. Some of these are about the proposed changes (understanding and communicating the reasons for change, understanding organisational culture, using research to know what does and does not work), some are about working with the people who will be involved in the change (setting the environment, getting to know and involving the people inside the organisation and the stakeholders outside it, finding leverage, setting goals and accountabilities) and some are about the person leading the change (being a good manager, being resilient, as well as overcoming fear and finding courage).

Ian MacLeod, who is both a manager and a practising conservator, lives up to the double meaning of his chapter title (change management in materials conservation) by providing additional, and sometimes different, perspectives on some organisational change lessons, as well as providing insights into the preservation function of museums. As an organisational change manager, he reiterates points made in the previous two chapters about the importance of involving those affected, of using (and in his situation, conducting) research, of aligning personalities with tasks, of drawing on overseas experience, and of having courage. He also demonstrates the effectiveness of measures that work in specific situations, such as introducing change gradually or without notifying anyone, and of bringing in contractors to introduce new processes. In terms of materials conservation, a key lesson is that it does not mean doing nothing, but instead it requires effort whether it be seamstresses 'stitching down degraded fibres of sacred and preciously embroidered fabrics onto sympathetic new support structures' or treating cannonballs excavated from the sea with appropriate chemicals to stop them from falling apart 'in a matter of hours'.

Anthropologist Francesca Merlan takes up a similar theme, elaborating on the requirement of energy and active production for maintaining continuity. Her focus is on culture, including but also beyond material artefacts. She contrasts anthropology—which is focused on continuity as well as change—with sociology, which as Craig Browne also demonstrates in his chapter, concentrates on change. Francesca explores the historical roots of the difference, stemming (simply put) from anthropology's historical and continuing, but no longer exclusive, focus on premodern societies, as compared with sociology's founding focus on understanding great changes involved in modernisation. The bulk of Francesca's chapter examines how investigation of Australian Indigenous culture has been distorted by the lens of continuity and how this has been exacerbated by the legal requirements placed on Indigenous people to achieve land rights. She uses two key examples: the lifestyles, especially religion and ritual, of the Mardudjara of Australia's Western Desert and the art of the Yolngu people of north-east Arnhem Land.

In complete contrast to the continuity focus, industry open innovation champion Sarah Pearson takes us to the fast-moving consumer goods sector. She presents two cases about the introduction of open innovation, which involves companies enhancing their internal research and development efforts with external input to solving specific problems or generating new products. She brings us back to the energy required to make change happen and also adds lessons from her practical experience working at Cadbury. Key success factors for the innovation she concentrates on include demonstrating early wins achieved either by working 'under the radar' or targeting 'low hanging fruit'; linking external searches to internal company needs, while maintaining an openness to serendipity; involving people widely across the company; and learning to fail fast, in other words halting unsuccessful activities quickly while also learning from them. The key drivers for open innovation are competition and opportunity, with companies seeking to shorten the time to develop new products and enter new markets, by harnessing—globally—ideas and skills that already exist in non-competing areas.

Economist Jim Butler's chapter, describing economics as the science of scarcity, provides further insight into the trend towards open innovation, where 'cost-reducing technological change' enables 'more efficient use of limited resources'. In addition to technological change, Jim explores two other main areas of change which concern economists—structural change and climate change. A common theme of all three is growing interest in causality, moving beyond simply accepting and describing change to understanding its economic determinants. This is a big shift, especially in the economics of technological change and climate change, where the determinants of change were previously seen to be 'exogenous' and therefore outside the domain of economics.

The final contribution in words and visual imagery by fine artist, researcher and teacher John Reid has three broad themes. One links back to the chapter on economics, where the recognition of universities as knowledge-based industries has affected the role of schools of art. In order to survive, artists have increased collaboration with scholars from other disciplines; the contribution of artists is to provide 'aesthetic assessments' of the topic or project. John predicts that artists will enhance that partnership role by adding other research methods and also project management skills to their repertoires. The other themes are the role of art in assisting with the perception of change by providing an aesthetic audit or archive of change, and art as a 'potent' agent for or against change.

The concluding chapter, which I have written, draws out insights from all of these contributions, as well as from the two-day symposium which brought together most of the authors. As mentioned above, it uses this range of perspectives to examine how better understanding change can improve research impact. Demonstrating research impact is gaining increasing prominence, as researchers and those who fund them want to see research findings move beyond providing greater understanding of a problem and also used to bring about improvement in the problem.

The chapter is also a case study of multidisciplinary synthesis. As I argue in the chapter, multidisciplinary synthesis requires a specific focus, but that focus can vary depending on who is undertaking the synthesis. My focus ties in with my role in the project as a specialist in the nascent discipline of Integration and Implementation Sciences (I2S). The primary focus of I2S is to improve research contributions to tackling complex problems—like global environmental change, organised crime and escalating health care costs—and to this end I2S is developing a repository of methods and associated concepts, along with illustrative case examples, that researchers can draw on. A detailed description of I2S can be found in Bammer (2013).

A core mission of I2S is the job which is currently no one's business, namely drawing together knowledge about change, so that it is better understood and managed, particularly by researchers contributing to tackling complex problems. While the primary focus in the immediate term is research impact, the longer-term goal is to catalyse the drawing together of knowledge about change to provide general principles to guide thinking about change, and a roadmap to the specific issues of interest to different disciplines and practice areas.

References

Bammer, G (2013) *Disciplining interdisciplinarity: integration and implementation sciences for researching complex real-world problems*. ANU E Press, Canberra. http://press.anu.edu.au?p=222171.

Bammer, G and Smithson, M (eds) (2008) *Uncertainty and risk: multidisciplinary perspectives*. Earthscan, London.

Bammer, G and the Goolabri Group (2007) 'Improving the management of ignorance and uncertainty. A case illustrating integration in collaboration.' In Shani, AB, Mohrman, SA, Pasmore, WA, Stymne, B and Adler, N, eds *Handbook of collaborative management research*. Sage, Thousand Oaks, CA: 421–37.

Ravetz, J (2008) 'Preface'. In Bammer, G and Smithson, M (eds) (2008) *Uncertainty and risk: multidisciplinary perspectives*. Earthscan, London: xiii–xvi.

Part 2
Perspectives

2. A Politician's View of Change

Kate Carnell

I cannot speak for all politicians. They are as diverse a group as any, with different backgrounds, education and beliefs. But you enter politics because you want to change things.

Politicians want to make their electorate, state and country a better place. Most start wide-eyed and optimistic. The mechanisms of government and the sheer difficulty of bringing about change often produce disenchantment and cynicism. The impediments to delivering real change start with your own party and supporters. Then there is the media, our relatively short political cycle, the bureaucracy, and intolerance to any political leader's policy failure.

This is my story, and my experience of change in politics.

Starting the journey

I bought my first pharmacy when I was 25 in the early 1980s. Back then lots of women were pharmacists but very few were owners. My first pharmacy was in a small suburban shopping centre in Canberra, one of those shopping centres that was under pressure from the ever-growing shopping malls and the expanding shopping hours of major supermarkets. More and more products that were traditionally pharmacy-only were 'going open' and being discounted in supermarkets, so smaller shopping centres were losing market share, and my pharmacy was losing many of its best-selling products to supermarkets. The question was what to do?

At this time, Canberra did not have self-government, even though it was the nation's capital. Decisions on things like planning and shopping hours were made by a federal minister who did not even live in Canberra and probably viewed the Australian Capital Territory (ACT) portfolio as a bit of a problem. The voters back in his or her electorate probably thought that doing good things for Canberra should not be a priority for their local member!

The ACT also did not have a branch of the Pharmacy Guild to represent local pharmacists. ACT pharmacists were part of the New South Wales branch, so ACT issues were virtually ignored.

I thought that I could do something to change these things, which might have indicated a level of self-belief or maybe just naivety—actually it was probably a mixture of both. My father had taught me that you could not expect things to change if you sat back, did nothing and whinged. In fact, he often said you have no right to complain if you are not willing to get involved in making change happen.

So I became involved in the local pharmacy association, became chairperson and started advocating for an ACT branch of the Guild. I was also appointed to the board of the local Chamber of Commerce and Industry and some other groups working for a better deal for local businesses and for more local representation.

After a couple of failed attempts, an ACT branch of the Pharmacy Guild was finally established in 1988 (ACT self-government occurred in 1989). I became president of the ACT branch and the first woman to be a national vice-president of the Pharmacy Guild of Australia. Obviously, these things happened due to the work of a lot of people, but it really reinforced for me that people can make a difference if they have a good, credible story to tell and the commitment to work to deliver the required changes.

After one particular public meeting where I had been encouraging a reasonably large group of small retailers to get involved in a campaign to achieve a better deal from shopping mall owners, a group of Canberra businesspeople approached me and asked me to stand for the ACT Legislative Assembly.

They argued that if I was serious about wanting real change for Canberra businesses I should stand. My initial response was to say no—there were many better qualified people than me. But after much soul-searching, and with a belief that you have to practice what you preach, I decided to give politics a go.

As a small business owner and mother of two primary school children, I felt I had a reasonable understanding of the challenges facing working couples with children and mortgages. I also had a strong vision for a city that was business-friendly, one where kids could get a great education and would be able to get jobs in either the public or private sector, and a city that was financially sustainable. Like most people, I wanted a health system that was efficient and fair and not bogged down by unnecessary bureaucracy. Probably the most challenging part of the vision—I really wanted Australians to be proud of their national capital!

I also aspired to see Canberra as a socially progressive city that addressed issues such as the damage caused by illicit drugs and AIDS with evidence-based policies, not prejudice. In their business, pharmacists see more of drug users than many other people do. Soon after I bought my first pharmacy, I became involved in delivering the methadone program and the first needle-exchange program in Canberra. Through this I became acutely aware that Canberra needed much better treatment for people unfortunate enough to be addicted to drugs, particularly heroin. To deliver real change and to save lives, it was important to stop treating people with an addiction as criminals, and start treating them as people with a medical problem. I learnt that for some people methadone did not work and they ended up back on heroin. Unfortunately, many of these people died as a result of the unpredictable quality of the illegal heroin they were using. The prevalence of AIDS among injecting drug users was also increasing, due to sharing of dirty needles.

I took these issues with me into politics. At least some of the solutions seemed obvious. AIDS was a serious problem and dirty needles and unprotected sex were causing the disease to spread, so giving heroin users clean needles would reduce infection rates, as would good access to information about safe sex and, of course, to condoms. Ensuring that brothels were legalised and subject to regular health checks would also help. Giving prescription heroin to people who had tried other programs to address their addiction seemed sensible if we were to save lives.

Pre-selection

Exposure to the pre-selection process involved learning that real change is about convincing people who do not want to be convinced! At the ACT Liberal Party pre-selection for the Legislative Assembly, I was asked questions like:

- are you pro-choice? (my answer was yes)
- would you support a republic? (my answer was yes)
- would you push for drug law reform in the Legislative Assembly? (my answer was yes)
- do you support equal rights for same-sex couples? (my answer was yes).

I also explained my vision for a financially sustainable city that was well managed with a great education system and a vibrant private sector. And, surprisingly, the party pre-selected me. Many socially conservative party members said, 'I don't agree with her on some things, but at least we know what she believes in.'

To achieve change you have to be true to your values and belief structures, otherwise people will, understandably, not trust you. If I had told the pre-selectors that I shared their socially conservative views, I do not believe I would have been successful—they would have known I was putting a spin on the truth.

I was elected in 1992. In 1993 I became Leader of the Opposition.

Leading the opposition

Canberra has always been a Labor-voting town but it was also home for nearly 350,000 people who wanted a good health and education system and jobs for their kids. Importantly, they wanted a well-managed, financially sustainable city that was a good place to bring up their children. Exactly the things I had entered politics to help deliver for Canberra.

Bringing about change in politics is interesting, to say the least. People (and the media) often say they want politicians who are only about getting the job done, not about the 'spin'. The dumping of Ted Baillieu (who resigned in March 2013 as Premier of Victoria) shows how wrong that is!

Ted is a good bloke, a hard worker, honest with good values, *but* he is not a salesman. In my view, his problem was he did not sell his vision and agenda to his party colleagues or the electorate. You could say that he did not spend enough time concentrating on the spin. Some might say that former Prime Minister Julia Gillard suffered from the same problem. Delivering real change in politics is not just about good policy. It is about being able to sell it to parliament, the electorate and the media.

We had to have a clear, simple set of messages and policies that we were passionate about delivering. There is no doubt that the KISS (Keep It Simple, Stupid) principle is important. Complicated messages are doomed to failure.

I really believe in the quote from General Colin Powell: 'Great leaders are almost always great simplifiers, who can cut through argument, debate and doubt, to offer a solution everybody can understand.' I always thought that this was something to aspire to if we were to get people to share our vision and give us their vote.

Electors needed to know what we stood for—and even if there were some things they did not agree with, they were willing to support us because the overall direction was right for Canberra.

I did not ask my Liberal Party colleagues to support my socially progressive policies, but told them I was happy to give them a free vote. This allowed my party colleagues to cross the floor on things they felt strongly about, and avoided unnecessary splits in party unity on issues that were not core Liberal Party policy.

So once the party had a solid set of policies and vision, we set about selling them to the media. The media, in my view, does not like to change its prejudices. Its members have a pack mentality and preconceived views on many things, and it takes *lots* of effort to change their collective minds! Not all journalists are like this, but I believe that most are. They did not see us as an alternative government.

To change this we decided we had to follow a simple rule. If we criticised the government in a press release or speech, we had to outline what we would do in government. It took six months but in the end the media were asking the Labor Party about our policy ideas. We were being reported as an alternative government.

To achieve change you have to communicate clearly and repeat your message time and time again. Some research suggests that people do not start absorbing a message until they have heard it at least seven times. And the message has to be credible, consistent and concise. We were elected in February 1995, forming a minority Liberal Government in the ACT Legislative Assembly. Now we had the opportunity to implement the changes we had promised.

In government

I have to say, I had no idea just how hard it is to deliver change in government.

Dealing with risk aversion

By its very nature, the public service is risk-averse and is therefore not quick to embrace new ideas. The challenge is to be clear about what you want and to set achievable goals with definite timelines. Sounds easy but it is not! Sir Humphrey (Appleby) was alive and well in some departments, and many of the things we wanted to do were described as 'courageous' and 'requiring more thought'. As a new and inexperienced government, we sometimes felt it was prudent to listen to this advice.

Myriad lobby groups give politicians often very conflicting advice. It is remarkable how many expert opinions there are backing up the different positions of these groups—and often these experts disagreed with each other! Listening to the community is important but the feedback is not homogenous. People only believe you have listened if you end up implementing the position they put forward. I remember at one point we had 293 different consultations under way and were being pilloried in *The Canberra Times* for not consulting.

To deliver positive change, we quickly had to learn how to separate self-interest from good policy. This was particularly the case in planning. Both from an environmental and a financial perspective, it was important that Canberra did not continue to grow and expand only in greenfield areas, creating more and more urban sprawl with the resulting infrastructure and environmental costs. The NIMBYs ('not in my back yard') outnumbered the BANANAs ('build absolutely nothing anywhere near anybody'), but both groups were very vocal. This made it incredibly hard to get sustainable, affordable planning laws through the ACT's Legislative Assembly. The fact that the Federal Government retained dual planning responsibility in the so-called 'Parliamentary Triangle' (a central area of Canberra) and on major entry roads made the job even harder.

The problem of multiple authorities was highlighted when we decided that a square in front of the Canberra Theatre, between the Assembly building and the Canberra Museum and Gallery, needed upgrading. It was a big grey square with a fountain that leaked. We wanted a public area that was exciting and appropriate for such an important space. Well, after ACT Planning, the National Capital Authority and various community consultation groups had had their say and $3 million had been spent, the ACT got a big grey square with a fountain that leaked! The various planning requirements and stakeholder group input had progressively removed all risk, innovation ... and excitement. We eventually fixed the leaking fountain.

It is important not to confuse committees, investigations and consultations with action. You will never have every possible bit of information or remove all the risk, so there is a time when it is important to go with your gut and 'just do it'.

Unfortunately, both the media and the public view government decisions that do not deliver desired outcomes very poorly. If a government supports a new initiative that does not work it will be on the front page of the paper, but the 200 that did work will not be reported. This can make politicians very risk-averse. It is often said that nobody ever got sacked for appointing IBM to do an IT project even if they ran over budget or over time, but if you contracted a local small or medium-sized business that did not deliver or (even worse) went broke, your job could be at risk.

The art of negotiation and compromise

The problem, of course, with a minority government is that you have to have the numbers in parliament to deliver any legislative change. This requires continuous negotiation and sometimes compromise. If you lose votes on the floor of the parliament too often, the media and the public will see a government unable to deliver on promises—even though it is not its fault!

So finding compromise solutions is important. That said, it is important not to compromise on values, ethical standards and core policy positions. If you do, the media and the electorate will understandably question what the government stands for, and that leads to a loss of trust—death for any government.

At one stage in my time as ACT Chief Minister, two of the three independent members whose support I needed to pass the government's budget refused to pass it unless I agreed to amendments to abortion laws that would require women to see pictures of what a foetus looks like at 8–12 weeks (the most common time for abortions to take place) and to establish a 48-hour 'cooling off' period.

I finally agreed to their demands but have regretted it ever since. Although I did support the cooling-off period, I did not believe that the pictures were right or reasonable. I should have let them vote against the budget—who knows whether they would have carried out their threat. If the government had fallen over this issue, voters might have taken a dim view of two independents using their numbers to unseat a democratically elected government.

I was publicly committed to pro-choice, so what was I doing supporting these changes to the abortion laws? I should not have compromised on the issue.

Key factors in dealing with some major policy challenges

The federal Howard Government was elected in 1996 and implemented significant change in the federal public service to address a large budget deficit. Canberra lost 9,000 jobs in 15 months. Unemployment went beyond 8 per cent and youth unemployment reached 40 per cent. The ACT experienced three consecutive quarters of negative growth, technically a recession. *The Canberra Times* ran front page stories of traffic jams of moving vans heading out of the city. Canberra had to change quickly.

We pulled together local business leaders and asked for help. The business community suggested that my government offer a small incentive to businesses that employed a young person and provided them with some training and experience. *The Canberra Times* committed to printing the names of participating companies, to publicly thank them. The aim of the program, Youth500, was to employ 500 young people for at least 12 months. Youth500 became Youth1000. Most Canberra businesses with the capacity to employ a young person did so—and the retention rate at 12 months was 85 per cent. This was achieved even though these businesses were doing it tough due to the federal cutbacks.

Canberra was under huge pressure, but Youth1000 showed that a shared goal can achieve great things and real change. Within two years, Canberra's unemployment rate was among the lowest in the country, growth was positive and 60 per cent of the workforce was in the private sector—a real change for a city that had traditionally been dominated by the public sector.

Even with the risk involved, we progressed with our policy to reduce drug-related deaths. This involved supporting a heroin trial in the ACT based on some comprehensive research done at The Australian National University. We managed to get support for the trial through the Assembly because of the leadership of one of the independent members, Michael Moore.

Initially most Canberrans did not support the trial, but over time they came to understand that the trial was aimed at saving lives. Even people who did not support the trial gave us the benefit of the doubt and did not stop supporting the government when irresponsible newspaper reporting suggested that Canberra would have free heroin on every street corner!

This was a very controversial policy but it shows that you can achieve change, even unpopular change, if your position is consistent and people understand that you really believe in the change. The change must be evidence-based, involve credible research and be supported by experts in the field.

All change requires leadership, but the sort of social change required for the heroin trial described above needs broad-based leadership and support, not just from politicians but from the community and academia. Broad support is needed because of the power of the media and the adversarial nature of our parliamentary system. It is easier to run a 'shock horror' story than a well-researched, balanced one.

Even with a minority government, we managed to implement a range of reasonably controversial changes, from selling half of the local electricity and water utility (ACTEW) to legalising X-rated videos, brothels and non-commercial surrogacy, starting the redevelopment of Kingston foreshore, and rolling out Canberra's own broadband network.

We achieved these changes by ensuring the media understood what we were doing and why. We also consulted widely, to encourage support from major stakeholders wherever possible. We worked very closely with the crossbenchers as, unfortunately, it is rare in our political system for the opposition to support the government on any major change if it is possible to get political mileage by putting forward an opposing view.

Policy failure and change fatigue

With new policy and change come some great successes, some average outcomes and a few failures. And the failures are seized on by both the opposition and the media. The media say that good news does not sell, so a feeding frenzy over a government initiative that has not worked is great copy.

The longer politicians are in power, the more things there will be that have not gone quite right—unless of course you do nothing. For me this started with the implosion of the old Canberra Hospital. This was an absolute tragedy with the death of a 12-year-old girl. There were multiple inquiries into what happened, with the final outcome being that the company doing the implosion got it wrong. The government was not found to be responsible, but at the end of the day, the buck stops at the top, as it should.

Events like this shake your confidence. You think you are doing the right thing—we embarked on an implosion of the hospital rather than a standard demolition to minimise the impact on the hospice that was next door to the hospital. The advice was that an implosion would mean that the worst of the demolition would be over in about eight weeks, compared with many months using traditional methods. After this event, it was hard not to become more risk-averse.

Then there was the redevelopment of Bruce (now Canberra) Stadium. We supported the redevelopment to make the stadium more appropriate and profitable for Raiders (rugby league) and Brumbies (rugby union) matches and so that Canberra could stage Olympic soccer (at the 2000 Sydney Olympics). The costs of the redevelopment blew out—as did the costs for two other stadiums being built at the same time: Olympic Stadium at Homebush in Sydney and Hindmarsh Stadium in Adelaide. The difference in Canberra was that we had a minority government with crossbenchers who had 'change fatigue'. With an increasing amount of mud sticking to the government and particularly to me as Chief Minister, the independent politicians were sick of justifying their support for changes the government wanted to make. As the government could not survive without the support of the crossbenchers and they had lost confidence in me, I resigned and handed the leadership to my deputy.

Change fatigue is a real thing in politics. With change comes risk and with risk comes the very real possibility of failure (or at least lack of success). I believe this is the reason many governments become increasingly risk-averse the longer they spend in office. This leads to more compromise and political leaders being seen as not standing for anything, a sure-fire formula for defeat at the polls.

Another reason for politicians being risk-averse is Australia's relatively short political cycle. The UK has five-year fixed terms—in Australia, we have three or four years, and the average term for a Federal Government is about two years and 10 months.

This does not give politicians long to implement changes that have any detractors—just about all major changes. There is a view among politicians that if you cannot implement your agenda in your first 18 months, you will not have the 'clear air' to do it at all in your first term. Voters may then decide your first term is your last!

Change is the lifeblood of most politicians—it is why we aspire to office. We all want to make a positive difference in our communities. How we manage that change within our political parties, within our communities, with the media or within parliament will determine whether we are successful or not.

There is one truism in politics: 'You never leave politics worried by the things you *did*, only by the things you did not do.'

3. Responding to Global Environmental Change

Mark Stafford Smith

Achieving change in individual and organisational behaviour to meet the challenges of global environmental change will be seen as a defining benchmark for our generation. Global environmental change challenges characteristically require inter-sectoral, multi-level responses within a fundamentally unpredictable complex systems framework. Here I focus on adaptation to climate change as an exemplar of these. Models of change that stress movement through phases of awareness, relevance, acceptance of agency and then action help to show that different motivators are required at different phases. Coupled with resilience theory and models of incremental and transformative change, they also help to identify what different modes of response should be targeted to different types of problem, and hence how engagement for change may be appropriately constructed. In the context of climate change adaptation, this leads to an enriched idea of adaptation pathways that meet many of the characteristics of global environmental changes.

The theme of this chapter is *requisite complexity* in responses to change—that is, 'one size does not fit all, but it is not helpful to have an indefinite number of sizes'. I explore this theme in the context of human change in response to global environmental change (e.g. Steffen et al. 2004). Responding to global environmental change in ways which are sufficiently but not excessively complex is a defining challenge for our generation, the first to really recognise that the human race is affecting sustainability at a global scale and the first, in science at least, to explore deeply the complex connectivities of social–ecological systems (Liu et al. 2007).

The nature and significance of global environmental change

Global environmental change refers to a suite of environmental impacts caused by human beings which are recognised as having effects that are global in scale. Indeed, the magnitude of these impacts has led to the proposal that we have entered a new geological epoch, the Anthropocene (Crutzen and Steffen 2003). An early recognised global environmental change was the hole in the ozone layer, where the emission of chlorofluorocarbon refrigerants mostly in the northern hemisphere was found to be dramatically affecting the ozone layer over Antarctica. Whilst climate change is today's iconic global environmental change, others include changes in the global water cycle, the global nitrogen and phosphorus cycles, ocean acidification, ecosystem loss and atmospheric pollution. These have been canvassed under the idea of nine planetary boundaries (Rockström et al. 2009) within which the world needs to stay to have confidence that the planet will continue to function in the relatively benign state that it has during the past 8,000 years. In this time, modern civilisation, agriculture, cities and technologies have developed. Of the nine boundaries, we have probably already transgressed three (Rockström et al. 2009). The concept of a 'safe operating space' with boundaries is a significant change from an engineering view of optimising our responses towards a specific desired future, since it does not seek to specify our collective actions within that space.

In general, these global environmental changes share some key attributes that interact with human decision-making. They all show a significant increase in their rates of change over the past 50 years—the so-called 'great acceleration' (see Figures 15 and 16 in Steffen 2010)—to the extent that the rates of human learning and decision-making processes risk being outstripped. They are all occurring at a spatial scale which seems far beyond the influence of individual humans. For most of them, it is certain that there is major change occurring on a decadal to centennial timeframe, but there is considerable uncertainty about where that change will end up and what impacts it will have. A large part of this uncertainty is a result of not knowing whether humanity will choose to respond to mitigate the changes.

This chapter takes climate change as an exemplar of the other global environmental changes. We now face the prospect of at least 2°C and up to 6°C of global warming by 2100 (IPCC 2007, Huntingford et al. 2012). Change is certain, but its magnitude depends greatly on human decisions. As with other global environmental changes, humanity must negotiate a balance between *mitigating* the magnitude of change and *adapting* to the changes which it is too late to mitigate. In some ways, adaptation to climate change has the same challenges as adapting to other drivers in society—planning for population increase, allowing for changing exchange rates, innovating into new technological markets. But whilst these contain uncertainty, only climate change exhibits so much certainty of major directional change over the long term, combined with uncertainty about the detailed trajectory.

This uncertainty presents a core challenge for climate adaptation, with many downstream implications. For example, issues of valuing the future compared with today; shifting risk management thinking from optimal solutions to robust decision-making; balancing short-term incremental change with harder, longer lead time, transformational change; placing everything in adaptive management and adaptive governance cycles rather than a one-off decision. A further key challenge is that adaptation responses need to be highly contextual; as a consequence, research tends to result in many case studies, but a limited ability to generalise these predictably for other contexts. We now turn to explore these issues.

Models of human response

A number of building blocks are emerging from the science of climate adaptation. To enable adaptation, people and organisations need to go through a sequence of steps (Figure 1) from initially understanding that there is an issue of climate change, to understanding their own vulnerability to climate change, to developing a sense of responsibility for responding to this vulnerability, to having a willingness to engage in adaptation planning, to acting on planning and implementation (Gardner et al. 2009). Recognising this sequence is important, because there are different drivers and barriers for moving from one step to the next, and people or organisations at different steps require different information to help them move onwards.

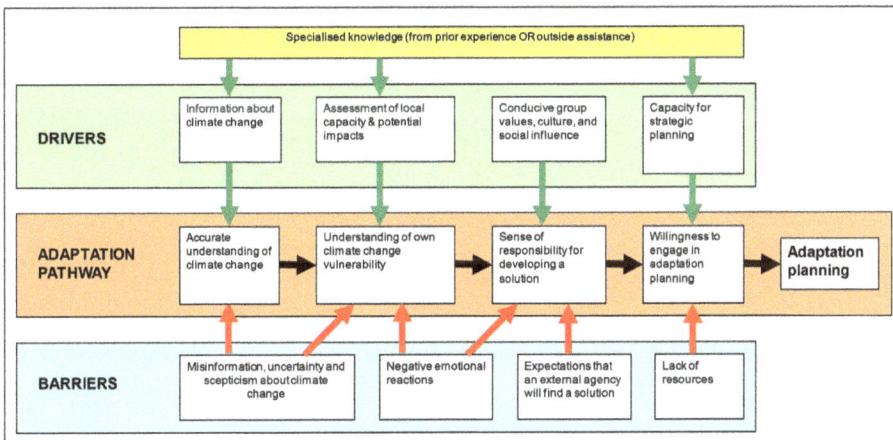

Figure 1 Steps people and organisations need to go through to adapt to global climate change, along with associated drivers and barriers.

Source: Modified from Figure 1 in Gardner et al. (2009).

Secondly, the characteristics of global environmental change problems noted above create specific difficulties for human cognition. Hamilton and Kasser (2009) note three categories of psychological strategies for responding to the prospect of severe climate change, ranging from various denial strategies, through a suite of maladaptive coping strategies, to genuinely adaptive coping strategies (see Table 1 in Stafford Smith et al. 2011). Understanding these is essential if people are to be facilitated through small steps on to the path of accepting the need to act; Crompton and Kasser (2009) suggest specific actions to encourage a move towards the adaptive strategies. However, there are also cognitive barriers to responding, particularly related to handling and misinterpreting long-term uncertainty (Weber 2006). Bazerman (2006) describes these as positive illusions (that a problem is not serious), egocentrism (interpreting events in a self-serving manner), over-discounting the future, privileging the status quo, and vividness (over-weighting personal experience). These mostly apply as much to organisational decision-making as they do to individuals, but are exacerbated by organisational silos and special interests that are legitimatised by corporate laws (e.g. the need to deliver short-term returns to shareholders). Collectively, these attributes provide hints towards facilitating change.

Thirdly, some change needs to be more than incremental (Kates et al. 2012, Park et al. 2012). Howden et al. (2010) explored the nature of incremental, transitional and transformational responses to climate change in agriculture, and noted that transformational change is more risky and expensive. It is also more cognitively challenging and has a longer lead-time (Stafford Smith et al. 2011). In reality, responses need to be seen as a continual cycle of incremental and transformational change (Park et al. 2012), adding further complexity to an overall adaptive cycle but converging with concepts such as triple loop learning (e.g. Chapin et al. 2009, Pahl-Wostl 2009).

Fourthly, there is a vast literature on organisational innovation, adoption and change (e.g. Greenhalgh et al. 2004, Pentland et al. 2011, Berkhout 2012). This is valuable in identifying many factors which may play a role in different contexts, such as leadership, structure, trigger events, resources and timing, but the literature struggles to get beyond shopping lists of such potential influences to be predictive in different contexts. Some of our own recent work has explored the issue of mainstreaming in the climate adaptation domain. In conversations with champions for adaptation in various organisations, for example, we have found that where the locus of influence for acting on climate change resides in the organisation's executive function, it is far easier to trigger implementation than when the locus is elsewhere. In the former case, interview responses focus on the nature of business-as-usual in different parts of the organisation. In the latter, conversations concentrate on the attributes of the champion, such as their ability to network with other parts of the organisation and in various ways achieve implementation despite (rather than because of) the structure.

Responses in climate adaptation

How should we respond to these issues in adapting to climate change, as an example of global environmental changes? First, let us distinguish three functionally different response roles. There is a commonplace narrative that asserts 'all adaptation is local', with the corollary that the role of government is simply to set the context within which local communities or businesses make decisions. In reality, adaptation decisions can be made at any scale, including in government, and so can 'policy' decisions that set the context for other decision-makers (Palutikof et al. 2013), but the two roles—in implementation and context-setting—are functionally useful to distinguish. The third role I wish to consider a little is that of researchers. Here I will abbreviate these functional roles as adaptation *action*, *policy* and *research* respectively.

Next, it is notable that climate change, as with many other environmental changes, has largely been approached through a problem-oriented framing. For good reason, climate scientists spent many years trying to show that there really was a problem which was worth tackling, and the Intergovernmental Panel on Climate Change process and report structure still emphasise the potential for climate change first, and its implications in terms of impacts and possible mitigation second. One result of this is the strong primacy of a hazard approach to impacts and vulnerability (Wolf 2012)—exposure and sensitivity defining impact, and impact and adaptive capacity defining residual vulnerability (Figure 2). Aside from a variety of technical and conceptual faults with this framing, it focuses attention on the *problem* of vulnerability rather than on potential response options; it also tends to give the impression that all actions will eventually be affected by climate change (potentially true), leading to paralysis or denial. Another result is that uncertainty in the climate projections is perceived to 'cascade' through impacts and vulnerability, with uncertainty increasing at each step to further challenge any ability to make decisions (Stainforth et al. 2007) (Figure 3).

These effects immediately play into undermining human responses. There is an increasing understanding that continuing to batter people with the problem rather than with solutions simply turns them off, particularly when that problem seems a long way into the future. And, whilst there are genuinely important uncertainties, overemphasising these again sparks all the cognitive challenges mentioned above. In fact, there has long been an alternative but muffled framing which is decision-centred rather than problem-oriented. This traces its antecedents to the adaptive management literature (e.g. Walters 1986, Walters and Holling 1990, Chapin et al. 2009), and has been readily available in the context of adapting to climate change for at least a decade through the efforts of UKCIP, formerly the UK Climate Impacts Programme (e.g. Willows and Connell 2003) (Figure 4). As decision-makers have increasingly turned to wanting to act on adaptation rather than just worry about whether climate change is real, this line of thinking has come more to the fore (Stafford Smith et al. 2011, Haasnoot et al. 2013), but is still not widely embedded in the thinking of adaptation policy, so that those seeking to plan for adaptation action often get stuck at the point of considering distant and uncertain impacts and vulnerabilities. Additionally, much research continues to emphasise the problem-oriented framing, due to the distance of most researchers from decision-makers, and a strongly entrenched dominance of climate science (Sarewitz and Pielke 2007).

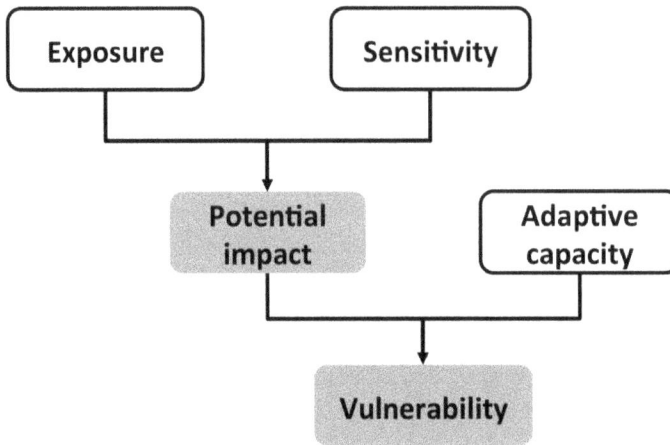

Figure 2 A common framing of impact and vulnerability.

This has technical and conceptual faults and focuses attention on problems rather than potential response options.

Source: Modified from Allen Consulting (2005).

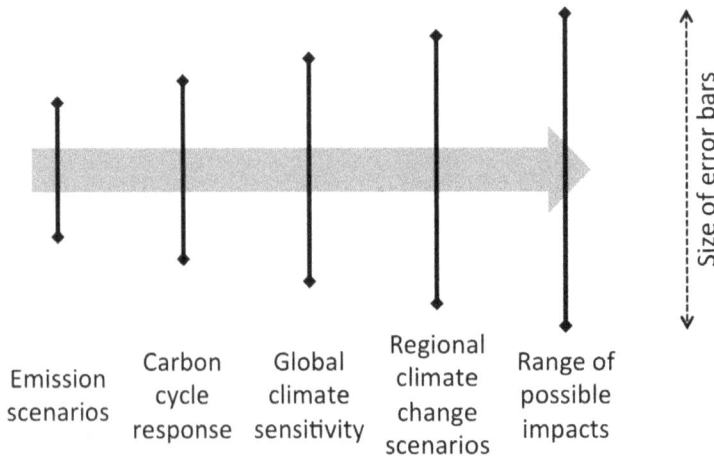

Figure 3 A perceived 'cascade' through impacts and vulnerability, with uncertainty increasing at each step.

This can undermine human ability to respond, and does not necessarily represent the relative importance of the uncertainties in an actual decision.

Source: Modified from Figure 2.2 in Parry et al. (2007).

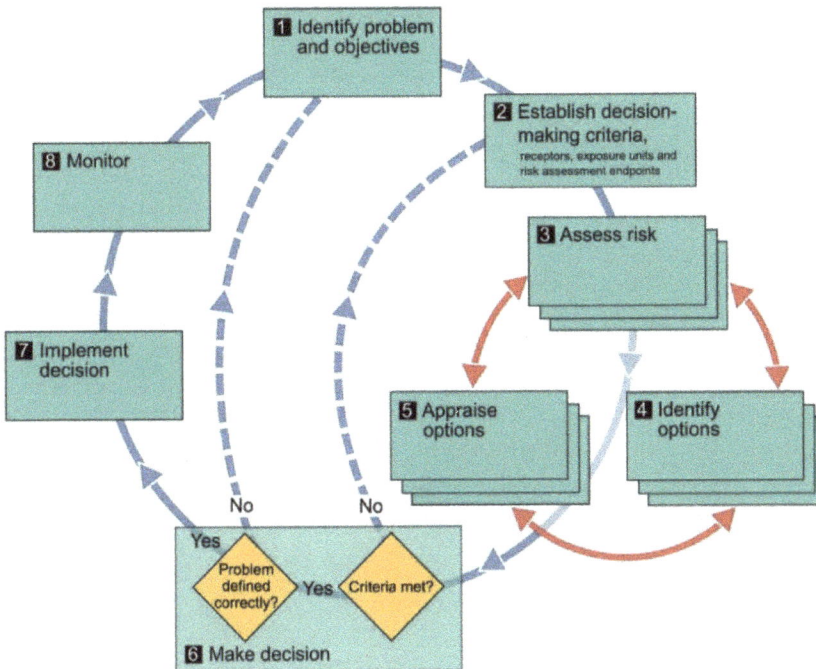

Figure 4 The UK Climate Impacts Programme (UKCIP) decision-centred model, which promotes more productive responses.

Source: Reproduced from Willows and Connell (2003).

A decision-centred framing resolves several problems. It asks, 'What decisions do either policy or action decision-makers face now?', and then, 'Which of these may be affected by future climate change?' Since most decisions have a lifetime that is quite short, this immediately narrows down the otherwise overwhelming suite of decisions that might be affected by climate change to a much smaller number (Stafford Smith et al. 2011). It also enables an assessment of the particular element of climate change that may affect each individual decision, and then a characterisation of the nature of uncertainty in that element, rather than being clouded by a pervasive sense of overall uncertainty. Indeed, when put in the context of other sources of uncertainty related to the decision, it may turn out that the climate uncertainty is not actually important—far from cascading, at times the implications of climate uncertainty may instead be attenuated. Where uncertainty remains, various ways of mitigating decision risk can be drawn upon (Hallegatte 2009) and the set of choices can be dynamically redefined through a series of potential adaptation pathways (Figure 5) out into the future wherein not all problems have to be solved at once (Haasnoot et al. 2013, Wise et al. 2014). Not all decisions can be so broken up, but most can: essentially decision-centred framing is replacing single shot, long-range artillery with its challenging need to get everything right in one go despite the risk of unexpected winds, with a game of golf, zigzagging adaptively up the fairway,[1] avoiding maladaptation and undesirable path contingency. Together these features facilitate adaptation action by making the process more relevant. They also highlight the need for adaptation policy decision-makers not to overemphasise vulnerability assessments. For researchers, a decision-driven conceptualisation would also better focus much adaptation research.

Reframing the issue not only helps reduce the cognitive gap between the information being provided and the decision-making environment of those actors who may need to respond, but also focuses attention on the context in which the decision is occurring. As reviewed by Wise et al. (2014), Voß et al. (2007) identify a typology of contexts along a gradient of increasing complexity based on levels of uncertainty in knowledge, goals and distributed power, which can guide the appropriate choice of methodologies (e.g. Randall et al. 2012). Where system functioning is well understood and future risks well characterised, goals or values are clear and there is a central decision-maker, problems are well suited to the rationalist reductionist approach to decision-making, and tools such as cost–benefit analysis are suitable. In relatively closed systems with a central locus of power and unambiguous goals (e.g. high reliability urban water supply systems), the 'knowledge problem' can be tackled through capability building, learning approaches and tools for decision-making under uncertainty (e.g. Dessai and van de Sluijs 2007, Hallegatte 2009). However, many complex systems contexts have a high degree of uncertainty in knowledge, as well as distributed power and ambivalent goals; in these there are no agreed values, and even the institutions intended to help resolve them may be contested or not exist, as can be the case in coastal responses to sea-level rise in Australia (Gorddard et al. 2012). In such circumstances, engagement processes, perhaps a deliberative democracy approach, and certainly an iterative approach to framing decision process are required, as is urged in strategic adaptive management (cf. Roux and Foxcroft 2011, Randall et al. 2012). It is worth noting, however, that these more complex approaches are expensive in time and energy, so it is essential to identify cases where simpler, cheaper approaches are sufficient, as opposed to cases where these are likely to fail so that more complex approaches are justified.

---

1   I am indebted to Paul Griffiths for this insightful metaphor from the sporting tradition of the philosophy of science.

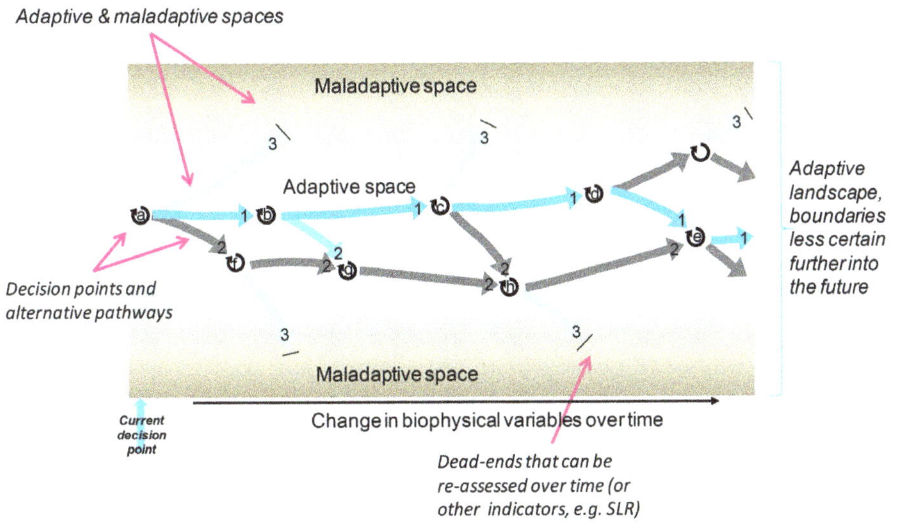

Figure 5 Conceptualising dynamic adaptation pathways.

A decision-maker at point (a) can envision various pathways of action across a landscape that is more-or-less adaptive (hitting the ball down the fairway and avoiding the maladaptive rough, in the golfing analogy). At point (a), some decisions are likely to be maladaptive and should be avoided; there remain multiple possible pathways, of which one seems best at the time of initial decision-making. Following the analysis, this first step can therefore be taken with confidence, knowing that re-appraisal at point (b) may mean choosing the shift to path (g)–(e) instead. It is important to explicitly define the decision's points, which may be points in time, or other triggers such as sea level rise.

Source: Adapted from Wise et al. (2014).

A decision-centred approach also emphasises the nature of the decision-maker themselves. Not only is this important in terms of the phases of readiness (Gardner et al. 2009) described earlier, but also in the ease of mainstreaming the topic even once the decision-maker is ready to consider it. If the implementation is close to current business-as-usual, it seems that the action can (and should for efficiency's sake) be readily mainstreamed; but where there is a major mismatch between the needed response and business-as-usual practices, then premature mainstreaming is likely to fail. This outcome is thus a conjoint property of both the needed response (itself related to the nature of the problem) and the characteristics of the decision-making individual or organisation—essentially a question of whether these aspects are 'in balance' or not. Even an organisation with very short-term planning horizons and low capacity may be able to cope with more incremental, shorter term, less contested responses, just as even a far-seeing, high capacity organisation may be challenged by very long-term transformative issues.

The concept of dynamic adaptation pathways can help to bring all these elements together and provide a structured approach of requisite complexity to complex decision-making that may otherwise dissolve into oversimplification or complexity-driven paralysis (Haasnoot et al. 2013, Wise et al. 2014).

Conclusions

Thus some simple guidelines can emerge for dealing with complex global environmental changes, which enable actors to structure their approaches in ways which are cognitively achievable and appropriate to their roles in decision-making. The choice of responses must take account of the nature of the problem, of the actors and of their normal modes of operating; focusing on any single dimension is bound to be inadequate. Lenses such as power and equity can be taken into these attributes. People, communities and institutions will be at different stages of acceptance and response and need different information and tools to assist them on to the next stage. The specific problems they face in their own context will require different levels of responses, from simple amendments to business-as-usual operations to deeply challenging transformative changes to ways of thinking, and different tools and approaches are again required for these. And different actors in society need to recognise and play their different roles in supporting the responses. These statements seem to be very obvious and widely documented in their parts; and indeed applicable in triggering adaptive responses to changes with similar complex characteristics that inhibit decision-making well outside the arena of global environmental change. Yet they have not been salient in the way in which the climate change issue has been progressed over the past few decades, perhaps partly because our collective understanding has not seen how these approaches apply in the context of global complex systems problems. It is time we changed this.

References

Allen Consulting (2005) Climate change risk and vulnerability. Final report to the Australian Greenhouse Office by the Allen Consulting Group. Australian Greenhouse Office, Department of the Environment and Heritage, Canberra.

Bazerman, MH (2006) Climate change as a predictable surprise. *Climate Change* 77: 179–93.

Berkhout, F (2012) Adaptation to climate change by organizations. *Wiley Interdisciplinary Reviews: Climate Change* 3: 91–106.

Chapin, FS III, Kofinas, GP and Folke, C (eds) (2009) *Principles of ecosystem stewardship: resilience-based natural resource management in a changing world*. Springer-Verlag, New York.

Crompton, T and Kasser, T (2009) *Meeting environmental challenges: the role of human identity*. WWF, Godalming UK.

Crutzen, PJ and Steffen, W (2003) How long have we been in the Anthropocene era? *Climatic Change* 61: 251–7.

Dessai, S and van de Sluijs, J (2007) Uncertainty and climate change adaptation—a scoping study (report for the Netherlands Environmental Assessment Agency). Copernicus Institute for Sustainable Development and Innovation, Utrecht University, Utrecht.

Gardner, J, Dowd, A-M, Mason, C and Ashworth, P (2009) *A framework for stakeholder engagement on climate adaptation*. CSIRO Climate Adaptation Flagship working paper no 3. CSIRO Climate Adaptation Flagship, Canberra.

Gorddard, R, Wise, R, Alexander, K, Langston, A, Leitch, A, Dunlop, M, Ryan, A and Langridge, J (2012) Striking the balance: coastal development and ecosystem values (CSIRO Climate Adaptation Flagship project report). Commonwealth of Australia, Canberra.

Greenhalgh, T, Robert, G, Macfarlane, F, Bate, P and Kyriakidou, O (2004) Diffusion of innovations in service organizations: systematic review and recommendations. *Milbank Quarterly* 82: 581–629.

Haasnoot, M, Kwakkel, JH, Walker, Warren E and ter Maat, J (2013) Dynamic adaptive policy pathways: a method for crafting robust decisions for a deeply uncertain world. *Global Environmental Change* 23: 485–98.

Hallegatte, S (2009) Strategies to adapt to an uncertain climate change. *Global Environmental Change: Human and Policy Dimensions* 19: 240–7.

Hamilton, C and Kasser, T (2009) *Psychological adaptation to the threats and stresses of a four degree world*. 'Four Degrees and Beyond' conference. Environmental Change Institute, Oxford University, Oxford.

Howden, SM, Crimp, SJ and Nelson, RN (2010) Australian agriculture in a climate of change. In Jubb, I, Holper, P and Cai, W (eds) *Managing Climate Change: papers from the GREENHOUSE 2009 Conference*. CSIRO Publishing, Melbourne: 101–11.

Huntingford, C, Lowe, JA, Gohar, LK, Bowerman, NHA, Allen, MR, Raper, SCB and Smith, SM (2012) The link between a global 2°C warming threshold and emissions in years 2020, 2050 and beyond. *Environmental Research Letters* 7, www.ceh.ac.uk/staffwebpages/documents/huntingford_et_al_12.pdf.

Intergovernmental Panel on Climate Change (IPCC) (2007) Summary for Policymakers. In Solomon, S, Qin, D, Manning, M, Chen, Z, Marquis, M, Averyt, KB, Tignor, M and Miller, HL (eds) *Climate Change 2007: the physical science basis*. Contribution of Working Group I to the Fourth Assessment Report of the Intergovernmental Panel on Climate Change. Cambridge University Press, Cambridge UK.

Kates, RW, Travis, WR and Wilbanks, TJ (2012) Transformational adaptation when incremental adaptations to climate change are insufficient. *Proceedings of the National Academy of Sciences* 109: 7156–61.

Liu, JG, Dietz, T, Carpenter, SR, Alberti, M, Folke, C, Moran, E, Pell, AM, Deadman, P, Kratz, T, Lubchenco, J, Ostram, E, Ouyang, Z, Provencher, W, Redman, CL, Schneider, SH and Taylor, WW (2007) Complexity of coupled human and natural systems. *Science* 317: 1513–16.

Pahl-Wostl, C (2009) A conceptual framework for analysing adaptive capacity and multi-level learning processes in resource governance regimes. *Global Environmental Change: Human and Policy Dimensions* 19: 354–65.

Palutikof, J, Parry, M, Stafford Smith, M, Ash, AJ, Boulter, SL and Waschka, M (2013) The past, present and future of adaptation: setting the context and naming the challenges. In Palutikof, J, Boulter, SL, Ash, AJ, Stafford Smith, M, Parry, M, Waschka, M and Guitart, D (eds) *Climate adaptation futures*. Wiley Publishing, Oxford: 3–29.

Park, SE, Marshall, NA, Jakku, E, Dowd, AM, Howden, SM, Mendham, E and Fleming, A (2012) Informing adaptation responses to climate change through theories of transformation. *Global Environmental Change* 22: 115–26.

Parry, ML, Canziani, OF, Palutikof, JP, van der Linden, PJ and Hanson, CE (eds) (2007) *Climate Change 2007: impacts, adaptation and vulnerability*. Contribution of Working Group II to the Fourth Assessment Report of the Intergovernmental Panel on Climate Change. Cambridge University Press, Cambridge UK.

Pentland, D, Forsyth, K, Maciver, D, Walsh, M, Murray, R, Irvine, L and Sikora, S (2011) Key characteristics of knowledge transfer and exchange in healthcare: integrative literature review. *Journal of Advanced Nursing* 67: 1408–25.

Randall, A, Capon, T, Sanderson, T, Merrett, D and Hertzler, G (2012) *Choosing a decision-making framework to manage uncertainty in climate adaptation decision-making: a practitioner's handbook*. National Climate Change Adaptation Research Facility / University of Sydney, Sydney.

Rockström, J, Steffen, W, Noone, K, Persson, Å, Chapin, FS III, Lambin, EF, Lenton, TM, Scheffer, M, Folke, C, Schellnhuber, HJ, Nykvist, B, de Wit, CA, Hughes, T, van der Leeuw, S, Rodhe, H, Sörlin, S, Snyder, PK, Costanza, R, Svedin, U, Falkenmark, M, Karlberg, L, Corell, RW, Fabry, VJ, Hansen, J, Walker, B, Liverman, D, Richardson, K, Crutzen, P and Foley, JA (2009) A safe operating space for humanity. *Nature* 461: 472–5.

Roux, DJ and Foxcroft, LC (2011) The development and application of strategic adaptive management within South African National Parks. *Koedoe* 53, article 1049: 5 pp, www.koedoe.co.za/index.php/koedoe/article /view/1049.

Sarewitz, D and Pielke, RA (2007) The neglected heart of science policy: reconciling supply of and demand for science. *Environmental Science & Policy* 10: 5–16.

Stafford Smith, M, Horrocks, L, Harvey, A and Hamilton, C (2011) Rethinking adaptation for a 4°C World. *Philosophical Transactions of the Royal Society A—Mathematical, Physical and Engineering Sciences* 369: 196–216.

Stainforth, DA, Downing, TE, Washington, R, Lopez, A and New, M (2007) Issues in the interpretation of climate model ensembles to inform decisions. *Philosophical Transactions of the Royal Society A—Mathematical, Physical and Engineering Sciences* 365: 2163–77.

Steffen, W (2010) Observed trends in Earth System behavior. *Wiley Interdisciplinary Reviews: Climate Change* 1: 428–49.

Steffen, W, Sanderson, RA, Tyson, PD, Jäger, J, Matson, PA, Moore B III, Oldfield, F, Richardson, K, Schellnhuber, HJ, Turner, BL and Wasson, RJ (2004) *Global change and the Earth system: a planet under pressure*. Springer-Verlag, Heidelberg.

Voß, J-P, Newig, J, Kastens, B, Monstadt, J and Nölting, B (2007) Steering for sustainable development: a typology of problems and strategies with respect to ambivalence, uncertainty and distributed power. *Journal of Environmental Policy and Planning* 9: 193–212.

Walters, CJ (1986) *Adaptive management of renewable resources*. Macmillan Publishing Co., New York.

Walters, CJ and Holling, CS (1990) Large-scale management experiments and learning by doing. *Ecology* 71: 2060–8.

Weber, EU (2006) Experience-based and description-based perceptions of long-term risk: why global warming does not scare us (yet). *Climatic Change* 77: 103–20.

Willows, R and Connell, R, eds (2003) *Climate adaptation: risk, uncertainty and decision-making.* UKCIP (United Kingdom Climate Impacts Programme), Oxford.

Wise, RM, Fazey, I, Stafford Smith, M, Park, SE, Eakine, HC, Archer Van Garderen, ERM, Campbell, B and Wolf, S (2014) Reconceptualising adaptation to climate change as part of pathways of change and response. *Global Environmental Change*, 28: 325–36.

Wolf, S (2012) Vulnerability and risk: comparing assessment approaches. *Natural Hazards* 61: 1099–1113.

4. Teleology, Cyclicality and Episodism: Three competing views of change in international relations

Michael Wesley

The discipline of international relations is divided by competing conceptions of change. International relations formed as a modern discipline in response to humanity's growing destructiveness as monarchs, states and societies repeatedly went to war with each other. Twentieth-century scholarship in international relations grew up alongside a hopeful project embodied in an international movement: that if subjected to rational research and the close attention of concerned citizens, inter-state relations could be prevented from descending into the carnage of another world war.[1]

The interwar years (1919–39) became the crucible in which this project was tested. Internationalism grew apace as a genuinely transnational movement, with the development of the Royal Institute of International Affairs (UK), the Council on Foreign Relations (US), the Australian Institute of International Affairs, the Institute of Pacific Affairs, and a range of like-minded institutions in many countries. Scholars such as James Bryce (1922), Goldsworthy Lowes Dickinson (1926), William Dunning (1923), Harold Laski (1935), Philip Marshall Brown (1923), Frederick Sherwood Dunn (1937), Thomas Lawrence (1919) and Sir Alfred Zimmern (1936) produced studies into the causes of war and international friction, and the prospects for these to be blunted by international law, international organisation, and the evolution of ethical forms of international thought. For a time, the combination of scholarship and activism appeared to be bearing fruit, with the formation of the League of Nations, the signing of the Kellogg–Briand Pact, and the drawdown of military arsenals in North America and Europe.

The problem was that Japan's Showa nationalists, Mussolini, Hitler and Stalin were not seized with such optimism. As Japanese, Italian, German and Soviet expansionism brought the world again to the brink of war, the occupant of the Woodrow Wilson Chair of International Relations at the University of Aberystwyth, EH Carr, published a trenchant critique of the idealist movement

---

1   Although modern international relations writing can be traced to the mid-nineteenth century (see Schmidt 1998) it is generally accepted that international relations coalesced as a self-conscious discipline after World War I, symbolised by the establishment of the first university chair in international relations at the University of Aberystwyth in 1919.

in international relations under the title *The twenty years' crisis* (1939). Joined on the other side of the Atlantic in 1946 by Hans Morgenthau's publication of *Scientific man versus power politics*, a burgeoning movement of 'realist' critique condemned utopian liberal scholarship for being overly prescriptive in its analysis, flawed in its basic understandings of human nature, and naive in its policy prescriptions. A clear implication of the realist critique was that idealism ironically makes war more, not less, likely.

International relations consolidated as a discipline after World War II, deeply divided by what came to be called its first great debate. Arguably, however, the idealist–realist divide continues as the major schism in the discipline, reproduced anew with each generation of scholars and each expansion of the discipline into new countries, because each side of the schism embodies a concept of change in international relations that is fundamentally incompatible with that of the other side. The two alternative conceptions of change can be termed 'teleology' and 'cyclicality'. More recently, a third conception of change has emerged, borrowing heavily from institutional analysis in political science, which can be called 'episodism'.

Teleology

The teleological conception of international relations is convinced that international relations can evolve and has evolved over time into more sophisticated, rational and just forms of relations. Scholars in this tradition point to a variety of data to support this conviction. The past century has seen, for example, an unprecedented proliferation of international institutions charged with regularising international relations and taming the excesses of power politics (Krasner 1983, Ruggie 1993). The occurrence of major war between states is in steady decline (Mueller 2004), although the bestiality of conflicts within states continues to climb (Rummel 1994). Transnational trade, investment and prosperity continue to rise, making sustained conflict simply too costly for states to contemplate (Rosecrance 1986). The great and bloody ideological contests of the past have been resolved (Fukuyama 1989). The spread of democracy and growth of conceptions of justice have tamed the ravages of power politics (Doyle 1986, Beitz 1979). The combination of technology, travel and transnational culture has bred a situation in which hostility between peoples has become unthinkable (Deutsch 1949, Cooper 1998).

At the base of the teleological conception is a profound belief in the power of rational human agency to alter the irrational outcomes of international relations. Ultimately, international relations is about the interaction of human beings, and as a result of this the closed system of states inevitably evolves into a more predictable and stable society of states based on shared norms, objectives and expectations (Bull 1977). For some writers in this tradition, rationality and progress are injected into the affairs of states by harnessing the cold reason of human interests to overwhelm the irrational passions of relations among societies (Mitrany 1943, Haas 1964). Others argue that international relations are driven by intellectual constructs, and thus progress is provided by changing the content and expectations of those constructs (Ashley 1984, Walker 1993).

Teleological approaches to international relations can be divided into liberal and critical variants. For liberals, progress in international relations results from the slow triumph of human interests over human passions, of material concerns over emotive drives. To liberal writers in international relations, all that is required is for the same concerns that underpin stable and prosperous domestic societies to be unfettered and allowed to construct a stable and prosperous international society (Keohane and Milner 1996, Moravcsik 1997). If allowed free play, rationality will free states from self-defeating, zero-sum conceptions of their interests, enabling them to develop positive-sum outcomes. Ultimately, long-run liberal international orders will foster liberal rationality within states, as they realise the benefits that arise from stability and liberal norms justify their own contributions to the perpetuation of the liberal order (Keohane 1984).

Critical variants of the teleological school are united by their conviction that scholarship and practice in international relations are mutually reinforcing. Any writer's perspective on world affairs derives from his or her preferences for and interests in the way the world works—or does not (Cox 1981). Typically, critical writers take aim at conservative or liberal conceptions of international relations, arguing that such frameworks provide intellectual justification for particular power orders or economic orders, which in turn reward their intellectual defenders. To critical writers, it is the task of international relations to expose the workings of the power and economic orders and their intellectual superstructures, making the act of international relations scholarship an emancipatory project. In stripping away the intellectual garb of the workings of the current order, critical writers intend to expose the inequities and injustices of the current system, as a first step to changing that system. In this conception, human agency in the evolution of international relations is refined down to the international relations scholar him/herself as the radical agent of change.

To the teleological view of international relations, change is progressive and unidirectional. It may alternate between periods of slower and faster evolution, but in general the thought of international affairs reverting to the instability, hatreds and hierarchies of a century ago is as ludicrous as believing in a return to the era of monarchs, empires and European supremacy. International relations has moved on from the issues that preoccupied the internationalists of the interwar years, and is focused on new global challenges, many of which are the product of the unprecedented period of peace and prosperity following the end of World War II. Old problems of national hatreds, ideological rivalry and zero-sum conflict are now found only in the margins of world politics, and can be eradicated there through the injection of evolutionary statecraft as surely as medieval diseases can be wiped out through the introduction of modern medicine. The future may not be as colourful as the past, but it will be safer, more prosperous, more just, and more sustainable (Fukuyama 1992).

Cyclicality

The cyclical conception of international relations is deeply sceptical of the claims of the teleological conception. Writers in the cyclical vein argue that all of the optimistic portents of positive evolution paraded by the teleologists are largely surface dressing, while the deep rationality of relations between societies remains much the same as it was at the dawn of recorded history. We have seen periods of peace and prosperity before, they point out, which usually come to an end in a catastrophic conflict that resets the basic ordering of power in the world. The last period of globalist euphoria ended in the slaughter of World War I. Sovereignty is not being quietly superseded by transnational flows of money, goods, people and ideas; rather, the state is quietly extending its tentacles into ever broader areas of national life (Weiss 1998). Neither are states ceasing to invest in ever more destructive weapons systems (Ball 1993). International organisations are not curbing national rivalries; they are the new vehicles for rivalry (Grieco 1990, Mearsheimer 1994). Democracy, technology and education have not eradicated passions so much as turbocharged them (Kagan 2008). The end of ideological contestation has not resulted in a liberal utopia so much as a new era of religious or civilisational conflict (Huntington 1993, Juergensmeyer 1993).

At the base of the cyclical view of change is a profound belief that one can dip into practically any period of international history and find remarkable parallels with international relations today. The observations of Thucydides' fourth-century BC *History of the Peloponnesian War* are much quoted by cyclicalists, as are those of his seventeenth-century translator, Thomas Hobbes (Lebow 2005). The lessons of history, for the cyclical conception, are that only sober study of the recurring patterns of history, and the realistic conduct of human affairs according to these patterns, are the best routes to security and prosperity. On the other hand, misinformed idealism of the teleological variety is the shortest route to instability and violence.

A view of human nature very different from the optimistic teleological view drives cyclical approaches to international affairs. However rational and virtuous humans are as individuals or within societies, as collectivities they become profoundly amoral (Niebuhr 1948). Whatever their morals or positive intentions, they are fated by the international structure of anarchy—whereby there is no power higher than the state, so each must look to protect its interests—to think and act in a profoundly self-interested way (Wight 1977). Because there is no higher authority to prevent predation, conflict and violence are ever present possibilities (Waltz 1959). As each state looks to bolster its own security, it thereby makes its neighbours less secure, prompting a never-ending 'security dilemma' that gives rise to high peacetime arms spending (Herz 1950). In such a state of nature, states and leaders may profess teleological principles, but these are most likely covers or vehicles for their power ambitions (Morgenthau 1948).

It is important to note that the cyclical view is not a theory of stasis; some evolution is acknowledged by writers within this tradition. They tend to see international history as the serial rise and decline of empires and great powers, which structure the world around them to suit their interests and to the preferences of their domestic orders and values (Knutsen 1999). Their rise is most often the result of material factors: economic dynamism, military technology, and/or demographic surges. The period of their ascendancy brings relative international peace, prosperity and progress (Kindleberger 1976). Often this period is marked by a rough balance between several great powers, the number of which determines the structure and stability of the international system at the time (Waltz 1979). But inevitably this period comes to an end, either due to the rise of competitors (Organski 1958) or because of the internal strains of maintaining hegemony (Kennedy 1988). The period of power transition, from one order to the next, is generally marked by great power war (Gilpin 1984).

Drawing inspiration from Machiavelli, cyclicalists believe the role of international relations is to provide clear policy advice on the current and future state of the cycle of history. It is their job to defuse any form of triumphalism, in which great powers can become convinced that history has ended with their ascendancy, and will stay that way (Layne 2003). By being clear-eyed about the inevitable cycle of history, they are able to provide policy advice that can minimise the violent aspects of power transition. In this sense, they are able to strike the occasional optimistic note, pointing to the US's peaceful usurpation of Britain's role as a world power in the mid-twentieth century, and the Soviet Union's peaceful implosion in the late twentieth century (Gaddis 1997). As such, theirs is not a rigidly mechanistic view of change. Surprising variation can occur despite the underlying logic remaining constant; as Mark Twain quipped, 'history seldom repeats itself, but it does tend to rhyme.'

Episodism

A third variant—very much a minority strain—has emerged between the absolutes of teleologism and cyclicality. This is a tendency to view change as episodic and unpredictable in its timing, extent and direction. It is a conception of international relations as a realm of human activity that tends towards routines and stasis, accreting over time structures and forces of inertia that are periodically overwhelmed by underlying change. It is an approach that remains unconvinced by the unidirectional optimism of the teleologists or the determining pessimism of the cyclicalists. It is unconvinced by the data of both schools, preferring to remain open-minded and empirically oriented in thinking about change in international relations.

A major element in the inertia of contemporary international relations is seen to be the increasing routinisation of international life. The remarkable proliferation of international institutions has been a major part of this. International institutions, it is argued, preserve the power structures and expectations that existed at the time of their establishment. This makes them extremely hard to adapt to the evolution of international relations, and equally hard to abolish, given the reputation capital and hopes that have been invested in them over the years. The solution to the declining relevance of existing institutions is rather to simply establish new ones—which turn out to be equally inflexible and of declining relevance over time. The result of constant institutional creation is a progressive crowding of diplomatic schedules and a growing routinisation of international life—at the expense of issues on which real initiative and action is needed (Wesley 2011).

Inertia is the result of the difficulty and cost of change and the investment of the powerful in current ways of doing things. Several factors play interlocking roles in supporting inertia and routinisation. Institutions and relationships often embody *high start-up and sunk costs*. Often they were negotiated at an opportune time that is unlikely to recur; inevitably they are seen, for all of their defects, as being better than no institution, agreement or relationship at all. Existing institutions exert strong *learning effects*, by favouring those who adapt their strategies and expectations to the existing rules. These are buttressed by *adaptive expectations* that favour existing ways of doing things over innovation. Bureaucratic objectives tend to be moulded by institutional possibilities, rather than vice versa. *Routinisation incentives* tend to multiply activities that comply with existing structures and crowd out opportunities for innovation. *Competency traps* breed familiarity with existing rules and bureaucratic training becomes oriented to most effectively using those rules (March and Olsen 1998).

The very anarchic nature of international relations means that established routines and institutions are heavily invested in, simply because they enable inter-state and intercultural interaction. Often such institutions are modes of communication (the dominant *lingua franca*) or transaction (the dominant international currency) that exhibit remarkable 'sticky power' simply because of their usefulness and the lack of viable alternatives (Mead 2004, Eichengreen 2009). Often their usefulness hides considerable weaknesses.

Ultimately, however, change will occur because humanity is subject to constant change: material, technical, developmental, moral. Eventually the sum of all of this underlying change will expose the inadequacies of existing routines, institutions and relationships. Europe's empires will collapse in the space of a decade. A Berlin Wall will be torn down overnight. Two planes will crash into the World Trade Centre. Depending on the gap that is drawn between existing routines and the new reality, a period of intense experimentation will follow—and the resulting routines, institutions and relationships will soon accrete all of the attributes of inertia.

Episodic change cannot be categorically classified as either teleological or cyclical. One instance—the fall of the Berlin Wall—may look like evidence of teleological progress, while another—the attack on the World Trade Centre—may be redolent with the rhymes of history.

Conclusion

Change remains a central problem in the discipline of international relations. As an intellectual exercise and a policy science, international relations is inescapably future-focused. Conditioned to the constant expectation of unforeseen developments, its reaction has been to study change in history as a way of projecting some predictability into the future. But the divides between its three perspectives on change—teleologism, cyclicality and episodism—are ultimately unresolvable. There is, quite simply, enough data to support each of these three positions. No event has yet enabled any of the variants to permanently discredit one of the others. And so international relations will continue to be a discipline united by its deeply divided conceptions of change.

References

Ashley, RK (1984) The poverty of neorealism. *International Organization* 38(2): 225–86.

Ball, D (1993) Arms and affluence: military acquisitions in the Asia Pacific region. *International Security* 18(3) Winter: 78–112.

Beitz, CR (1979) *Political theory and international relations*. Princeton University Press, Princeton.

Brown, PM (1923) *International society: its nature and interests*. Macmillan Company, New York.

Bryce, J (1922) *International relations*. Macmillan, London.

Bull, H (1977) *The anarchical society: a study of order in world politics*. Macmillan, London.

Carr, EH (1939, 2nd ed 1964) *The twenty years' crisis, 1919–1939*. Harper and Row Publishers, New York.

Cooper, R (1998) *The breaking of nations*. Atlantic Books, London.

Cox, RW (1981) Social forces, state and world orders: beyond international relations theory. *Millennium* 10(2) Summer: 126–55.

Deutsch, K (1949) *Political community in the North Atlantic area*. Princeton University Press, Princeton.

Dickinson, GL (1926) *International anarchy 1904–1914*. The Century Co, New York.

Doyle, M (1986) Liberalism and world politics. *American Political Science Review* 80(4) December: 1151–69.

Dunn, FS (1937) *Peaceful change: a study of international procedures*. Council on Foreign Relations, New York.

Dunning, W (1923) Liberty and equality in international relations. *American Political Science Review* 17 (February): 1–16.

Eichengreen, B (2009) *Exorbitant privilege: the rise of the dollar*. Oxford University Press, Oxford.

Fukuyama, F (1989) The end of history? *The National Interest* 16 (Summer): 3–18.

Fukuyama, F (1992) *The end of history and the last man*. Penguin Books, London.

Gaddis, JL (1997) *We now know: rethinking Cold War history*. Oxford University Press, Oxford.

Gilpin, R (1984) *War and change in world politics*. Cambridge University Press, Cambridge.

Grieco, J (1990) *Cooperation among nations*. Cornell University Press, Ithaca.

Haas, EB (1964) *Beyond the nation-state: functionalism and international organisation*. Stanford University Press, Stanford.

Herz, J (1950) Idealist internationalism and the security dilemma. *World Politics* 2: 157–80.

Huntington, SP (1993) The clash of civilizations? *Foreign Affairs* (Summer): 22–49.

Juergensmeyer, M (1993) *The new Cold War? Religious nationalism confronts the secular state*. University of California Press, Berkeley.

Kagan, RD (2008) *The return of history and the end of dreams*. Atlantic Books, London.

Kennedy, P (1988) *The rise and fall of the great powers*. Random House, New York.

Keohane, RO (1984) *After hegemony*. Princeton University Press, Princeton.

Keohane, RO and Milner, HV (1996) *Internationalization and domestic politics*. Cambridge University Press, Cambridge.

Kindleberger, C (1976) *The world in Depression, 1929–1939*. University of California Press, Berkeley.

Knutsen, T (1999) *The rise and fall of world orders*. Manchester University Press, Manchester.

Krasner, SD (1983) *International regimes*. Cornell University Press, Ithaca.

Laski, H (1935) *World politics and personal insecurity*. McGraw-Hill, New York.

Lawrence, T (1919) *The society of nations: its past, present and possible future*. Oxford University Press, New York.

Layne, C (2003) *The peace of illusions*. Cornell University Press, Ithaca.

Lebow, RN (2005) *The tragic vision of politics*. Cambridge University Press, Cambridge.

March, JG and Olson, JP (1998) The institutional dynamics of international political orders. *International Organization* 52(4): 943–69.

Mead, WR (2004) *Power, terror, peace and war*. Knopf, New York.

Mearsheimer, JJ (1994) The false promise of international institutions. *International Security* 19: 5–49.

Mitrany, D (1943) *A working peace system*. Royal Institute of International Affairs, London.

Moravcsik, A (1997) Taking preferences seriously: a liberal theory of international politics. *International Organization* 51: 513–53.

Morgenthau, HJ (1946) *Scientific man versus power politics*. University of Chicago Press.

Morgenthau, HJ (1948) *Politics among nations*. Knopf, New York.

Mueller, J (2004) *The remnants of war*. Cornell University Press, Ithaca.

Niebuhr, R (1948) *Moral man and immoral society: a study in ethics and politics*. Scribner's Sons, New York.

Organski, AFK (1958) *World politics*. Knopf, New York.

Rosecrance, R (1986) *The rise of the trading state*. Basic Books, New York.

Ruggie, JG (1993) *Multilateralism matters: the theory and praxis of an organizational form*. Columbia University Press, New York.

Rummel, RJ (1994) Power, genocide and mass murder. *Journal of Peace Research* 31(1): 1–10.

Schmidt, BC (1998) *The political discourse of anarchy: a disciplinary history of international relations*. State University of New York Press, Albany.

Walker, RBJ (1993) *Inside/outside: international relations as political theory*. Cambridge University Press, Cambridge.

Waltz, KN (1959) *Man, the state and war*. Columbia University Press, New York.

Waltz, KN (1979) *Theory of international politics*. Addison-Wesley, Boston.

Weiss, L (1998) *The myth of the powerless state*. Polity Press, Cambridge.

Wesley, M (2011) *There goes the neighbourhood: Australia and the rise of Asia*. Newsouth Books, Sydney.

Wight, M (1977) *Power politics*. Penguin, London.

Zimmern, A (1936) *The League of Nations and the rule of law*. Macmillan and Co., London.

5. Change is Central to Sociology

Craig Browne

Change is a central problem for the discipline of sociology. It is often claimed that sociology originated as a discipline to comprehend the major changes that characterised modern society, especially those bequeathed by two revolutions: the French Revolution and the Industrial Revolution. Sociology approaches the question of change at a number of different levels, and major theoretical traditions can be demarcated in terms of their conceptions of change, particularly with respect to their interpretations of the origins, agencies, scale, preconditions, consequences and potentials of change. As a discipline that is in dialogue with the present state of society, sociologists' thinking about change is affected by contemporary trends and developments. Sociologists have recently been very much concerned with whether the topic of their investigation has changed, particularly with the question of whether the global has replaced the national as the context of social relations. C Wright Mills once described the best work in sociology as establishing a connection between history and biography. The sociological imagination enables individuals to turn their personal experience of private troubles into public issues that are recognised as shared (Wright Mills 1959). Sociology accomplishes this reflection through disclosing general patterns in social relations and revealing connections between different dimensions of society.

Sociologists often think about change in a comparative and constructionist manner, since they seek to demonstrate that what is assumed to be natural and permanent is actually a product of historical processes and culturally specific practices. From this perspective, modern capitalist society is considered to be particularly dynamic and transformative; it incorporates elements of change in the processes of its reproduction, and supposedly renders earlier and less competitive methods of production and organisation obsolete. Sociologists have been concerned with the effects that the major institutions of modern society have on individuals and their living conditions—institutions like capitalism, the state, bureaucratic administration, industrialisation and modern cities. The major sociological theories of change generally contain some critical and diagnostic conception of modern life. Emile Durkheim proposed that a sense of normlessness or *anomie* was promoted in individuals by certain tendencies of modern society. Max Weber suggested that modern capitalism and industrialisation may lead to an 'iron cage' of unending accumulation and labour. Karl Marx contended that capitalist production was based on systematic exploitation and human alienation. And Georg Simmel pointed to the indifference that individuals develop through their experience of life in large cities and the practices of quantification that are associated with the use of money. Important works of contemporary sociology continue the critical diagnostic approach to change, but there are also recent positive assessments of changes and their potentials. Manuel Castells, for instance, has drawn attention to how the use of social media and information technologies gives individuals the prior experience necessary to participate in new kinds of leaderless organisation. The experience of networked association is then translated into the practices of movements like those of the Arab Spring and the Occupy protests (Castells 2012).

Sociologists have equally been concerned with questioning notions of the inevitability of change. Sociological research has regularly demonstrated that change has been limited in major areas of social relations, especially those to do with longstanding inequalities. Sociologists quite often find discrepancies between the widespread social perceptions of changes in the circumstances of subordinated social groups and their actual conditions. For example, the overall remuneration of female labour compared to male labour has not changed as much as might be presumed from the enacting of equal pay legislation in Australia several decades ago. These kinds of discrepancies highlight the complexity of explaining change and the constraints upon changing enduring dimensions of society. Sociologists appreciate that it may be necessary to take into account how one change may facilitate or limit another—for example, there has been a substantial increase in part-time employment during the period since the legislation of equal pay for men and women. Sociologists are then very interested in how institutions and social structures, like class and patriarchy, are reproduced and limit change. It is impossible to address the question of change without engaging with some of the basic dilemmas of sociology. One of these dilemmas is the extent to which social institutions are the intended product of social action.

Before considering some basic dilemmas that shape sociological thinking about change, I will introduce the early sociological interpretations of change. Although the consolidation of sociology as a discipline disqualified many of the early speculative theories of social evolution, I suggest that their interest in long-term historical processes has contemporary relevance. Sociology undoubtedly contains a diversity of approaches to change, but the differences between them reflect the positions taken on some basic dilemmas. I then outline several particularly significant conundrums and emphasise the importance of how explanations of change seek to interrelate social action and social structure. After sketching these dilemmas, I overview the most important classical sociological theories of change and explain how Emile Durkheim, Max Weber and Karl Marx provided profound and contrasting conceptions of the dominant processes that shape modern societies. In 'Modernity and modernities: Multiple and successive', I then examine how sociologists have sought to rethink the dynamics of social transformation and to understand the implications of the modernising of societies that historically held different cultural, especially religious, perspectives from those that shaped European modernity. It has already been noted how sociological investigations regularly generate empirical evidence of persisting inequalities. The section that follows is an excursus on some influential recent perspectives that qualify the notion of change and question the role that notions of change play in contemporary discourses. Although these critical standpoints are considered to be somewhat deficient, they importantly contribute to greater theoretical reflexivity. Indeed, the penultimate section, 'Contemporary sociological interpretations', highlights how the most novel current approaches to change respond to these qualifying perspectives, including through their exploration of the relationship between social critique and change. This section also sketches how interpretations of a new phase of modernity reframe the dilemma of the relationship between action and structure, considers the interpretations of social movements as initiators of change and sources of resistance to change, outlines several accounts of the paradoxical character of the social processes that are transforming contemporary societies and subjects' experiences, and notes the recent sociological concern with elucidating social creativity. Finally, the 'Conclusion' does not so much synthesise the various lines of analysis as underline how disagreements between them derive from different responses to some commonly shared assumptions.

Early sociological images of change

The way that sociologists think about change has changed. Sociologists have largely left behind the interpretations of change that they inherited from nineteenth-century thought, specifically those notions derived from philosophies of history and theories of evolution. Nineteenth-century sociology and proto-sociology incorporated a strong sense of human progress and elaborated corresponding typologies of the evolutionary development of society, for example, suggesting that there has been a transition from more simple to complex social structures. In this way, these early sociologists sought to establish the direction or teleology of change. Borrowing from natural scientific thinking of the time, they considered that the evolution of society was a process of adaptation and early sociological theories were concerned with society as a whole, or a holistic system that combined and coordinated different institutions, like the family, law and production. Although the influence of the tradition of the philosophy of history may have been less pervasive upon nineteenth-century sociology, the assumption that the evolution of society belonged to a common history of the human species was derived from it. This justified thinking about change in universalistic terms. Despite European society being taken to be the most advanced and superior, the investigation into what Raewyn Connell describes as global difference, that is, the inquiring on a global scale into the diversity of societies and the multitude of practices, beliefs and organisation, gave rise to questions that remain relevant to sociological reflection on large-scale social development (Connell 1997, 2007). These questions include whether change is a linear sequence of development and what is the basis for comparing changes in societies that are at different levels of development.

The questions that early sociologists posed about change have not entirely disappeared. Rather, assumptions about the overall development of society and social evolution are probably still implicit in sociological analyses that are addressed to other topics, like gender and education, sexuality and consumption. Connell argues that in the early decades of the twentieth century the leading sociological theme of global difference came to be replaced by a concern with the problems internal to the urban Metropole. Major strands of sociological thought have subsequently been criticised for their alleged retreat from history and exclusive concern with present-day society. It has been recently suggested that in order to address the recent global financial crisis and its implications, it is necessary for sociology to renew its interest in long-term, large-scale historical processes (Calhoun 2011, Postone 2012). Independent of the financial crisis, this interest has been a defining feature of the recent work on multiple modernities and, as will be discussed later, this approach proposes that different civilisations constitute the cultural background to major changes, like political revolutions and the varying patterns of modernisation.

Basic dilemmas of sociological thinking about change

Sociological conceptions of change reflect some of the basic dilemmas that confront the discipline. In my opinion, the notion that society is constituted through the actions of subjects is a basic supposition of sociological reasoning. At the same time, sociological analyses equally highlight the extent to which subjects are not autonomous and the persistence of social relations of domination that limit subjects' actions and capacities to enact change. From this latter perspective, society appears more like an objective reality that constrains subjects and is itself an independent force. This character of society is realised in various institutions or social systems, like those of the economy, the law, the family, the political order, and enduring structures, like those of class and patriarchy. These institutions and systems pre-exist individual subjects and they appear to change of their own volition, that is, somewhat independently of the actions and interactions of subjects.

The global financial crisis may be a useful illustration of this apparent objectivity and externality of the social. The crisis involved the actions of individuals but it may have been conditioned to a greater extent by the structural problems of the global financial system, including the excessive expansion of unstable financial instruments, like derivatives and credit default swaps. Individuals participate in the financial system, yet their power to control this institution may be limited. Individuals are nevertheless significantly affected by the financial system's problems, such as through becoming unemployed as a result of the recession that follows from the financial crisis. The basic dilemma that sociology addresses recurs in the case of seeking to understand the potential of individuals either to transform the global financial system or to simply rectify its existing structural problems. Of course, there are many additional considerations that should be taken into account in a sociological analysis of the global financial crisis, including the position taken on the relationship between the state and the market in capitalist societies.

Karl Marx famously contributed one of the most lucid articulations of this basic dilemma of sociology, although any contemporary reiteration would alter its gendered formulation: 'Men make their own history, but they do not make it just as they please; they do not make it under circumstances chosen by themselves, but under circumstances directly encountered, given and transmitted from the past' (Marx 1977, 301; first published 1852).

The dichotomy that shapes this dilemma in sociology is often described as that between social action and social structure. It is a dichotomy that can be readily seen to converge with others, like that between the individual and society, or that between the small scale and large scale: micro and macro. For some sociologists, these distinctions do not exist, because, for example, they argue that the individual is always a social being and cannot be separated from society. To my mind, this is to draw the wrong conclusion from a valid contention about the social being of the individual. The problem contained in the dilemma of the double character of society is not limited to specifying the relevant dichotomy; it is equally that of explaining the connections and interpenetrations that exist between social action and social structure. The actions of individuals and groups are not independent of their structurally based social positions, such as those of class and gender. Action is contingent on the resources of wealth and power, or, to use Pierre Bourdieu's term, capital that is at their disposal (Bourdieu 1990). This means that there are significant differences in the ability of individuals to control and modify their life situations. Indeed, a good deal of sociological research is concerned with detailing how these differences manifest themselves in the interaction between individuals, for example, in terms of the differences in the degree of autonomy that individuals possess at work, or how differences in capital shape individuals' interaction with social institutions, such as in the case of the effects of class background on educational outcomes.

In developing a theory that seeks to reconcile social action and social structure, Anthony Giddens (1979, 1985) proposes that structure should be conceived as both constraining and enabling. Structure is, in his opinion, somewhat like language, because language makes possible the production of sentences and limits sentences to those consistent with its rules. Just as communication serves to reproduce language, Giddens argues that structure should be conceived as the medium and outcome of action. The class structure, for instance, shapes the actions of individuals at work or school and it is, in turn, reproduced by these actions. Leaving aside the question of whether this conceptualisation is satisfactory, it is intended to capture the dynamic features of social life and the modifications that can ensue from variations in social action. According to Giddens, social agency is the capacity to pursue different alternatives. This implies that certain dimensions of change depend on the knowledge, competence and abilities of subjects. In a number of works, Giddens argues that contemporary subjects' increasing reflexivity about their living conditions is deployed by them to reshape these conditions, for example, their knowledge about divorce rates comes to be incorporated into the practices of constructing intimate relationships (Giddens 1992).

The connection that Giddens draws between social structure and social action has been criticised by sociologists who consider that it is important to emphasise the difference between them. One of the arguments that these critics make is that structure and action can change independently of each other and that a change in one may not produce a change in the other. In concrete terms this means, for instance, that changes in the interaction between individuals in work contexts and the norms that inform action need not imply a corresponding change in the principles that organise the relationship between business organisations or the system of ownership of the economic system as a whole. The distinction that I have just sketched between different types and levels of social coordination is close to the distinction sociologists draw between social integration and system integration. For instance, the education system contributes to social integration through the socialising function of schooling and system integration through enabling the allocation of individuals to different positions in the division of labour. Now, these two functions may be complementary, but they involve different imperatives. Nevertheless, the discordance between social and system integration can become a precipitating condition for social change. Sociological analyses of some major contestations, like those of May 1968 in France and of the 2011 Egyptian uprising, have drawn attention to the underlying discontent and alienation that resulted from the rising expectations of an increasingly educated youth and the actual limited opportunities in those societies at the time for either employment or rewarding work commensurate with qualifications.

Classical sociological conceptions of change

How sociologists think about change has been indelibly influenced by the work of the founding figures of the discipline of sociology. The writings of the classical sociologists, particularly Emile Durkheim, Max Weber and Karl Marx, were deeply concerned with the problem of historical transition and understanding the profound difference between modern industrial capitalist society and all preceding forms of society. These classical sociologists contributed detailed accounts of substantial historical changes and a series of theoretical concepts to explain the processes and mechanisms of change. In each case, the conception of change exemplifies aspects of their methodological perspective and their more general image of society or social relations.

For Durkheim, sociological explanations should be distinctively concerned with the social or collective, because the social has emergent properties that transcend the combination of individuals. It is at the level of the social that Durkheim sought to explain the modern division of labour and its implications. He argued, after Herbert Spencer, that social differentiation was the key process that drove the change in the division of labour and that this produced significant and unprecedented institutional separations, such as between home and work (Durkheim 1984, first published 1893). However, Durkheim considered that individuals are integrated into society through their adherence to shared norms and beliefs. Consistent with the idea of a historical transition from simple to complex social structures, Durkheim contrasted the pre-modern form of social integration, 'mechanical solidarity', with the more dynamic modern form of integration, 'organic solidarity'. Mechanical solidarity is based on the similarity of the living conditions—work, family, consumption, education and so on— of the members of a community. By contrast, organic solidarity is based on the principle of cooperation across difference and it enables social cohesion in contexts of increasing social complexity. Durkheim believed that society is a moral entity and that excessive social differentiation can lead to breakdowns in the normative integration of individuals into society, something that he sought to illustrate through a study of suicide as a social phenomenon (Durkheim 1952, first published 1897).

There are several things worth noting about Durkheim's conception of change and these features are relevant to functionalist sociological explanations. Durkheim implies that crises and social breakdown can generate responses that restore the social order. In this way, change is modification. Durkheim's vision supported French Republicanism. He sought to show how individual autonomy is reconciled in modern societies with the overarching social structure. Social differentiation makes possible a greater concern with the realisation of individual potentiality, and the division of labour provides opportunities for individuals to pursue specialised interests. Although Durkheim sought to demonstrate the unique or *sui generis* character of the social, there is the problem of the notion of social differentiation's potential circularity. It seems to better describe the consequences of change than to explain its sources. In several of his works after *The division of labour in society* (1984, first published 1893), Durkheim developed themes that have preoccupied more recent sociological thinking. Notably, he sought to reveal the social basis of classification and cognitive categories, like time and space. In addition, he developed an interpretation of the social creation of meanings and values. In *The elementary forms of religious life* (1995, first published 1912), he suggested that rituals and ceremonies can generate intense experience of the social bond and that this *collective effervescence* has the power to transform the symbolic meaning of objects and things, for instance, making a sacred totem out of a previously profane object.

Max Weber contended that a historical approach is fundamental to sociology and he wrote extensively about diverse contexts of change. Weber argued that sociology is concerned with social action and the meanings that individuals attach to these actions. In his famous work *The protestant ethic and the spirit of capitalism* (1930, first published 1905), Weber sought to demonstrate how the 'salvation anxiety' that protestant theologies promoted influenced the capitalist spirit of continuous accumulation. The protestant ethic made the types of action that facilitate capitalist accumulation practically effective, specifically through the ascetic avoidance of unproductive consumption, the regulated and efficient use of time, and the constant reinvestment of the self and profits in the business enterprise. Besides its explanation of social institutions in terms of individual actions and their combination, several features of Weber's approach to change can be gleaned from his interpretation of the 'elective affinity' between the protestant ethic and the spirit of capitalism. Weber emphasises the significance of cultural meanings and values, since these provide action with motivations and purposes for change. Yet change is the product of the historical conjuncture and the interplay of various factors. The expansion of capitalism was an unintended outcome of the protestant anxiety over salvation and it is part of a broader tendency of rationalisation that occurred in various spheres of Western society (Weber 1958, originally 1917).

For Weber, change is always the result of a combination of ideal and material interests. It depends on the particular social and historical context whether social agents' ideal interests, in things like value commitments, religious beliefs and reputation, prevail over material interests in the accumulation of wealth or subsistence. Weber showed how the interplay of factors, like ideal and material interests, the moral and the instrumental, are critically important to the historical institutionalisation of change. Weber spoke, for example, of the 'routinization of charisma' in the history of religious movements and the shift that this often entailed from a prophet's personal authority to the impersonal authority of the church. The latter represents an instance of bureaucratic rationalisation and a change in the conditions of legitimacy. Weber offered a railway metaphor to describe how 'world images', such as those of religions like Christianity, Buddhism and Hinduism, have 'like switchmen, determined the tracks along which action has been pushed by the dynamics of interest' (Weber as quoted in Swedberg 1998, 134). The prevalence of rationality in modern Western societies, Weber argued, was related to the historical processes of the 'disenchantment of world', that is, the elimination of notions of the world as inhabited by spiritual forces and influenced by magical powers.

Weber's analysis of the religious and cultural background to modern capitalism has often been interpreted as a response to the materialist perspective of Marxism, and sociological thought has sustained its dialogue with the work of Karl Marx. The problem of change was not simply a matter of description and explanation for Marx; it was a question of developing a theory that could become an informant of struggles for changing society. Marx's conception of change is dialectical, but the dialectical method has several connotations. Probably owing to its original connection to the practice of dialogue, the dialectical approach to change is relational. Marx argued that historical change has been driven by the struggle between classes. Marx sought to show how class conflict is based in the interdependency between classes and the manner in which the dominant class reproduces itself through the exploitation of the labour of the subordinate class. Marx's dialectical approach emphasised how contradiction and negation are sources of major historical change. The contradictions of capitalist production were not just limited to the exploitation of the majority by a minority. Marx contended that eventually the forces of production—that is, the technology, labour and organisation of production—would come into conflict with the social relations of production, in other words, with the capitalist system of private ownership. Marx's dialectical approach is meant to convey the dynamic of change and how the negation of the capitalist social order is developing within it; for example, Marx claimed that increases in capitalist production entail an expansion of the working class and that the working class have an interest in abolishing the conditions of their subordination.

It should be clear already that Marx's conception of change places particular emphasis on production. On the one hand, Marx considered that the major episodes of transformation were changes in the modes of production, such as from feudalism to capitalism. On the other hand, Marx suggested that changes in the culture and other institutions of society, like the legal system and the political order, are conditioned by the system of production. Many of the details of Marx's arguments have been contested, but the link that he sought to develop between social conflict and change has been extended and revised. In some cases this has been done by treating conflicts other than those of class as being of equal or greater importance to change, as, for example, in the case of the arguments of feminist sociologists concerning gender or the Weber-influenced conflict sociology highlighting the relative independence of conflicts over social status and political authority. There is another noteworthy way in which Marxism has influenced sociological thinking about change. This derives from the need to explain the confounding of Marx's expectations. In other words, it is the question of why the working class has not pursued the revolutionary abolition of capitalism? It would be impossible here to briefly survey the variety of answers that have been given to this question, but Marxists have regularly drawn attention to role of ideology and the function of the state in order to explain the absence of change. For instance, it has been suggested that the ideologies of capitalist society, like the notion that reward is commensurate with individual achievement, have concealed the exploitation of labour and that the institution of the welfare state supported a class compromise by alleviating more extreme forms of inequality.

Modernity and modernities: Multiple and successive

The writings of the classical sociological theorists laid the foundations for sociological approaches to modernity. Modernity represents not only a major change from the social order of the past, but also a constant tendency towards transformation in the present. In a sense, modernity is precisely the attempt to apply or realise this insight into the changing character of modern society. This is one reason why there is a strong connection between the ideal of autonomy and modernity. Modernity involves then a specific cultural outlook and a set of social institutions; it originated in Europe several centuries ago and has subsequently spread across the globe. Sociologists broadly agree that modernity concerns the relating of the present to the future but disagree over the probable changes and their consequences. Changes during the past few decades have compelled sociologists to revise elements of their interpretations of modernity, particularly changes like the modernisation of East Asian societies and the Iranian Revolution. It had previously been presumed that modernisation would lead all societies or nation states to share a common pattern of institutions and cultural values. In effect, change would lead to a convergence in the form of modern societies and underpinning this assumption was the equating of modernising change with other notions, especially those of progress, rationalisation and development.

The perspective of multiple modernities commences from the questioning of the notion of historical convergence of modern societies. It emphasises instead the variations in the constitution of modernity due to the background cultural context and the historical period of modernisation. For example, China's recent modernisation occurred during a period when most European societies had already undergone several phases of industrial modernisation. For this perspective, modernity is considered to accentuate human agency and this is manifested in the mobilising of significant political and religious movements, such as nationalist, communist and fundamentalist movements. The multiple modernities perspective traces differing trajectories of modernisation and institutional configurations to the influence upon modernising initiatives of prior cultural meaning systems, especially religious, and preceding structures of political authority, such as the power of the centre compared to the periphery, the social complexion of elites, and judicial authority, all of which have resulted in kinds of path dependencies that effect change. These religious–cultural meaning systems generally have civilisational dimensions, owing to the scope of the world religious background and the internal variations of a common cultural framework, such as results from conflicts over theological authority and the formation of different religious denominations and sects. The world-images, to return to Weber's phrase, of different civilisations provide responses to profound questions, like the nature of authority, the basis of justice, the purpose of living, and the difference between immanence and transcendence. From these somewhat abstract considerations, the multiple modernities perspective has generated rich and complex historical sociologies of change, for instance, elucidating the connection between earlier antinomian strands of religion and more recent fundamentalist mobilisations, the manner in which the Soviet model of modernisation was conditioned by the synthesis between revolutionary movement and imperial background, and the variations within and between European and Asian capitalism (Arnason 1993, 1998, 2002, 2005; Eisenstadt 1999, 2000).

Peter Wagner (2012) suggests that the multiple modernities perspective's accentuation of the cultural programs of civilisations may obscure the extent to which moments of crisis and conflict result in radical breaks with prior cultural meanings and institutions. Wagner proposes instead the idea of successive modernities. He emphasises how shifts ensue from the changes in the rules and conventions of social practices, especially insofar as this relates to the application of knowledge to generic problems, like those of political power, economic allocation, and legitimate knowledge. Wagner (1994) argued that in the first few decades of the twentieth century, the early liberal phase of modernity gave way in the face of economic and political crises to another phase. Organised modernity entailed a greater degree of state coordination, the expansion of bureaucratic capitalist organisation, the development of social policy and mass consumption based on standardised production. In short, the successive phases of modernity result from the loss of legitimacy of formerly dominant understandings and the diffusion across major social institutions of another set of common principles and practical orientations, as well as the creation of new social organisations. Wagner claims that two broad notions have shaped modernity, those of liberty and discipline. Liberty and discipline form the points of reference for modern endeavours to modify society and to control processes of change. In part, the dynamic of modernity can be traced to the institutional and everyday practical attempts to make liberty and discipline mutually reinforcing and the changes that ensue from the persistent tension or conflict between autonomy and control.

Wagner argues that around 1970 the phase of organised modernity entered into crisis and it is in the process of being succeeded. The crisis of organised modernity is evident in its core framing dimensions of the state, the nation and class coming under challenge, the connected tendency for individuals to have a more differentiated relationship to collective categories, like class and citizenship, as well as a more general redefining of social identities, the emergence of post-Fordist discourses of deregulation and flexibility, and the questioning of social scientific knowledge's ability to predict and produce an accurate representation of the world. The notion of successive modernities does, nevertheless, imply significant continuity, and change remains a matter of the different institutional articulations of the core orienting notions of autonomy and control. Although Wagner's conception of the transition from organised to 'extended liberal modernity' is founded on several distinctive theoretical assumptions, the method of demarcating and contrasting the contemporary period and its types of dominant institutions with those of the preceding period is typical of sociological approaches to change. In fact, there has been a plethora of theoretical conceptions that have developed to explain similar empirical developments and that consider that the period roughly between the late 1960s and early 1980s marks a significant transition in Western capitalist societies. These conceptions of change often employ binaries like those between industrial and post-industrial society, simple modernisation (the original change from feudal–agrarian social structures to capitalist–industrial social structures) and reflexive modernisation (the modernising of already modern societies through science and technology, the extension of welfare rights to citizens, and the increase in female labour market participation, for example) (Beck 1992, Beck et al. 1994).

Before considering these conceptions in more detail and some recent modifications in sociological thinking about change, I will comment on a couple of rather different and much more sceptical sociological approaches to change. Significantly, the perspectives of multiple and successive modernities are sociological responses to notions of a movement beyond modernity and the postmodernist challenge to modernist conceptions of reason, progress, autonomy and subjectivity. Postmodernist questioning of these conceptions was influenced by the structuralist approach that had developed in linguistics and the extension of its method to disciplines like anthropology and sociology.

Recent sociological qualifications of change

It is worth reflecting on some recent sociological arguments qualifying change, especially because approaches seeking to account for change sometimes developed in response to them. I have noted that empirical sociological enquiries into social inequalities have produced findings that qualify ideas about change and social mobility. Now, this kind of research can enable a more exacting understanding of the conditions of change, but for the most part it does not actually question the meaning of the category: 'change'. By contrast, neo-structuralist perspectives analyse change as a sign or cultural schema. Structuralism considers that the meaning of *change* derives from its position in a system of signs and its difference from, or negation of, other significations and categories, like the antonyms of stasis, permanence, or stability. This means that the category of change is open to the criticism of relying on questionable binaries and oppositions; for example, I distinguished changing modern societies from less dynamic traditional societies in order to introduce sociological perspectives on change. Michel Foucault claimed that modern discourses that espouse change, such as those of therapy and management, are modes of power that operate through a subject's internalising their meanings and by excluding other meanings (Foucault 1980a). The notion of unintended consequences is a feature of many sociological conceptions of change, but Foucault's historical genealogies show how movements for humane punishment, sexual liberation and liberties were themselves implicated in the extension of power and resulted in the more intensive disciplining of prisoners, the regulation of sexual identities, and the consolidation of governmentality (Foucault 1978, 1980b, 2003).

Bourdieu criticised structuralist analyses for subordinating the temporal dimension of social life, but he retained structuralism's relational approach to symbolic meaning. Bourdieu developed the relational conception in his empirical sociological studies of the dynamics of struggles over recognition in different fields of social life, including those of art, consumption, academia and education (Bourdieu and Passeron 1977, Bourdieu 1984, 1988). In these investigations, Bourdieu noted how the category of change is mobilised in conflicts and how it can serve both to legitimise and to undermine legitimacy. It is probably a banal, though nevertheless true, insight that individuals towards the top of a field or social hierarchy generally argue for either the preservation of the existing order or for managed change. However, social fields are arenas of struggles. Bourdieu suggested that groups contesting the current structure of a field seek to establish different principles and criteria as the basis for organising and evaluating practices in that field. Bourdieu's thesis is that the principles and criteria that individuals and groups promote are closely aligned with their social position, for example, those subordinated in a field due to factors like age, training, accreditation, and patronage may try to reclassify prevailing forms and label a musical style or literary genre 'old-fashioned'. Whether this contestation ultimately changes the field depends on many factors, but Bourdieu's main point is that the power to construct symbolic value is unevenly distributed and that this inequality limits change or influences the perception of the changes that are considered possible.

There are a number of reasons why Bourdieu's sociology constitutes a highly attenuated conception of change. First, it suggests that the category of change belongs to the struggle within the field and the competition between fields. There is no disinterested conception of change. Change is perceived and enacted relative to the position individuals occupy in social space, for example in terms of class distribution or the gender division of labour. Second, this means that what appears to be change may be just a matter of composition, since it might be the outcome of a struggle between different factions of the same group. It is in these terms that one may perceive how an agenda for change may be promoted by one segment of the bourgeoisie against another, such as financial capital in relation to manufacturing capital. Bourdieu tries to reveal the rules that are involved in the value placed on change, for instance, the value of change is downplayed in the tendency of the former members of the French aristocracy to either inherit furniture or buy antiques. In his late political interventions, Bourdieu criticised neoliberal globalisation and argued that the notion it perpetuated of the necessity of change is a myth that financial elites used to disempower opponents and resistance (Bourdieu 1998, 2001).

In my opinion, the criticism that Bourdieu privileges reproduction over change is largely correct, although it would be more valid to claim that Bourdieu aims to show the amount of effort that goes into sustaining social reproduction and that this can include aspects of change. The denial or veiling of effort is part of the logic of reproduction, because social legitimacy is regularly achieved by the perception of a person and practice as given, natural and normal. This includes everyday practices like speaking a certain way and eating certain kinds of foods. Bourdieu proposes that early socialisation has an enormous bearing on later outcomes and this means that more effort may be involved in subordinate individuals' and groups' attempts to change their situation. On the one hand, this is because social position is manifested in the person's body (Bourdieu 1990b). Many embodied social practices may be quite resistant to conscious modification, yet represent the unrecognised components of social assessment. On the other hand, social actors have an intuitive understanding of probability in social life. Consequently, they are always making implicit assessments about what they can achieve and the amount of effort that would be involved in significant change. Sociology, in Bourdieu's opinion, 'unveils the *self-deception*, the collectively entertained and encouraged lying to oneself which, in every society, is at the foundation of the most sacred values and, therefore, of all social existence' (Bourdieu 1990a, 188).

Contemporary sociological interpretations

It is impossible to survey the wealth of empirical sociological research into changes in specific dimensions of contemporary society, like the family, health, cities, law, sport, sexuality and so on. These dimensions of society have dynamics that are specific to them, especially in the cases of systems and fields that can be shown to have internal organising properties, like competition in markets and capital accumulation in the economic system. Dimensions of society, like the family and education, are equally transformed by broader general changes in society. The sources of changes that affect several dimensions of society are typically conveyed by categories that define the period's dominant tendencies, such as those of globalisation, neoliberalism, new capitalism, the consumer society, the risk society, and the information age. In the most innovative cases, the perceived changes in dominant social tendencies go together with modifications in theoretical explanation. Yet most sociological interpretations of dominant tendencies are based on some combination of the factors and considerations that have been noted. For example, Haferkamp and Smelser (1992, 2) claim that any theory of change must contain the three elements of 'structural determinants', 'mechanisms and processes', and 'direction and consequences'. Nevertheless, contemporary sociology contains important proposals regarding modifications in the constituents of these three elements and the relations between them.

Sociologists concerned with globalisation have questioned the adequacy of explanations of change that focus on endogenous developments in a nation-state. In their opinion, exogenous developments are increasingly important in determining changes in specific dimensions of society. For example, Saskia Sassen (2006) has shown how the disparities between Sydney and Melbourne in income and household property prices increased during the period after financial deregulation and with the growth in the global trade in currencies. In some cases, sociologists relate contemporary changes to practices and institutions that are perceived to now have a greater impact on social relations and social interaction, like digital media, information technologies, consumerism, and 'creative industries'. These are considered to generate change through either directly altering other dimensions of society or by the thinking and practices associated with them becoming paradigmatic. It is suggested that the organising principles of consumerism or the new media may infiltrate other dimensions of social relations, like education or politics, and come to reshape them. In my opinion, despite their sensitivity to novel innovations in the present, these approaches tend to confuse specific developments with general tendencies and they are consequently theoretically flawed and sometimes empirically deficient. For example, Richard Florida's thesis of the rise of the creative class and creative cities is a work of social science that has had considerable popular impact, but its analysis depends on stretching the category of creative occupations and exaggerating the significance of lifestyle considerations compared to other factors (Florida 2003; and see Murphy 2012). In my opinion, these kinds of approaches are more interesting as extrapolations about potential futures, and they can be considered to participate in what Alain Touraine (1977, 1981) terms the conflicts over *historicity*, that is, the conflicts over the construction of the future.

Touraine argues that social movements seek to realise cultural models that challenge those of capitalist business organisations and the technocratic versions of the state. For example, the ecological movement contests models of industrial development, and the peace movement presents an alternative conception of security. Social movements are, of course, directly concerned with the promotion of change and resistance to change. In recent sociology, there have been two particularly influential conceptions of how social movements seek to bring about change. The first conception is sometimes known as resource mobilisation theory and it is principally concerned with political contestation (McCarthy and Zald 1977, Jenkins 1983). It tends to focus on how social movements influence and transform political processes through mobilising resources and citizen participation. For this conception, contestation is provoked by inequalities and competing interests. These considerations are to a certain extent present in the second conception, but it differs in its greater accentuation of how social movements transform cultural meanings and social identities, for instance, feminists engaged in processes of consciousness-raising and argued that the 'personal is political'. This second conception, associated with theorists of new social movements like Touraine and Alberto Melucci (1996), considers that the changes promoted by social movements occur more in everyday life and civil society, that is, change is initially to some extent independent of the state, and social movements enable individuals to explore alternative ways of living. The state is then compelled to adapt to the cultural transformation and the contestation over the cultural model it represents. The contrasting interpretations of how social movements generate change can be found in recent analyses of global social movements. Geoffrey Pleyers (2010), for instance, distinguishes between two strands of alter-globalisation: the 'way of reason', which seeks to present a superior political and economic rationality to that of existing globalisation; and the 'way of experience', which prioritises the experience of another reality to that of global capitalism through radical democratic participation and opportunities for creative self-expression (see also McDonald 2006).

One of the more recent ways in which change has been thought about in sociology is in terms of the disputes and justifications that take place in social life. This represents an interest in norms and values, but it focuses on their instantiation and practical application in social interaction, rather than on the antecedent socialisation. It implies that the social agency of individuals has greater latitude than is the case in sociologies that emphasise the structural constraints on action. The proposed model of change is based on a kind of pragmatic analysis, one that is 'capable of taking account of the ways in which people engage in action, their justifications, and the meaning they give to their actions' (Boltanski and Chiapello 2005, 3). Luc Boltanski and Laurent Thevénot, the initiators of this pragmatist program, had previously collaborated with Bourdieu. Their book *On justification* is a departure from Bourdieu's critical sociology and the seminal text of this sociology of critical capacity (Boltanski and Thevénot 2006). Although it is based on different theoretical foundations, Michael Pusey's book *Economic rationalism in Canberra* might be considered an Australian sociological investigation into a change in the regime of justification and the implications of adoption of the principles of economic rationalism, or the neoliberal prioritising of the market (Pusey 1991).

Boltanski and Thevénot argue that a variety of formats of justification can be brought into play in contexts of social dispute. Drawing on the history of political philosophy, they identify several different grammars or 'regimes' of justification, which they term *polities*. These are polities because they each appeal to some image of the common good and each of them involves a specific kind of attribution of value. For example, rankings in an 'industrial polity' will be based on perceived professional abilities and the achievement of efficiencies, whereas in the 'inspired polity' justifications reference the grace of the spiritual figure or the inspiration of the artist. It is not difficult to perceive how this schema would draw attention to the importance of classification to disputes, such as whether the criteria of the 'domestic' or 'market' polity should be applied—or are being applied—to a situation, and how conflict ensues from the confrontation of one system of value with another. This is a perspective that is particularly relevant to clarifying how individuals change their actions, as well as how they may resist change, but its significance for thinking about change was probably only fully revealed in the book Boltanski later wrote with Eve Chiapello, *The new spirit of capitalism* (Boltanski and Chiapello 2005).

The new spirit of capitalism addresses questions that had originally been left outstanding but which are significant for the application of this approach to change: how do *polities* originate and become institutionalised at a societal level? The argument that Boltanski and Chiapello propose is that the new spirit of capitalism was consolidated in response to the contestation of the late 1960s and 1970s. It institutionalised a new polity or regime of justification: the *project* polity. Boltanski and Chiapello reveal the change in justification through an analysis of the changes in the discourse of managerial texts. The *project* polity refers to the network as the organising principle of social relations at work, rather than industrial capitalism's model of a more permanent and vertical structure. The network model is more flexible and transitory, social agents combine for the duration of a project and then move on to another project. In fact, the *project* polity incorporates, at least at the level of legitimating discourse, many of the qualities that had been opposed to capitalism during the preceding period of contestation, like those of self-organisation and horizontal structures. Boltanski and Chiapello are then able to show how the spirit of capitalism was modified in response to critique, especially the critique of industrial alienation that was inspired by artistic values like creativity and self-expression. In other words, this is an institutional change that is connected to changes in the grammar of justification. Indeed, it represents a way in which the tensions and contradictions of the capitalist social order were resituated and transformed, or as Boltanski and Chiapello term it, subjected to the processes of displacement. The critique of capitalism had the effect of dismantling some of capitalism's former legitimating justifications and the practices that corresponded to them, whilst the incorporating of certain elements of this critique in the new spirit of capitalism had as one of its effects the fracturing of some of the preceding period's industrial and political alignments. Further, the changes were not precisely those that the contestation derived from critique intended. The demand for flexibility acquired different connotation through its insertion in the grammar of the market and became used to justify the institution of more tenuous and insecure conditions of employment.

Sociological interpretations of contemporary change are not just concerned with the distinction of the present from the past but also the tendencies that are likely to shape the future development of society (see Browne 2005, 2008). As a result of the dissolution of notions of the convergence of modern societies and Marxist visions of a future transition from capitalism to socialism, perspectives on the future are more open to diverse possibilities and they are, at the same time, rather more circumspect. Yet modernity is still viewed as sustained by its orientation towards future change, through science and technology's self-surpassing dynamics, the commitment to the new of modern art, and the everyday experiences of time as quantified and a resource. These dynamics of modernity are considered to be implicated in the dissolving of some of the constraints on individual agency in contemporary capitalist societies, as exemplified by Giddens' notions of the 'disembedding' of social relations and globalisation as 'action at a distance', Ulrich Beck's vision of the risk society and individualisation, and Zygmunt Bauman's conception of liquid modernity (Giddens 1990, Beck 1992, Bauman 2000, Beck and Beck-Gernsheim 2002). Notions of the acceleration, contingency and uncertainty of contemporary social relations are typically connected with conceptions of the enhanced, or obligatory, individual agency in the present. That is, institutions like the welfare state and the family are considered to have changed in ways that foreground individual agency—for example, in contemporary capitalist societies, health and retirement are considered to be less simply states of being and more conditions that are amenable to shaping through individual choice and decision. Of course, these current developments are the result of longer term trends like the decline in the size of the family, the changes in divorce law, and the welfare state's institution of the social rights of citizenship.

At the same time, sociological interpretations of change in advanced capitalist societies tend to be fairly circumspect in their projections about the future. In my opinion, this is partly because of empirical changes that are counter to former visions of social progress, particularly the rising inequalities in the distribution of wealth and income over recent decades, the perception of increased insecurity in employment, along with paradoxically in the Australian context an increase in the average weekly working hours of full-time employees, political disaffection, distrust of institutions and ideological uncertainties, and the predicament of the ecological crisis (Browne 2005). For these and other reasons, the perceived increase in social agency does not necessarily represent an increase in individual autonomy and control over the sources of social change. Rather, the opposite appears the case. Sociological commentaries tend to highlight individuals' experiences of being affected by social processes that are outside their control and the sense that major institutions, especially the state, are less able to provide social protection to individuals against regressive social change (see Hage 2002, Pusey 2003). It was in terms of this kind of dilemma that I examined the question of whether there is a new nexus of change located in the tension between globalisation and democracy, one which overlays the dynamics of class conflict and reconfigures them (Browne 2002). Despite existing transnational institutions, like the European Union, arguably exacerbating the tension between globalisation and democracy, it remains an open question whether transnational institutions will modify this tension through processes of democratisation and lead to the institution of new dimensions of citizenship rights and the collective regulation of global markets (see Habermas 2001).

There is another noteworthy development in sociological thinking about contemporary change. It is the recognition of the significant social innovations that are taking place outside Europe and North America. In part, this recognition is a consequence of the uncertainty about the future in advanced capitalist societies and changes in the global order of international relations. Nevertheless, the perceived changes are not limited to those of political power and economic development. Rather, it is the recognition of the emergence of novel capacities for change and the experience in societies from the capitalist periphery of the necessity for changes that address historical injustices, particularly those deriving from colonial domination and previous authoritarian regimes. It has been suggested, for example, that Brazilian experiments in participatory democracy, like the initiation of 'participatory budgeting' and the World Social Forum in Porto Alegre, are social innovations of general significance and may represent the nucleus for new kinds of collective self-determination (see Santos 2005, Domingues 2012, Wagner 2012).

Although this sketch of contemporary sociological interpretations of change is admittedly selective, it is possible to perceive how the basic dilemma of the relationship of social structure and social action continues to shape debates within the discipline over change. Similarly, sociologists continue to explain changes through the elaboration of theoretical conceptions of the contemporary phase of modernity and its distinction from preceding forms or phases of modernity. These conceptions are generally based on interpretations of the alterations in modernity's dominant institutions. For instance, it is common to encounter arguments about how capitalism is being rendered resurgent, the sovereignty of the nation-state may be diminishing, and welfare state restructuring is generating, to use Barbara Misztal's term, the challenges of vulnerability (Misztal 2011). One of the ways in which recent sociological thinking about change may differ from earlier perspectives is in its greater appreciation of social creativity and the semantics of institutions. Social creativity is not only highlighted in relation to the practices of social movements and as a feature of the legitimating ideology of capitalism's new spirit, but it is also considered an important part of the mobilisation of collective identities and the genesis of meanings or values. The inconsistency between the self-representation of the social order and its institutional reality remains a significant source of social conflict and potential change.

Conclusion

The discipline of sociology has produced a plethora of interpretations of change. This is not surprising insofar as sociology is concerned with modern social institutions and the dynamic character of social relations. Yet conceptions of change are highly contested in sociology. There are substantial disagreements over the relative importance of different dimensions of society, and sociology regularly demonstrates how social structures limit change in areas like wealth distribution, educational attainment and health outcomes. For similar reasons, sociologists often draw attention to the discrepancies between intended changes and actual outcomes, particularly because they disclose the effects that one part of society can have on another. Sociologists then take into account recurrent patterns and social complexity, but they are equally concerned with social actors' motivations and the meanings that change has for them. I have proposed that the way that sociologists think about change is generally shaped by their approach to the dilemma of the relationship between social action and social structure. The conception of the relationship of action and structure has normative, as well as analytical, implications. It can serve to clarify the socially instituted degree of human autonomy and human capabilities. In my opinion, sociological typologies of development and delineations of contemporary modernity's dominant tendencies have similar implications. These provide insights into the potential of unfolding change and the conditions that enable individual and collective autonomy.

The reflexivity about social life that sociological knowledge generates has the potential to shape change through informing social action. However, my analysis of contemporary perspectives disclosed a considerable uncertainty. Change is depicted as accelerating but its long-term consequences are thought to be either unknown or suffused with risk. Globalisation suggests an expansion of social interconnections but possibly at the cost of a decline in the ability to coordinate and control social processes. Modernity appears close to becoming a global condition, yet the similarities in social organisations and everyday practices do not mean that future changes will not be heavily conditioned by historically important differences in cultural orientations, political authority and social identities. Sociologists could be faulted for presuming that modern societies change, yet any reckoning of the differences between social conditions in the middle of the last century and the present reveals significant modifications in various spheres of social life, including those of family forms and intimate relations, employment patterns and work, political institutions and nation states, transport and communication. In some of these spheres, what seemed impossible has been realised and many former justifications of social oppression are no longer legitimate, but sociologists are now more reluctant than their predecessors to equate change with progress. No doubt this reluctance reflects how sociological interpretations are conditioned by empirical developments and the shifts in cultural understandings of concepts like change. Finally, sociologists continue to consider that individuals are to varying degrees capable of modifying aspects of their life-situations and identities but that major changes in social structures are conditioned by the strains, conflicts and contradictions of a social order.

References

Arnason, JP (1993) *The future that failed*. Routledge, London.

Arnason, JP (1998) *Social theory and Japanese experience*. Kegan Paul, London.

Arnason, JP (2002) The multiplication of modernity. In E Ben-Rafael (ed.) *Identity, culture and globalization*. Brill, Leiden: 130–54.

Arnason, JP (2005) *Civilizations in dispute*. Brill, Leiden.

Bauman, Z (2000) *Liquid modernity*. Polity Press, Cambridge.

Beck, U (1992) *Risk society*. Sage, London.

Beck, U and Beck-Gernsheim, E (2002) *Individualization*. Sage, London.

Beck, U, Giddens, A and Lash, S (1994) *Reflexive modernization*. Polity Press, Cambridge.

Boltanski, L and Chiapello, E (2005) *The new spirit of capitalism*. Verso, London.

Boltanski, L and Thevénot, L (2006) *On justification*. Princeton University Press, Princeton.

Bourdieu, P (1977) *Outline of a theory of practice*. Cambridge University Press, Cambridge.

Bourdieu, P (1984) *Distinction*. Routledge and Kegan, London.

Bourdieu, P (1988) *Homo academicus*. Polity Press, Cambridge.

Bourdieu, P (1990a) *In other words*. Polity Press, Cambridge.

Bourdieu, P (1990b) *The logic of practice*. Polity Press, Cambridge.

Bourdieu, P (1998) *Acts of resistance*. The New Press, New York.

Bourdieu, P (2001) *Firing back*. The New Press, New York.

Bourdieu, P and Passeron, C (1977) *Reproduction in education, society and culture.* Sage, London

Browne, C (2002) A new nexus of social change? In BE Hanna, EJ Woodley, E Buys and J Summerville (eds) *Social Change in the 21st Century Conference Proceedings*, Brisbane.

Browne, C (2005) Hope, critique and Utopia. *Critical Horizons* 6(1): 63–86.

Browne, C (2008) The end of immanent critique? *European Journal of Social Theory* 13: 459–79.

Calhoun, C (2011) Series introduction: from the current crisis to possible futures. In C Calhoun and G Derluguian (eds) *Business as usual—the roots of the global financial meltdown.* New York University Press, New York: 9–42.

Castells, M (2012) *Networks of hope and outrage.* Polity Press, Cambridge.

Connell, RW (1997) Why is classical theory classical? *American Journal of Sociology* 102(6): 1511–57.

Connell, R (2007) *Southern theory.* Allen and Unwin, St Leonards.

Domingues, JM (2012) *Global modernity, development and contemporary civilization.* Routledge, London.

Durkheim, E (1952, originally published in 1897) *Suicide.* Routledge and Kegan Paul, London.

Durkheim, E (1984, originally published in 1893) *The division of labour in society.* Macmillan Press. Houndsmill.

Durkheim, E (1995, originally published in 1912) *The elementary forms of religious life.* The Free Press, New York.

Eisenstadt, SN (1999) *Fundamentalism, sectarianism, and revolution.* Cambridge University Press, Cambridge.

Eisenstadt, SN (2000) Multiple modernities. *Daedalus* 129(1): 1–29.

Florida, R (2003) *The rise of the creative class.* Pluto Press, North Melbourne.

Foucault, M (1978) *Discipline and punish.* Penguin, Harmondsworth.

Foucault, M (1980a) *Power/knowledge*, C Gordon (ed.) Harvester Press, Brighton.

Foucault, M (1980b) *History of sexuality,* vol 1. Vintage, New York.

Foucault, M (2003) *Society must be defended.* Penguin, London.

Giddens, A (1979) *Central problems in social theory*. Macmillan Press, London.

Giddens, A (1985) *The constitution of society*. Polity Press, Cambridge.

Giddens, A (1990) *The consequences of modernity*. Polity Press, Cambridge.

Giddens, A (1992) *The transformation of intimacy*. Polity Press, Cambridge.

Habermas, J (2001) *The postnational constellation*. Polity Press, Cambridge.

Haferkamp, H and Smelser, NJ (1992) Introduction. In H Haferkamp and NJ Smelser (eds) *Social change and modernity*. University of California Press, Berkeley: 1–33.

Hage, G (2002) *Against paranoid nationalism*. Pluto Press, Leichhardt.

Jenkins, C (1983) Resource mobilization theory and the study of social movements. *Annual Review of Sociology* 9: 527–53.

Marx, K (1977, originally published in 1852) The eighteenth Brumaire of Louis Napoleon. In D McLellan (ed.) *Karl Marx: selected writings*. Oxford University Press, Oxford: 300–25.

McCarthy, JD and Zald, MN (1977) Resource mobilization and social movements: a partial theory. *American Journal of Sociology* 82: 1212–41.

McDonald, K (2006) *Global movements: action and culture*. Blackwell Press, Oxford.

Melucci, A (1996) *Challenging codes: collective action in the information age*. Cambridge University Press, Cambridge.

Misztal, B (2011) *The challenges of vulnerability*. Palgrave Macmillan, London.

Murphy P (2012) *The collective imagination—the creative spirit of free societies*. Ashgate, Farnham.

Pleyers, G (2011) *Alter-globalization*. Polity Press, Cambridge.

Postone, M (2012) Thinking the global crisis. *South Atlantic Quarterly* 111(2) (Spring): 227–49.

Pusey, M (1991) *Economic rationalism in Canberra—a nation-building state changes its mind*. Cambridge University Press, Melbourne.

Pusey, M (2003) *Middle Australia*. Cambridge University Press, Melbourne.

Santos, B de S (ed.) (2005) *Democratizing democracy—beyond the liberal democratic canon*. Verso, London.

Sassen, S (2006) *Cities in a world economy*, 3rd ed. Princeton University Press, Princeton.

Simmel, G (1950) The metropolis and mental life. In KH Wolff (ed.) *The sociology of Georg Simmel*. The Free Press, New York: 409–24.

Swedberg, R (1998) *Max Weber and the idea of economic sociology*. Princeton University Press, Princeton.

Touraine, A (1977) *The self-production of society*. University of Chicago Press, Chicago.

Touraine, A (1981) *The voice and the eye: an analysis of social movements*. Cambridge University Press, Cambridge.

Wagner, P (1994) *Sociology of modernity*. London, Routledge.

Wagner, P (2008) *Modernity as experience and interpretation*. Cambridge, Polity Press.

Wagner, P (2012) *Modernity—understanding the present*. Cambridge, Polity Press.

Weber, M (1930, originally published in 1905) *The Protestant ethic and the spirit of capitalism*. Unwin Hyman, London.

Weber, M (1958, originally delivered as a lecture in 1917) Science as a vocation. In C Wright Mills and H Gerth (eds) *From Max Weber*. Routledge, London.

Wright Mills, C (1959) *The sociological imagination*. Penguin, Harmondsworth.

6. Advertising and Change: Message, mind, medium, and mores

Dee Madigan

For an industry that is a slavish follower of trends, advertising has an uneasy relationship with change. This is slightly surprising given that the whole purpose of our industry, its *raison d'être*, is to change people—whether it is changing their minds in terms of which brand they choose or changing their behaviour. But whilst we are very up to date on the various psychologies of change and how best to motivate people to change, our own industry has been particularly slow to do so. Watching daytime TV ads, in which a woman's happiness and social standing amongst peers is tightly linked to the cleanliness of her toilet, you could be forgiven for thinking advertising was stuck in the 1950s.

Nevertheless, advertising, like all industries, has changed and will continue to change. And the drivers of change within the advertising industry can be roughly broken down into the mind, the medium, the mores and, as always, the money. In this chapter I trace the major changes in the advertising industry and couple them with my practitioner perspective on how the advertising industry seeks to make change happen through a slightly different set of 'M's: the message, the mind, the medium and the mores.

It was the Industrial Revolution, one of the greatest changes to our society, that spawned advertising as we know it. Previously advertising had been mostly at the point of sale and/or was the realm of the grifter and snake oil salesman (there would be many who would argue that this is still the case!).

In the late nineteenth century, companies started making mass-market products. In the early twentieth century, consumer credit on smaller household goods became available. So for the first time ever we had mass-produced products and masses of people with the money to buy them (whether they could afford them or not!). We had a product, a target audience and, with the increase in national newspapers and the advent of radio, we had a medium. Where previously most advertising had been at the point of purchase or as small advertisements in local newspapers, suddenly national advertising campaigns were required, which meant that copywriters, art directors and so on were needed, and the advertising agency as we know it today was born. Total advertising spending in the United States grew from approximately $200 million in 1880 to nearly $3 billion in 1920.

The message

While many of the early advertisements were simply product benefit style advertisements, an increasing understanding of the psychology of the consumer (or how to best manipulate the mind) led to fundamental changes in the industry. Great ad men of the past like PT Barnum instinctively knew what would make people want something, but in the 1950s the relationship between advertising and psychology was formalised when advertising agencies began to use psychologists and other behavioural experts to help develop advertising campaigns.

The realisation that people were not nearly as rational as they themselves thought was perhaps one the biggest changes in the industry. Basically, how a product makes you feel is as important as what it does. This is why, when we get a brief to write an ad, it is as much or more about the consumer insights as it is about the product.

This is particularly the case in parity products, i.e. those which have no real discernible difference between them. Tampons are an excellent example. Having spent the best part of two decades doing the advertisements for Carefree tampons, I learned that it was the visual and emotional cues that worked to change buying behaviour far more strongly than research and development features like an extra groove in the tampon. This is why nearly every advertisement for this company's product took place on a foreign beach. (Also I love to travel!)

In terms of these psychological drivers of change, Abraham Maslow's publication of his theory of human motivation had a massive impact in the industry. We still use it today. In his paper, Maslow (1943) said all human decision-making is motivated by unfulfilled needs and that people seek to satisfy their needs and desires in a certain hierarchy, known nowadays as Maslow's hierarchy. These needs could then be used as a basis for understanding why a consumer makes a decision to buy a particular product or a service.

The hierarchy of needs begins with basic life survival needs, and then the model progresses through to safety and security, love and belonging, self-esteem, and finally self-actualisation. As people meet the needs at the first level, they move toward the next, then the next and so on. Think of it as a pyramid, with basic survival needs at the bottom and self-actualisation at the top. In advertising terms, the closer to the base of the pyramid you can create the need that your product answers, the more successful you can be. Volvo, for example, has created one of the world's strongest brands based on the second-level need of safety and security.

We often see entirely non-essential items marketed to meet this second-level need. The space under our kitchen sinks is full of products we do not really need but we have purchased because somehow we have bought into the marketing that they are important for the heath/security of our family. If you pay attention to marketing language, you will see words that connect a product to this need like 'Protect your family' and 'Don't put your children's heath at risk'. The advertisements are usually aimed at mothers, using kids' health as the bait. Maternal guilt is a prime motivator for advertisers. We even managed to put tampons into the security category—'Simply no better protection'.

I also did the first advertising campaign for Barely There Pantyliners (if you are a female creative in an ad agency and there's a feminine hygiene brief, it lands on *your* desk, no matter what). Pantyliners were unusual in that they were a brand new category of product. We had to create a need from scratch. In the end I used an old adage and modernised it. 'My grandmother said you should always wear fresh underwear in case you get hit by a bus. I (as she looks at a cute guy) can think of a much better reason.' Basically, protect yourself from feminine odour in case you get lucky. A stretch perhaps, but it was Johnson & Johnson's most effective advertisement in the world that year.

When physiological and safety needs are fulfilled, the person can move up to the third level of needs in Maslow's model, the social need—belonging. Human beings have an innate need to be emotionally involved. We need relationships, whether that is as a couple or as a social group. We need to love and be loved. The explosion and profitability of dating sites is testament to how powerful this need is. In fact, the success of social media is based on this. Marketing to teenagers often uses this need because the need to fit in, to belong, is particularly high at that age. The eternal advertising mainstay is 'buy this and you will be loved'.

The next level in Maslow's hierarchy of needs is the need for esteem. People want and need to be respected and we need to feel good about ourselves. And this is where much advertising lives, often because we are selling products that people really do not need. L'Oréal's 'Because you're worth it' is the perfect example.

And then finally, at the top of the triangle, is the need for self-actualisation. Very little advertising leverages this higher order need except perhaps universities and various Buddhist courses!

One of the more interesting examples demonstrating the pitfalls of employing Maslow's hierarchy without thinking it through was in trying to reduce the road toll. In the 1980s, advertising agencies on the Roads and Traffic Account were doing amazing, gut-wrenching, incredibly graphic advertisements in which young guys died as a consequence of speeding on the roads. They were highly awarded advertisements, and every creative wanted to work on them. There was just one small problem. They did not work.

They used the base level of Maslow's hierarchy, survival, as the motivator to change behaviour, which on paper makes absolute sense, until you delve into the psychology of the target audience. Young guys are uniquely unmotivated by fear of death. They simply think it will not happen to them. They feel invincible, so the advertisements did not work for them. And what was equally interesting was that there was no flow-on effect into the rest of the community either, because the advertisements were so horrific that people literally looked away rather than watch. This was an essential lesson for the advertising industry—if the fear factor is so high, people self-protect by tuning out, so absolute fear is no good at changing behaviour.

We finally realised that what did work for our young men with a death wish was far higher up Maslow's hierarchy but far more motivating for them—the fear of not belonging. And this is why the 'little pinkie' advertisement has been a far greater success.[1] Death does not work to change their behaviour, but fear of belittlement by their friends does.

The mind

As well as the messaging itself, one of the great changes in advertising is a greater understanding of how stimulus works on the mind. The beautiful, long copy advertisements of the 1950s and 60s are long gone, because they were not effective. They were based on the assumption that people spend time reading and thinking about advertisements. They do not. And we discovered that the last thing an advertisement should do was actually encourage rational thought. It was not just that rational, deliberative thought was not an effective driver of purchase. We discovered something far worse. Encouraging consumers to *think* actually reduced the chance of getting them to buy.

And so the power of visuals was born. During the 1960s, the visual image started to supplant text as our primary mode of communication. Today, if you flick through a magazine, almost all the advertisements have a big picture and few words. You would think this would make my job as a writer easier, but it does not. It means you have to communicate the same information in far fewer words.

---

1   See www.youtube.com/watch?v=JqWO7fzwSLM.

But the reason we use visuals is because images work so differently from words. Pictures circumvent consumers' critical thought. Visuals are registered before you have had time to analyse them, so they become truth in your head, even when they are not. Seeing is believing even if what you are believing in is a fantasy—which is the other reason why images work better than words, because we fantasise in pictures. In advertising, a picture really is worth a thousand words. In fact, advertisements went from 15 per cent mainly pictorial in 1978 to 40 per cent by 1988.

This understanding of the power of visuals also gave rise to the importance of the logo. A lot of people think of a logo as a brand. I often get clients saying they want to change their branding, when in fact all they want is a new logo and somehow they think that will do. It will not, and is the reason why most rebranding exercises fail. If you truly want to change a company, changing the logo simply will not work. Like anything, change works best when you start from the centre and work your way out.

A logo is only a shortcut to a brand. This visual representation of the brand (rather than a straight brand name) allowed consumers to remain engaged in the visual processing of the advertisement, without having to switch to verbal processing. Logos also transcend language barriers so there are cost efficiencies, which is an important thing in an increasingly global marketplace.

People do not often buy a product or a logo, they buy a brand. And a brand is essentially the relationship you (the seller) have with your consumer—how they *feel* about you. It is who you are, what you offer, how that offer is experienced and exists as much internally as externally in a company. Basically, it is a promise kept. 'Keeping on brand' has been an advertising catchphrase ever since the 1960s. And the intangible value of brand equity is considered a quantifiable amount. Companies with strong brands are worth more on the stock market. And brands are properties to be protected. Not just brand names but brand properties are trademarked, like Cadbury purple and the Coca-Cola font.

Psychology has continued to drive change in advertising. Many agencies are now investing serious money in neuropsychology, which involves basically hooking people up to machines and watching brain patterns to see how advertising affects us in a physiological way. That is because even when we asked people in research groups why they buy one particular brand over another, they would give us answers that were simply not being reflected in the actual data, and we realised that people are not always themselves aware of what changes their own behaviour. By skipping the conscious and going straight to the unconscious, we can get a truer idea. There are a whole lot of ethical questions raised over this, of course, but if you think change and advertising have an uneasy relationship, the relationship of ethics and advertising is somewhat worse.

The medium

The medium has also been one of advertising's great drivers of change. The changes in the medium created by technological advancements have necessarily dictated changes in advertising. The printing press and the rise of national newspapers led to the first print advertising. This was followed by radio with its famous soap operas—radio drama sponsored by cleaning products from Proctor and Gamble's range.

Then came TV and with it the bigger budget big brand advertisements. In the US, the year 1948 is considered the year television advertisements came into their own, not the least because for the first time, enough people owned TVs to make it financially worthwhile to advertise on them. The first television advertising was the 'one sponsor per show' style, e.g. The Colgate Hour. The stations and advertising agencies realised that selling blocks of time in shows to multiple sponsors meant multiple streams of revenue per show, and the 'ad break' as we now know it was born. By the time television came to Australia in 1956, the format of TV ads had begun to be well established.

By the early 1970s the remote control was in nearly every household and the video recorder was gaining popularity. This meant advertisers had to work harder to engage audiences who could now mute, change channels or fast forward an ad. Previously a big enough media spend meant people saw your ads whether they were good or not but suddenly the entertainment value of an advertisement—the engagement—rose in importance. And the 'idea' became king. An advertisement had to have an idea created from a 'unique selling proposition' to cut through the clutter.

Since then, there has been an ongoing tussle between advertising agencies and clients over how much entertainment (i.e. the idea) versus how much 'boring product stuff' there should be. Creatives like myself are forever trying to convince clients (quite rightly) that no one is actually obliged to look at their advertisement, which means that they really have to make it entertaining. And clients are forever pointing out (quite rightly) that a really entertaining advertisement that says nothing about why people should buy the product is a waste of money. The holy grail is, of course, an idea that entertains but is built around the product benefit that answers an emotional need.

Another change has been in the growing number of channels on which you can potentially reach your target. When I started in advertising, people used to watch one of three channels, listen to one of a handful of analogue radio stations, and read one or two newspapers. Even though we did not know much about them (beyond basic demographic information), we at least knew where to reach them, and they were pretty much a captive audience.

The advent of pay TV meant that consumers split themselves up according to viewing habits, which was a double-edged sword for us because whilst it meant we could target more accurately, it also meant that the audience was more fragmented and therefore harder to reach. Basically, although the content of TV advertisements has changed to reflect societal changes, and although there have been some technological changes, and increased demographic information about target audiences, the basic TV advertisement format remains the same mass interruption model of advertising that was there when I started.

The internet changed everything.

My first agency had two computers in the library connected to the internet on which we could do research. Within a few years we were all connected. It helped that we had Malcolm Turnbull's Ozemail as a client. But for a few years, we still tried to do banner advertisements (the usually rectangular ads at the top of many websites) pretty much as print advertisements online.

Gradually we realised that this medium required a completely different way of thinking to drive consumer change, particularly once the social network began, and everyone in the advertising industry went around with either gloom or glee on their faces, depending on the level of their digital capability. 'Interruption is dead, long live engagement'. Soon every agency boasted a digital department filled with hipsters in low-slung pants who walked around the agency saying wisely, 'It's all about starting a conversation' and 'You have to build your communities'.

Clients listened to their advertising agencies and ploughed millions of dollars into online campaigns, and then learnt the hard way that engagement without persuasion is, for an advertiser, an utter waste of money. One of the most famous examples of this was Pepsi, who in 2010 decided to withdraw all money from traditional media and plough it into a social marketing campaign. The campaign rang all the bells, with 80 million votes registered, nearly 3.5 million 'likes' on the Pepsi Facebook page and almost 60,000 followers on Twitter. The only problem was that it did not sell Pepsi. It failed to change behaviour. Pepsi lost 5 per cent of market share in one year and, for the first time ever, dropped from being the number two soft drink in the US.

What had been forgotten was everything that Maslow had taught us, along with the importance of a creative idea. You can know everything about your target audience, but unless you motivate them to purchase with creativity and an answerable need, it is money wasted. In fact, one online experiment used blank banner advertisements (banners with nothing at all in them) and they still scored higher click-through rates (i.e. the rates at which people click on an advertisement, supposedly to purchase or find out more information) than micro-targeted Facebook ads.

That is not to say everyone gets it wrong. Companies like Red Bull quickly changed their offering from simply selling energy drinks to creating their own online and offline content, and companies who set themselves up to sell online have done very well too, though many retailers still struggle with online for a whole plethora of reasons. Nonetheless the times they are a-changing—the new media is here and that is where the consumers are, so that is where the advertisers have to be. Smart, agile companies are making it work.

The mores

The other massive way the internet has changed advertising is that for the first time the consumer truly had power, and the ability to talk back. Many brands, so quick to embrace new media, have been burnt. The 'hashtag' has become the 'bashtag' enough times to scare even the bravest companies off Twitter. Formerly, if customers were unhappy with a product or service, they wrote a letter to the company and complained to their ten closest friends. Now they can tell hundreds of thousands of people in real time. If anything, the internet has meant many advertisers had to lift their game in terms of the quality of their products and services.

For the first time in history there is also an asset value, not just a moral value, in ethical corporate behaviour. The companies themselves have had to become advertisements for their products. Companies can no longer make happy bouncy TV ads while they act like corporate bastards behind closed doors. The massive availability of information online about companies means they can be judged, and are judged, on their corporate behaviour.

As societal mores change, these are of course reflected in the advertising. But to some, advertising plays a bigger, more sinister, active role as the agent of unwanted and evil change, for example: 'Junk food ads are making our kids fat!' and 'Advertising with unrealistic body sizes is causing anorexia.'

To some, advertising is the cause of all society's ills, while others say it simply reflects changes that are happening. The truth, as always, lies between the two. Advertising does reflect society but it is never a true reflection. We airbrush truth to be more persuasive, distorting reality along the way. This of course has an effect on the way we see ourselves. It is churlish of advertisers to say we are not responsible for negative changes in our society because 'it's just advertising' and 'everyone knows ads aren't real', when literally billions of dollars are spent on working out better ways to change people's behaviour—to change their minds, to change their purchasing decisions, to change how they feel about their lives and what might make them happier.

While many of the changes are part of the bigger picture (or bigger problem!), other changes in advertising reflect changes for good in our society. The portrayal of women in advertising, for example, is certainly better than it was, and we now see a broader range of cultures in our advertising. Although sometimes I know that feels a bit 'politically correct' and trite, in casting for advertisements we have to tick cultural boxes.

Advertising has also copped a lot of flak for its sexualisation. The truth is that sex sells. It always has, because we are hardwired to notice sexual content. Certainly what are considered acceptable levels of sexiness now are very different from 50 years ago, but that is a societal trend. A hundred years ago, an ankle was considered sexually arousing; nowadays it is a breast. This is a trend reflected through all forms of media and in society at large. A look at *Video Hits* on a Saturday morning shows far more sexual images than advertising generally does, certainly advertising that has a family classification.

The law has also changed things. We simply cannot make the types of claims the snake oil salesman got away with. So these days much of our craft and effort goes into implying all the same things without actually saying them. If you really think about it, a claim like 'No other tampon gives you better protection' simply means it is a parity product, but we have made it sound like a superior product. And now every claim we make has to be qualified. The threat of a lawsuit by competitors and consumers means asterisk usage (where an asterisk is linked to a qualifying statement at the bottom of the ad, usually in small typefont) has increased dramatically.

As we continue to learn more about how to manipulate the mind, as technology continues to change the mediums we use, and as society's mores change to reflect the times, one thing will never change. Somewhere, somehow, advertisers will always be trying to sell you something.

Reference

Maslow, AH (1943) A theory of human motivation. *Psychological Review* 50: 370–96.

7. Media Advocacy for Public Health

Simon Chapman

This chapter describes two sets of insights about using the media to advocate for the health of the public. The first comes from my involvement in the campaign for plain packaging of cigarettes and other tobacco products. Second, I describe the results of a study examining the characteristics of influential Australian public health researchers, particularly their use of the media.

Insights from the campaign to secure plain packaging of tobacco products

On 1 December 2012 Australia became the first nation in the world to implement plain packaging of all tobacco products, after the legislation was supported by all three of Australia's main political parties. No country had ever mandated the entire appearance of packaging for any consumer product, so this historic legislation was at once exceptional, radical and a massive affront to the global transnational tobacco industry, which had for over 100 years packaged its products in highly consumer-tested boxes designed to maximise the appeal of both smoking and each brand.

How did this historic development happen?

The idea of requiring tobacco packs to be 'generic' or plain, with brands distinguished only by their names on the box in a standard font, was first suggested by a Canadian doctor from Vancouver, Gerry Karr, in 1986 (Lee 1986). After some advocacy for the concept in New Zealand, an unsuccessful attempt to see the idea implemented in the early 1990s in Canada, and some early testing of the likely impact in Australia, it went dormant for another decade as the powerful tobacco industry successfully framed the proposal as a fool's errand for any government to consider.

With tobacco advertising being rapidly eroded globally, the pack was coming into its own as the frontline of marketing and branding, as several researchers were pointing out (Slade 1997, Wakefield and Letcher 2002, Wakefield et al. 2002). In 2006, I commenced a National Health and Medical Research Council project grant examining the future of tobacco control. As part of this, in August 2007 we published an online review (Freeman et al. 2007) of the limited experimental evidence on the idea, together with insights into the importance of packaging, found in internal tobacco industry documents and the tobacco retail trade press. A peer-reviewed version subsequently published (Freeman et al. 2008) contained a detailed description of what plain packaging would need to embrace if it was to avoid subversion from an industry well practiced in that art from decades of evading advertising restrictions.

Working in public health research, where the whole idea is to produce work that is useful to informing public opinion and leveraging policy interest, I have never seen the sense in publishing work that is only read by a few hundred colleagues closeted behind journal subscriptions and paywalls. So I often push my research, distributing it to relevant people and writing journalistic pieces to accompany the publication of my scholarly papers.

I circulated the paper widely among my Australian colleagues and to some 5,000 members of a closed global internet listserv, GlobaLink. My sense was that the main objective at the time was to first reoxygenate the dormant concept among the global tobacco control community, to allow it to become part of the narrative of what was needed if nations were to get serious about continuing the reductions in smoking and in the many diseases it causes.

I did not, however, write my normal newspaper opinion page or online blog article to accompany the paper. I sensed that plain packaging was an issue that would first need considerable selling within the public health community, who would need to be comfortable enough with it to become enthusiastic supporters once it got out there as a policy being advocated for adoption. Being novel and never implemented before, it needed to be workshopped in preparation for the inevitable major attacks it would attract.

Over my career, I have spent interminable hours sitting on a large number of committees. Often these are inconsequential and deaden the spirit, but occasionally they can be catalysts to important outcomes. In 2008, I was appointed to the Tobacco Task Force of the Preventative (sic) Health Task Force, an initiative of the Commonwealth Department of Health and Ageing that had been established as a direct response to the newly elected Rudd Labor Government's explicit emphasis on the importance of prevention in health policy reform. With 50 or so others, I had been invited to a briefing by the new Health Minister, the Hon. Nicola Roxon. Her presentation commenced with and dwelt on prevention, not in its normal role as a policy confection to be sprinkled on the more dour real meat and potatoes of health policy such as hospitals and treatment services, but as a primary consideration. Here was a rare government sending direct and forceful signals that prevention was to be taken seriously. Roxon at once seemed one of us, inhabiting the same population-focused values as the public health community.

On the first day the task force met, its chair, Mike Daube, emphasised that his brief had been to convene a committee of experts who should be in no doubt that the government wanted recommendations that would really make a difference. We took turns to propose sometimes bold but always evidence-based actions. An increased tobacco tax was unanimous, but the substantial size of the proposed increase we agreed on (25 per cent) reflected the spirit of the government's clear interest to take prevention seriously.

I predictably recommended plain packaging, which was again unanimously accepted by the committee. I recall remarks about 'we can be bold here … it's important that we get it out there on the agenda, even though it will probably take years to get up'. That was the spirit of our recommendation. I doubt there was anyone in the room who expected that the proposal would have any life other than as a historic but merely 'noted' recommendation in a report.

The proposed legislation was first announced on 29 April 2010, at a press conference held by Prime Minister Kevin Rudd and his health minister, Nicola Roxon, although late night television broke the news the night before, after Roxon's office had called me and others at about 6 pm. Dr Angela Pratt, Roxon's chief of staff, told me deadpan, 'I thought you might like to know that we'll be announcing tomorrow that we'll be introducing plain packaging'. I could almost see her beaming down the phone. From that moment, those working in population-focused tobacco control in Australia did little else for the next two years than concentrate our efforts to ensure the announced bill would be passed.

Policy reform

The confluence of a newly elected government with a prevention reformist agenda; the presence in that government of a passionate, highly educated and articulate minister with accessible staff; the opening of a window of opportunity in the form of a task force charged with maximising policy impact; and a small, closely networked and highly experienced circle of policy entrepreneurs advocating for change, epitomise several of the key ingredients of John Kingdon's analysis of policy reform (Kingdon 2003). But these features were all proximal factors that leave unexplained how a radical idea like plain packaging, when landing on the desk of a new government, found such favour. Proximal factors such as those which Australian tobacco control enjoyed with plain packaging are doubtless necessary to such policies gaining traction, but they are hardly sufficient, as the long trail of policy detritus of excellent, evidence-based proposals that got nowhere should make obvious. It has long been banal to note that policy adoption is not simply a matter of presenting the best facts and evidence to policymakers and sitting back to watch evidence triumph over other considerations. With rare exceptions, policy entrepreneurs and advocates need to engage in serious, extended and highly strategic efforts to ensure that evidence is communicated in ways that make it publicly and politically compelling, so that inaction is not an option. Policy solutions need to be framed in ways that make their rejection problematic. 'Killer facts' (Bowen et al. 2009) need to be mined from eye-glazing data; memorable sound bites (averaging 7.2 seconds) (Chapman et al. 2009) constructed and rehearsed; analogies forged with other issues known to have widespread support; and instinctive understanding developed of the importance of subtext and values referencing in effective communication (Chapman 2007).

While the proposal for plain packaging was novel, the case for it rested on the same long-running narratives that had seen governments of all persuasions incrementally ban all forms of advertising and promotion, commencing with the TV and radio direct advertising in 1976. The 'can't be half pregnant' (Chapman 2004) imperative allowed Roxon and public health advocates to argue that with plain packaging, they were simply finishing the job of banning tobacco advertising because frank admissions by the industry were abundant that packaging was now the frontline of tobacco advertising in 'dark markets' like Australia (Chapman et al. 2003).

Dominant public discourses involving routine framings of the tobacco industry as nefarious, duplicitous, venal, being corporate Pied Pipers, purveyors of deadly products and being indifferent to the health of Australians (Christofides et al. 1999) have been current for at least 40 years. These have grown ever more heated as tobacco use and the industry promoting it become increasingly denormalised (Chapman and Freeman 2008) as smoking prevalence continues to fall. With only 15 per cent of Australians smoking today, and 90 per cent of smokers regretting ever having started (Fong et al. 2004), only 1.5 per cent of Australian adults are smokers who enjoy being smokers. And only a fraction of these are likely to be smokers who care enough to speak out against effective tobacco control measures. Many smokers in fact support tobacco control because they believe it might help them to stop. During the campaign to defend the bill, Roxon said repeatedly that she has never met a smoker who hoped their own children would grow up to become smokers.

Because of three decades of advocacy and incremental government action, smoking has become an issue with vanishingly few champions in Australia. Any political party seen to be going out of its way to support the tobacco industry's interests risked sending a message that would resonate with a very small proportion of the community.

From the moment the government's intentions on plain packaging were announced, a series of major enabling goals became evident. These included ensuring that the research informing the design of the new packs would maximise the main goals of the policy: to make cigarette packs look as unappealing as possible, and to maximise the impact of the graphic health warnings. Legal expertise was also vital in preparing for the anticipated challenges in both Australian courts and internationally, in forums such as the World Trade Organization, and in drafting the legislation itself. The Health Department needed to steel itself for an obstructionist campaign involving massive requests from the tobacco industry under Freedom of Information, fishing for any document that might assist their efforts to derail the policy.

But one of the most important tasks was to ensure that the government's commitment to the legislation received widespread public and all-party political support, the latter being vital because the government held power only with support of minor parties and independent crossbenchers. It became quickly apparent that the bill was highly likely to pass even without the Opposition's support. But it was unanimously agreed that it would be important to gain Opposition commitment too, to ensure ongoing support not only for this bill, but for future tobacco control initiatives in the event of a subsequent change of government.

For this to have happened, and to understand why a proposal as radical as plain packaging was picked up politically and eventually supported by all political parties when the bill was voted on, it is necessary to understand the central place that media advocacy has had in the DNA of Australian tobacco control leadership.

Using the media to meet the nation's most senior politicians

I speak with many researchers who express frustration at the rare opportunities they get to meet with politicians and senior policymakers. I probably get to meet with politicians and senior policymakers only a few times each year myself, if that. But I tell colleagues and students that I 'meet' these people many times each month, often at times when they are most relaxed and receptive. I had never met Nicola Roxon until invited to her 2008 prevention forum. As we met, she said 'I feel I have known you most of my life', referring to my long involvement in news media. So while I had never previously had the opportunity to put proposals to her directly, it was immediately clear that I had done so on innumerable occasions as she awoke to radio news and commentary, in her car as she drove to work or around on weekends, via her newspapers, through television news and via any online feeds she may have followed. Her cabinet colleagues would also all need to be voracious news consumers, so when health portfolio items arose, they too would be acquainted with the public narratives about these issues that have been circulating in news media.

Many researchers today remain ambivalent about media engagement and some are 'deeply distrustful' (US House of Representatives Committee on Science 1998). The values implicit in Sir William Osler's 1905 advice that doctors should not 'dally with the Delilah of the press' (Osler 1905) remain alive today in academic research circles, particularly in disciplines 'where practitioner or liberal educational values counsel modesty and impartiality' (Orr 2010, 23) Concerns are sometimes muttered about the impropriety of researchers actively engaging with the media to publicise their research and, particularly, to advocate for policy—an activity said by some to politicise science (Weigold 2001).

Wilkes and Kravitz's study of first authors whose research had received press coverage found that, while most authors were satisfied with the coverage, a substantial minority thought that media attention 'gives the impression that the researcher is seeking publicity' and 'creates jealousy among colleagues' (Wilkes and Kravitz 1992). Such concerns were echoed in a major study undertaken for the Royal Society in which 20 per cent of British scientists believed colleagues who appeared in the media were 'less well regarded' by their peers—seen as selling out or seeking self-publicity. To this minority, public engagement was something 'light' or 'fluffy' and 'done by those who were "not good enough" for an academic career' (People Science & Policy 2006, 11).

The potential pitfalls of media engagement are well documented, focusing on concerns about sensationalised framing and the misrepresentation inherent in reducing scientific and conceptual complexity to sound bites (Orr 2010, Parry 2002, Schwitzer et al. 2005). Consequently, the literature is full of instances of poor relations between researchers and journalists (Valenti 1999, Maille et al. 2010). For example, 60 per cent of British researchers want to engage with policymakers about their research, but far fewer want to talk to journalists (31 per cent) (People Science & Policy 2006, 9), despite common knowledge that politicians are voracious consumers of news where they daily encounter expert and public opinion directly relevant to their portfolios.

Nevertheless, many researchers engage often and effectively with the media, believing media coverage of their work has significant benefits (Gascoigne and Metcalfe 1997, Gething 2003). Independent health experts are the sources most trusted by journalists covering health issues (Leask et al. 2010); experts are the second most frequent category of news actor in Australian television health news stories, after those experiencing health problems (Chapman et al. 2009).

Yet many researchers remain ambivalent about media engagement, despite strong political encouragement to do so (Department of Innovation, Industry, Science and Research 2010).

Previous studies on how scientists communicate with the media have focused on understanding factors associated with this engagement, particularly challenges and barriers (Dunwoody and Ryan 1985, Peters 1995, Gascoigne and Metcalfe 1997, Poliakoff and Webb 2007, Besley and Nisbet 2011). These include confidence in talking to the media (Poliakoff and Webb 2007), the reaction of colleagues (Gascoigne and Metcalfe 1997), and concerns about the accuracy of reporting (Peters 1995). However, until we began our work examining leading public health researchers, there had been little research on why and how such researchers engage in public discussion of their research and policy and the strategies they use to overcome these barriers and challenges.

Insights from leading 'influential' public health researchers[1]

In 2009–10, I worked with others on a project looking at the characteristics of influential Australian public health researchers (Chapman et al. 2014, Haynes et al. 2011a, 2011b, 2012). We interviewed 36 researchers who had been voted as the six most influential researchers in six fields of public health (alcohol, illicit drugs, injury prevention, obesity, skin cancer prevention and tobacco control). In interviews lasting 60–90 minutes, we asked them to try and reflect on why they believed they had been thus ranked by their research peers. We also interviewed senior policymakers (politicians, their staff, senior bureaucrats) and asked them to reflect on how they came to learn about public health expertise, to use and trust such experts and to regard them as influential.

Three-quarters of Australian politicians we interviewed on how politicians identify expertise placed great importance on media profile, with media presence sometimes disturbingly considered as commensurate with expertise: 'the media is used as a proxy for being an expert in the area'. For one political adviser, it was the only means of identifying experts: 'I have absolutely no idea how I would go about identifying someone if there wasn't an obvious expert prominent in the media' (Haynes et al. 2012).

---

1   The unattributed quotations in this section come from interviews with leading influential public health researchers. They are unattributed to protect confidentiality. See also Chapman et al. 2014, Haynes et al. 2011a, 2011b, 2012.

Perceptions of the media

Our informants considered news media to be both peerless in their power to influence, and a potentially problematic but vital channel for researchers who wished to advance research-informed policy. The sheer reach of media surpassed any academic forum for research dissemination:

> I spoke on [a radio program] last night for example, and there probably would have been, at minimum, 100,000 people listening to that, which is an audience that you would never dream of speaking to in a scientific conference.

Television was seen by some as the most powerful medium:

> If you want to see change, the television screen is really the way to do it. The television screen of the mid-twentieth century has changed more health policy than the Gutenberg revolution of the mid-fourteenth century has or ever will.

The ability of the media to affect policy agenda-setting was of paramount interest to most researchers. Media coverage of health issues had 'brought the community along' with new ways of thinking about public health: 'Without … the softening up that the media did, it [tobacco control legislation] would not have been as acceptable as it ultimately was to the community.' This critical mass of public interest and support could then provide the catalyst for policymakers to back proposals:

> Doing things that will attract media attention and getting good media coverage is another way of getting policy into action indirectly by preparing the community for things or creating a demand in the community that then starts to be felt politically which ultimately leads then through to action in the political sphere as well as more widely in the community.

The major concern of researchers was about possible misrepresentation caused by the media's insistence on simplification resulting in inadequate contextualisation of data or commentary; because of lazy and factually incorrect reporting; or media spin (deliberate efforts to selectively frame the meaning of research, often for sensationalist purposes).

A clear majority (86 per cent) agreed that public health researchers have a duty to increase public awareness of their work and the same percentage agreed that public health researchers had a duty to influence policy and practice.

Media engagement was seen as integral and vital here: 'If you're trying to influence policy, which is really what we were trying to do, we had to put information into the public arena.'

Some interviewees had encountered colleagues who questioned the motivation of media-engaged researchers, seeing their promotion of research as an unseemly, 'ego-driven, empire-building' activity.

These critical colleagues dismissed those who engaged with the media as 'self-promoting' or 'show ponies', terms 'designed to circulate the view that proper science is science which does not seek to promote or publicise its findings'.

Strategies used by influential researchers

All but one of our interviewees regularly engaged with the media because of the 'huge advantage' it provides in 'getting your research out there'. In many cases, this had led to an advantageous media profile that, once established, became almost self-perpetuating with the media returning regularly and the researcher gaining further opportunities to promote research: 'They see that you can articulate an issue and so you tend to get called and that kind of snowballs into becoming the "go to" person.'

Establishing this relationship was seen to be dependent on several attributes: managing simplification, framing, having an opinion, being available and institutional capacity and support.

Managing simplification

Given that the average duration of comments on Australian television news is 7.2 seconds (Chapman et al. 2009), being 'media-friendly' meant 'being able to collapse your complex important findings into the briefest sound bites' and 'knowing what to pick. What is it out of your research that the media is actually going to be interested in?'

The measured and qualified language of science was seen as having little place in media commentary:

> The media's not interested in people who say on the one hand and on the other hand and on the third hand and on the fourth hand. Academics might be interested in that sort of nonsense but no one else is.

The challenge was for researchers to find ways of truncating research, while maintaining its integrity.

Several also noted the importance of modern information technology in providing research detail that the media so often omitted: 'The advent of the web has made it a lot easier to live with simplification in the media and then put all the complexity on the web.'

Framing

Using sound bites effectively not only provided the simplification that media coverage required, it also helped to frame key research findings and implications (Entman 1993, Lakoff 2004), rather than allowing journalists to decide which points were most salient and how they should be presented. Researchers who were able to find accessible but accurate ways of conveying research findings were regarded as highly successful and influential media operators:

> He can spin things really well. I don't mean that in a negative way—he is somebody who has the most fantastic media style, is across the issues … explains the issues endlessly to the media, to the general public and to the bureaucrats in ways that people can readily understand.

Having an opinion

Some interviewees had encountered colleagues who believed researchers should just 'stick to the facts' in interviews. This position was echoed by just two researchers who agreed that '[i]t is not appropriate for me to express my opinions about public health policy'. They argued that extrapolating policy implications from data was outside a researcher's remit: 'I think my public face while I am wearing a researcher's hat is to provide the data and to ensure that the data that are being discussed are the right data and are accurate.' However, the overwhelming majority (94 per cent) disagreed, arguing that the public expects experts to go beyond reciting and clarifying facts to provide commentary, to 'translate' data and explain its meaning for policy: 'They want to see what professor so and so says about it' because 'people always want to know what the policy implications are'.

While nearly everyone would consider it appropriate for experts to appear in news media to explain the facts, journalists and the public expect that experts should also have views worth hearing about what should be done. This is particularly so in public health, where much news is problem-focused. Discussions about problems invariably move from descriptions of the problem, to a focus on those responsible for the problem and its solution (Iyengar 1994). Any public health expert who tried to avoid discussion of such solutions would rapidly find themselves marginalised as an authority. The public would reason, 'What sort of an expert is this, who knows so much about the problem but doesn't seem to have any views about what should be done to fix it?'

Being available

All but one of our interviewees regarded 'being available' to the media as being a component of their professional role. Consequently, these researchers all agreed with the statement that 'I generally respond to media requests to promote awareness of my research', thus being 'assiduous in courting the media and being available at reasonable and unreasonable times when they contact you'.

Some had come to know journalists personally and often assisted them behind the scenes. Several spoke of the symbiosis between the need of researchers to gain public and political attention for their issues and the need of journalists for reliable and credible sources to help them provide authoritative stories. This occasionally led to openings for researchers to suggest stories: 'There were a few journalists who had me on their books and if it was a quiet news day they'd give me a call.'

Institutional capacity and support

Researchers were divided on academic institutional support for research-related media engagement. Many pointed to the lack of encouragement inherent in traditional academia which focuses on 'teaching and research rather than service to the community or being a public intellectual':

> None of this gets counted in an academic's workload or output. It is something that individual senior researchers, in Australia at least, have tended to take on for themselves because they are passionate about public health. Not because they get paid for it.

But others remarked that this neglect was fading fast, with universities highlighting and rewarding their media-active staff and requiring researchers to keep records of media appearances for institutional profiles:

> The sort of mentality that I'm talking about ... 'Don't do anything to publicise your research', it's almost evolving away from that in leading research universities ... They encourage their staff to engage with the community and with policymakers.

This attitude had evolved to such an extent in some universities that some of the most media-engaged researchers were promoted as peer role models: 'If you go to the faculty website ... there is a page where it says "featured academics". I am one of them. I am probably featured because others understand that I embody that approach to my research and that's acknowledged within the faculty as something that they wish to encourage.'

Discussion

While almost all of the peer-rated influential researchers we interviewed recognised the importance of media engagement, they were also sensitive to concerns about its inherent constraints, the dilemmas posed by differences between journalistic and academic cultures and the reputational risks from an injudicious embrace of media celebrity. The major concerns were the news media's insistence on brevity and simplification, and the resultant dumbing down of complexity, and intolerance of inconclusiveness in encapsulating commentary within sound bites. This group of researchers appeared to have developed strategies to overcome these constraints, such as interacting with media workers that they knew and trusted. To most, these concerns were offset by the judgment that to absent oneself from the media was to almost guarantee the irrelevance of one's research to public and political debates about health policy.

Overall, the opportunity that media engagement provided for researchers to contribute to research-informed public awareness and debate was regarded not only as appropriate by most of our influential interviewees, but as a critical aspect of their professional duty to advance public health. It seems these researchers recognise that the nature of media coverage is shaped, in part, by those who initiate stories, meaning that researchers can not only generate media interest in public health research and research-informed policy, but can also set in motion the framing of such stories and influence their effect on public health policy.

In conclusion, this study showed that a willingness and capacity to engage with mass media was seen as an essential attribute of influential public health researchers by most influential Australian researchers. Most of these researchers were comfortable in performing this role and made themselves available to the media to comment on their own research and that of others in their field, and on matters of public health policy relevant to their expertise. This was done with awareness of the limitations of the media and of the difficult path that must be followed in making policy recommendations without being seen as a policy advocate who ventures beyond the evidence or selects evidence to advance a particular policy agenda.

References

Besley, J and Nisbet, M (2011) How scientists view the public, the media and the political process. *Public Understanding of Science* doi:10.1177/0963662511418743. Epub 30/8/2011.

Bowen, S, Zwi, A and Whitehead, M (2009) Killer facts, politics and other influences: what evidence triggered early childhood intervention in Australia? *Evidence and Policy* 5(1): 5–32.

Chapman, S (2004) 'Half-pregnant': occupational health policy on environmental tobacco smoke. *Occupational and Environmental Medicine* 61(5): 383–4. Epub 20/4/2004.

Chapman, S (2007) *Public health advocacy and tobacco control: making smoking history*. Blackwell, Oxford.

Chapman, S and Freeman B (2008) Markers of the denormalisation of smoking and the tobacco industry. *Tobacco Control* 17(1): 25–31. Epub 26/1/2008.

Chapman, S, Byrne, F and Carter SM (2003) 'Australia is one of the darkest markets in the world': the global importance of Australian tobacco control. *Tobacco Control* 12 Suppl 3:iii: 1–3. Epub 3/12/2003.

Chapman, S, Haynes, A, Derrick, G, Sturk, H, Hall, WS and St George, A (2014) Reaching 'an audience that you would never dream of speaking to': influential public health researchers' views on the role of news media in influencing policy and public understanding. *Journal of Health Communication* 19(2): 260–73.

Chapman, S, Holding, SJ, Ellerm, J, Heenan, RC, Fogarty, AS, Imison, M, MacKenzie, R and McGeechan, K (2009) The content and structure of Australian television reportage on health and medicine, 2005–2009: parameters to guide health workers. *Medical Journal of Australia* 191(11–12): 620–4. Epub 24/12/2009.

Christofides, N, Chapman, S and Dominello, A (1999) The new pariahs: discourse on the tobacco industry in the Sydney press, 1993–97. *Australian and New Zealand Journal of Public Health* 23(3): 233–9. Epub 1/7/1999.

Department of Innovation, Industry, Science and Research (2010) *Inspiring Australia: a national strategy for engagement with the sciences*. Report to the Minister for Innovation, Industry, Science and Research. Commonwealth of Australia, Canberra, available from www.innovation.gov.au/General/Corp-MC/Documents/InspiringAustraliaReport.pdf.

Dunwoody, S and Ryan M (1985) Scientific barriers to the popularization of science in the mass media. *Journal of Communications* 35(1): 26–42.

Entman, RM (1993) Framing: towards clarification of a fractured paradigm. *Journal of Communications* 43(4): 51–8.

Fong, GT, Hammond, D, Laux, FL, Zanna, MP, Cummings, KM, Borland, R and Ross, H (2004) The near-universal experience of regret among smokers in four countries: findings from the international tobacco control policy evaluation survey. *Nicotine & Tobacco Research* 6 Suppl 3:S341–51. Epub 1/4/20051.

Freeman, B, Chapman, S and Rimmer, M (2007) The case for the plain packaging of cigarettes. Aug 1 [cited 2013 Mar 20], available from papers.ssrn.com/sol3/papers.cfm?abstract_id=1004646.

Freeman, B, Chapman, S and Rimmer, M (2008) The case for the plain packaging of tobacco products. *Addiction* 103(4): 580–90. Epub 15/3/2008.

Gascoigne, T and Metcalfe, J (1997) Incentives and impediments to scientists communicating through the media. *Science Communication* 18(3): 265–82.

Gething, L (2003) 'Them and us': scientists and the media—attitudes and experiences. *South African Medical Journal* 93(3): 197–201.

Haynes, A, Derrick, G, Chapman, S, Gillespie, J, Redman, S, Hall, W and Sturk, H (2011a) Galvanisers, guides, champions and shields: the many ways that policymakers use public health researchers. *Milbank Quarterly* 89: 564–98.

Haynes, AS, Derrick, GE, Chapman, S, Redman, S, Hall, WD, Gillespie, J and Sturk, H (2011b) From 'our world' to the 'real world': exploring the views and behaviour of policy-influential Australian public health researchers. *Social Science & Medicine* 72(7): 1047–55.

Haynes, AS, Derrick, GE, Redman, S, Hall, WD, Gillespie, JA, Chapman, S and Sturk, S (2012) Identifying trustworthy experts: how do policymakers find and assess public health researchers worth consulting or collaborating with? *PLoS ONE* 7(3): e32665. Epub 10/3/2012.

Iyengar, S (1994) *Is anyone responsible? How television frames political issues.* University of Chicago Press, Chicago.

Kingdon, J (2003) *Agendas, alternatives, and public policies*, 2nd ed. Longman, New York.

Lakoff, G (2004) *Don't think of an elephant!: know your values and frame the debate—the essential guide for progressives.* Chelsea Green Publishing, White River Junction, Vermont.

Leask, J, Hooker, C and King, C (2010) Media coverage of health issues and how to work more effectively with journalists: a qualitative study. *BMC Public Health* 10(1): 535.

Lee, B (1986) Sell tobacco in no-frills wrappers, urge doctors. *The Journal* 1 October.

Maille, M, Saint-Charles, J and Lucotte, M (2010) The gap between scientists and journalists: the case of mercury science in Quebec. *Public Understanding of Science* 19: 70–9.

Orr, G (2010) Academics and the media in Australia. *Australian Universities Review* 52: 23–31.

Osler, W (1905) *Aequanimitas with other addresses: internal medicine as a vocation*. P Blakiston Son & Co, Philadelphia.

Parry, V (2002) Scientists as communicators: how to win friends and influence people. *Journal of Molecular Biology* 319(4): 973–8.

People Science & Policy (2006) *Factors affecting science communication*. Report for the Royal Society, Research Councils UK, and Wellcome Society. London, available from www.peoplescienceandpolicy.com/downloads/Science_communication_quantitative_report_NAV.pdf.

Peters, H (1995) The interaction of journalists and scientific experts: cooperation and conflict between two professional cultures. *Media, Culture & Society* 17(1): 31–48.

Poliakoff, E and Webb, T (2007) What factors predict scientists' intentions to participate in public engagement of science activities? *Science Communication* 29(2): 242–63.

Schwitzer, G, Mudur, G, Henry, D, Wilson, A, Goozner, M, Simbra, M, Sweet, M and Baverstock, KA (2005) What are the roles and responsibilities of the media in disseminating health information? *PLoS Medicine* 2(7): e215.

Slade, J (1997) The pack as advertisement. *Tobacco Control* 6(3):169–70. Epub 1997/12/13.

US House of Representatives Committee on Science (1998) Senate committee hearing: National science policy study part VI: Communicating science and engineering in a sound-bite world. Washington, DC, available from commdocs.house.gov/committees/science/hsy134000.000/hsy134000_0f.htm.

Valenti, J (1999) How well do scientists communicate to media? *Science Communication* 21: 172–8.

Wakefield, M and Letcher, T (2002) My pack is cuter than your pack. *Tobacco Control* 11(2):154–6. Epub 30/5/2002.

Wakefield, M, Morley, C, Horan, JK and Cummings, KM (2002) The cigarette pack as image: new evidence from tobacco industry documents. *Tobacco Control* 11 Suppl 1: I73–80. Epub 15/3/2002.

Weigold, M (2001) Communicating science: a review of the literature. *Science Communication* 23: 164–90.

Wilkes, MS and Kravitz, RL (1992) Medical researchers and the media: attitudes toward public dissemination of research. *JAMA* 268(8): 999–1003. Epub 26/8/1992.

8. Is the Intelligence Community Changing Appropriately to Meet the Challenges of the New Security Environment?

Grant Wardlaw

The changed intelligence environment

Pity the intelligence policymakers or officials attempting to design the ideal organisation to meet the changed strategic and operational environment that now faces them. The world has changed so much since the end of the Cold War that it is in many respects almost unrecognisable.

Many see a clear divide between the 'old' and 'new' threat environments. Treverton (2009), for example, sees the 'old', characteristic of the Cold War era, as concentrated on large, slow-moving targets (for example, Soviet political–military establishment, strategic missile systems) and a shared frame of reference between agencies that facilitated communication with policymakers and made it easy to slot in new information. The focus was on intelligence puzzles—questions for which there were answers if only the veil of secrecy could be penetrated. By way of contrast, 'new' issues are the transnational threats, such as terrorism, weapons of mass destruction, and transnational organised crime, which are small and constantly changing targets with no permanent addresses. They are constantly and rapidly evolving, they exploit our societal vulnerabilities, and they are intelligence mysteries—questions whose answers are inherently unknowable in detail (often because even the targets do not know precisely what they are going to do until they do it).

The implications of this change of targets are substantial. The threats are increasingly diffuse, transnational in nature and cannot be dealt with by single states. The information required to produce intelligence analyses comes from many different sources—often not secret—which need to be shared with a growing number of partners, many of whom are outside government. In an era of terrorism and transnational organised crime, the focus of much intelligence is prevention of individual or small group acts, rather than the intentions and behaviour of states. The nature of the targets means that more emphasis is being placed on human sources (such as spies, informants, interrogation of suspects) than on the technical approach (such as satellite surveillance, communications interception) that came to dominate the Cold War. New technologies of surveillance that are applicable to the new targets raise serious questions about civil liberties and this may limit their use. The nature of the new targets means that the boundaries between domestic and foreign intelligence and between national security intelligence and law enforcement intelligence are increasingly being blurred, if not becoming irrelevant. The danger of intelligence gaps arising has increased because, when compared with the attack preparations of states, those of targets such as terrorists may be more difficult to discern and thus offer less strategic warning (Maddrell 2009).

Analysts coming from a Cold War background were used to vertically integrated intelligence systems focused on a monolithic target (primarily the Soviet Union). The target itself evolved slowly and the analysts had years to develop a good understanding of it (AFCEA 2005). But the current environment for analysts is quite different. The threats are many and diverse in nature. Information has exploded in amount and ubiquity, and sorting for relevance has become one of the most critical jobs of the intelligence analyst. Timelines are very compressed and the requirements of the intelligence clients are more numerous, diverse and immediate. Interaction between analysts and clients is now the norm, while it used to be strongly discouraged. The operational tempo places great strain on intelligence systems and makes it difficult to schedule time for thinking, mentoring and self-development. Analysis needs to be networked, rather than the relatively solitary business it has traditionally been.

It is likely, then, that the nature of intelligence systems and practice requires both fundamental change and a capacity for continuous adaptation if these are to keep pace with the changing environment. This chapter attempts to assess the extent to which the intelligence community has been up to this challenge. It outlines some of the debates about what change is necessary, describes some changes that have taken place and asks how significant (and fit for purpose) the changes that have occurred have been.

Managing change in an intelligence context

The intelligence community faces all of the challenges of managing change according to accepted change management principles (see, e.g. Jones et al. 2004 for a brief outline of these principles). There are, however, some important context issues that affect the ability of intelligence to change meaningfully. The first is the obvious observation that using the word 'community' to describe the organisation and operations of intelligence disguises the fact that the community is really a collective term for a number of individual agencies and units. These operate often quite separately, have specific mandates that sometimes put them at odds with each other, and individual agency cultures that do so even more. So change in the community can and does occur at different times and speeds, in different manners and with more or less success in different agencies.

Policymakers have realised that this makes it very difficult to achieve more directed and comprehensive change across the community and have moved to address the issue from a strategic perspective. For example, one of the prime objectives of recent policy in Australia, especially following the release of the first National Security Statement in December 2008 and the National Security Strategy of March 2013, has been to consciously create a national security community, of which the national intelligence community is a subset. The strategy has included new coordinating mechanisms, strategic documents guiding planning, priority setting and budget management, and the creation of the position of National Security Adviser to provide leadership to the national security community. The lack of an adequate evaluation strategy, however, makes it difficult to judge accurately how far this approach has both harmonised approaches to change and been successful in changing intelligence appropriately to meet the threat environment.

A second issue is that the pressure on intelligence to change its way of operating most often comes from alleged intelligence 'failures', accusations of politicisation of intelligence, and scandals (usually involving alleged intelligence abuses). Bad publicity, poor performance, and failure are all quite common drivers of change in other settings (e.g. business) too. But in these settings it is rare that the pressure falls on a whole community or industry. In the case of an intelligence failure, it is the whole intelligence community that feels the pressure for change. This is typically driven by media hype, and suggested reforms are often simply imposed by government fiat.

Resistance to change is common in all settings, and the intelligence community is no exception. The community often disagrees with the diagnosis of the issue (for example, many would argue that intelligence failures are more often policy failures—see, e.g. Marrin 2011), the solutions are often imposed without serious consideration of expert intelligence opinion (which is often accused of merely protecting agency interests or established, comfortable ways of doing things) and some parts of the community feel that they are immune from criticism even if it may rightly apply to other parts. As Barger (2004, 23) notes:

> Intelligence professionals often have a visceral reaction to calls for new reforms, largely because the connotation of reform suggests an approach to remedy a perceived failure, implies no willingness on the part of the Intelligence Community to change, and is regarded as punitive.

> Most insiders would argue that intelligence reform efforts have resulted
> in more regulation and bureaucracy and little, if any, improvement
> in intelligence performance.

The result, again, is uneven approaches to change across the agencies that
comprise the intelligence community. Consequently, some experts argue
that reorganisation in response to change should be resisted more often than
it is 'because the costs of reorganisation are always substantial, because it is
disruptive and creates negative side effects, while the benefits often prove
dubious' (Betts 2008, 6). Betts recommends that we should focus on changes
that do not require major reorganisation—advice that seems to resonate with
Australian approaches over the last three decades.

Ironically, in the post-9/11 era an almost universal response by governments to
intelligence failures has been to increase the resources going to the community,
so that it has grown substantially over the past decade. This has introduced
another layer of complexity to the manner in which agencies respond to change.
Not only are they grappling with a rapidly changing threat environment and
constantly shifting government requirements, but they are facing all of the
problems of managing rapid growth—a major change issue in its own right.
While there are positives here, particularly with the recruitment of younger,
more technically savvy people who might be more attuned to the contemporary
threats and information technology, there are also major problems with
integrating large numbers of inexperienced officers. There is often a clash
of workplace expectations between old hands and new recruits and there
are limitations in developing and introducing new methods and structures
when a largely untrained workforce is deployed in a high-tempo operational
environment.

More recently, the situation has been further complicated by the international
financial situation which has seen a cutting of intelligence budgets in some
countries and at least stabilisation of resources in an environment which sees
continued growth in intelligence taskings. In essence, the agencies are being
asked to do more with fewer resources. So the challenge facing some intelligence
agencies is managing downsizing at the same time as managing an apparently
insatiable appetite for intelligence. Managing changes to culture, operating
procedures and analytical methodologies will be especially challenging where
the fiscal realities of the present rub up against change fatigue in the agencies
and security fatigue in the community (in the latter case, especially in the
absence of any actual serious national security incidents).

How is intelligence changing?

It is useful to distinguish two ways in which the intelligence community adapts to changes in its environment (Nicander 2011). The most obvious (and most publicised) form of change is reactive. The community changes because of external demands, most often made as a result of a perceived intelligence failure (e.g. the 9/11 terrorist attacks) or an obvious major change in the operating environment (e.g. the end of the Cold War). The community (or some elements of it) may also adapt proactively, by changing practices or organisation as a result of either observing or anticipating changes in the environment (e.g. the emergence of new threats or wider issues such as the introduction or spread of technologies). Such changes will usually be internally driven rather than externally imposed and would be largely characterised as being innovation.

An important change that intelligence agencies have to deal with is the context for oversight of their activities. Traditionally, intelligence has been shrouded in secrecy, with intelligence activities protected from public gaze by both convention and draconian laws forbidding disclosure of sources and methods, information and even the existence of the agencies themselves. In Australia, for example, the existence of the Australian Secret Intelligence Service (ASIS) was not acknowledged by government until 1977, although it was established in 1952. It was not put on a legislative footing until 2001. However, the exposure of illegal activities by intelligence agencies in a number of countries, the occurrence of intelligence 'failures', and the changing nature of the targets—which have drawn an ever-widening number of organisations into the system of providing information or assessments—have all combined to bring intelligence much more into the public arena. The nature of the new information environment of ubiquitous information technology, social media and 24-hour news cycles has made it impossible for the governments to monopolise information in ways they used to, and media coverage and official inquiries are revealing more and more, at least on a general level (and sometimes quite specifically), about the agencies, their missions and capabilities and their activities.

Two other developments have also contributed to the increasing transparency. One is the increasing willingness (indeed, some would say enthusiasm) for politicians to release intelligence publicly to support political decisions. This was essentially the argument that was at the heart of much of the angst over the Iraqi weapons of mass destruction issue. The second is that, now that the targets are often terrorists and criminals whom states want to bring to justice, it is necessary if they are to be tried in ordinary courts that the use of intelligence in apprehending the offenders is revealed and tested in court. This means that it may sometimes be difficult to protect intelligence sources and methods.

On the whole, intelligence has responded very conservatively to this problem, challenging the right to access the intelligence which is also the evidence that a judge or jury would need to weigh up. Responses have mostly been to restrict access to intelligence either by legislative provisions or by proposing (and, in some jurisdictions, establishing) special courts that are not open to the public, have security-cleared judges and lawyers, and have different rules of evidence from ordinary courts. So far the arguments on these issues have largely been in a counterterrorism context, but they are now beginning to arise in ordinary criminal cases where transnational crime is said to be involved. Although there is an increasing trend to view high-end crime (transnational organised crime, cybercrime, significant financial crime) as a national security threat, it is going to be more difficult to argue that there should be severe restrictions on the rules of evidence and the law governing criminal investigations, just because intelligence has been the genesis of the evidence against an accused person.

But it is in this area of the intersection between traditional national intelligence and criminal intelligence that many of the responses of intelligence to change are thrown into sharp relief. Law enforcement agencies have significantly increased their intelligence capabilities in the last decade, both in size and sophistication. Originally the need to support the new counterterrorism responsibilities assumed by police drove the need to interact more comprehensively with the national intelligence community. Law enforcement agencies rapidly expanded their collection and dissemination of intelligence on terrorism to share with the national agencies, and the latter were required to share terrorism-related intelligence with law enforcement. The interaction also led to the increasing incorporation into law enforcement intelligence of national intelligence methodologies, so that the two communities are converging in terms of intelligence doctrine and processes. This convergence is something that some police intelligence officials have resisted, believing that the incorporation of military intelligence methods (in particular) into policing reflects either a takeover of police approaches or a lack of understanding of how intelligence applied to crime problems differs from its application in security settings.

This provides an interesting case study of how two parts of the larger intelligence community using the same intelligence terminology can differ so much in their approaches to the business of intelligence and in how to manage the intersections between their two domains. It is also a case study in how there can be demonstrable change (e.g. significant reorganisation) but still disagreement about the significance or impact of the change on the critical problems identified. In this case, while the language is the same, there are substantial differences in areas such as intelligence collection tasking and management and in analysis, which actually make communication and collaboration between the two communities difficult at times and certainly hamper the effectiveness of the overall system. This fact is often obscured by the official rhetoric about how far-reaching the changes have been and how well the agencies get on with one another. This is not to deny the changes that have taken place. In many ways the degree of interaction between law enforcement and national intelligence agencies would have been unimaginable 15 years ago. But observers looking at the fundamentals of intelligence in the same time span, or looking back to the post-World War II intelligence era, might find little that has essentially changed in the craft of intelligence. Since the world has certainly changed, is it realistic to expect that the basic concepts and operating methods of intelligence can have changed so little and still have a system that delivers quality advice to its clients?

One other issue is important in the attempts of intelligence to manage change in the relationship between law enforcement and national (especially foreign) intelligence—that is, the increasingly blurred lines between intelligence collection for police and for security use. The debate arose initially in the context of counterterrorism work, but is now especially relevant domestically with the designation of transnational crime as a national security issue. There has been pressure to allow foreign intelligence collectors to use their resources to spy on Australian citizens and, in some cases, to do so within Australian borders. The arguments are based on the alleged seriousness of the threat and the argument that some of the old boundaries are artificial and outdated. Similar calls have been made in other countries.

The arguments are complex, but it is easy to see why law enforcement agencies would be frustrated with some of the current restrictions. They argue that they are not being allowed to keep pace with technologies that criminals exploit and that the resulting criminality poses serious threats to national wellbeing that could be avoided if traditional intelligence collection and sharing restrictions were to be changed. The reality is that there is an inherent tension between what law enforcement perceives to be its intelligence collection needs and the collection technologies that they believe they should be able to employ, and citizen concerns about civil liberties. As Betts (2008, 11) notes: 'At some point, optimising intelligence collection and maximising civil liberties come into conflict, and which takes precedence is likely to depend on how alarmed or relaxed the public is about national security.' Managing change in this area is likely to be one of the most difficult for the intelligence community. The intelligence community must understand how both it and its adversaries can exploit evolving technological capabilities, and integrate this knowledge into its business practices. New technological capabilities also raise questions of balance between a state's rights to intrude on its citizens' privacy and the citizens' right to privacy. It involves judgments about the seriousness of the threats and how they are communicated to the public and government in a manner that is not merely self-serving.

On past indications it would not be unreasonable to conclude that police and intelligence agencies have focused almost exclusively on perceived obstacles to operational effectiveness and have little time for arguments about either the consequences of further erosions of privacy or questioning of whether or not the intrusions are proportionate to the threats. This will probably not be a sustainable position as the technologies of surveillance and data integration become even more powerful and the debate about civil liberties becomes more of a mainstream issue. If this happens, intelligence will have to be much more adept at providing a convincing case for increased capabilities and powers and will almost certainly need to manage increased oversight of its activities if additional powers are to be granted. The situation is made more complex by the public reaction to intelligence abuses. Writing about US intelligence, Treverton (2009) argues that the intelligence community faces the challenge of both reforming itself and restoring the social contract with the public, after scandals such as the treatment of insurgents and terrorist suspects in places such as Abu Ghraib and Guantanamo Bay. As a consequence, he claims: 'Intelligence agencies labour under the weight of having been deemed not just incompetent [in terms of failures such as 9/11] but malignant' (Treverton 2009, 64) and will not be given the powers and capabilities they need to respond effectively to the changing world. This is not just a problem for US agencies. Intelligence is now seen as an international community. Issues affecting one country's activities and policies tend to flow over to other jurisdictions, especially where there is a close relationship between them.

National differences

A number of observers have claimed that there are national differences in which ways of handling change predominate. As one might expect, it is widely agreed that change is externally imposed in the case of perceived failure. Studies in the US, UK and Australia have all shown that organisational change, either at the agency or the system level, is the preferred solution to failure. But each country seems different in the degree of enthusiasm for organisational solutions. Significant organisational change is the norm in the US after a perceived failure of intelligence. In the most recent example, after the terrorist attacks of 9/11 and the furore over the role of intelligence in the claims of Saddam Hussein's possession of weapons of mass destruction, the US government substantially reorganised its intelligence community. It did so following the critical findings of various commissions of inquiry (e.g. National Commission on Terrorist Attacks upon the

United States 2004, Commission on the Intelligence Capabilities of the United States Regarding Weapons of Mass Destruction 2005). The changes involved the creation of the position of Director of National Intelligence, new organisations (such as the National Counterterrorism Center) and significantly changed roles and functions for some agencies. Similar findings from inquiries in the UK (e.g. Lord Butler 2004) did not result in such significant organisational changes. The equivalent inquiry in Australia (the Flood Review; Australian Government 2004) produced even less organisational upheaval and the most recent inquiry (the Cornall Review; Australian Government 2011) also concluded that fundamental change, particularly in structure, was not required. Interestingly, this review claimed that a transformation had already taken place in the Australian intelligence community in response to the changing environment. But the evidence for this was that budgets had substantially increased, and that agencies were working more closely together than previously and were working in some new areas (such as people smuggling). This is hardly transformational and there was no discussion of fundamental changes in the way the community goes about its business.

In examining Australian responses to the challenges of responding to change, Wesley (2006) noted that such reform as has occurred has been a reaction to controversies and reviews but has always been informed by three organising principles. These are:

- functional specialisation in intelligence (i.e. different types of intelligence collection are the responsibility of separate specialised agencies)
- separation of intelligence collection from intelligence assessment
- separation of domestic and foreign collection and assessment.

If these principles are used as yardsticks against which to measure the extent of change in the community, I can only agree with Wesley's conclusion that recent reforms in Australia 'have reinforced, rather than challenged, the basic organising principles according to which [the Australian intelligence community] has always operated'. This conclusion is further reinforced by the Cornall Review which argued that 'there is no need to consider any significant restructure of the existing agencies at present although the agencies will have to consider carefully how they will adapt in response to the future challenges they face within those existing structures and cooperation arrangements' (Australian Government 2011).

The reasons for resistance to change are somewhat different in the US. Nicander (2011), for example, argues that generally the US intelligence community moves slowly in response to change, partly because of the strength of organisational cultures and the ability of the US to 'throw money at the problem', thus building new capacity or capability, often in new agencies or structures, with a corresponding unwillingness to fundamentally assess the way business is done at a systemic level. Thus, the US can have substantial change, but possibly without really adapting to the changes in the environment in anything other than a superficial or partial manner.

This brief comparison points to one difficulty in reaching general conclusions about how intelligence deals with change. The manner in which change occurs will likely vary, often substantially, depending on which country is being examined. A number of authors have pointed to the different ideas about intelligence that guide national approaches to practice. Davies (2010), for example, claimed that British intelligence culture tends to be integrative in nature while the US culture tends to be disintegrative. As Duyvesteyn (2011, 527) observes: 'These distinctive cultures are prone to specific weak points; integrative cultures are highly sensitive to groupthink and disintegrative cultures to turf wars.' In an earlier discussion of intelligence culture, Davies (2002, 62) had also pointed to the significant divergences in the concept of intelligence between the US and the UK. He notes wryly that in the mid-1990s, official committees in both the US and the UK examined intelligence methods in the other's intelligence community but in their final reports '[n]either side found anything to incorporate from the other's methods, and yet neither seemed to detect that they were talking—and hence thinking—about entirely different things when they were talking about intelligence'. Probably more importantly, however, the same observation could be made even *within* national intelligence communities. This is certainly true of the foreign intelligence and criminal intelligence communities. These differences make the task of harmonising effective change in the broader intelligence community that much more difficult and underpin a number of implementation problems.

How much change in intelligence is required to manage the changed threat environment?

According to Lahneman (2007), experts on intelligence community change fall into one of three categories based on the degree of change that they believe is required to deal with the changing environment. The first group believes that significant reform is not necessary. They claim that views that intelligence is not sufficiently attuned to change are too influenced by so-called intelligence failures. (The argument here is that failure to predict a specific threat or event is evidence that intelligence is not able to keep up with the changing threat environment.) But the non-reformers argue that since we cannot eliminate surprise altogether, the occurrence of occasional surprises does not necessarily indicate anything about the adequacy of the system. In this group, even those who recognise that some changes are necessary believe that there are greater dangers in wholesale change motivated by specific failures.

A second group of experts believes that the intelligence community is so poor at keeping up with change that it requires significant change to the way it does business and that this change needs to be transformational if it is to make a real difference. Finally, a third group falls somewhere between the other options, believing that intelligence faces such a changed (and continually changing) environment that significant reform is necessary—*but* that the change should be evolutionary rather than revolutionary.

Strangely, although there is a large literature on the changing strategic, political and social environment which is driving changes in intelligence community targets, there is a relative dearth of attention paid to how intelligence is changing conceptually to deal with these changes. Most attention is paid to intelligence community reorganisation, but not much to thinking about whether or not intelligence theory and practice should change also. As one commentator has noted: 'Very little has been written about how intelligence community agencies—traditionally rigid organisations in the core of the state apparatus— evolve and adapt to new circumstances when no market or other competitive mechanisms are present' (Nicander 2011, 535). That may be about to change, however, since one of the new trends evident in the intelligence environment is that there are now competitors to traditional agencies, ranging from clients who see themselves as analysts to commercial practitioners who claim to offer better, faster or newer services than some government organisations.

So is intelligence adapting adequately to the changed environment?

Responding adequately to changes in the new, complex and fast-moving security environment requires that intelligence has the capacity to analyse threats in a systemic manner—to see them as being interconnected and interdependent, with changes in one having impacts on others. But in reality most analysis is still stove-piped (that is, held and worked on in relative isolation from other analytical areas), generally on an issue or geographical basis. This makes it very difficult to see the connections between the threats.

Dupont (2013), commenting on the new National Security Strategy in Australia, claims,

> The Australian national security community does not yet have the analytical tools or rigorous methodologies for assessing and prioritising complex risks and anticipating system-threatening tipping points. The need for new analytical tools and methodologies was clearly identified ... [in the 2008 National Security Statement] but there is no evidence they have been developed or applied.

This view is echoed by Zegart (2005) who, commenting on the US scene, claimed that the intelligence community failed to adapt to the rise of terrorism after the Cold War. She acknowledges that there has been substantial change, but notes that organisations are always changing. But she argues that change is not as relevant as adaptation—the question is, do the changes matter and does the rate of change keep pace with the rate of change in the environment? Zegart lists a number of impediments to adaptive reform and argues that important amongst these is the fact that government agencies are built to be reliable, consistent and predictable—not adaptive. Unfortunately, 'the very characteristics that give an organisation reliability and fairness reduce the probability of change' (Zegart 2005, 96).

But adaptability is exactly the characteristic that intelligence needs, to keep up with the changing environment. A senior analyst with the Central Intelligence Agency (CIA) has nicely summarised some of the characteristics of the changed environment for intelligence (Andrus 2005). Foremost among these is the fact that intelligence, especially in some of its new support to military operations and crisis roles, increasingly works in a 'real-time, worldwide decision and implementation environment' where the 'total "intelligence–decision–implementation" cycle time can be as short as 15 minutes' (Andrus 2005, 63). This is a huge change from the way intelligence has operated in the past. Tactical and strategic superiority now requires a very different way of organising intelligence and different ways of assigning responsibilities to its staff. Andrus makes the point that these compressed cycles are just the way the environment generally is organised these days, but that makes changes and individual events very hard to predict. It follows (Andrus 2005, 63) that the intelligence community

> is faced with the question of how to operate in a security environment that, by its nature, is changing rapidly in ways we cannot predict ... [So] the Intelligence Community, by its nature, must change rapidly in ways we cannot predict.

But Andrus is wary of reorganisation as the basis of the solution. By its nature, reorganisation is both predictable and slow. 'By the time any particular reorganisation has taken effect, the causes that spawned it will have been replaced by new and different causes' (Andrus 2005, 63–4). Importantly, though, this judgment itself is at the core of the debate over the differing views on the correct manner in which the intelligence community should manage change. Is change as fast and as continuous and as fundamental as Andrus and like-minded experts believe? This is a critical question to resolve before deciding on the right approach to take.

However, while the preponderance of expert opinion (clearly contrasting with the opinion of politicians) is that reorganisation is not *the* answer to managing change in the intelligence world, it is almost certainly *part* of the solution. As previously noted, one of the biggest changes affecting intelligence has been the move from a focus essentially on one huge national security problem (the USSR) to an environment of many targets of a vastly different nature (for example terrorism, organised crime, weapons proliferation), requiring many more locations, smaller footprints, very mobile targets and different collection and assessment methodologies. As Hammond (2010) points out, it is unlikely that the 'best structure' for addressing the USSR intelligence target will be the same as for the much different and more diffuse threats of today. While there have been many experiments with different structures since the Cold War, none could be described as truly revolutionary. This is partly explained by institutional inertia and cultural resistance, but a more fundamental reason is that there is simply no agreement across the board as to the nature of the intelligence enterprise. This comes as something of a surprise to community outsiders but, as Hammond (2010, 687) rightly observes,

> What allows these debates to continue after so many decades is the fact that most of the key issues remain unresolved, both theoretically and empirically … Indeed, knowing how to think about this design problem in any theoretically fundamental manner is problematical, and what some observers think they know (e.g. about the virtues of centralised control and management, or about the virtues of decentralised competition) has not been subjected to rigorous theoretical or empirical evaluation.

The need to change is not just about new methods or structures. A crucial question is that of whether or not changes in the intelligence environment will change or are changing the intelligence process itself (i.e. how intelligence is developed and used). For example, there is a growing literature detailing dissatisfaction with the traditional intelligence cycle—the model which is supposed to describe and guide the conduct of intelligence through from tasking to dissemination to users (see e.g. Davies 2012, Hulnick 2006 and 2013, Richards 2012). Some experts have claimed that while much is different, there has been little real change. Lahneman (2010, 206), for example, claims that the (US) intelligence community 'still looks and operates substantially as it did at the end of the Cold War'. A seasoned CIA officer, after noting the huge changes that have occurred in the environment in which intelligence operates, goes on to say: 'Yet the DI's [Directorate of Intelligence's] approach to analysis has hardly changed over the years. A DI analyst from decades ago would recognise most of what a typical analyst does today' (Medina 2002, 23). Although that judgment was made over a decade ago, many commentators believe the same is substantially the case today. So a recent analysis (Agrell 2012) found that, while the intelligence environment and the conduct of intelligence in terms of technology, collection ability and focus have all changed significantly since the end of the Cold War, there has been no corresponding change in the underlying theory of intelligence or the industrialised knowledge production system. He believes that intelligence is significantly under-theorised and that the knowledge production system must evolve to meet new information processing and sense-making realities.

With such disagreements on fundamentals and the corresponding lack of data, it is not surprising that views on how well intelligence manages change often sound more like personal opinion than solid analysis. Nevertheless, many writers agree with Bruce (undated) that the intelligence practices required by the current environment require far greater adaptability than they are designed for, especially if they are to keep up with the changes in the environment.

Bruce proposes that we need to analyse adaptations across four different domains. The first is functional—what is it that intelligence organisations do? What are their principal functions and missions? Second is the cultural domain—what are the attitudes, values and beliefs that define the profession? Third is the question of change mechanisms—what processes are (or are not) built in to ensure adaptation? And, finally, there is the structural dimension—what are the organisational forms that characterise the agencies and the community? Bruce believes that a detailed analysis of these domains can produce a useful classification into 'old' and 'new' approaches to intelligence that could help design a truly adaptive intelligence community. We are a long way from that point at present. But Bruce (2006) also sounds a note of caution about adaptation that often seems to be overlooked—adaptation is a two-way street. As intelligence gets better at finding and understanding its targets, the smarter targets also adapt to evade intelligence. The effectiveness of intelligence will decline if its adaptive cycle falters at any point.

Some have argued that intelligence changes most when an event (usually characterised as an intelligence failure) acts as a wake-up call which focuses attention on a new threat or issue and stimulates new thinking and approaches or a redirection of effort. Broader studies of organisational change (see, for example, Clarke 2006) have found that organisations seldom take significant action to improve security or safety without the impetus of a disaster affecting them or their interests. Disasters or failures thus act as focusing events that stimulate change. Kingdon (1995) asserts that studies of focusing events show that policy change is more likely if the events highlight widespread problems (often indicating the issues are already on someone's agenda) and potential solutions have already been proposed. Exposure of novel problems is less likely to drive policy change. Further, the impact of focusing events is not necessarily long-lasting.

These findings have important implications for intelligence change. As Dahl (2010) points out, incidents such as the 9/11 terrorist attacks are often described as focusing events for the intelligence community. Certainly the attacks provoked a flurry of inquiries, recommendations, budget increases, legislative changes and intelligence reorganisations, not only in the US but around the world. But there is a wide range of opinions about the extent to which they were focusing events that had long-term effects or meant deep change to the way intelligence goes about its business. For example, Zegart (2007) believes they were not focusing events, arguing that change leading to significant performance improvements has been stymied by organisational and bureaucratic limitations. On the other hand, Dahl (2010 797) believes,

> The history of unsuccessful terrorist plots within the US in recent years does, in fact, suggest that the 9/11 attacks acted as a wake-up call that jolted the intelligence community and policy makers into a new understanding of the danger from home-grown as well as international terrorism.

It seems to me that this is a premature judgment. It may reflect little more than a willingness to change priorities—and so to change targeting and analysis— in this one field of intelligence, but might not indicate changes in the field of intelligence itself. Of course, this begs the question of how much fundamental change is really necessary and also underscores both the conceptual difficulty in designing an evaluation strategy for intelligence and in collecting and accessing relevant data. Dahl's work has, however, made an important initial contribution to analysing the influence of focusing events and wake-up calls on intelligence success and failure, and is particularly relevant in pointing out the role that decision-maker receptivity to new directions in threats or intelligence itself plays in successful implementation of meaningful change.

While Zegart (2007) claims that the intelligence system as a whole is not designed to cope well with change, others have examined the possibility that particular parts of the system have, in effect, been designed *not* to adapt. Peterson (2009), for example, discusses the central role given to intelligence requirements (the specification of the information that is needed to fill gaps in knowledge) to drive collection and analysis, and concludes that the strength of this approach—efficient allocation of scarce resources and a focus on meeting client needs—is also its Achilles heel because it ensures that most effort is put into filling gaps in existing knowledge rather than challenging assumptions and creating new insights. As Peterson (2009, 27) sees it:

> We mobilise the intelligence system to seek greater and greater clarity based on old insights and fail to develop new insights that reflect changing circumstances. We begin to seek information that helps us execute our chosen courses of action while ignoring information that suggests flaws in our original assumptions.

In other words, the requirements system itself limits the ability of the community to detect change and to make sense of it.

Especially in an era when so much emphasis is put on meeting client demands (as in the wider, non-intelligence, world) we may actually be cutting off the raising of new issues for analysis or policy consideration. Client demands for certainty—especially in an environment in which decision-makers want to (unrealistically) reduce risk to zero—can mean that the system fails to develop novel insights that may be critical for future challenges. This is true both at the operational and strategic levels. This does not mean the abandonment of the current system—which does have virtues—but it indicates that the system needs modification to ensure some capacity to collect on areas not of current concern. As Peterson (2009 33) concludes:

> If our decision makers accept that intelligence cannot provide certainty and our intelligence community gives priority to equipping them with insights necessary to support decision making under uncertainty, then we will be much more capable of anticipating events, avoiding surprise, and maintaining the strategic initiative in an ever changing world.

Treverton and Gabbard's (2008) report on the tradecraft of intelligence analysis reflects similar concerns. Following an extensive review of the way analysts work in the US intelligence community, they concluded that the traditional approaches are not optimised either to take advantage of changing technology and methodologies or to keep pace with the threat environment. They found (Treverton and Gabbard 2008, 33–4),

> Analysts still mostly work alone or in small groups. Their use of formal analytic methods, let alone computer-aided search engines or data-mining, is limited. Their basis for analysis is their own experience, and their tendency is to look for information that will validate their expectations or previous conclusions.

This approach is the opposite of what many regard as the appropriate set of behaviours in a world of many, small, rapidly emerging and changing targets, of information overload and of the availability of sophisticated analytical methods and technologies. Such a world requires an analytical community that is collaborative, often virtual and linked by robust tools and datasets. The new targets also require collaboration with a host of partners outside the formal intelligence community. The information and knowledge required for many contemporary intelligence issues lie in industry, non-government organisations and the academic community. Intelligence contact with these partners has increased substantially out of necessity but is still often hampered by old-fashioned notions of secrecy and by an intelligence agency attitude that treats partners just as sources. This latter attitude is unsustainable. Notions of secrecy will have to evolve if the collaboration is to be truly successful.

My own experience with police intelligence would lead to similar conclusions in that environment. Advanced analytical techniques are seldom employed and collaborative technologies not exploited. The confining effects of organisational culture are also very apparent. Clients focus on immediate operational outcomes in matters that they already know about, and have little appetite for additional or novel areas for exploration. Resource management almost always drives collection priorities to immediate operational support. Perhaps more surprisingly, there is little interest amongst analysts to explore new approaches. Those who do so tend to be alone in their excitement about new methods and get little support or time allocated for experimentation with them. Overall, there is little indication that intelligence is changing fundamentally in order to keep up with the changing environment. This is particularly obvious in the lack of support for strategic intelligence that is aimed at looking widely at the operating environment for signs of new developments. Such work, while seen by some as potentially interesting, is seen by most as operationally irrelevant. The tyranny of the present stifles the long view and the opportunity to be prospectively adaptive.

The limitations on the ability of analytical areas to change mean that effective intelligence in the new environment is threatened by 'a convergence of societal and governmental trends that make it extremely difficult to hire the right people, train them or allow them to collaborate effectively' (Hart and Simon 2006, 35). Although there is widespread recognition of the human resources challenges that the changed environment has brought to intelligence (see e.g. O'Brien 2008), very few of the current reforms to the community attempt to comprehensively address the recruitment, retention, workplace environment, cultural and organisational issues that arise.

Conclusion: How significant are the changes?

How significant and appropriate to the challenges of the new environment are the changes that have taken place? There does seem to be a general appreciation of the extent of the changes that have occurred in the intelligence operating environment. Most official reviews and intelligence scholars and commentators agree that the shift from an almost single-minded focus on the Cold War to the new agenda of transnational and 'new security' threats necessitates substantial changes to the intelligence community. The rapidly evolving information technology revolution is also noted as driving new challenges and opportunities for intelligence. All agree that this means new targets to be pursued, new technologies to be embraced and new partners to be engaged. There is considerable disagreement, though, about whether or not this necessitates fundamental change to the very nature of the intelligence enterprise—an 'intelligence transformation' or a 'revolution in intelligence affairs' (Lahneman 2007, 2011) to parallel the much-discussed 'revolution in military affairs' (Gray 2004).

In asking whether or not a revolution in intelligence affairs is occurring, Lahneman (2007) suggests that the answers to four questions will help determine the extent to which real change is taking place. Adapting questions originally asked about the revolution in military affairs in a seminal article by Eliot Cohen (Cohen 1996), he asks: Will developments in intelligence change how it is developed and used (process changes)? Will they change the structure of the intelligence community (organisational changes)? Will they create new elites in the intelligence community (skill set changes)? And will failure to embrace the changes affect the national security of countries that do not move with the environment (changes in effect)?

Lahneman judges that the answer to all four questions is yes, and that a revolution in intelligence affairs is already under way. Others are not so sure. An American intelligence community working group tasked to examine intelligence analysis concluded that 'for all the experimentation with technology and intelligence production over the years, intelligence products have remained remarkably unchanged: they are primarily static, branded and stove-piped' (Anon 2012). Treverton (2009, 55) believes that 'the carousel of reorganisation has produced more shuffle than substance'. However, the intelligence literature is littered with reports of either attempts to change the system (or parts of it) or suggestions of how the community should respond to the changes it faces. Whatever the merits of individual change proposals and attempted implementation, it will be useful for the intelligence community to take note of the lessons of other transformation efforts in large organisations. Barger (2004) argues that looking at these experiences teaches that three things seem to characterise successful transformations: a deliberate and focused attempt to think strategically about the business of the organisation *before* any attempt to change it; a core group who develop a new idea and stay long enough to see changes through; and a method of critically analysing change proposals to evaluate how well they would serve all (or the most important) of the organisation's strategic objectives.

My own view of where we are at present is that there is plenty of activity, some of it cosmetic and designed to meet political objectives. Some is potentially substantial change which is muted in implementation by organisational resistance and the difficulties inherent in culture change, and some is significant but too limited in scope to affect the intelligence enterprise overall. So there are questions about how real many of the changes are, how widespread they are at a fundamental level within the intelligence community, and whether or not many of the changes are actually adaptive. Given the importance to security and safety of getting intelligence right, and in view of the vast amounts of money expended on intelligence internationally, assessing the ability of the community to successfully adapt to change is a subject worthy of much more study and debate.

References

Agrell, W (2012) The next 100 years? Reflections on the future of intelligence. *Intelligence and National Security* 27(1): 118–32.

Andrus, D (2005) The wiki and the blog: toward a complex adaptive intelligence community. *Studies in Intelligence* 49(3): 63–70.

Anon (2012) Products or outputs? Probing the implications of changing the outputs of intelligence. *Studies in Intelligence* 56(1): 1–11.

Armed Forces Communications and Electronics (AFCEA) (2005) *Making analysis relevant: it's more than connecting the dots.* A White Paper prepared by the AFCEA Intelligence Committee, Fairfax VA.

Australian Government (2004) *Report of the inquiry into Australian intelligence agencies.* Canberra.

Australian Government (2011) *2011 Independent review of the intelligence community report.* Canberra.

Barger, D (2004) It is time to transform, not reform, U.S. intelligence. *SAIS Review* 24(1): 23–31.

Betts, R (2008) *21st century intelligence: progress and limits*. Address to the Canadian Association of Security and Intelligence Studies, Ottawa, 30 October.

Bruce, J (2006) Denial and deception in the 21st century: adaptation implications for Western intelligence. *Defense Intelligence Journal* 15(2): 13–27.

Bruce, J (undated) *Dynamic adaptation: a twenty-first century intelligence paradigm*. Unpublished PowerPoint slides from the author.

Clarke, L (2006) *Worst cases: terror and catastrophe in the popular imagination*. University of Chicago Press, Chicago.

Cohen, E (1996) A revolution in warfare. *Foreign Affairs* 75(2): 37–54.

Commission on the Intelligence Capabilities of the United States Regarding Weapons of Mass Destruction (2005) *Report to the President of the United States, 31 March 2005*.

Dahl, E (2010) Missing the wake-up call: why intelligence failures rarely inspire improved performance. *Intelligence and National Security* 25(6): 778–99.

Davies, P (2002) Ideas of intelligence: divergent national concepts and institutions. *Harvard International Review* 24(3): 62–6.

Davies, P (2010) Intelligence culture and intelligence failure in Britain and the United States. *Cambridge Review of International Affairs* 17(3): 495–520.

Davies, P (2012) *The intelligence cycle is dead, long live the intelligence cycle: rethinking an intelligence fundamental for a new intelligence doctrine*. Paper prepared for the Annual Convention of the International Studies Association, San Diego, 1 April.

Dupont, A (2013) National security dilemma: new threats, old responses. *Australian Financial Review* 15 March: 1.

Duyvesteyn, I (2011) Intelligence and strategic culture: some observations. *Intelligence and National Security* 26(4): 521–30.

Gray, C (2004) *Strategy for chaos: revolutions in military affairs and the evidence of history*. Frank Cass, London.

Hammond, T (2010) Intelligence organizations and the organization of intelligence. *International Journal of Intelligence and CounterIntelligence* 23(4): 680–724.

Hart, D and Simon, S (2006) Thinking straight and talking straight: problems of intelligence analysis. *Survival* 48(1): 35–60.

Hulnick, A (2006) What's wrong with the intelligence cycle? *Intelligence and National Security* 21(6): 959–79.

Hulnick, A (2013) *Intelligence legoland: seeking better models of the intelligence process.* Paper prepared for the Annual Convention of the International Studies Association, San Francisco, 3–6 April.

Jones, J, Aguirre, DeA and Calderone, M (2004) 10 principles of change management, *Strategy+Business,* Booz and Co, 15 April, available at www.strategybusiness.com/media/file/resilience-04-15-04.pdf.

Kingdon, J (1995) *Agendas, alternatives and public policies,* 2nd ed. HarperCollins, New York.

Lahneman, WJ (2007) Is a revolution in intelligence affairs occurring? *International Journal of Intelligence and CounterIntelligence* 20(1): 1–17.

Lahneman, WJ (2010) The need for a new intelligence paradigm. *International Journal of Intelligence and CounterIntelligence* 23(2): 201–25.

Lahneman, WJ (2011) *Keeping US intelligence effective: the need for a revolution in intelligence affairs.* Scarecrow Press, Lanham MD.

Lord Butler (Chair) (2004) *Review of Intelligence on Weapons of mass destruction: report of a committee of privy counsellors,* HC 898. Stationery Office, London.

Maddrell, P (2009) Failing intelligence: U.S. intelligence in the era of transnational threats. *International Journal of Intelligence and CounterIntelligence* 22(2): 195–220.

Marrin, S (2011) The 9/11 terrorist attacks: a failure of policy not strategic intelligence. *Intelligence and National Security* 26(2): 182–202.

Medina, C (2002) The coming revolution in intelligence analysis: what to do when traditional models fail. *Studies in Intelligence* 46(3): 23-29.

National Commission on Terrorist Attacks upon the United States (2004) *The 9/11 commission report.* WW Norton and Co, New York.

Nicander, L (2011) Understanding intelligence community involvement in the post-9/11 world. *International Journal of Intelligence and CounterIntelligence* 24(3): 534–68.

O'Brien, K (2008) *The changing security and intelligence landscape in the 21st century.* International Centre for the Study of Radicalisation and Political Violence, London.

Peterson, S (2009) *US intelligence support to decision making*. Research Paper. Weatherhead Center for International Affairs, Harvard University, Cambridge MA.

Richards, J (2012) *Peddling hard: further questions about the intelligence cycle in the contemporary era*. Paper prepared for the Annual Convention of the International Studies Association, San Diego, 1 April.

Treverton, G (2009) Intelligence test. *Democracy Journal* 11 (Winter): 54–65.

Treverton, G and Gabbard, C (2008) *Assessing the tradecraft of intelligence analysis*. Rand Corporation, Santa Monica CA.

Wesley, M (2006) *Between probity and proficiency: challenge and change within the Australian intelligence community*. Commentary no. 88. Canadian Security Intelligence Service, Ottawa.

Zegart, A (2005) September 11 and the adaptation failure of U.S. intelligence agencies. *International Security* 29(4): 78–111.

Zegart, A (2007) *Spying blind: the CIA, the FBI, and the origins of 9/11*. Princeton University Press, Princeton NJ.

9. Evolutionary Change: Nothing stands still in biology

Lindell Bromham

The world around us is the product of evolution—not just the actual biological organisms such as the trees, birds and insects, but also many features of the environment such as the soil, atmosphere and buildings, which have been constructed by the actions of organisms over time. This life-built environment is in a constant state of change, as are all the biological lineages that inhabit it. So if you want to understand the world around you, then a passing familiarity with the nuts and bolts of evolutionary change is an important part of your intellectual toolkit.

Understanding the processes of evolutionary change is also essential to grasping biological phenomena that affect our everyday lives, such as recognising the way that your antibiotic prescription contributes to the incidence of untreatable infections, or judging whether genetically modified food is dangerous. While most people in our society recognise that the species alive on earth today are descended from earlier types, common notions of evolutionary change such as 'the survival of the fittest' can just as often mislead as enlighten. Evolution is at the same time breathtakingly simple in mechanism, and devilishly complex in outcome.

In this chapter, I briefly summarise the basics of evolutionary change: how genomes change, species evolve, and biodiversity is shaped over time. The point I wish to emphasise is that evolutionary change is continuous and inevitable—nothing stands still in the biological world. Because DNA replication is almost but not entirely perfect, mutations arise in each generation. Some of these mutations rise in frequency until they become permanent changes to the genetic material that characterises a population. Over generations, in every population, genetic change accumulates, driving a process of divergence that ultimately results in the formation of new species. As new species arise, others are lost to extinction, so the composition of the biosphere is in constant flux. The changing nature of species and communities shapes the environment, creating a constantly shifting biological landscape that all species must adapt to. Our own species has had to adapt to changing conditions, even as it has dramatically changed the environment of nearly all other species in the biosphere.

I also want to highlight the way ideas change over time, using a few key debates to demonstrate that evolutionary biology itself is in a constant state of flux, as new ideas prompt the search for new data or novel analyses, and these new data and analyses generate further new ideas. One of the main themes that has threaded through many debates in evolutionary biology since its inception is whether evolution is primarily driven by small changes accumulating slowly and gradually over long periods of time, or rapidly in occasional bursts of large changes. Although the nature of the data has changed dramatically, now that we have access to whole genome sequences of an increasing number of species, many of the core ideas have parallels to debates that have waged since Darwin's revolutionary publication *On the origin of species* (1859).

The best place to start if you want to understand evolutionary change is to consider the raw material of evolutionary change: a mutation occurring in an individual's DNA.

We are all mutants

Life depends on DNA copying. Whenever a cell gives rise to a new cell, its genome, consisting of all the DNA that is inherited as a coherent unit, must be copied in its entirety (Figure 1). Because the integrity of genetic information is critical to survival, the genome is copied with astounding accuracy, with only a few mistakes made for every hundred million nucleotides ('letters') of DNA copied. But because genomes of most complex creatures are so big (in the case of humans, roughly 3 billion nucleotides of DNA), and are copied dozens of times in a typical generation from parent to offspring, even this vanishingly small error rate results in new mutations with every generation. Similarly, damage to DNA, such as that caused by mutagenic chemicals or ultraviolet light, is usually perfectly repaired by a barrage of specialised cellular equipment, but the occasional missed or misrepaired damage slips through the net, permanently changing the DNA sequence. The upshot is that each new individual might have 100 or more entirely new mutations that neither of the parents carried (Nachman and Crowell 2000).

Mutations, whether created by mistakes in copying or unrepaired damage, are accidents. They are not deliberate changes, and they occur with no regard for consequences. Mutations that change DNA sequences that encode the instructions for growth, survival and reproduction will tend to be harmful. This is because a random change to organised information almost never results in improvement (you can test this next time you write an email by randomly replacing words with alternatives chosen by a blind draw from the dictionary). Very, very rarely will a random change to the useful information in the genome make that individual function better, thus imparting a greater chance of successful reproduction and representation in coming generations. However, some mutations may be neither harmful nor beneficial. A mutation that occurs in a part of the genome that does not contain important instructions for making or maintaining the organism may make no difference to its carrier's chances of survival and reproduction. Even some mutations that occur in essential genes may have little impact on the organism's success, for example if the DNA or protein sequence is altered but it still functions as normal. These 'neutral' mutations can be carried by an individual without cost or benefit.

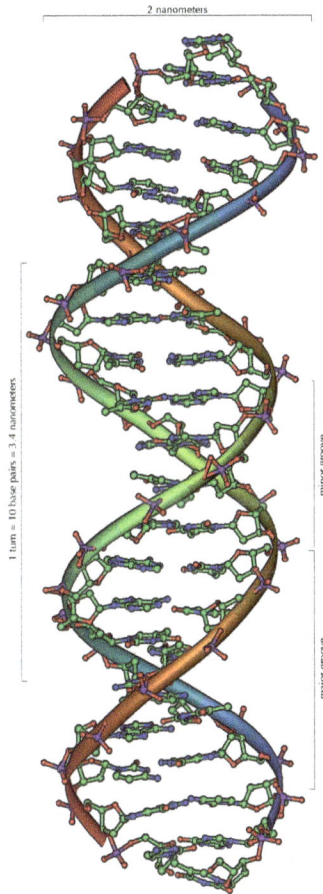

Figure 1 The most beautiful molecule in the world: A short section of a DNA double-helix.

DNA is the heart of the living world, beautiful not only in form but also in function. The DNA molecule is made of two intertwined strands made of linked phosphate and sugar (ribose) molecules, with four kinds of nitrogenous bases (A, C, T and G) making the steps of the spiral staircase. The bases pair between the strand, each base matched to its complement—A pairs with T, and G pairs with C. This means that one strand of DNA can act as a template to create a new strand containing the matching base sequence, and that new strand can act as a template to create a sequence identical to the original strand. In this way, the genetic information can be faithfully copied from cell to cell, from generation to generation.

Source: Figure created by Michael Ströck, available through WikiCommons at commons.wikimedia.org/wiki/File:DNA_double_helix_horizontal.png.

How can accidental changes to the information in the genome be the basis of the evolution of complex and well-adapted life? Random mutations may be the raw material of evolution, but they are sorted by natural selection.

If a mutation harms its carrier's chances of surviving and reproducing, then, by definition, that mutation is less likely to end up in a healthy offspring in the next generation. So harmful mutations will either fail to make it into the next generation at all (if they result in death or sterility) or will diminish in numbers with each generation (if they reduce the chance of survival and reproduction). This filtering out of harmful mutations is referred to as 'negative selection' and it is the only process that prevents evolutionary change at the genomic level. If there is a sequence in the genome that is very similar, or identical, in many different and otherwise divergent species, then that sequence must be so important that changing it almost always results in negative consequences. For example, there is a protein sequence in the active site of the enzyme DNA polymerase (an essential part of the cellular equipment that copies DNA: Figure 2) that is so similar in bacteria, animals, plants and fungi that we can infer that, for billions of years, almost any mutation that ever occurred in this particular DNA sequence was removed from the population by negative selection (Bromham 2000, Patel and Loeb 2000).

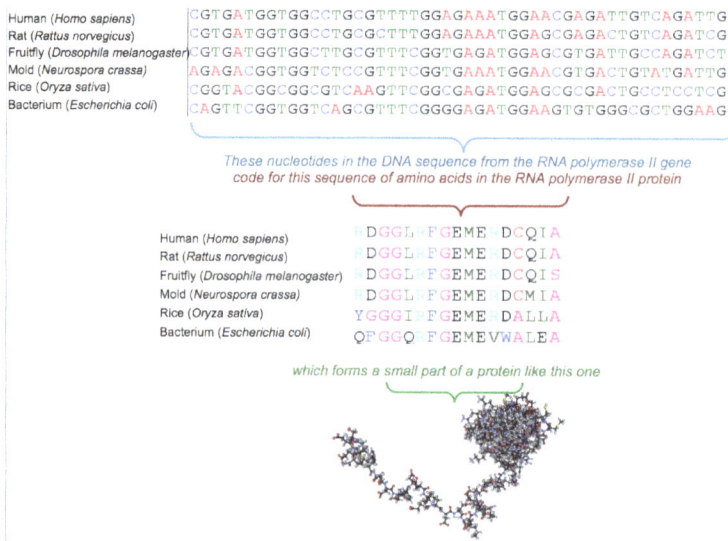

Figure 2 Family resemblance: Selection maintains important DNA sequences against change.

The information needed to build an organism is coded in the genome in the four bases of DNA (represented by the letters A, C, G and T). In this example, the DNA sequence is part of the RNA polymerase II gene that makes an essential part of the cellular machinery. Each three bases are translated into one amino acid. Amino acids are the subunits of proteins represented by 20 different letters (for example, the conserved motif RFGEME can be translated as the amino acid sequence arginine–phenylalanine–glycine–glutamine–methionine–glutamine). Each of these amino acids forms one tiny piece of a peptide chain which will fold into a specific three-dimensional structure and join with other proteins to form a working enzyme.

Source: Figure created by Lindell Bromham.

Very occasionally, a random change in the genome sequence will somehow increase the individual's chance of surviving and reproducing. For example, a chance mutation in a blood protein gene that makes it more efficient at taking up oxygen at low barometric pressure might increase the chances of survival of an individual living at high altitude, who will then be more likely to leave descendants who also carry copies of that mutation (Bigham et al. 2010). By definition, any change that increases the chances of successful reproduction will have a tendency to end up in more members of the next generation, and therefore will tend to increase with each passing generation (as long as it remains at a relative advantage). This is positive selection, the process that people associate with the phrase 'survival of the fittest'.

Beneficial mutations will tend to increase in frequency until they replace all alternative versions in the population, and harmful mutations will tend to decrease in frequency until they disappear from the population. But what about mutations that have little or no effect on the chances of successful reproduction, for example a change in a part of the genome that does not code for anything important, or change to the DNA sequence of a gene that does not alter the function of the gene product? These 'neutral' mutations will not increase their chances of appearing in the next generation, but neither will they harm their carrier's chance of reproduction. So whether or not they are passed on down the generations depends entirely on chance. Many will disappear when their carriers fail to reproduce, but others will, by chance, increase in frequency if their carriers happen to have many descendants. And occasionally, by sheer luck, some of the neutral variants will just happen to increase in frequency until they replace the other variants in the population. So not all evolution at the genetic level is due to natural selection—some of it is the result of the random sampling of alternative DNA sequences that occurs every generation. For example, it has been estimated that there are around 35 million differences in the DNA sequences between the chimpanzee and human genomes, but a substantial proportion of these mutations will have no impact on the ability to build, maintain and operate an ape (Varki and Altheide 2005). The silent differences between the genomes of humans and chimps cannot have been influenced by selection, so they must have evolved by drift (random sampling of functionally equivalent sequences).

So the first two fundamental processes of evolution are mutation—whereby heritable change is generated—and substitution—whereby a mutation rises in frequency over many generations until it replaces all alternative traits in the population. This process may seem very obvious, but it is worth keeping these basic mechanisms in mind in order to appreciate the inevitability of evolutionary change. First, mutations constantly arise irrespective of their usefulness or harm. Mutations are accidents, most of which are bad, some of which do no harm, and very few of which are improvements. Second, if a mutation is to become a fixed part of a species makeup it must go through the process of substitution. Any characteristic shared by an entire sexually reproducing species must have started in a single individual (or several, due to recurrent mutation) then increased in frequency until it replaced all alternatives. Third, the role of chance in the process of substitution is often underestimated. Random mutation and chance substitution, even in the absence of natural selection, can give rise to evolutionary diversity and complexity. To understand why, we should consider a third fundamental process in evolution: divergence.

The inevitability of change

From a genomic point of view, evolutionary change is inevitable; mutations constantly arise, and though many will be removed by natural selection, others will become a fixed part of the genome, through chance or selection. Even species that appear not to change over time are in constant flux at the molecular level. Species referred to as 'living fossils', such as the coelacanth, may remain virtually unchanged to the eye for tens of millions of years, but their genomes have continued to steadily accumulate change (Lampert et al. 2012). The only thing that can halt evolutionary change is negative selection (removal of harmful mutations).

The continuous action of mutation and substitution results in divergence. If populations are divided by any means then any changes that accumulate in one population are not shared with other populations, and so the populations become progressively more different over time as they acquire more and more unique changes. When two populations are so different that individuals from one population will not interbreed with another, we tend to call them separate species. So anything that divides populations and stops them sharing any new mutations will kickstart the process of divergence that may ultimately lead to the formation of new species. However, there has been a lot of debate about which mechanisms are the main drivers of speciation.

Darwin focused on what is now often referred to as ecological speciation, when natural selection drives populations to become adapted to different conditions (Darwin 1859). Under this view of evolutionary divergence, sections of a widespread population gradually accumulate adaptations that better equip them to survive and breed in their own particular circumstances. At first we might recognise these as variants within the same population, then as they became more distinct we might regard them as local races. As more differences accumulate between the populations, they may be referred to as subspecies. Eventually they become so distinct that we could happily recognise two separate species, which may be so divergent that they rarely, if ever, interbreed in nature. According to this Darwinian view of speciation, the distinction between local varieties, subspecies and species may be blurred as populations gradually accumulate more and more differences.

But what prevents the mutations that arise in one section of the population from flowing through to all other parts, eroding the differences between local races? In the mid-twentieth century the focus of speciation research shifted toward the nature of the barriers that divided populations, preventing gene flow and thus allowing the build-up of unique genetic changes in subpopulations (Mallet 2010). Geographic barriers are the most obvious example, as when a mountain range or river prevents individuals from meeting and mating. But barriers to interbreeding might come about through behaviour, for example through changes to mating rituals, or temporal separation, such as different flowering times. Once barriers to interbreeding arise, by whatever means, any mutations that occur in one population cannot move into the other population. Each population therefore accumulates a different set of mutations, which go on to create unique patterns of substitutions, fuelling continual divergence. Selection might then favour the evolution of mate recognition that prevents individuals wasting time mating with members of different populations, reinforcing the lack of gene flow and further enhancing their divergence.

In recent decades, advances in technology have allowed an intense focus on the genetic basis of speciation (Wolf et al. 2010). Some scientists look for specific genes involved in particular speciation events (Nosil and Schluter 2011). For example, a number of 'speciation' genes have been identified, such as *Odysseus* (*OdsH*) in fruit flies and *Prdm9* in mice, that seem to disrupt normal chromosome pairing in hybrids (Bhattacharyya et al. 2013). These genes prevent gene flow by making it impossible for individuals produced by cross-species mating to have their own offspring (Orr et al. 2004). Other scientists take in the broader picture, investigating genome-wide processes that contribute to the divergence between populations. For example, speciation can occur when one lineage undergoes a complete doubling of the genome: the differences in chromosome numbers between populations can create a barrier to the formation of viable hybrids, preventing further interbreeding (Rieseberg and Willis 2007)

But even small genetic changes can contribute to the formation of a new species. For a mutation to become fixed in a population, it must be able to work with the other traits present in the population. This is because any particular mutation can only be passed on to the next generation if the individual that carries it survives and breeds. In a sexually reproducing population, each new individual born has a selection of the different variants for each gene that are currently in that population's gene pool. Any individual with a set of gene variants that do not work well together will have a reduced probability of reproducing, and so those particular variants will have less chance of making it into a successful offspring in the next generation. In each generation, any mutation is tested against different sets of genetic variants sampled from the population. It can rise in frequency if, on average, individuals carrying that mutation do relatively better than others in the population. So for a mutation to become fixed in a population it must generally work well with the other genetic variants that it may find itself sharing an individual body with.

But the mutations present in one population have not been tested for harmonious operation with the variants present in other populations, and this means that the particular genetic variants in one population may be incompatible with those found in its sister population. So when individuals from two populations mate and produce a hybrid, their offspring might inherit substitutions from one population that do not work well with the changes accumulated in the other population, resulting in unfit hybrids with disharmonious genomes. The more genetic differences between the populations, the greater the chance that a combination of genes from the two populations will contain unviable combinations of mutations (Welch 2004).

Finally, it is important to note that, while the focus of the preceding discussion was on the divergence that pushes populations apart, separated populations occasionally come back together again. In some cases, this might be through 'de-speciation', where the ecological differences between species niches collapse (McKinnon and Taylor 2012). In other cases, long-diverged lineages can form viable hybrids that give rise to new species (Abbott et al. 2013). In fact, the analysis of whole genomes of an increasingly wide range of species has revealed that the barriers to gene exchange between lineages are sometimes more permeable than had been supposed. Genes can move between distantly related lineages, a phenomenon referred to as horizontal gene transfer (to distinguish it from the vertical transfer of genes from parent to offspring). For example, bacterial species can exchange genes for drug resistance (Ochman et al. 2000). Parasite genes have made their way into hosts and host genes into parasite genomes (Mower et al. 2004). It has even been suggested that seaweed consumption has promoted the transfer of genes from marine bacteria to the gut bacteria of people in Japan, so now the gut bacteria can manufacture enzymes that can digest the polysaccharides found in nori (which is made from the red alga *Porphyra*: Hehemen et al. 2010). The result is genomes that are a patchwork of genes with different histories: for example, a gene that plays a key role in the formation of the human placenta is derived from a virus (Mi et al. 2000). So while evolution is commonly displayed as a tree, with branches splitting again and again to form a large number of separate twigs, sometimes evolutionary history might be better thought of as a net, with strands both dividing and intertwining.

Generation of biodiversity

The inevitability of evolutionary change—mutations will always arise, some will become a fixed part of the gene pool, so populations will always diverge—means that new species are constantly arising. But species are also continually lost to extinction. Species extinction—the death of all members of a species so that their unique genetic heritage is irreversibly lost—is as normal a part of evolution as the generation of new species.

Extinction is a familiar concept to us. We are constantly reminded of lost forms, from dodos to dinosaurs, and concerned by the prospect of imminent extinction of species under threat, such as polar bears, orange-bellied parrots, or the Lord Howe Island stick insect. But the fact of extinction is a relatively recent discovery. Fossils must have been unearthed throughout human history, but if you do not know that the biological world has a long hidden history, it might not be obvious that fossils are the remains of extinct species (Rudwick 1976). For example, it has been suggested that the remains of ice age beasts in Europe could have been interpreted as the bones of heroes of legend, and that ceratopsid dinosaur bones exposed in the Gobi desert may be the source of tales of gryphons (Mayor 2000). When dinosaur skeletons found in England were identified as the remains of giant reptiles, no longer to be seen alive, it proved beyond doubt that the biological world had changed dramatically over time.

If species are forever gained and lost, does the biosphere steadily accumulate species, or does it maintain a steady state, with new species replacing old species in the economy of nature? You would think that this would be a simple question to answer, simply by counting the number of species over time. But new data and new analyses provide continual fuel to an ongoing debate.

One of the key pieces of evidence has been numerical analyses of taxonomic diversity from the fossil record, plotting the total number of recognised species over time (or, more commonly, higher taxonomic groups of related species such as genera and families). Figure 3 shows a typical example. Two patterns stand out on this graph. First, the number of recorded genera has a clear increase over time, with the highest diversity towards the present day (on the right hand side of the graph). Second, the increase in diversity has not been constant over time; there are occasional catastrophic losses of diversity identified as mass extinction events, which tend to be followed by rapid increases (Jablonski and Chaloner 1994).

Biodiversity during the Phanerozoic

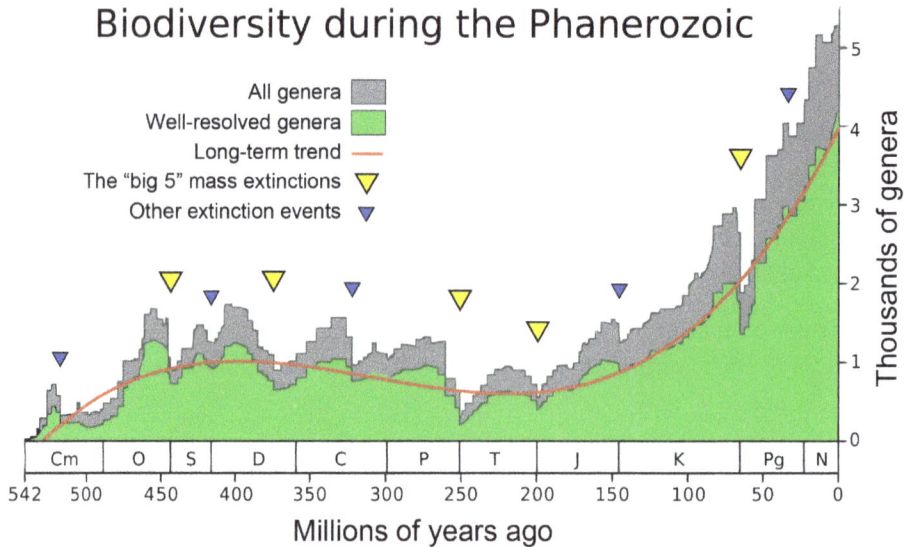

Figure 3 Biodiversity over evolutionary time, estimated from the fossil record of marine animals from the beginning of the Phanerozoic (542 million years ago) to the present day.

While this count of the number of identified genera (groups of related species) per time period seems to show a clear increase toward the present, there are a number of biases that could produce this trend. Although there are a number of extinction events identified on this graph, these are also a matter of debate. A mass extinction is recognised as a period when a higher than usual number of species make their last appearance in the fossil record, but this will be affected not only by biological or geological events, but also by the resolution of the fossil record, and by dips in the amount of sedimentary rock available for palaeontological sampling (Peters and Foote 2001, Smith 2001).

Source: Figure created by Albert Mestre, based on the analysis of Rohde and Muller (2005), available through WikiCommons at commons.wikimedia.org/wiki/File:Phanerozoic_Biodiversity.svg.

But this figure highlights the complicated nature of scientific research and discussion. Rarely can data be taken at face value; all patterns must be interpreted in light of potential biases in data collection and analysis. There are many reasons why the number of species (or other taxonomic groups) recorded for each geological time period might not be an unbiased estimate of how many species actually existed at any point in time. For example, if more scientific effort is directed at a particular period, then we would expect more species to have been described from that period, just as we would expect a higher species count from a well-studied rainforest than one that had rarely been sampled. So not surprisingly, periods that have been more intensively studied may have higher recorded biodiversity (Lloyd et al. 2012, Sheehan 1977). The amount of available fossil-bearing rocks will also influence the number of fossil species that have been discovered (Smith 2001). Instead of resulting from an increase in biodiversity over time, the upswing in species towards the present may reflect the 'Pull of the Recent': we are more likely to have data on recent taxa than those from the distant past. So we cannot take the uncorrected counts of described species over time as evidence for increase in biodiversity, without correcting for ascertainment bias. However, different statistical corrections lead to different conclusions, so at this point in time, we cannot be sure of the answer to the apparently simple question of whether or not biodiversity has increased over time (Peters and Foote 2001).

Figure 3 points to another very important pattern read from the fossil record: the boom and bust pattern of biodiversity over time. Extinction is a constant feature of evolution, but a number of mass extinction events are recognised where the number of taxa that make their last appearance is higher than expected. These dips in the diversity curve have been interpreted as evidence for occasional periods of upheaval when a global catastrophe, such as a massive meteor strike, prolonged period of volcanism, or rapidly changing climate results in above-average species losses.

But, as with so many ideas in evolutionary biology, there is vigorous debate concerning the meaning of the dips and peaks in the diversity curve. Some analyses identify as many as 18 mass extinction events, others find only a few outliers from the background extinction rate, while some consider that all extinction events form a continuum of magnitude from which no particular events stand out (Bambach 2006, Jablonski and Chaloner 1994). Furthermore, some of the dips in the diversity curve may be due to slow rates of origination of new lineages, rather than raised extinction rates (Bambach et al. 2004). It has even been suggested that the diversity curve is, for the most part, indistinguishable from a random walk in extinction and origination rates (Cornette and Lieberman 2004). So a consideration of global diversity patterns over time illustrates the important point that rarely in evolutionary biology can we simply read past patterns and processes straight from the raw data. All hypotheses require testing that takes into account the unavoidable biases inherent in all observations.

Steps or leaps?

There is, and has always been, controversy about the nature of evolutionary change. Just as discussions about the process of speciation have changed over time, these debates over the tempo (pace) and mode (mechanism) of evolutionary change illuminate how evolutionary biology is shaped over time as new evidence is uncovered, and new ideas discussed.

One of the earliest debates was on the nature of the mutations that drive the formation of new species. Darwin argued strongly for gradual divergence, with populations steadily acquiring nearly insensible changes, until the summed differences were great enough to form distinct gaps between species. Darwin used the phrase *'Natura non facit saltum'*—nature does not leap (Darwin and

Wallace 1858). But not all of his contemporaries were convinced that the myriad of tiny variants found naturally in all populations could ever be sufficient to explain the distinct gaps between recognised species. Instead, some considered that the differences they observed between species were of a different kind from the variations typically found in populations. Scientists in the mutationist school felt that the 'unbridgeable gaps' between species, families and orders could only be created by leaps in form, arising from rare macromutations (genetic changes of large effect). Discussion of the mutationist model of evolution in the mid-twentieth century focused on the concept of the 'hopeful monster', a hypothetical individual born with a macromutation that makes it so strikingly different from other members of its species that it gives rise to a new distinct lineage. Under this hypothesis, the differences between species are not simply a sum of the tiny variations that occur every generation: new species arise by leaps and bounds rather than by very many small steps.

The mutationist school of thought was displaced by the rebirth of Darwinian evolutionary theory in the mathematical framework of population genetics. These mathematical models showed how, despite the intuitive implausibility, it was indeed possible for natural selection to drive significant changes between populations simply through the accumulation of tiny changes, each one of small effect, over very many generations. Furthermore, the mathematical models suggested that macromutations were less likely to contribute to the formation of evolutionary novelty, because a single, large change has a high probability of reducing fitness, so is unlikely to survive and breed.

But ideas similar to the mutationist view continue to be debated, for example in the new field of 'evo-devo' (evolutionary development). Many scientists working in this field have discussed the evolutionary potential of mutations in developmental genes which cause dramatic changes in body plan, for example changing the number or type of wings and other appendages (Marshall et al. 1999). It has been suggested that notable differences between distinct kinds of animals might be attained through relatively few mutations of large effect, rather than by the gradual accumulation of tiny differences (Gellon and McGinnis 1998). But while these mutations have been instrumental in understanding development (the process whereby the information in the genome is used to build and operate an individual's body), their role in evolution of the major different kinds of animals is less clear (Bromham 2011, Hoekstra and Coyne 2007). The question is not whether such developmental macromutations can arise in populations, but whether they can give rise to new kinds of species when they do. For a hopeful monster to survive, the new trait must be sufficiently well integrated not simply to permit survival, but to give an advantage over other forms in the population that would allow it to compete and thrive (Maynard Smith 1958). For example, an extra set of wings is not much good if your neural circuitry is not wired up to allow you to fly with them.

Tempo and mode

The tension between gradualism (moving forward by many tiny steps) and saltationism (leaping forward by few large jumps) pervades many aspects of evolutionary biology. As with most aspects of biology, there are examples of both and it is often impossible to draw a clean line between the two extremes. For example, a new plant variety may arise in a single generation by hybridisation, or it may arise over many generations by a series of successive tweaks to existing traits (Soltis and Soltis 2009). A bacterial strain may acquire antibiotic resistance by gradual steps, through natural selection on mutations to its existing genes (Normark and Normark 2002), or it may become resistant in a single leap when it acquires a gene from another strain (Ochman et al. 2000). There has been an ongoing debate about the relative contributions of cumulative tiny steps and large single leaps to the generation of biodiversity.

This debate for and against Darwinian gradualism crystallised around discussion of the punctuated equilibrium hypothesis (Maynard Smith 1981). This hypothesis has been interpreted in many ways, but the essence is that most of the major changes that generate biological diversity occur not through the continuous collection of small variants but in rapid bursts of change associated with speciation events. Evidence for 'punc eq' (pronounced 'punk-eek') came largely from the fossil record, where some species were reported to persist for millions of years with little change, then to be rapidly replaced by a new, related species (Stanley 1979). This pattern was interpreted as a signal that speciation primarily occurred when a small subpopulation became isolated from a larger established population, and it was often implied that the genetic change underlying the rapid change was not driven by the gradual action of natural selection (Gould 1980).

But, as with everything in evolutionary biology, there is always more than one way to interpret observations. Punctuated equilibrium was promoted as a refutation of Darwinian orthodoxy (Gould 1980, 1997), but no one, including Darwin, ever expected that the pace of morphological evolutionary change would be uniform over time. The gradual model refers to the expectation that most evolutionary change is built from the accumulation of small changes over generations, which does not rule out acceleration in the rate of change when the environment changes rapidly. Bursts of change can also correspond to the influx of new genetic variants by mutation or migration (Elena et al. 1996). Negative selection can hold traits in stasis by removing variants that arise by mutation (Coyne and Charlesworth 1997).

In the often vituperative debate between the two schools of thought, punc eq was labelled 'evolution by jerks', and Darwinian gradualism was called 'evolution by creeps'. One of the underlying causes of the animosity was a cultural difference: punctuated equilibrium was proposed, and largely championed, by palaeontologists who study large-scale changes in biodiversity over time as recorded in the fossil record (Sepkoski 2012). Many of the critics were 'neontologists' (biologists who work on living species), particularly those who focused on the population genetic basis of evolution. Perhaps as a consequence of these differing viewpoints, it has been sometimes unclear whether the debate is about pattern or process. Gradual cumulative change in a population over hundreds of thousands of generations may appear instantaneous in the fossil record (Maynard Smith 1983), and observable population genetic change can occur in bursts (Coyne and Charlesworth 1996). So it is difficult to assess whether rapidity of change in the fossil record rejects the Darwinian model of evolution, unless we have a clear idea of how fast is too rapid to fit the gradualist model of many tiny steps.

Molecular clocks

The punctuated equilibrium debate has now moved to the realm of the genome. When the genetic revolution made it possible to compare biomolecular sequences from different species, a surprising pattern began to emerge. When the amount of divergence between sequences was plotted against evolutionary time, a strikingly linear relationship emerged: the longer two species had been evolving separately, the more differences you would observe between their genomes (Bromham and Penny 2003). This was surprising, as it had been expected that molecular evolution would track adaptation, changing at different rates in different lineages or evolutionary periods.

A whole new body of theoretical work arose to explain the observation of an apparently steady accumulation of genetic changes over time. If most changes at the molecular level had no significant effect on an organism's chances of survival and reproduction, then those mutations would not be removed by negative selection nor promoted by positive selection, so would simply accumulate at a rate determined by the mutation rate. Whatever the cause, the apparently clock-like evolution of molecules over time promised a new way of estimating the time scale for evolution: simply comparing gene sequences from different species could tell you how long it was since they had last shared a common ancestor. One of the first molecular clock estimates prompted a radical revision of our own place in the evolutionary tree, showing that humans and chimpanzees shared a common ancestor only a few million years ago, in contrast to the commonly held belief that they were separated by tens of millions of years of evolution (Sarich and Wilson 1967).

The molecular clock hypothesis has matured since then and, like so many things in evolutionary biology, turns out to be a lot more complicated than might have been hoped. Not surprisingly, the rate of molecular evolution varies dramatically across the genome: important sequences change slowly because most mutations are removed by negative selection, large parts of the genome change more readily because mutations in them do not seem to affect survival and reproduction, and some parts of the genome are under positive selection that promotes a faster rate of change. More intriguingly, the rate of molecular evolution also varies between lineages: for example, a typical gene in a mouse evolves roughly three times faster than the equivalent gene in a human. Some progress has been made in untangling the causes of variation in the rate at which genomes evolve (Bromham 2009). Since most mutations in the genome arise from copy errors, genomes that are copied more often accumulate changes more rapidly, so it is not surprising that mice, which can have 50 generations in the time it takes for a human baby to grow up and reproduce, would accumulate more genetic changes. The copy error effect might also explain why rate of molecular evolution is related to plant height (because shorter plants undergo more cell divisions per year: Lanfear et al. 2013), why social insects have faster rates of molecular evolution (because queens can lay thousands of eggs: Bromham and Leys 2005), and why most new mutations in the human genome originate in fathers (because it takes more cell generations to make sperm than eggs: Li et al. 2002).

But there are other differences in molecular rate between lineages that are harder to explain. One is the emerging evidence that biodiverse lineages—those that have produced more living species than their relatives—have higher rates of molecular evolution (Barraclough and Savolainen 2001, Lanfear et al. 2010). This observation has given rise to the claim that the genome evolves in a punctuated manner, with most substitutions occurring in bursts associated with speciation events (Pagel et al. 2006). However, an alternative model is more akin to the Darwinian gradualist view. We have already seen that the accumulation of mutations in separated populations results in the accretion of hybrid incompatibilities: sequence variants that work well in the context of one population, but when mixed across population boundaries produce disharmonious hybrids. Rates of mutation are influenced by all manner of species traits, such as body size, generation time, fecundity, longevity and mating system (Bromham 2009). If mutations drive substitutions, and if substitutions drive hybrid incompatibility, then might we not expect lineages with greater mutation rates to more rapidly form new species? Evidence points to a relationship between mutation rates and rates of diversification in at least some cases (Duchene and Bromham 2013, Lanfear et al. 2010).

The link between species diversity and molecular evolution is now well established, but distinguishing the direction of causation is not simple. At this stage, we cannot say for sure whether the process of diversification speeds the rate of genome divergence, or whether the rate of accumulation of changes in the genome is a driver of the evolution of biodiversity. So in the post-genomic era, the debates that have been threaded through the whole history of evolutionary biology—many slight variations versus few key macromutations, gradualism vs punctuation—have been carried through to a consideration of the patterns of changes in DNA sequences.

Keeping up with a changing world

No species exists in isolation; all must persist in the face of constant change if they are to avoid extinction. The environment of a species is partly determined by the abiotic conditions (such as the minimum temperature, average rainfall, or available nutrients), and partly by other species, either directly (e.g. predation, herbivory, parasitism, competition) or indirectly (e.g. decomposition, nutrient cycling, reef-building). Species both create and respond to changing environments, creating a tangled web of interactions in space and time.

Changes in global climate may explain some of the broadscale patterns in biodiversity over time (Ezard et al. 2011, Mayhew et al. 2012). Climate change, in space or time, can drive the formation of new species by favouring individuals better able to survive and thrive under the new conditions, resulting in directional trends in species traits such as temperature tolerance (Hua and Wiens 2013). As the climate changes, species must either move to track favourable conditions, adapt to a new set of conditions, or go extinct. The average species duration is measured in millions of years, so most persist through at least some degree of climate change (Dawson et al. 2011, Moritz and Agudo 2013). For example, any species alive today is descended from a lineage that survived the dramatic cycles of cooling and warming that characterised the Pleistocene era (spanning the period from approximately 2.5 million years ago to 11,000 years ago). Given that life on earth depends on the ability of species to change in response to a changing climate, why are biologists so concerned about species extinction under ongoing climate change?

Climate change in the Anthropocene may have a more severe extinction cost than past climate oscillations for several reasons. First, the pace of climate change is so rapid that many species may be left behind. The speed of climate change is reflected in changes in species reproduction and distribution which are observable over short time periods in a wide range of ecosystems—examples include earlier grape harvests, range shifts in butterflies, loss of populations of high altitude mammals, extinction of frog species in cloud forests of Central America, decrease in sea-ice dependent algae and krill, and increase in prevalence of pathogens in coral reefs (Hoegh-Guldberg and Bruno 2010, Parmesan 2006, Webb et al. 2011). Second, while some species may be able to shift their geographic range to track the changing climate, species with fragmented or isolated habitats may not be able to move between isolated remnants of suitable habitat. Montane species are a particular cause for concern. Warming temperatures correspond to an upward trend in the distribution of some species, with low altitude species shifting higher up mountains, tracking suitable conditions. But species already on mountain summits cannot go higher, and moving across lowlands to ever higher mountaintops or higher latitudes may be impossible. Third, species already under stress may be limited in their ability to respond to a changing environment. Reduced population size due to habitat modification or other stresses will reduce the ability of a population to respond through adaptation, because selection for new traits that allow persistence under changed conditions will be less effective in small populations (Orr and Unckless 2008). For example, it has been estimated that increase in global temperature after the last ice age led to a 90 per cent reduction in the suitable habitat for woolly mammoths, reducing the population to such a low level that they were particularly vulnerable to human impact (Nogués-Bravo et al. 2008). Many scientists are using ecological and evolutionary modelling to try to predict which species will be able to adapt to a rapidly changing climate and which will not (Moritz and Agudo 2013). Evolutionary biologists are beginning to explore the constraints on 'evolutionary rescue', where genetic change allows a lineage to persist in conditions that would have been lethal to its recent ancestors (Bell 2013). Rapid environmental change may leave insufficient time for potentiating mutations to build increased tolerance in the population (Lindsey et al. 2013).

But within the tolerable range of conditions, success or failure may be determined largely by interactions with other species, whether direct or indirect, so modelling the climatic niche may not be sufficient to predict species response to climate change (Dawson et al. 2011). For example, the movement of species across the landscape may place even greater pressure on locally endemic species, by bringing novel combinations of species into competition with each other (Hoegh-Guldberg and Bruno 2010, Sinervo et al. 2010). Where adaptation to a changing climate might promote directional selection pressure, adaptation to other species involves chasing a moving target. This view of evolutionary change in response to the changes in other species is often referred to as the Red Queen model, after the Lewis Carroll character who says that 'it takes all the running you can do, to keep in the same place' (Carroll 1871). The most obvious expression of the constant evolutionary chase is in the arms races between predators and prey, plants and herbivores, pathogens and hosts.

I began this chapter by pointing out that much of the environment we experience is constructed by living species. Humans are perhaps one of the most obvious examples of the life-built environment, with the activities of our own species leaving few other species wholly unaffected. Evolution has not stopped in these highly modified environments, but continues to drive change in response to this rapidly changing world. For example, bird populations living around highways have been shown to evolve longer wing-lengths, because the shorter-winged individuals are more likely to end up as roadkill and therefore have fewer descendants in subsequent generations (Brown and Bomberger Brown 2013). In many instances, the evolutionary response of other species to the changing environment may be not in people's best interests, such as in the rapid evolution of antibiotic resistance in harmful bacteria. Any significant interaction with other species sets up a strong selection pressure, whether it is the impact of commercial fishing selecting for reduced body size at maturity in fish, the evolution of myxomatosis resistance in rabbits, or the alteration of bird song in noisy urban environments. But understanding evolutionary principles allows these processes to be managed and monitored. For example, strategies employed to prevent crop pests from evolving resistance to the insecticides produced by genetically modified crops have thus far been largely successful (Tabashnik et al. 2013). While evolutionary change is inevitable, understanding evolutionary principles helps us to mitigate biodiversity loss and manage our own interaction with the changing biological world.

Conclusion

The biological world is in a constant state of flux. The processes of mutation, substitution and divergence occur continuously, though they may vary in rate or pattern over time, space, between different lineages or in different parts of the genome. Studies of the patterns of change in biodiversity over time have supported very different views of the mechanisms of evolutionary change, with some biologists favouring a model of continuous change through the accumulation of many small variations, and others promoting a model of discontinuous evolution, where evolutionary change is concentrated into bursts of significant change followed by long periods of stasis. These issues have been debated since Darwin's day, and are reinvented in each age and adapted to new data sources. The explosion of availability of DNA sequences has provided a new platform on which these old arguments are being played out.

Recognising the causes and consequences of evolutionary change is an essential part of appreciating the world around us. But it also complicates our understanding of our interaction with the natural world. How can we preserve biodiversity in an ever changing world? Which species will track the rapid environmental change the world is experiencing, and which will fail to do so? Viewing ourselves as part of a dynamic, ever changing biosphere is critical to human prosperity. Nothing stands still in the biological world.

Acknowledgements

I am grateful to Camile Moray, David Duchene, Brett Calcott and Xia Hua for their valuable feedback.

References

Abbott, R, Albach, D, Ansell, S, Arntzen, JW, Baird, SJ, Bierne, N, Boughman, J, Brelsford, A, Buerkle, CA, Buggs, R, Butlin, RK, Dieckmann, U, Eroukhmanoff, F, Grill, A, Cahan, SH, Hermansen, JS, Hewitt, G, Hudson, AG, Jiggins, C, Jones, J, Keller, B, Marczewski, T, Mallet, J, Martinez-Rodriguez, P, Möst, M, Mullen, S, Nichols, R, Nolte, AW, Parisod, C, Pfennig, K, Rice, AM, Ritchie, MG, Seifert, B, Smadja, CM, Stelkens, R, Szymura, JM, Väinölä, R, Wolf, JB and Zinner, D (2013) Hybridization and speciation. *Journal of Evolutionary Biology* 26(2): 229–46.

Bambach, RK (2006) Phanerozoic biodiversity mass extinctions. *Annual Review of Earth and Planetary Sciences* 34: 127–55.

Bambach, RK, Knoll, AH and Wang, SC (2004) Origination, extinction, and mass depletions of marine diversity. *Paleobiology* 30(4): 522–42.

Barraclough, TG and Savolainen, V (2001) Evolutionary rates and species diversity in flowering plants. *Evolution* 55: 677–83.

Bell, G (2013) Evolutionary rescue and the limits of adaptation. *Philosophical Transactions of the Royal Society B: Biological Sciences* 368:20120080.

Bhattacharyya, T, Gregorova, S, Mihola, O, Anger, M, Sebestova, J, Denny, P, Simecek, P, and Forejt, J (2013) Mechanistic basis of infertility of mouse intersubspecific hybrids. *Proceedings of the National Academy of Sciences USA* 110(6): E468–77.

Bigham, A, Bauchet, M, Pinto, D, Mao, X, Akey, JM, Mei, R, Scherer, SW, Julian, CG, Wilson, MJ, López Herráez, D, Brutsaert, T, Parra, EJ, Moore, LG and Shriver, MD (2010) Identifying signatures of natural selection in Tibetan and Andean populations using dense genome scan data. *PLoS Genetics* 6(9): e1001116.

Bromham, L (2000) Conservation and mutability in molecular evolution. *Trends in Ecology and Evolution* 15: 355.

Bromham, L (2009) Why do species vary in their rate of molecular evolution? *Biology Letters* 5: 401–04.

Bromham, L (2011) The small picture approach to the Big Picture: using DNA sequences to investigate the diversification of animal body plans. In K Sterelny and B Calcott (eds) *The major transitions in evolution revisited*. MIT Press, Cambridge [UK].

Bromham, L and Leys, R (2005) Sociality and rate of molecular evolution. *Molecular Biology and Evolution* 22(6): 1393–1402.

Bromham, L and Penny, D (2003) The modern molecular clock. *Nature Reviews Genetics* 4: 216–24.

Brown, CR and Bomberger Brown, M (2013) Where has all the road kill gone? *Current Biology* 23(6): R233–34.

Carroll, L (1871) *Through the looking glass: and what Alice found there*. Macmillan, London.

Cornette, JL and Lieberman, BS (2004) Random walks in the history of life. *Proceedings of the National Academy of Sciences USA* 101(1): 187–91.

Coyne, JA and Charlesworth, B (1996) Mechanisms of punctuated evolution. *Science* 274: 1748.

Coyne, JA and Charlesworth, B (1997) On punctuated equilibria: a reply to Eldredge and Gould. *Science* 276(5311): 337–41.

Darwin, C (1859) *On the origin of species by means of natural selection: or the preservation of favoured races in the struggle for life*. John Murray, London.

Darwin, CR and Wallace, AR (1858) On the tendency of species to form varieties; and on the perpetuation of varieties and species by natural means of selection. *Journal of the Proceedings of the Linnean Society of London. Zoology* 3: 45–50.

Dawson, TP, Jackson, ST, House, JI, Prentice, IC and Mace, GM (2011) Beyond predictions: biodiversity conservation in a changing climate. *Science* 332(6025): 53–8.

Duchene, D and Bromham, L (2013) Rates of molecular evolution and diversification in plants: chloroplast substitution rates correlate with species richness in the Proteaceae. *BMC Evolutionary Biology* 13: 65.

Elena, SF, Cooper, VS and Lenski, RE (1996) Mechanisms of punctuated evolution. *Science* 274: 1748–9.

Ezard, THG, Aze, T, Pearson, PN and Purvis, A (2011) Interplay between changing climate and species' ecology drives macroevolutionary dynamics. *Science* 332(6027): 349–51.

Gellon, G and McGinnis, W (1998) Shaping animal body plans in development and evolution by modulation of Hox expression patterns. *BioEssays* 20: 116.

Gould, SJ (1980) Is a new and general theory of evolution emerging? *Paleobiology* 6(1): 119–30.

Gould, SJ (1997) Darwinian fundamentalism. *New York Review of Books* 44: 34–7.

Hehemann J-H, Correc, GL, Barbeyron, T, Helbert, W, Czjzek, M and Michel, G (2010) Transfer of carbohydrate-active enzymes from marine bacteria to Japanese gut microbiota. *Nature* 464(7290): 908–12.

Hoegh-Guldberg, O and Bruno, JF (2010) The impact of climate change on the world's marine ecosystems. *Science* 328(5985): 1523–8.

Hoekstra, HE and Coyne, JA (2007) The locus of evolution: evo devo and the genetics of adaptation. *Evolution* 61(5): 995–1016.

Hua, X and Wiens, JJ (2013) How does climate influence speciation? *American Naturalist* 182(1):1–12.

Jablonski, D and Chaloner, WG (1994) Extinctions in the fossil record [and Discussion]. *Philosophical Transactions of the Royal Society of London. Series B: Biological Sciences* 344(1307): 11–17.

Lampert, KP, Fricke, H, , Hissmann, K, Schauer, J, Blassmann, K, Ngatunga, BP and Schartl, M (2012) Population divergence in East African coelacanths. *Current Biology* 22(11): R439–40.

Lanfear, R, Ho, SYW, Love, D and Bromham, L (2010) Mutation rate influences diversification rate in birds. *Proceedings of the National Academy of Sciences USA* 107(47): 20423–8.

Lanfear, R, Ho, SYW, Davies, TJ, Moles, AT, Aarssen, L, Swenson, NG, Warman, L, Zanne, AE and Allen, AP (2013) Taller plants have lower rates of molecular evolution: the rate of mitosis hypothesis. *Nature Communications* 4: 1879.

Li, WH, Yi, S and Makova, KD (2002) Male-driven evolution. *Current Opinion in Genetics & Development* 12: 650–6.

Lindsey, HA, Gallie, J, Taylor, S and Kerr, B (2013) Evolutionary rescue from extinction is contingent on a lower rate of environmental change. *Nature* 494: 463–6.

Lloyd, GT, Pearson, PN, Young, JR and Smith, AB (2012) Sampling bias and the fossil record of planktonic foraminifera on land and in the deep sea. *Paleobiology* 38(4): 569–84.

Mallet, J (2010) Why was Darwin's view of species rejected by twentieth century biologists? *Biology and Philosophy* 25(4): 497–527.

Marshall, CR, Orr, HA and Patel, NH (1999) Morphological innovation and developmental genetics. *Proceedings of the National Academy of Sciences* 96: 9995–6.

Mayhew, PJ, Bell, MA, Benton, TG and McGowan, AJ (2012) Biodiversity tracks temperature over time. *Proceedings of the National Academy of Sciences USA* 109(38): 15141–5.

Maynard Smith, J (1958) *The theory of evolution*. Penguin Books, London.

Maynard Smith, J (1981) Did Darwin get it right? *London Review of Books* 3(11): 10–11.

Maynard Smith, J (1983) The genetics of stasis and punctuation. *Annual Review of Genetics* 17(1):11–25.

Mayor, A (2000) *The first fossil hunters: paleontology in Greek and Roman times*. Princeton University Press, Princeton NJ.

McKinnon, JS and Taylor, EB (2012) Biodiversity: species choked and blended. *Nature* 482(7385): 313–14.

Mi, S, Lee, X, Li, X, Veldman, GM, Finnerty, H, Racie, L, LaVallie, E, Tang, XY, Edouard, P, Howes, S, Keith, JC Jr and McCoy, JM (2000) Syncytin is a captive retroviral envelope protein involved in human placental morphogenesis. *Nature* 403: 785–9.

Moritz, C and Agudo, R (2013) The future of species under climate change: resilience or decline? *Science* 341(6145): 504–08.

Mower, JP, Stefanović, S, Young, GJ and Palmer, JD (2004) Plant genetics: gene transfer from parasitic to host plants. *Nature* 432(7014): 165–66.

Nachman, MW and Crowell, SL (2000) Estimate of the mutation rate per nucleotide in humans. *Genetic*s 156(1): 297–304.

Nogués-Bravo, D, Rodriguez, J, Hortal, J, Batra, P and Araújo, MB (2008) Climate change, humans, and the extinction of the woolly mammoth. *PLoS Biology* 6(4): e79.

Normark, BH and Normark, S (2002) Evolution and spread of antibiotic resistance. *Journal of Internal Medicine* 252(2): 91–106.

Nosil, P and Schluter, D (2011) The genes underlying the process of speciation. *Trends in Ecology and Evolution* 26(4): 160–7.

Ochman, H, Lawrence, JG and Groisman, EA (2000) Lateral gene transfer and the nature of bacterial innovation. *Nature* 405(6784): 299–304.

Orr, HA and Unckless RL (2008) Population extinction and the genetics of adaptation. *American Naturalis*t 172(2): 160–9.

Orr, HA, Masly, JP and Presgraves, DC (2004) Speciation genes. *Current Opinion in Genetics & Development* 14(6): 675–9.

Pagel, M, Venditti, C and Meade, A (2006) Large punctuational contribution of speciation to evolutionary divergence at the molecular level. *Science* 314(5796): 119–21.

Parmesan, C (2006) Ecological and evolutionary responses to recent climate change. *Annual Review of Ecology, Evolution, and Systematics* 37: 637–69.

Patel, PH and Loeb, LA (2000) DNA polymerase active site is highly mutable: evolutionary consequences. *Proceedings of the National Academy of Sciences* 97: 5095–5100.

Peters, SE and Foote, M (2001) Biodiversity in the Phanerozoic: a reinterpretation. *Paleobiology* 27(4): 583–601.

Rieseberg, LH and Willis, JH (2007) Plant speciation. *Science* 317(5840): 910–14.

Rohde, RA and Muller, RA (2005) Cycles in fossil diversity. *Nature* 434(7030): 208–10.

Rudwick, MJ (1976) *The meaning of fossils: episodes in the history of palaeontology.* University of Chicago Press.

Sarich, VM and Wilson, AC (1967) Immunological time scale for hominid evolution. *Science* 158(805): 1200.

Sepkoski, D (2012) *Rereading the fossil record: the growth of paleobiology as an evolutionary discipline.* University of Chicago Press.

Sheehan, PM (1977) Species diversity in the Phanerozoic: a reflection of labor by systematicists? *Paleobiology* 3: 325–9.

Sinervo, B, Mendez-de-la-Cruz, F, Miles DB, Heulin, B, Bastiaans, E, Villagrán-Santa Cruz, M, Lara-Resendiz, R, Martínez-Méndez, N, Calderón-Espinosa, ML, Meza-Lázaro, RN, Gadsden, H, Avila, LJ, Morando, M, De la Riva, IJ, Sepulveda, PV, Rocha, CFD, Ibargüengoytía, N, Puntriano, CA, Massot, M, Lepetz, V, Oksanen, TA, Chapple, DG, Bauer, AM, Branch, WR, Clobert, J and Sites, JW Jnr (2010) Erosion of lizard diversity by climate change and altered thermal niches. *Science* 328(5980): 894–9.

Smith, AB (2001) Large-scale heterogeneity of the fossil record: implications for Phanerozoic biodiversity studies. *Philosophical Transactions of the Royal Society B* 356: 351–67.

Soltis, PS and Soltis, DE (2009) The role of hybridization in plant speciation. *Annual Review of Plant Biology* 60(1): 561–88.

Stanley, SM (1979) *Macroevolution: pattern and process.* WH Freeman and Company, San Francisco.

Tabashnik, BE, Brévault, T and Carrière, Y (2013) Insect resistance to Bt crops: lessons from the first billion acres. *Nature Biotechnology* 31(6): 510–21.

Varki, A and Altheide, TK (2005) Comparing the human and chimpanzee genomes: searching for needles in a haystack. *Genome Research* 15(12): 1746–58.

Webb, LB, Whetton, PH and Barlow, EWR (2011) Observed trends in winegrape maturity in Australia. *Global Change Biology* 17(8): 2707–19.

Welch, JJ (2004) Accumulating Dobzhansky-Muller incompatibilities: reconciling theory and data. *Evolution* 58(6): 1145–56.

Wolf, JBW, Lindell, J and Backstrom, N (2010) Speciation genetics: current status and evolving approaches. *Philosophical Transactions of the Royal Society B* 365(1547):1717–33.

10. Demographic Change:
How, why and consequences

Peter McDonald

Change is inherent to demography because demography is the study of how and why populations change. Without change, demography does not exist as a discipline.

In its simplest definition, demography is the scientific study of human populations. According to Landry (1945), the term demography was first used by the Belgian statistician Achille Guillard, in his 1855 publication *Éléments de statistique humaine, ou démographie comparée*. However, John Graunt's *Natural and political observations mentioned in a following index, and made upon the bills of mortality*, published in 1662 in London, is generally acknowledged to be the first published study in the field of demography. The book demonstrated the usefulness of compilations of information relating to the population of London by presenting statistics on a wide range of characteristics such as employment, age and sex composition, health and environment. Graunt also published an early version of the life table which, having been further developed by Edmund Halley and Joshua Milne, led to the publication in 1840 of the first official life table by William Farr, compiler of scientific abstracts in the General Register Office of England and Wales. The statistical concepts of the life table remain today the fundamental elements of demographic method. The life table, perhaps better termed a death table, is a description of how the number in a population, all born on the same day, falls with age until all have died.

This chapter begins with a more detailed description of demography in terms of life transitions before moving on to a discussion of the measurement of these transitions. Next, it addresses the theory of how and why transitions occur and the association of demography with the theoretical approaches of other disciplines. Transitions are the determinants of demographic change but, as elaborated in this chapter, demography is also concerned with the consequences of change. The distinction between determinants and consequences is the basis of the subsequent discussion of policy in demography as mitigation (influencing the determinants) or adaptation (dealing with the consequences). The chapter ends with how demographers deal with future change.

Demographic transitions

The life table describes the ages at which an event, death, occurs in a population. It provides the risk of death at any age in the population. More generally, demographic methods are concerned with describing whether and when events occur to human populations. The main events studied are childbearing, death, disease, disability, migration, entry to and exit from relationships, education and employment, and housing types or tenures. However, demographic methods can be and are applied to a much wider range of events that are experienced by human populations, theoretically to any changes in the lives of the members of a population. The study of the occurrence of several different events during a person's lifetime is referred to as life course analysis (Uhlenberg 1996).

In more conceptual terms, demography examines transitions from one state of being to a different state of being where these transitions are set in space and time. Demography is concerned with how, when, why, where and to whom these transitions occur. Measurement in demography applies concepts and methods from statistics and mathematics. Most significantly, demography measures the probabilities that a group of people in one state will remain in that state or move to another state in a fixed period of time.

The ultimate states of being are life and death and the life table describes rates of transition from life to death at any given age. Births come into being through transitions in women's (and potentially men's) childbearing histories as they move at different ages from having had no births to having one birth, or from one to two, and so on. The main focus in the demography of fertility is upon women because the range of their fertile years is narrower than is the case for men. Rates of transition from one birth to the next are called parity progression rates. There is a further dynamic involved here because as women move from one age to the next age, their chances of transitioning from one parity to the next also change, thus affecting the number of births. Parity progression is also affected considerably by the time since the previous birth (McDonald and Kippen 2011). This is an example of how decisions related to the timing of a transition affect the chance that the transition will occur and, in macro-terms, how decisions on the timing of births affect the total number of births in a given time period. This latter macro-consequence is referred to by demographers as a 'tempo effect'. Today, in countries with low birthrates, changes in the timing of births, tempo effects, are the main reason that fertility rates change from one year to the next (Bongaarts and Feeney 1998).

In addition to the fundamental demographic events of birth and death, the concepts and methods of demography provide a statistically robust way of examining numerous population transitions such as:

- between relationship statuses
  - singlehood to marriage
  - singlehood to living together
  - living together to marriage
  - marriage to separation
  - separation to divorce
  - divorce to remarriage
- between different living arrangements
  - at home with parents to a group household
  - a group household to a couple relationship
  - children at home to the 'empty nest'
  - a couple relationship to living alone
  - living alone to an aged care facility
- between different labour force statuses
  - out of the labour force to employment
  - employment to unemployment and vice versa
  - employment to retirement
- between different health statuses
  - no chronic illness to chronic illness
  - one stage of a chronic illness to another stage
  - an acute condition to recovery
  - fully able to disabled
  - one stage of disability to another stage
- between different health behaviours
  - a smoker to a non-smoker
  - a healthy weight to obesity
  - active to sedentary
- between education states
  - secondary school to vocational training
  - secondary school to university
  - university to graduation
  - graduation to employment
- between housing situations
  - renting to purchasing
  - purchasing to full ownership
  - from an apartment to a separate house

- between places of residence
  - living in a small country town to living in a metropolis
  - living in one country to living in a different country
- between different states of income and social security
  - living on a wage to living on a social security payment
  - moving from one social security payment to another.

Demographic method

The ways of measuring these transitions can be quite complex when, in a given period of time, people can make a number of different transitions. For example, in a given year, a person may be (in statistical language) 'subject to the interrelated risks' of partnering, moving residence, and changing housing type. In the same period, they are subject to the risk of death or leaving the country in which they are living. Demography handles these multiple possibilities through increment–decrement life tables that measure how people move in and out of multiple states during a year (Preston et al. 2001). However, full application of the increment–decrement approach to transitions is highly data intensive and this is why demographers are very concerned with the collection of detailed, quantitative information on populations. High-quality data across time also allows the calculation of relative degrees of uncertainty related to transitions between states of being (Clark 2003).

Theory in demography

Theory in demography relates to explanation of why and when events occur to people; for example, explanation of:

- long life
- teenage pregnancy
- early school drop-out
- housing tenure
- contracting a disease such as HIV/AIDS and how long people live after contracting a particular disease
- why people move from rural to urban areas or change their country of residence
- why people end their relationships.

Like other disciplines, demography draws upon knowledge in other disciplines to develop its theory. The main disciplines that contribute to demographic theory are economics, sociology, anthropology, epidemiology, geography, public health, biology, ecology and environmental science. Theory in demography is established very largely through statistically oriented comparative analysis: comparisons across space and time and across different subgroups of the population. In this regard, demography is inherently comparative. The methods used are primarily quantitative but the complexity of human behaviour often means that qualitative research methods are required.

As most life course transitions involve a decision on the part of the person making the transition, theory in demography relates to sociology, anthropology, psychology and economics. In relation to sociology and anthropology, the decisions of individuals are taken within an institutional context, and that context may favour or constrain the decision being considered. For example, very low rates of fertility in a country have been attributed to institutional constraints upon decision-making about births stemming from how women are supported in that society (McDonald 2000). Also in relation to decision-making about births, the theory of planned behaviour has been applied from psychology (Klobas 2011) and utility theory from economics (Becker 1981). Todaro (1969) provides an economic behavioural model to explain the decision to move from a rural area to a city. The same model has been used extensively to explain other population movements. Thus, theory in demography is also inherently about change: why is it that people decide to move from one state of being to another?

Consequences of demographic change

Demography is concerned also with the outcomes for populations of the occurrence of 'demographic' events, that is, with the impacts that demographic changes have upon society and the economy. Most basically, it is concerned with a population's size, age structure and geographic distribution, which are the outcomes of the events of birth, death and migration. The important demographic measure, the rate of population growth, a measure of change, is an outcome of the rates of birth, death and migration. To understand past and present rates of population growth and to predict future rates, it is necessary to have an understanding of past and present rates of birth, death and migration. More broadly, demographic events affect the composition of the population according to a wide range of characteristics: age, location, marital or relationship status, parenthood status, education, employment, occupation, industry employed in, illness, disability, housing, ethnicity, religion, and so on. Population characteristics in turn influence a wide variety of other behaviours such as consumption, voting, and leisure.

In recent times, a great deal of attention has been focused on the demographic phenomenon of population ageing and its implications. Ageing is fundamentally the consequence of changes in age structure brought about by a long history of fertility decline, a history as long as 100 years. For example, ageing in Australia in the next 30 years is the consequence of changes in birthrates from the 1930s onwards. In this example, demography is concerned with very long-term change. Ageing, unlike most other demographic changes, is highly predictable because of its long-term nature; ageing is already built into the existing age structure of the population and eventuates simply by people alive today getting older with no decision-making being involved.

Policy: Mitigation and adaptation

Policy in demography is concerned with the implementation of measures that might influence the course of demographic decision-making and hence influence the course of demographic change (mitigation). As examples of mitigation policy, the birthrate may be influenced negatively through the provision of methods of contraception or positively through benefits provided to those having children. International movements of population are enhanced or constrained by national immigration policies. Public health policy has the aim of reducing rates of mortality and morbidity. Extension of education will be influenced by compulsory schooling or by means of assisting young people to stay in education. Population growth in a particular locality will be influenced by the availability of jobs or housing.

Mitigation policies are potentially controversial. In the age of eugenics, policy called for fertility rates to be lowered among people with so-called 'inferior' characteristics. Government family planning programs have been coercive and family size limitation has been associated with sex-selective childbearing. Today, many countries are attempting to increase their birthrates through policies that redistribute public resources to those who have children. Governments prevent or restrict non-citizens from entering their country, often using draconian measures. Or they run sophisticated immigration programs designed to attract highly skilled people from other countries. Some governments restrict the movement of people within the country or sometimes they sponsor such movement. Laws related to sexual behaviour, abortion or divorce can be controversial. More generally, it is often suggested that governments have no business intervening in the private (demographic) affairs of their citizens. In simple terms, mitigation policy is difficult and not suited to the faint-hearted practitioner.

Because demographic mitigation policies are often directed to the most intimate or fundamental areas of people's lives, demography becomes associated with ethics and human rights. For example, studies in demography are concerned with such issues as the provision of reproductive health rights to all members of a population, social practices that slow the reduction of maternal mortality, human trafficking, the closing of borders against family reunion and the relative rights of citizens and non-citizens.

On safer ground, demographic policy is also concerned with adjusting to the consequences of demographic decision-making (adaptation). A very large segment of the activities of government is related to adaptation to demographic change including provision of housing, transport, infrastructure, population-related environmental initiatives, energy and water use, food production, provision of educational institutions, location of shops and services, aged care facilities and hospitals. Demographers become involved in these decisions of government through the forecasting of future needs based upon estimation of future demographic change.

In addressing population policy itself, governments are often trading off between mitigation and adaptation to demographic changes. For example, the government of Japan for many years has been attempting unsuccessfully to increase the nation's birthrate but now it is planning for the very old society that Japan's very low fertility will generate. Following similar unsuccessful attempts to raise the birthrate, the Singapore government is turning to large-scale immigration. Likewise, in 2011, the Australian Government in stating its population policy put all its emphasis upon adaptation:

> It is more useful for governments, businesses and communities to focus on ways of improving our wellbeing, protecting our environment and making better use of the resources we have, rather than trying to determine an absolute limit to our population and focusing efforts on restricting growth in order to not exceed this 'limit'.[1]

In contrast, over the past 40 years, many developing country governments have put considerable effort, often very successfully, into family planning programs in order to reduce birthrates and population growth. The fall in birthrates from high levels to contemporary relatively low levels over the past 40 years has been one of the most spectacular successes of mitigation policy in human history. If the world birthrate had remained at its 1970 level, the population of the world in 2050 would have been 16 billion compared with a current projection of the 2050 population of 9 billion.

---

1   Department of Sustainability, Environment, Water, Population and Communities (2011) 25.

Forecasting future change

The ultimate in the study of change is predicting future change. Because of the urgency of the planning needs of government as referred to above, demographers become involved in forecasting future demographic change. Booth (2006) provides a review of methods of forecasting demographic change. She describes three basic approaches to demographic forecasting: extrapolation of past trends, expectation of future behaviour provided by respondents in surveys or through the opinions of experts (Bayesian models), and theory-based structural modelling involving exogenous variables. A fourth approach, not forecasting in Booth's terms, is to make projections of the future based upon a range of reasonable but hypothetical scenarios (assumptions) about the future. With this last approach, the approach used by most national statistical offices, users are invited to make their own choices from among the various scenarios provided.

With a long history of a wide range of error in demographic forecasts or projections, some demographers favour stochastic projections that provide a central forecast with a range of predicted error around the forecast (Hyndman and Booth 2008, Bell et al. 2011). Using stochastic projections, 95 per cent confidence limits can be placed around predicted future levels of population. However, the 95 per cent confidence limits for Australia's population predicted in stochastic population projections by Hyndman and Booth (2008) and by Bell et al. (2011) do not even overlap with each other, despite just a three-year difference in the publication of their results. Despite claiming to build in the conception of risk, this example indicates that stochastic projections claim a spurious degree of accuracy. These two projections differed dramatically from each other because, between the two projections, Australia's international migration level rose very considerably. In both these cases, the projections were strongly influenced by contemporary demography and, despite using different methods to project the future, the conclusion that contemporary demography would extend into the distant future prevailed. Thus, in considering the future, demographers seem to be reluctant to view it as radically different from the present. In this aspect of change, demographers are not well equipped in theory or in method.

References

Becker, G (1981) *A treatise on the family*. Harvard University Press, Cambridge MA.

Bell, M, Wilson, T and Charles-Edwards, E (2011) Australia's population future: probabilistic forecasts incorporating expert judgment. *Geographical Research* 49(3): 261–75.

Bongaarts, J and Feeney, G (1998) On the tempo and quantum of fertility. *Population and Development Review* 24(2): 271–91.

Booth, H (2006) Demographic forecasting: 1980–2005 in review. *International Journal of Forecasting* 22(3): 547–81.

Clark, J (2003) Uncertainty and variability in demography and population growth: a hierarchical approach. *Ecology* 84(6): 1370–81.

Department of Sustainability, Environment, Water, Population and Communities (2011) *Sustainable Australia — sustainable communities. A sustainable population strategy for Australia*. Commonwealth of Australia, Canberra.

Hyndman, R and Booth, H (2008) Stochastic population forecasts using functional data models for mortality, fertility and migration. *International Journal of Forecasting* 24(3): 323–42.

Klobas, J (2011) The theory of planned behaviour as a model for reasoning about fertility decisions. *Vienna Yearbook of Population Research* 9(1): 47–54.

Landry, A (1945) *Traite de demographie*. Payot, Paris.

McDonald, P (2000) Gender equity, social institutions and the future of fertility. *Journal of Population Research* 17(1): 1–16.

McDonald, P and Kippen, R (2011) *Forecasting births*. Feature article, ABS Catalogue Number 2051.0. Australian Bureau of Statistics, Canberra.

Preston, S, Heuveline, P and Guillot, M (2001) *Demography: measuring and modeling population processes*. Blackwell Publishing, Oxford.

Todaro, M (1969) A model of labour migration and urban unemployment in less developed countries. *The American Economic Review* 59(1): 138–48.

Uhlenberg, P (1996) Mutual attraction: demography and life-course analysis. *The Gerontologist* 36(2): 226–9.

11. Conceptual Change and Conceptual Diversity Contribute to Progress in Science

Paul Griffiths

[W]e must sharpen our conceptual tools as best we can and have faith that in using them to untangle the complexity we shall see how to fashion better ones.

— Hinde 1985, 990

Key theoretical constructs are frequently defined in different ways by different practitioners. The idea of a biological species is perhaps the most famous example. The many competing 'species concepts' are the subject of both an enormous literature in biology (Mayden 1997) and a substantial body of commentary in the history and philosophy of science (Wilkins 2009). Such conceptual diversity is often viewed as dysfunctional, leading to miscommunication between practitioners from different fields, making their findings incommensurable with one another, and generally impeding scientific progress. For example, many have argued that the multiple meanings of the term 'innate' impedes progress in understanding behavioural development for these reasons (Mameli and Bateson 2006; Linquist et al. 2011). Similarly, eminent emotion researcher Klaus Scherer has argued that lack of a shared definition of emotion holds back research through the failure to 'define central working concepts in the universal, invariant, and consensual fashion generally required by a systematic scientific approach' (Scherer 2005 696).

In this chapter I want to explore the opposite possibility. The existence of multiple competing definitions of a construct, and the corresponding different conceptions or ways of thinking about that construct can be a functional part of the scientific process. The example I will use to make this point is the gene. In our work on this key biological construct, my collaborators and I argue that constructs like the gene concept exist to serve ongoing projects in which scientists try to derive empirical generalisations of increasing scope and reliability (Stotz et al. 2004, Griffiths and Stotz 2006, 2013). For the scientific practitioner, concepts are tools that classify experience in ways that meet their specific needs and which are reshaped in the light of new empirical findings. This attitude is sometimes made explicit, but is implicit whenever scientists describe a statement as a 'definition' and yet regard it as hostage to future empirical findings, as they commonly do. Practitioners adjust both the extension of these concepts, in order to encompass sets of instances with as much in common as possible, and the intension of these concepts, so that statements that were once true by definition become open to empirical testing, and vice versa. If scientific concepts are evolving tools, it should not be the aim of philosophers of science to identify one correct conception associated with a word or phrase. An alternative aim, and the one that we have adopted in our work, is to examine how conceptual differences reflect different scientific requirements. The needs of a particular research field can be conceived as an epistemic 'niche' and changes in the concept over time can be seen as responses to changes in the niche. As a result of such conceptual evolution, what was originally a shared concept between two or more communities of researchers can become a range of related but distinct concepts.

In his discussion of the diversity of emotion definitions Scherer identifies the problem as 'the need to resort to everyday language concepts' and the 'inherent fuzziness and the constant evolution' of such concepts (Scherer 2005, 696). I believe this to be a misdiagnosis. The difference between scientific and everyday concepts does not lie in the precision and stability of the former. The term 'gene' is perhaps the most successful example of the introduction of a new technical term into the life sciences (Johannsen 1909), yet its definition has changed continuously since that introduction and remains highly controversial today. The spectacular success of the molecular biosciences did not require a precise and stable definition of 'gene'. Nor has that success led to a precise and stable definition. Instead, 'we are currently left with a rather abstract, open and generalized concept of the gene, even though our comprehension of the structure and organization of the genetic material has greatly increased' (Portin 1993, 173).

The first person to stress that the categories which 'carve nature at its joints' need not be clearly defined was the Victorian polymath William Whewell (1971, first published 1860). Whewell remarked that science makes rapid progress whenever it discovers 'groups made by nature, not by mere definition', such as the chemical elements and biological species. The ability to *define* such a category is neither necessary nor sufficient to make it valuable to science. The Aristotelian category of superlunary objects (objects outside the moon's orbit) is precisely defined but scientifically useless. Conversely, the definition of the gene remains controversial, but a vast amount of successful scientific work has been done with that concept.

In the next section, I outline two conceptions of the gene, the Mendelian conception introduced by Johannsen in 1909 and the molecular conception that emerged in the early 1960s through the work of Francis Crick, James Watson, Seymour Benzer, and others. I will show that these two very different ways of thinking about genes coexist in biology even today. The term 'gene' can be understood in two different ways by investigators, and sometimes even by the same investigator at different points in a single research project. Although these two ways of thinking often converge on the same sequences of DNA, sometimes they do not, and this need not cause any difficulty for science. My discussion of this example will illuminate how such slippage of meaning can be functional rather than dysfunctional.

The evolution of conceptual diversity in genetics

The gene as it was conceived in classical Mendelian genetics—the research tradition that flourished in the first half of the twentieth century, before the advent of molecular biology—was not an observable entity, but it was something different from the unobservable entities postulated by earlier particulate theories of inheritance, such as Darwin's 'gemmules' (Darwin 1868). The gene was a practical tool for predicting and explaining the outcome of breeding one organism with another. The gene was not merely postulated to explain the success of Mendelian genetics; it played a key role in the highly successful practice of 'genetic analysis'—analysing the pattern of inheritance between organisms and using these analyses to answer all sorts of biological questions, from Thomas Hunt Morgan's discovery of chromosomal sex determination (Morgan 1917) to Muriel Wheldale's pioneering studies of plant pigments (Wheldale 1916).

Geneticists certainly hoped that the gene would be shown to exist as a physical reality within the cells of the organism. But the practical role of the gene in genetic analysis meant that the gene would remain an important and legitimate idea even if this did not work out. Morgan remarked in his Nobel Prize acceptance speech that 'at the level at which the genetic experiments lie, it does not make the slightest difference whether the gene is a hypothetical unit, or whether the gene is a material particle'.[1] When Morgan contrasted a 'hypothetical unit' to a 'material particle' I believe that he was envisaging something like a centre of mass in physics. When two bodies act on one another, for example by being at the two ends of a lever, their masses are distributed throughout each body. But when we calculate how the bodies will affect one another, the whole mass is assigned to a single, infinitesimal point—the centre of mass. The centre of mass is not a material particle, but every object has a centre of mass. In the same way, even if there were no straightforward material particles corresponding to genes, genes could still play a critical role in the calculus of heredity.

---

1   Morgan, TH (1933) Nobel lecture, nobelprize.org/nobel_prizes/medicine/laureates/1933/morgan-lecture. html, retrieved 29 January 2011.

Historian of genetics Raphael Falk (1984, 2009) described this situation by saying that the gene of classical Mendelian genetics had two separate identities. One identity was as a hypothetical material unit of heredity, and some genetic research was directed to confirming the existence of these units and finding out more about them. But the gene had a second, and more important, identity as an instrument used to do biology. The future development of genetics was the result of the interplay between these two identities.

The continued development of genetic analysis, and particularly the work of Seymour Benzer which showed the need to distinguish the unit of genetic function from the units of mutation and recombination (Benzer 1957), combined with Francis Crick and James Watson's work on the structure (Watson and Crick 1953) and function (Crick 1958) of DNA to produce a new, molecular conception of the gene as a distinctive kind of DNA sequence. This is the gene presented in biology textbooks today.

Each gene has a promoter region that acts as a signal to the machinery that transcribes the DNA into RNA. This is followed by an open reading frame, a series of nucleotides that correspond to the series of RNA codons that specify the amino acids in a protein, beginning with a start codon and ending with a stop codon. The gene of molecular biology is thus a linear image of a gene product—an RNA or a protein—in the DNA.[2]

The fact that molecular genes are defined in such a way that the nucleotide sequence of a gene has a linear correspondence to the sequence of its products is the key to the practical utility of the molecular gene concept in research and in biotechnology. It is the basis of most of the techniques, whether chemical or computational, by which biologists identify and manipulate those molecules. This is true despite the extent to which transcriptional and post-transcriptional processes can distort this relationship in multicellular organisms. As Karola Stotz and I have argued, the fact that the 'picture' of the product in the DNA is sometimes a cubist picture does not stop biologists from figuring out the relationship between DNA and product (Griffiths and Stotz 2007, 2013).

Today the molecular, material identity of the gene is the most prominent, but not because Mendelian conception of the gene was shown to be in error and replaced. Instead, as I will now show, the Mendelian conception continues to exist alongside the molecular conception and plays a critical role in research to this day.

---

2   I owe this expression to Rob D Knight.

The emergence of the molecular conception of the gene appears to be a successful example of the research strategy of identifying a causal role and seeking the concrete occupant of that role (Lewis 1966). In this case, the role was that of the Mendelian gene, something whose distinctive pattern of transmission from one generation to the next explains many of the phenomena of heredity. It is natural to suppose that the occupant of that role turned out to be the molecular gene—an open reading frame with an adjacent promoter region. But the relationship is not that simple. The role-occupant framework for thinking about conceptual change starts from the observation that some concepts can be analysed using the causes and effects of the thing being conceptualised (its 'causal role'). Lightning was originally known only as something that causes bright flashes in the sky during thunderstorms and whose destructive effects we see as lightning strikes. When it was shown that the flashes and destructive strikes are the effects of atmospheric electrostatic discharges, it followed necessarily that lightning is atmospheric electrostatic discharge.

This framework seems on first inspection to describe what happened in the transition from Mendelian to molecular genetics: with the unravelling of the genetic code and of the basic processes of transcription and translation in the 1960s, the two identities of the gene in classical genetics—the Mendelian and the hypothetical material—converged on a single identity, the molecular gene. Looked at more closely, however, the causal role of the gene had been significantly revised to take account of findings about the material gene. In classical Mendelian genetics, the gene played three theoretical roles. It was the unit of mutation: changes in genes give rise to new, mutant alleles of the same gene. It was also the unit of recombination: crossover between chromosomes either separates genes that were previously linked or links genes that were previously inherited independently. Finally, the gene was the unit of function: the genotype that interacts with the environment to produce the phenotype is a collection of genes, and any effect of genotype on phenotype can be traced back to some gene or combination of genes.

It was natural to project these ideas from Mendelian genetics onto the gene as a hypothetical material entity and to expect that the material gene would be a unit of mutation, of recombination, and of genetic function. But the new, molecular concept of the gene did not live up to that expectation. A mutation is something that can happen to any stretch of the DNA molecule, not only to genetically meaningful units such as molecular genes. Recombination is a highly regulated process involving chromosomes and an accompanying cast of enzymes. In analysing this process, there is no need to divide the DNA itself into 'units of recombination'. Recombination can occur within a molecular gene so that one part of one allele is recombined with the complementary part from its sister allele, as well as occurring between whole alleles, and it can occur between segments of DNA that are not molecular genes at all. So the new conception of the molecular gene was one in which the gene is only the unit of function and not the unit of mutation or recombination. While the molecular conception of the gene grew out of the earlier conception, it did not do so by the discovery of a material unit that fulfilled the role of the Mendelian gene.

In the light of these observations about the development of the gene concept, I can now explain why the Mendelian conception of the gene persists alongside the molecular conception, rather than being reduced to it as lighting was reduced to atmospheric electrostatic discharge. The concept of the molecular gene applies only to sequences that have a structure something like that described above and that act as the template for making a gene product. But in humans, for example, only 1 per cent to 2 per cent of the DNA consists of sequences used to make proteins. Some—currently controversial—proportion of the remaining sequence is used to make functional RNAs. But much of the sequence is not transcribed to make a product, and does not have the structural features, such as promoter regions, which make transcription possible. There are many segments of chromosome that have some effect on the phenotype and hence behave as Mendelian alleles but that do not count as genes under the new molecular conception. Any difference in the sequence of DNA that causes a difference in phenotype will function as a Mendelian allele, but it need not be an allele of any molecular gene.

It would be foolish to redefine *allele* in a way which restricts the term to alleles of molecular genes, because the fact that these other sequences are behaving as Mendelian alleles is not something to gloss over. If there is an inherited cause of phenotypic differences, we want to know about it! Conversely, the molecular gene cannot be redefined as any piece of DNA that can act as a Mendelian gene, because this would render it unsuitable for the purpose for which it is used in molecular biology—namely, to identify sequences that have a linear correspondence to the biomolecules made from the DNA.

These observations would be a mere quibble if the possibility of the two conceptions coming apart were merely theoretical, or even if it were very rare. But this is not the case. There are many other ways that DNA sequences can play a role in the development of phenotypes besides acting as linear templates for the synthesis of biomolecules. When one of these other pieces of DNA comes in two or more forms with different phenotypic effects, they will behave as Mendelian alleles and can be investigated via genetic analysis. Even if they are not called genes, they are treated as (Mendelian) genes, and sometimes they *are* called genes but only when speaking in an appropriate context. Such is the flexibility of scientific language. For example, when a medical geneticist is seeking the 'genes' for a disorder, she is looking for Mendelian alleles: sections of chromosome whose inheritance explains the phenotypic differences observed in patients. Translated into molecular terms, these sequences may or may not turn out not to be molecular genes. It is entirely possible that they will be segments of DNA that fulfil other, regulatory functions.

A clear example of the continuing coexistence of the Mendelian and molecular identities of the gene comes from studies of the gene *Lmbr1* in the mouse and its homologue on human chromosome seven (Lettice et al. 2002). This locus is known to house an allele that produces abnormal limb development in both mice and humans. But further molecular analysis of that locus shows that the molecular gene within which the mutation is located is not a molecular gene that plays a role in the development of these abnormalities. Instead, there is a sequence embedded in a non-coding stretch within that gene that acts to regulate the gene 'sonic hedgehog' (*shh*).

The gene *shh* is located about one million DNA nucleotides away on the same chromosome and is known to be important in limb development. The regulatory sequence at the original locus is called an 'enhancer' in molecular genetics, not a gene, since it does not code for a product. It is not a functional component of the molecular gene within which it is physically located, since this mutation does not affect the product of that gene or the post-transcriptional processing of that product. But this mutated regulatory sequence is the Mendelian allele for the abnormal limb development. Conversely, *shh* is a paradigmatic molecular gene, but there exists no allele of *shh* that causes (is the Mendelian allele for) this kind of abnormal limb development. What is happening here is that in one experimental context—that of hunting for the mutation responsible for the phenotype—the idea of gene assumes its Mendelian identity, while in the other context—that of analysing the DNA sequence—the idea of gene assumes its molecular identity. These two identities of the gene often converge on the same sequence of DNA, but sometimes they do not.

The relationship between Mendelian and molecular conceptions of the gene defies at least the simplest form of the role-occupant analysis of scientific progress that I described above. Biologists were looking for the physical occupant of the role of the Mendelian gene. But what they found, and what molecular geneticists call a gene, occupies only part of that role, and the original role remains important, too. Molecular biology enriched genetics with a new way of thinking about genes, and biologists today have both these ways of thinking about genes in their toolkit. They move smoothly between these two contextually activated representations of genes as they move from one research context to another.

The function of conceptual diversity in genetics

The case of Mendelian and molecular genetics shows how conceptual diversity can be a functional part of scientific practice. The two conceptions of the gene are tools used to do different kinds of scientific work. One is used in genetic analysis to locate the pieces of DNA that make a difference to some phenotype. The other is used to identify pieces of DNA that play one specific role in the production of gene products—that of the template for transcription. Both ideas are useful and neither can be replaced by the other.

One suggestion might be that the term 'gene' should be reserved for one sense and another term introduced for the other sense. This kind of stipulation may sometimes be useful. However, one of these two ideas developed out of the other, and during the period in which this was happening the effect of demanding that the term be used only in accordance with one definition would have been stifling. It would have prevented the emergence of a new meaning in response to the needs of a particular kind of experimental practice. Scientists need to be able to flexibly redefine theoretical constructs to fit the phenomena they are uncovering. But sometimes, when different groups are studying different phenomena, they need to redefine them in different ways. At the end of such a process it may be possible to distinguish the two constructs and give them separate names. But the period when productive conceptual innovation is happening is precisely the period when this cannot be done, both because the two ways of thinking have not yet been clearly distinguished and because it is not yet clear that there are two different phenomena that need to be distinguished.

Even when two or more different conceptions of a construct have emerged, it is not clear that stipulating that a term be used in only one sense can be more than a temporary expedient to ensure clarity in a particular paper or in a particular program of research. Scientific change is not a series of discrete steps, but a continuous process. As well as major events of 'conceptual speciation' there are minor local variants that arise and die out again, as scientists explore possible ways to think about a topic. It is by stretching and warping constructs in this way that science hits on novel and productive ways of classifying nature.

Dysfunctional conceptual diversity

But while conceptual diversity can be functional, it is not always so. In the paper discussed in my introduction, Scherer (2005) argued that the continuous interchange between the language of psychology and vernacular language is a fundamental problem for emotion theory. This may be correct, but I suggest the problem is not that ordinary language transmits its imprecision to the language of science. The real problem is more or less the opposite. The ties between scientific and ordinary usage prevent concepts from evolving to meet the needs of scientists.

This dysfunctional pattern can be seen with the idea of innateness. It is a truism that the term 'innate' is vague and ambiguous. According to ethologist Patrick Bateson (1991),

> At least six meanings are attached to the term: present at birth; a behavioral difference caused by a genetic difference; adapted over the course of evolution; unchanging throughout development; shared by all members of a species; and not learned.

More recently Matteo Mameli and Bateson systematically reviewed the scientific use of the term 'innate' and identified no less than 26 proposed definitions. They judged eight of these to be both genuinely independent definitions and potentially valuable scientific constructs (Mameli and Bateson 2006).

The work that my collaborators and I have conducted on the concept of innateness suggests that this ambiguity leads to unproductive slippage of meaning because the use of the term 'innate' cannot evolve freely into any specific scientific niche. This is because it is strongly anchored in a vernacular conception of innateness that conflates the various different constructs that could each be of scientific value in their own right (Griffiths 2002, Griffiths and Machery 2008, Griffiths et al. 2009, Linquist et al. 2011).

What is the vernacular conception of innateness? Just as there are commonsense ideas about heat and about dynamics, ideas which formal education wholly or partially replaces with scientific conceptions of these domains (Clement 1983, McCloskey 1983), there are commonsense ideas about biology, ideas commonly referred to as 'folk-biology' (Atran 1990, Medin and Atran 1999). Prominent amongst these is the idea that some traits are expressions of the inner nature of animals and plants, whilst other traits result from the influence of the environment. The idea that living things have inner natures that make them the kind of organism that they are is intimately linked to the very idea of heredity. The hereditary traits of an animal are those that are passed on as part of its nature. Natures also explain the stability of some traits within a single lifetime—people do not expect a black sheep to grow white wool after shearing, because the colour of its wool is part of its nature. Like 'folk physics', these 'folk-biological' ideas work reasonably well for hunting, farming, and traditional stockbreeding.

Griffiths (2002) hypothesised that the vernacular concept of innateness is an expression of an implicit theory that organisms possess inherited 'inner natures' (1) that cause them to possess species-typical properties, (2) whose development is resistant to environmental influences, and (3) that are functional (they have a purpose). That is, when biologically naive subjects believe a trait is innate, they believe that it is an expression of an organism's inner nature, and hence that the trait will possess all or some combination of the three features of species—typicality, developmental fixity, and purposive function. We have given these three factors the more convenient labels *typicality*, *fixity* and *teleology*, and we understand each as a broad, conceptual theme:

- *Typicality*—the trait is part of what it is to be an organism *of that kind*; every individual has it, or every individual that is not malformed, or every individual of a certain age, sex or other natural subcategory.

- *Fixity*—the trait is hard to change; its development is insensitive to environmental inputs in development; its development appears goal-directed, or resistant to perturbation.

- *Teleology*—this is how the organism is *meant* to develop; to lack the innate trait is to be malformed; environments that disrupt the development of this trait are themselves abnormal.

Using vignettes of behavioural development we showed that manipulating information about these three factors predicts a substantial amount of the variance in a subject's willingness to classify the resulting behaviour as innate. We also showed that there is no interaction amongst the three factors, which we interpret to mean that our subjects understand all three as independent signs that the behaviour flows from the animal's inner 'nature' (Griffiths et al. 2009). In a series of further studies we replicated these results and extended them to elucidate what biologically naive subjects mean when they describe behaviour as 'in the DNA' (Linquist et al. 2011). So we now have some empirical warrant for our claim that the vernacular concept of innateness is driven by these three independent criteria.

There have been several attempts to clarify the concept of innateness by stipulation. Unsurprisingly, most of these pick one of the three features just discussed and stipulate that this alone is to be meant by 'innate'. One approach identifies innate traits with those characteristic of an entire species and acquired traits with those that vary between populations and individuals, the factor we call typicality (e.g. Stich 1975). A second approach identifies innate traits with those that can be explained by natural selection, the factor we call teleology (e.g. Lorenz 1966). A third distinguishes two different patterns of interaction between genes and environment and identifies one pattern with the innate and another with the acquired. This defines innateness as the factor we call fixity (e.g. Ariew 2006).

We have also found that scientists who subscribe to one of these stipulative definitions nevertheless continue to respond to our manipulations of the other factors that are part of the vernacular conception of innateness when classifying behaviour as innate or acquired. The entrenched, vernacular understanding resists the scientific imperative for the concept to evolve to represent only one of the potentially valuable constructs confounded in the vernacular conception.

Conclusions

1. Conceptual change in science can be understood as the evolution of constructs to fit a changing epistemic niche. This evolution is driven by the need of scientists to group phenomena together in ways that facilitate reliable inductive generalisation. On occasion this can result in conceptual 'speciation' in which a construct evolves into two or more distinct constructs.

2. The adoption of stipulative definitions can only ever be a temporary expedient. Efforts to rigorously police scientific usage would be dysfunctional because they would prevent scientific concepts from exploring new niches.

3. Another factor that can obstruct conceptual evolution is the existence of an entrenched intuitive conception which obstructs the emergence of new conceptions to serve specific scientific purposes.

Acknowledgements

This research was supported under Australian Research Council's Discovery Projects funding scheme (project number DP0878650).

References

Ariew, A (2006) Innateness. In Matthen, M and Stevens, C (eds) *Handbook of the philosophy of science*. Elsevier, Amsterdam: 567–84.

Atran, S (1990) *Cognitive foundations of natural history: towards an anthropology of science*. Cambridge University Press, Cambridge.

Bateson, PPG (1991) Are there principles of behavioural development? In Bateson, PPG (ed.) *The development and integration of behaviour: essays in honour of Robert Hinde*. Cambridge University Press, Cambridge: 19–39.

Benzer, S (1957) The elementary units of heredity. In McElroy, WD and Glass, B (eds) *A symposium on the chemical basis of heredity*. Johns Hopkins Press, Baltimore: 70–133.

Clement, J (1983) A conceptual model discussed by Galileo and used intuitively by physics student. In Gentner, D and Stevens, AL (eds) *Mental models*. Erlbaum, Hillsdale NJ: 325–40.

Crick, FHC (1958) On protein synthesis. *Symposia of the Society for Experimental Biology* 12: 138–63.

Darwin, CR (1868) *The variation of animals and plants under domestication*. John Murray, London.

Falk, R (1984) The gene in search of an identity. *Human Genetics* 68: 195-204.

Falk, R (2000) The gene: a concept in tension. In Beurton, P, Falk R and Rheinberger, H-J (eds) *The concept of the gene in development and evolution*. Cambridge University Press, Cambridge: 317-48.

Griffiths, PE (2002) What is innateness? *The Monist* 85(1): 70–85.

Griffiths, PE and Machery, E (2008) Innateness, canalisation and 'biologicizing the mind'. *Philosophical Psychology* 21(3): 397–414.

Griffiths, PE, Machery, E and Linquist, S (2009) The vernacular concept of innateness. *Mind and Language* 24(5): 605–630.

Griffiths, PE and Stotz, K (2006) Genes in the postgenomic era. *Theoretical Medicine and Bioethics* 27(6): 499–521.

Griffiths, PE and Stotz, K (2007) Gene. In Ruse, M and Hull, D, eds *Cambridge companion to philosophy of biology*. Cambridge University Press, Cambridge: 85–102.

Griffiths, PE and Stotz, K (2013) *Genetics and philosophy: an introduction*. Cambridge University Press, New York.

Hinde, RA (1985) Was 'the expression of emotions' a misleading phrase? *Animal Behaviour* (33): 985–92.

Johannsen, W (1909) *Elemente der exakten erblichkeitslehre*. Gustav Fischer, Jena.

Lettice, LA, Horikoshi, T et al. (2002) Disruption of a long-range cis-acting regulator for *Shh* causes preaxial polydactyly. *Proceedings of the National Academy of Sciences* 99(11): 7548–53.

Lewis, DK (1966) An argument for the identity theory. *Journal of Philosophy* 63(1): 17–25.

Linquist, S, Machery, E, Griffiths, PE and Stotz, K (2011) Exploring the folkbiological conception of human nature. *Philosophical Transactions of the Royal Society B* 366: 444–53.

Lorenz, KZ (1966) *Evolution and the modification of behaviour.* Methuen & Co, London.

Mameli, M and Bateson, PPG (2006) Innateness and the sciences. *Biology and Philosophy* 21(2): 155–88.

Mayden, RL (1997) A hierarchy of species: the denouement in the saga of the species problem. In Claridge, MF, Dawah, HA and Wilson, MR (eds) *Species: the units of biodiversity.* Chapman & Hall, New York: 382–423.

McCloskey, M (1983) Intuitive physics. *Scientific American* 248: 122–30.

Medin, D and Atran, S (eds) (1999) *Folkbiology.* MIT Press, Cambridge MA.

Morgan, TH (1917) The theory of the gene. *American Naturalist* 51: 513–44.

Portin, P (1993) The concept of the gene: short history and present status. *The Quarterly Review of Biology* 68 (2): 173-223.

Scherer, KR (2005) What are emotions? And how can they be measured? *Social Science Information* 44(4): 695–729.

Stich, S (1975) *Innate Ideas.* University of California Press, Los Angeles.

Stotz, K, Griffiths, PE and Knight, R (2004) How scientists conceptualise genes: an empirical study. *Studies in History and Philosophy of Biological and Biomedical Sciences* 35(4): 647–73.

Watson, JD and Crick, FHC (1953) Molecular structure of nucleic acids: a structure for deoxyribose nucleic acid. *Nature* 171: 737–8.

Wheldale, M (1916) *The anthocyanin pigments of plants.* Cambridge University Press, Cambridge.

Whewell, W (1971, first published 1860). *On the philosophy of discovery.* Burt Franklin, New York.

Wilkins, JS (2009) *Species: a history of the idea.* University of California Press, Berkeley.

12. Mental Illness and Psychiatry Have Seen Substantial Change—But There is Still a Long Way To Go

Beverley Raphael

The spectrum of health and illness

The spectrum of what can be defined as health and illness has been progressively changed, by both the recognition of diverse diseases and how they are characterised, and the emergence of new patterns of problems. These new, emergent patterns of distress, impairment, 'strange' phenomena and suffering may be those associated with, for instance, a new infectious disease arising from viral mutation, or a new pattern of problems resulting from environmental or other hazards, or with socially driven behavioural change, or existing behaviour newly described, for instance, narcissistic personality disorder. Behavioural changes, whether the result of internally driven processes (such as chemical factors, e.g. neurotransmitters) or externally (as with adversity, violence, abandonment) may also lead to consistent patterns of suffering and dysfunction, which become defined as 'disorder'. Syndromes—patterns of symptoms—may constitute physical or psychiatric disorders that can be recognised and diagnosed as such and treated.

The consideration of the spectrum, or more specific patterns of symptoms that are categorised as illness, is important in identifying what is normal compared to what is pathological. The consideration of which symptoms, how many, for what duration, what levels of impairment are associated with disease or disorder, is important, but often difficult to separate from the human condition, particularly in terms of mental illnesses and disorders. This theme of the spectrum is important in considering change as it is relevant to psychiatry. It has been in recent years a rapidly advancing discipline involved with defining and classifying disorders, identifying causes, and providing effective treatment. But its interfaces with people's lives are often variable. The question of what is disorder is relevant to the changing conceptualisation of illness.

This is exemplified by debates about the suffering of grief, as for example over the loss of a loved one. Freud (1917) described the symptoms of mourning and melancholia and the normality of the former, along with the pathology of the latter. Lindemann (1944) described the symptomatology and management of acute grief. Engel (1961) asked 'Is grief a disease?' in a paper which argued that it was not. Many researchers in this field have continued to ask such questions, on issues including sadness and depression, shock, and post-traumatic stress disorders. And studies have evolved to lead to a recognition of prolonged grief, perhaps a disorder, a severe and disabling condition that could be treated—and currently argued in terms of its inclusion in the new edition of the *Diagnostic and statistical manual of mental disorders* of the American Psychiatric Association DSM V. At the same time others grieve for the loss of sadness as part of life and of human experience (Horwitz and Wakefield 2007).

This concept of life and human behaviour versus madness is highlighted when violence is addressed. When is this darker side of human nature part of the human condition, and when is it a psychiatric disorder? How can it be explained by syndromes of lack of control, rage disorders, or the consequence of psychosis, or response to perceived threat? When is the violent person not guilty because of mental illness—or more simply, when is that person bad, evil, a psychopath? The spectrum, the explanation, the definitions and naming, the environment, the purposes and effects of violence reflect the complexity of the life versus disorder questions.

The argument of the spectrum could continue—for instance, when does fear become an anxiety disorder? Or when do the multiple and prevalent psychotic-like experiences become an illness such as schizophrenia? When do passionate enthusiasms and driven activities become bipolar disorders, and when does forgetfulness in old age become dementia? When do the behavioural differences of children become disorders? These issues can be cogently argued against the diagnostic criteria developed from research and consensus. What is life and what is a disorder is much clearer when the differences are profound, but less so at the edges.

So the questions of change that arise here are those of the forces that have led to the recognition and effective treatment of many psychiatric or mental health problems, and how they deal with the boundaries of life versus disorder. At the same time, they call for research and knowledge development to find out why we have not or cannot prevent or cure the disorders that are so closely linked to our lives.

Societal and cultural dynamics of definition, diagnosis, prevalence and treatment

Over time many societal and cultural dynamics have contributed to the naming, defining and treating of illnesses—from the 'humours' to plague and madness, to name a few. Understanding the causes and nature of problems of disease and sickness has developed through observation, efforts to deal with the condition, clinical or healing work, and science and knowledge that have progressively led to strategies for the definition, diagnosis and treatment of these forms of ill health.

Among diseases, psychiatric conditions—mental ill health—have been uncertain and complex, often poorly understood. Those dealing with the mentally ill were once known as alienists. Psychiatry has, however, changed to become a specialist medical discipline, one with its own professional training following a general medical degree, and its craft grouping, a college of like experts. In the years of its progressive change to this status, it has faced many challenges ranging from the stigma, fear, and discrimination experienced by mentally ill patients, and those who treat them, to the ebb and flow of anti-psychiatry movements.

Psychiatry is a complex discipline with multiple interfaces with other disciplines in related fields: psychology; general medicine where its separation from medical practice has led to the development of subspecialties such as consultation-liaison psychiatry; paediatrics and child psychiatry; geriatric psychiatry; neuropsychiatry with neurology; and similarly neurochemistry and other biologics; and biological psychiatry. These subspecialisations continue to evolve as branches, but perhaps with less than optimal definition and multidimensional interactions for change.

It has often also been hypothesised that societal change influences the types of mental health problems that become prevalent, or are identified as prevalent. It was suggested that Freud's models, including the rise of psychoanalysis, were strongly influenced by the rise of physics. There is no doubt that earlier times, and even some currently, were principally informed by concepts of 'bad spirits'. War provides another example. 'Shell shock' affected soldiers of World War I, who were initially treated as cowards. This changed to 'combat fatigue' with World War II, and subsequently to post-traumatic stress disorder, which research has now defined, and for which it has delivered a number of scientifically valid treatments. Mild traumatic brain injury provides the most recent example of a related syndrome. Simple singular solutions are, however, infrequent.

'Madness' or psychosis has been the most feared and stigmatised domain of psychiatric illness, with biological changes, the genetic variables revealed in the increased risk shown by family members, and the influence of environments such as cannabis use in the early teenage years. The rapid development of science for medication treatments has brought important changes in outcomes for many people suffering illnesses like schizophrenia. Nevertheless, fear and stigma continue. Perhaps the ultimate change is the role of people who are themselves ill in this way, having a 'Mad Pride' march to challenge other views.

The dominant models of psychiatric disorder are seen as based on Western cultural interpretations and values, and this is seen by some as a hegemony that is powerfully propagated.

Cultural understanding and belief have influenced the response to madness, in particular, psychosis. Formerly those affected were seen as having been taken over by an evil spirit and they were abandoned, chained up or locked away. In the earlier phases of recognition of this illness, this was also the pattern of care in what is now defined as the developed world. Change has occurred, even for those severely ill in this way, with the development of antipsychotic medications and other psychosocial interventions. These multiple treatment strategies have led to a life that can be lived in the community, not an institution of containment. However, for many with such severe illnesses, lifelong dependency, disability and dysfunction may persist so that the search for better treatment continues. One such valuable change has been the development of the 'recovery' movement, implemented in ways to empower those affected, and to bring a framework for belief, action, and hope.

The search for ways to prevent psychoses continues in research and service provision. There are now initiatives which seek to prevent the development of full-blown disorders by strategies which identify and treat those in the early stages of psychosis in the adolescent years. The Early Psychosis Prevention and Intervention Centre program 'EPPIC' (McGorry 2010) initiated in Australia is an important strategic change where the strong commitment of leaders in this field led to government commitment at policy, program and funding levels that supported widespread implementation.

The global need for change in the recognition of psychiatric disorders has been driven by the World Health Organization (WHO), with its focus on low and middle income countries. It has supported research to identify the extent and patterns of mental health need, i.e. mental illness, through initiatives such as the World Mental Health Survey; the reporting of policies, programs and service levels through the WHO Atlas project; as well as global programs supporting education, training and program development. Education and training to build expertise in low and middle income countries continues to be critical for change to more effective and humane treatments for those with severe psychiatric disorders. This extends from basic levels with primary care, through to psychiatric nurses and psychiatrists as well as psychologists and other allied health workers. The core essential provision of psychotropic medications is delineated and provided as far as possible. These changes, driven at a global level, continue to improve care and outcomes for those with severe mental illnesses. More specific focused programs to facilitate education and change include programs such as AsiaLink, an Australian/Asian program within which sits Asia Australia Mental Health, funded through both philanthropy and government. These programs have involved sophisticated educational initiatives with China and other Asian partnerships, achieving significant positive program development attuned to the defined needs of the participating countries.

One of the continuing challenges at a global level is the ongoing impact of adverse social determinants on mental health and wellbeing in all countries, but especially in low and middle income settings. These and other indices of adversity continue to have negative impacts, including those related to experience of violence, dislocation from home and country, and exposure to war and conflict. Increasingly in recent years, mass natural disasters such as earthquakes, hurricanes and cyclones, forest fires, drought, and floods have caused trauma, death and destruction, bringing adverse mental health consequences for significant numbers of affected populations. The response to these may also be influenced by the culture of belief in fate, acts of God, and acceptance of the specific cultural interpretations relevant to such events. Human-caused disasters such as terrorism have even more severe impacts for mental health.

Culture is, of course, central to how we interpret our world. The loss of cultural recognition and identity can add an extra burden of distress affecting mental health. The failure to recognise cultural values of the other may mean that their mental health needs are not understood. Nor may Western models of understanding or treatment be well received. Culturally informed practice is an important component of care. In Australia and other culturally diverse societies informed by multicultural programs, policies and service development can be attuned to cultural diversity. Recognition of our own culture and its beliefs and practices is also essential for developing true collaborations in service and care models. This change is progressive, from 'them' to 'us': the 'other', the 'alien', the 'unknown' can be perceived as threatening.

Mental health and mental illness across the lifespan

As different cohorts—generations of baby boomers, X, Y, Z, and others—evolve over time, some generations are seen as having certain problems, and other factors also draw particular attention, such as the improvements in physical health and longevity.

Traditionally mental illness was seen in terms of psychosis, madness, and melancholia. Adult illnesses were, and still are, the principal focus. They are more overt, associated with heightened acute risk (e.g. violence, suicide) and onset in adolescent or early adult life. These are 'the mentally ill', suffering from, and diagnosed as having, 'serious mental illness'. This is, sadly still a defining term, rather than a person 'living with' a specific disorder.

With the ageing population there is concern for their mental health needs, especially proper recognition and treatment of their psychiatric disorders. Epidemiological research makes clear that there is a lower prevalence of psychiatric disorders generally in these years—but there is a high prevalence of dementia, with many in institutional care. The debate that remains is about in what category these illnesses of dementia sit, particularly whether or not they are psychiatric syndromes, as well as who is responsible for care. Research for prevention and treatment is extensive with these, as with any types of illness. As with other psychiatric disorders, comorbidity is frequent, for instance with depression, anxiety disorders, etc. Research-driven understandings are occurring, but these are chronic diseases and we have not yet found a way of change—by name or intervention—to make them go away, to prevent or cure them.

Conditions affecting children have had increasing attention, not necessarily because of a full understanding of the extent of their prevalence, but because of a growing body of research that makes it very clear that many, if not most, of the psychiatric problems of adult life begin from the earliest times. The role of the perinatal, early childhood and the early years is significant, with not only the genetic influences, but the gene–environment interactions, and the environments themselves.

The names given to disorders potentially excluded children from mental health or psychiatric assessment and care. Those with 'conduct disorder' were seen as being in need of other types of behavioural management, or discipline, as were those with other externalising conditions. The internalising, quiet behaviours were often seen as good, not causing problems. The progressive building of strong child psychiatry services, informed by a growing body of research in this field, has led to very significant developments. There have been excellent prevention and early intervention findings and randomised controlled trials of treatment for anxiety disorders, for instance.

Burgeoning research in the past decade has identified the vital role of early experiences of adversity in contributing in major ways to the development of mental disorders in childhood, adolescence and adult life, and even old age. These damaging experiences may occur in the spectrum 'family life difficulties'. Most likely to be associated with adverse health and mental health outcomes, however, are child abuse and neglect, especially child sexual abuse (penetrative) and other forms of violent abuse.

While studies also show the possibility of 'resilience' in the face of adverse environments, it is only in the most recent times that more population-based strategies have been implemented to build such strengths. 'Kids Matter', a universal primary school program, is one such evidence-based initiative that is currently being put in place across Australia. Triple P (Positive Parenting Pre-schoolers; Sanders 2013), developed in Australia, is established in many places internationally, but for multiple reasons not widely implemented in Australia. In addition, youth programs for adolescents such as 'Headspace' and the EPPIC early psychosis programs are being widely implemented on the basis of research and the costs of not changing, as established by research. Nevertheless, challenges to change come in many shapes and sizes, and from many sources: costs, lack of perceived benefits, and other political priorities, to name a few.

So across the lifespan of those who may develop a psychiatric disorder there are multiple challenges and changes—but the burden of mental ill health, measured at a population level, remains high.

Models and systems of care

Models and systems for the care and treatment of those with diagnosed mental disorders or mental illnesses have progressively changed and continue to do so. At earlier times, containment was the major management strategy for those who were ill, usually in asylums, which were large and often very dehumanised institutions. This was followed by deinstitutionalisation through the 1960s and 1970s, a movement that was facilitated by the availability of the new medications such as antipsychotics and antidepressants. Models of community care came into being. Nurses, psychiatrists and other professionals made home visits and community mental health centres were established. Psychiatric units were developed as part of general hospital services.

These changes were seen as positive and valuable, although some elements of the old models of care persisted. These included the identification of people as 'the mentally ill', and as needing to be managed as though they could not know what was best for them. More importantly however, ideology continued the separation of mental health from health more broadly in terms of systems and the basis of care. 'Mental illness' programs, despite the growth of important services, often failed to address associated and frequent comorbid physical illness.

Systems of care changed in Australia, as in other countries, with the development and implementation of a national mental health policy and associated programs. These changes brought additional development with accountability, reporting requirements, funding base delineation, and health care utilisation statistics. Such policies are regularly updated and jurisdictions are engaged in implementing the proposed elements of service delivery. In addition to the progressive development of these frameworks, there have been improvements in services and outcomes for a great many of those affected. Regular data reporting of progress of change is provided through government agencies such as the Australian Institute of Health and Welfare.

Service systems and models of care, including specific hospital-based inpatient services, focus chiefly on those with 'serious mental illness', i.e. psychosis, severe depression and suicidal behaviour. Less severe cases were and are managed through community programs, for instance psychological counselling services, and primary care general practitioners. As indicated earlier there has also been growth in child and adolescent services.

Special program initiatives have also progressed, but not necessarily become formal parts of services systems and care delivery. Prevention programs, although well supported by research, remain a low priority despite their potential value. They do not have change drivers and traction, despite potential cost benefits, compared to youth programs focused on treatment such as 'Headspace' and the EPPIC early psychosis program which have had passionate drivers and change-based implementation.

Multidisciplinary teams have been a core component of mental health programs, bringing together diverse views in decision-making for clinical issues of concern. However, rather than reflecting the diverse expertise of different disciplines, at times there is still a culture of the core mental health professional or worker. Using a generic conceptualisation rather than specifying what is required has sometimes hindered opportunities for change and innovation.

Service systems and models of care have continued to evolve and change in some ways, but not in others. The use of mental health units as specialist components of emergency departments and to provide emergency assessment, triage and management, sometimes occurred early (for example in the Royal Brisbane Hospital) but was resisted elsewhere because of the 'separation' ideology of mental health service models. Nevertheless such change has been driven forward and reflects a more modern, humane, less stigmatised process than the former model of the 'police van at the hospital back door'.

The separation of mental health from health, and of mental illness from the diverse and multiple specialised components of disease and illness management in the broader illness field, has reflected what could be considered a more limited and less sophisticated approach.

Specialised programs focused on different psychiatric disorders have only started to appear in recent years. And even though the costs and burden of these multiple psychiatric disorders is very significant, sophisticated, focused clinical programs such as those for cancer, heart disease and the like have not been well developed for mental health disorders. This is further compounded by the merging into chronic disease concepts—that illnesses like psychiatric disorders are not cured, require ongoing care, and are highly likely to recur. One may well ask where are the concepts of prevention and cure for psychiatry? Why are they so little believed in, and committed to, in our models and systems of care?

Hopeful, committed, skilled people advocate and work to improve mental health, and to lessen the human and social costs of mental illnesses. New systems and models continue to develop, such as mental health commissions, the 'recovery' movement, community care, and mental health online services. The evolution of change and its drivers occurs at multiple levels.

Drivers of change

Change continues to evolve for mental health, often from diverse processes. Further questions are: what change, why, and what are the outcomes? Does the change that occurs make things better or worse—better in terms of more positive health, lower costs, greater productivity, happiness or mental health? Or does it lead to greater suffering, increased pathology, impairment, and death? Our measures may not be adequate to answer these questions.

There are many drivers of change, and also resistances and barriers. Drivers include the ongoing pressures of a persistent problem, frustrations regarding the inability to access services at times of need and consistent pressures of severe demand. The issues themselves—such as the contributions of child abuse and neglect to mental ill health and suffering—may be drivers for both change and resistance, the latter coming from fear of the unfamiliar, the opening of Pandora's box. There are a number of influences driving change for mental health and for psychiatry.

Science, its processes and outcomes

It is clear that the findings of scientific research in the mental health field have been, and continue to be, very powerful influences. These have ranged from those leading to the development of effective medications to treat psychiatric disorders to the systematic exploration of symptom patterns, syndromes and their change over time, providing a shared base for understanding (as reflected in the World Health Organization's International Classification of Disease and the *Diagnostic and statistical manual* of the American Psychiatric Association).

The labelling and naming of disorders may change over time as they are further understood, as reflected in the trauma syndromes, depression, typologies of psychoses, autism spectrum, and attention deficit hyperactivity disorder (ADHD). The passionate curiosity of scientists in this field, the search to know to the fullest degree the brain and the mind and their relationships to pathology, has led to rapid advances in neuroscience as relevant to psychiatric disorders. Genomics, the chemistry of the brain and its transmissions, and more recently the recognition of neuroplasticity, have been important. There are also aims of enhancing understanding of and response to psychiatric disorders through prevention and treatment. The extensive programs from molecular psychiatry to translational psychiatry (Licinio 2013) aim to bring science to the coalface of treatment and care.

The findings of science are widely propagated through publication, conferences and the like, building the knowledge base. But essential to change is the integration of relevant research into the real world of treatment, to make mental health better. Translation, integration and embedding research into the understanding of psychiatric disorder is critical in driving change for the future. Major systems of research such as the US National Institute of Mental Health contribute to such research/change processes, the more so when linked to service delivery programs.

The rapidity of scientific development in this field, both basic science research, and social and other sciences, leads to a critically evolving challenge. How can we utilise the future developments of these fields, of society, of science, of technology, to address the rapidly advancing 'rolling front end' of problems and need, as suggested by the World Health Organization's Norman Sartorius in 1994. Future focus is critical for effective change.

Social, environmental and cultural processes

The evolution of social processes, as well as environmental and cultural themes, inevitably brings potential change to mental health and to the understanding and management of mental illnesses. War, dislocations, psychological damage through conflict, loss of social status, breakdown of social environments and support networks, along with stresses such as the global financial crisis, may all make people more vulnerable and in need of psychiatric care. Strong social cohesion and social capital may protect and enhance health and health care.

Negative change may result from social exclusion and all its associated wounds, as shown by the experience of Indigenous Australians, and also by indigenous people in many other countries. Progressive socially and politically driven changes, including recognition of culture, have provided positive frameworks, but the ways forward (Swan and Raphael 1995) constitute a long journey. In Australia's case, special initiatives such as 'Closing the Gap' are making improvements, and recognition, respect, the Apology, education, and valuing this oldest surviving culture will all help to build positive social and emotional wellbeing, and promote culturally appropriate treatments for those with mental illnesses.

New displaced populations such as refugees (the 'boat people') also highlight needs for change for better mental health. Adverse social determinants, societal discrimination, and the politics of power can lead to negative change processes, or challenge change to contribute to positive mental health outcomes.

Stigma and discrimination have been a focus for strategies for change, with many agencies promoting programs to counter them. The UK's well funded, multifaceted program for mental health, 'Time to Change', has recently been evaluated, highlighting the importance of these issues as obstacles for mental health programs. Though change for the better was achieved, there are still many ongoing issues. Like all change intentions, there are multifaceted outcomes (Sartorius 2013).

Social and cultural processes can also define what illness is and what it is acceptable to do about it. This is particularly the case for psychiatry problems because of the overlap and interfaces with life, highlighted earlier in this chapter. The influence of social and cultural processes was discussed by psychiatric and anthropological colleagues (Hansen et al. 2013) exploring from social determinants, social science and population health points of view whether there were changes in environmental factors causing an actual increase in mental health problems; whether diagnostic criteria were applied differently; or whether diagnostic criteria could have been written in a way that could include people who did not have pathology—just the human spectrum.

Hansen and colleagues from the New York University Langone Health Center intend to set up a new independent research and review process to focus on such perspectives on mental health.

Technological advances, knowledge expansion and communication

The ability to spread knowledge through the internet, Google, the e-revolution, and the breadth of media coverage has been of value across many domains relevant to health and mental health. There is now constant exposure, in Australia at least, to information about mental illnesses and the range of associated problems. Technological advances have also provided platforms for assessing and treating these disorders (Looi and Raphael 2007).

Furthermore, technological changes in and of themselves have stimulated, threatened and universally engaged the human population across all age groups. The change processes are massive in terms of access, connectivity and instantaneity of information. These are all changing mental health in new ways, for instance with 'i' disorders (Rosen 2012), Facebook support and information to deal with emergency threats (Taylor et al. 2012), trauma help lines, and treatments facilitated by technologies of the internet. Some exposures are said to create problems, for instance children's repeated exposure to very traumatic experiences on television replays, or addiction to violent computer games.

Technological advances mean that social and physical opportunities and environments will continue to change rapidly, perhaps in unanticipated ways, and technologies can now influence the nature and functioning of brain and mind. The two-way neurology–engineering models, and real world brain–technology interfaces are examples for the future, as are brain–computer interfaces.

These changes continue to escalate, alongside many other questions of demand and response. Instantaneity will challenge human adaptation, and mental health and wellbeing—for better and for worse, but inevitably for the future.

The voices of the people

'The people' are many. They are those most severely affected and their families—the consumers and the carers. Their voices grow progressively stronger and they are being heard. In addition, studies examining the 'burden of disease' show the importance of psychiatric problems, with depression alone being a major component. This has been a driver that has influenced governments, funding bodies and organisations nationally. Ongoing studies in Australia, both those examining the prevalence and impairments associated with psychiatric illnesses, and reported studies of the broader social and economic 'burden', bring a strong rationale for the need to better address these problems.

Voices that are the most potent, the voices that have driven change, are those of people themselves. The power and expertise of the consumer movement in mental health in Australia has been supported by the Department of Health's *Mental health statement of rights and responsibilities* (1991), which has developed over time. Voices of advocates and supporting organisations arguing for representation, respect and formally having a say, as well as presenting stories of cost, burden, and human experience, have all been potent for change. They have rightly demanded recognition of the need for effective safe services, access, quality care, and support systems for carers. Non-government agencies, for instance SANE Australia (a leading national mental health non-government organisation) and the Consumer Advisory Group of the Australian state of New South Wales and such bodies in other states and territories have added their contributions. These voices now have formal and required representation at all levels of service, government, and community, with mottos such as 'Nothing about us without us'. Other consumer movements monitoring the nature and bases of care systems are also strong, influential and easily identifiable.

All these voices, those of the people, professionals, the public, the scientists and the wider community, have driven and are ongoing drivers of change.

Conclusions

Many changes have happened to improve the treatment and care of people with mental illnesses across the human lifespan and, as described above, there have been many drivers of such changes—most powerfully the voices of the many communities involved. Change is continuous, evolving, and developing with a growing world of people who will face differing future challenges: climate change, technological advances and inventions that will transform our lives, and perhaps even life on Mars (Kaku 2011).

There is more change to come. The true challenges for mental health are to resist the seductions of conservatism that hold us to familiar ideologies, and to tune to opportunities for change—change that involves risk, hopes to prevent illness, to build with courage and strength, to listen and learn from the multiple expertises within and outside this specialised field, for the future.

Many changes have occurred for mental health, mental illnesses and psychiatry—but many more are needed. These include the capacity to know and manage issues of change such as:

- Are mental health problems getting worse—more prevalent, more severe? Have they changed; if so, how and why?
- Why is it so difficult to change to prevention, early intervention and treatment with cure for mental illnesses?
- Why is mental health still so separated from health and identified by the challenges of 'serious mental illness'?
- Why are there no answers to questions about why so many children and young people have mental illness, and what changes will make things better?
- And why are we not able to ride the waves of change affecting the human condition, the spectrum of health and mental health problems, for more positive futures for our children?

References

Australian Department of Health (1991) *Mental health: statement of rights and responsibilities* (see www.health.gov.au/internet/main/publishing.nsf/Content/1A5FE569B1D0E391CA257BF0001A9342/$File/rights.pdf).

Engel, GL (1961) Is grief a disease?: a challenge for medical research. *Psychosomatic Medicine* 23 (January): 18–22.

Freud, S (1917) *Mourning and melancholia. The Standard Edition of the Complete Psychological Works of Sigmund Freud*, vol. XIV (1914–1916): *On the history of the psycho-analytic movement, Papers on metapsychology and other works*, 237–258s.

Hansen, HB, Donaldson, Z, Link, BG, Bearman, PS, Hopper, K, Bates, LM, Cheslak-Postava, K, Harper, K, Holmes, SM, Lovasi, G, Springer, KW and Teitler, JO (2013) Independent review of social and population variation in mental health could improve diagnosis in DSM revisions. *Health Affairs* 32 (May): 984–93.

Hortwitz, AV and Wakefield, JC (2007) *The loss of sadness*. Oxford University Press, New York.

Kaku, M (2011) *Physics of the future: the interventions that will transform our lives*. Penguin Books, London.

Licinio, J (2013) Translational psychiatry: leading the transition from the cesspool of devastation to a place where the grass is really greener. *Translational Psychiatry* 1: e1; doi:10.1038/tp.2011.3 2158–3188.

Lindemann, E (1944) The symptomatology and management of acute grief. *American Journal of Psychiatry* 101: 141–8.

Looi, J and Raphael, B (2007) Reflection on therapy in the era of the internet. *Australasian Psychiatry* 15(4) August: 334–7.

McGorry, P (2010) *Early psychosis guidelines writing group, Australian clinical guidelines for early psychosis*, 2nd ed. Orygen Youth Health, Melbourne.

McGorry, P (2011) *Early psychosis feasibility study report.* Prepared by Orygen Youth Health Research Centre.

Rosen, L (2012) *iDisorder: the psychology of technology.* Palgrave McMillan.

Sanders, M (2013) *Triple P-Positive Parenting Program: review of evidence.* Parenting and Family Support Centre. University of Queensland, Brisbane, March.

Sartorius, N (1994). 'The Rolling Front End'. Talk presented at Psychiatry Meeting, Indianapolis.

Sartorius, N (2013) Time to change. *British Journal of Psychiatry* 202: S108–09.

Swan, P and Raphael, B (1995) *'Ways Forward': national consultancy report on Aboriginal and Torres Strait Islander Mental Health, Parts l and ll.* Commonwealth of Australia, Canberra.

Taylor, M, Wells, G, Howell, G and Raphael B. (2012) The role of social media as psychological first aid as a support to community resilience building: a Facebook case study from 'Cyclone Yasi Update'. *Australian Journal of Emergency Management* 27(1): 20-6.

13. Education Reform: Learning from past experience and overseas successes

Robyn M Gillies

There is no doubt that the first decade of the twenty-first century has been characterised by an exponential increase in demands for knowledge—techno-scientific, medical, social, educational, environmental, and so on—with the clear intention of transforming how we live as individuals and as a society, and of sustaining this transformation. Globalisation has increased the mobility of people, resources, and ideas. This has had an enormous impact on education and the role it must play in fostering the development of creative and informed citizens who are able to participate fully in a dynamic and changing world (Department of Education, Employment and Workplace Relations 2011, Sahlberg 2011). As a consequence, education is no longer seen as producing skilled labour to meet the demands of an industrial market-driven economy characterised by centrally planned and imposed policies and practices to meet prescribed system performance targets. Rather it is seen as the *engine* through which educational change can occur. We expect that schools will produce students who can bring significant improvements to the knowledge and skills needed for national economic competitiveness and increasing ecological sustainability (Hargreaves 2012).

In an attempt to ensure that these expectations are met, various Australian governments have enunciated policies which acknowledge that high quality schooling is central to achieving this vision. The *Adelaide Declaration of the National Goals of Schooling* (1999),[1] for example, acknowledged that 'Australia's future depends upon each citizen having the necessary knowledge, understanding, skills and values for a productive and rewarding life in an educated, just and open society'. It provided broad directions to help schools and education authorities achieve these goals for students. The *Melbourne Declaration of Educational Goals for Young Australians* (2008)[2] built on the *Adelaide Declaration* by recognising that globalisation and technological change place greater demands on education and skill development. People with university or vocational education qualifications have better prospects for employment than young people who leave school before they have completed high school.

---

1   Adelaide Declaration of the National Goals of Schooling (1999) www.mceetya.edu.au/mceecdya/nationalgoals/index.htm, retrieved 7 February 2013.
2   Melbourne Declaration of Educational Goals for Young Australians (2008) deewr.gov.au/melbourne-declaration-educational-goals-young-people, retrieved 17 January 2013.

These declarations with their associated goals recognise that Australia's future depends on all young people having the opportunity to receive a quality education to be able to participate in an increasingly globalised and complex world. National and state governments have invested billions of dollars in the last decade to:

- ensure that all young people have the right to 12 years of education
- provide a national curriculum that will enable students to acquire the knowledge, skills, and competencies needed to participate in the social, cultural, and economic development of the nation
- fund both pre-service and in-service teacher education programs to expose teachers to the latest innovations and applications in teaching, that can be used to support student educational needs and meet society's expectations.

With this investment, issues are raised about whether our schools are equipped to prepare students to meet the needs and challenges of the twenty-first century. Are we getting value for the investments we have made? There is enormous pressure on education authorities, schools, and teachers to be accountable for the education students receive. Recent debates in the media about the variability in the academic standards set by universities for admission into pre-service teacher education programs and the quality of the training received contribute to the anxiety teachers feel and the concerns the public have about teachers' competence to deliver quality education programs that reflect community expectations.

In this chapter, I discuss the types of pressures that exist, such as those that arise from national and international assessments of student achievements, enabling performances to be compared across schools and different educational jurisdictions; teacher responses to these assessment pressures, including the focus on teaching content that is likely to be tested, and the effect this has on narrowing students' curriculum experiences; teacher responses to the new national curriculum and associated changes in pedagogical innovations and practices that are required, and the effects that these changes and expectations are having on how educators think about change, and respond to it.

National and international assessment programs

In the last decade there has been an unprecedented rise in standardised assessment in schools. For example, all students in years 3, 5, 7 and 9 participate in the National Assessment Program in Literacy and Numeracy to determine whether they are meeting key performance outcomes. Results released publicly allow comparisons across schools and educational jurisdictions. While the original intention was to address the academic gap emerging between students and the inequities evident in divergent outcomes between schools, one unfortunate consequence has been that these data now act as league tables with potential to affect the reputation of schools that do not perform as well as expected and, possibly, their ability to attract and retain teachers and students. This alone creates enormous pressure on teachers to ensure that students meet national minimum standards and preferably perform at or above national standards, irrespective of socio-economic circumstances and support.

How then do teachers respond to these pressures? A recent survey of 8353 teachers and principals, commissioned by the Whitlam Institute and conducted by Dulfer and colleagues (2012), found that 73 per cent of teachers taught to the test (i.e. they cover content that is likely to be tested, rather than allowing the test to uncover gaps in student learning), with 46 per cent holding weekly practice tests five months before testing with the National Assessment Program in Literacy and Numeracy. This focus on testing appeared to account for 69 per cent of teachers reporting that they spend less time on teaching subjects that were not tested. Apart from the narrowing of the curriculum that often results from this type of testing (Smeed 2010), testing itself appears to adversely affect a significant number of students. Ninety per cent of teachers in the study by Dulfer and colleagues reported that the tests stressed some students. Sixty-two per cent of teachers had students who were physically distressed as a consequence.

Other assessments in the national assessment program include the Trends in International Mathematics and Science Study,[3] an international assessment of mathematics and science in years 4 and 8. This assessment is organised around a content dimension, that is, the subject matter to be taught, and a cognitive dimension (the thinking processes expected of students as they engage in the required content). While Australia's performance levels are above the scale centre point of 500 for students in years 4 and 8, they are markedly lower than student scores in Singapore, the Republic of Korea, Finland, Chinese Taipei and Japan and, in some cases, markedly lower than those in the Russian Federation, Czech Republic and Slovak Republic.

The Program for International Student Assessment is also included in the National Assessment Program. The Program for International Student Assessment aims to evaluate education systems worldwide every three years by assessing 15-year-old student competence in reading literacy, mathematical literacy, and scientific literacy. The purpose is to determine how well students are prepared to meet the challenges of the future, assess if they can analyse, reason

---

3   timssandpirls.bc.edu/index.html, retrieved 7 July 2014.

and communicate their ideas effectively, and identify if there are some ways of organising schools and school learning that are more effective than others. While Australian students performed above the Organisation for Economic Co-operation and Development average, their scores in reading, mathematics, and scientific literacy were significantly lower than such countries as China (data based on Shanghai), Finland, Hong Kong, Singapore, Japan and Korea. Moreover, Australia's position in these rankings has remained virtually static for the last decade, even though we now know more about the factors that contribute to the success these countries consistently demonstrate.

Finally, the results for the Progress in International Reading Literacy Study, an international assessment of reading comprehension at year 4 that is conducted every five years, were released recently. Australia was ranked 27th out of 49 participating countries. While Australia did perform significantly higher (527) than the centre point of 500 on the scale, it ranked significantly lower than 21 other countries including Portugal (541), Hungary (539) and the Slovak Republic (535), raising concerns that our students were not performing as well as expected in the international rankings.

In summary, the results of the various assessments included in the National Assessment Program show that most Australian students are reaching expected benchmarks, or performing better than many other countries in the international mathematics and science study,[4] the program for international student assessment, and the literacy study. However, concern exists that, even though there has been heavy government investment in education, Australian students are still not able to compete with Finland or a number of our Asian neighbours—average student performances on these international assessments have not changed for over a decade. The increased accountability that principals and teachers often feel as a consequence of these programs of assessment has resulted in some schools changing the curriculum to reflect the demands and requirements of these testing regimes (Smeed 2010). This action by itself has led some to question what we teach and how we teach and the effect teachers are having on student learning.

Reforming the curriculum: teacher reactions

The Australian Curriculum is currently being developed and phased in by the Australian Curriculum, Assessment and Reporting Authority, which is responsible for developing the different subjects from the Foundation Year to Year 12. The Australian Curriculum is guided by two key documents:

---

4   The Trends in International Mathematics and Science Study.

the Melbourne Declaration on Educational Goals for Young Australians and the Shape of the Australian Curriculum. It includes a range of subjects such as English, arts, health and physical education, mathematics, science, history and geography.[5]

While every effort has been made by the authority to liaise closely with the states about implementation of the different phases of the Australian Curriculum, it appears that many teachers are still scrambling to understand the content and the processes involved in teaching the various subjects. The authority is also responsible for collecting, managing, analysing, evaluating and reporting statistical and related information about educational outcomes, including national measures for reporting the performance of Australian schooling. It is therefore easy to understand the concerns of many teachers that priority is attached to testing and measuring student performances, often at the expense of building caring teacher–student relationships, work that teachers have traditionally seen as part of their role in school (Mausethagen 2013). It is no wonder many feel increasingly disempowered and professionally marginalised (Ball 2008, Priestley et al. 2012).

Although it is still too early to evaluate the impact that the new national curriculum is having on teachers, it is possible to look at how teachers have reacted in the past to curriculum reforms that have been imposed on schools. Day and colleagues studied the commitment of 20 teachers to change in Australia and England. They found that as governments have intervened in the governance and curriculum of schools, teachers' work became 'increasingly performance orientated and audit driven, more directly accountable to a range of stakeholders, and enlarged and intensified' (Day et al. 2005, 564–5). Clandinin and colleagues (2009, 141) recognised that teachers live and work in 'school landscapes' that are constantly changing. Tensions are created as teachers struggle with the shifting professional knowledge landscapes that are at variance with the narratives they live by or the knowledge and practices they have as teachers. Moreno (2007) argues that in many cases these changes and their intensification have brought about a crisis in professional identity.

Others have reported similar experiences of teachers struggling to adjust to reform agendas that impose beliefs that challenge their professional identities. Kelchtermans (2005), for example, reviewed the professional biographies of a number of experienced primary teachers in Belgium. This revealed that they often felt powerless, threatened and vulnerable when they were not in control of the processes and tasks they felt professionally responsible for as teachers.

---

5   www.acara.edu.au/default.asp.

Change!

Teacher strategies for managing imposed change

Teachers are very adroit at responding both overtly and covertly to imposed change. In a large-scale survey of public school teacher perceptions of imposed curriculum reform and how they coped, McCormick et al. (2005) found that many often resorted to 'palliative' coping strategies that involved cutting back and slowing down or engaging in activities that were not work-related, rather than using strategies for confronting the problem. These findings led the authors to conclude that palliative coping strategies are less likely to be effective and more likely to lead to teachers experiencing higher levels of stress in the long term. Furthermore, important problems may not be solved, and this is likely to impede the attainment of the educational authority's curriculum reform goals. These findings led the authors to argue that curriculum reform cannot be carried out in a vacuum. Teacher perceptions of the educational system within which they work are likely to influence their interpretations of the reform and its implementation.

Troman (2008) investigated the identities and commitment to teaching of primary teachers in schools where there was a focus on how the school could maximise student test scores on high-stakes tests. Although the six schools in this study were from both high and low socio-economic areas, the author reported that they all engaged in various strategies to compensate for the high-stakes testing that existed in their schools. The schools in high socio-economic areas introduced curriculum enrichment experiences for their students while the schools in low socio-economic areas adopted nurturing programs to compensate for perceived academic and social deprivation of students. These actions, Troman argued, demonstrated teachers' attempts to mediate performative school cultures through their involvement in nurturing and creative projects. The actions involved increased personal effort and commitment in attempting to defend their professional values and their own identities, while adjusting to their school's commitment to high-stakes testing.

There is no doubt that teachers are experiencing enormous stress associated with the way schools change with the different policy demands, albeit with policy associated with high-stakes testing regimes and curriculum reform or professional identities. However, despite working in such contexts, Groundwater-Smith and colleagues (2001) and Hargreaves (2005) found that significant numbers of teachers remain committed to their profession, dedicated to their students, and willing to embrace innovative and cooperative teaching practices. Moreover, many recognise and manage various competing agendas by being more strategic and political in defending their professional identities while simultaneously adjusting to their public commitments in performative school cultures (Troman 2005). Kelchtermans (2005) also reported that teachers hold strong beliefs about what education means, and that reform agendas which impose different normative beliefs may not only trigger intense emotions but also elicit micro-political responses of resistance or proactive attempts to influence particular situations.

Change that works

The tension teachers feel from different reform agendas and change is very real. Yet it is possible, Levin (2007) argues, to have large-scale education reform that does make a difference for students, does generate public support, and does engage teachers and other education staff in a positive way. This was achieved in Ontario by the provincial education authority when it crafted a strategy to improve elementary students' literacy and numeracy, reduce class sizes, and increase high school graduation rates. By partnering with key stakeholder groups (education authorities, school boards, and provincial organisations of teachers, principals and other partners), policies and strategies were put in place that emphasised professional capacity-building, strong leadership, judicious targeting of resources (i.e. extra funding and staff) and effective parent and community engagement initiatives. These changes occurred in a context that demonstrated respect for staff and their professional knowledge so that all public statements by the government were supportive of public education and teachers. Furthermore, induction procedures rather than tests were introduced for new teachers and professional practice-sharing was encouraged. The results obtained indicate that more students per year now achieve the provincial standard for literacy and numeracy, student skill levels have increased, high school graduation rates have risen, and attrition rates for teachers leaving the profession have decreased. Thousands of teachers are participating in professional development programs and more teachers are reporting satisfaction with their work. Levin notes that the success of these efforts has resulted in more positive public positions by different stakeholder groups, including school boards and teacher unions.

Other successful reform efforts have been conducted in Finland, Singapore, and Hong Kong where students consistently perform significantly above the international average on such assessments as the Program for International Student Assessment, and Trends in International Mathematics and Science Study. This leads many educators to ask what these countries are doing that is contributing to this success. Hargreaves and Shirley (2009, 84) provided some insights when they commented that Finland's mediocre performance experienced a turnaround when the government actively made the decision to design 'a creative, high-skill, high-wage knowledge economy in which people invent, apply, share and articulate knowledge at a level that surpasses all competitors'. The results, Sahlberg (2011) reports, are that Finland has been a consistent high performer on the Program for International Student Assessment and the Trends in International Mathematics and Science Study without adopting policies on standardised teaching and learning practices, student testing, test-based accountability, and competition (these policies have been adopted by countries such as Australia, the US, the UK, Canada, Japan and New Zealand).

While Sahlberg (2011) is careful not to criticise countries that adopt these policies, he does emphasise that Finland has been successful with alternative policies revamping their educational system, so the emphasis is on investing in teachers and principals as professionals, encouraging teachers and students to try new ideas, and promoting teaching renewal while respecting schools' pedagogical legacies. Sahlberg argues that by having confidence in their teachers and schools, creativity and innovation are fostered as teachers design and pursue high quality learning and shared goals.

Singapore is another country that is a consistent high performer on the Program for International Student Assessment and the Trends in International Mathematics and Science Study. Like Finland, the government set about creating a national vision of what needed to happen if the country was to remain competitive and exceptional in the global economy. Education is seen as key to achieving this, and the government has invested heavily in it (Hargreaves 2012). It also built professional partnerships with teacher groups and actively encouraged public collaboration as a way of building a national commitment and forging a common purpose to achieving this vision. In this sense, the education system contributes to nation building and collective identity, attracting high calibre individuals to the teaching profession. Teachers are paid on a level similar to other professionals such as engineers to attract them to teaching. All teachers receive up to 100 hours of professional training each year which is paid for by the Ministry of Education. In contrast, most Australian states provide 25–30 hours.

In Singapore, there is a system-wide emphasis on developing a teacher-led culture of professional excellence which aims to promote ongoing professional learning. This is based on the belief that learning is lifelong when the learner exercises initiative, solves problems, innovates, and contributes to the greater good. Teachers are encouraged to share and collaborate with colleagues, both within and across schools, as a way of enhancing their professional knowledge and instructional practices. Teachers also have opportunities to follow different career paths with flexibility of movement between them and continuous monitoring and mentoring to ensure they are progressing satisfactorily in their career aspirations. Furthermore, students are very much seen as partners in change and in leadership, and are encouraged to be involved through mentoring and coaching programs that provide them with opportunities to lead and initiate change. Their involvement is seen as critical to encouraging them to accept responsibility as young citizens and invest in the success of the educational system of which they are part.

Hong Kong, like Singapore, is another high-performer on the Program for International Student Assessment and the Trends in International Mathematics and Science Study, possibly because it has embraced many of the educational practices of Finland and Singapore. It recognises that its market economy and progress rest on the talents of its people. Education is seen as an important government priority—23 per cent of its total budget is devoted to education. Curriculum reform has been at the forefront of educational change and innovation with an emphasis on student-centred learning, the development of higher level thinking skills and people skills, and a more flexible curriculum aimed at developing the whole child. In recent years, the government has invested heavily in small class teaching and teacher professional development as ways to promote quality teaching and learning in the schools and to build professional coalitions with schools in other bureaus of education in the region.[6]

Factors mediating success

Given the achievements of Ontario, Finland, Singapore and Hong Kong on international student assessments, what factors do they have in common that might contribute to this success? All governments have been able to articulate a clear national or provincial vision for education that is inspiring and inclusive of all its citizens. Hargreaves (2012, 12) argues that 'it is inspiring visions rather than imposed system targets that are more likely to move a whole system forward successfully and sustainably'.

Second, all governments have invested heavily in education to ensure that schools are able to achieve the vision. Money has been spent on curriculum reform, teacher professional development and training, and resources, including both personnel and material.

Third, these communities have been encouraged to help define and shape the education agenda through school boards, councils, and parent activities. Hargreaves (2012, 12) maintains that 'keeping the public informed of and being engaged in the development and change within the education system reduces public anxiety and helps parents and others to align their focus and to support schools'.

---

6   Schleicher, A (2012) Hong Kong's success in PISA: one system, many actors, oecdeducationtoday.blogspot. com.au/2012/05/hong-kongs-success-in-and-pisa, retrieved 13 January 2013.

Fourth, teachers are encouraged to reflect on their practices, to critique and challenge current ideas with the focus on improving how they teach. To achieve this, these governments have all invested heavily in professional development and learning initiatives to ensure teachers have the latest evidence-based research and practices.

Finally, students have been encouraged to be partners in the change process through different leadership initiatives such as tutoring less able students, mentoring students from disadvantaged backgrounds, participating in school-based decision-making, and suggesting changes to promote better educational outcomes for all. In short, students are seen as having the ability and capacity to contribute to how education is delivered in their schools.

Many of the factors that are evident in high-performing nations are also identified by John Hattie (2011) in his book *Visible learning for teachers*, where he identifies the attributes of schooling that truly affect student learning. Based on more than 800 meta-analyses of research articles, Hattie argues that the quality of teaching makes the difference. Teachers are the major source of controllable variance in the school system. Using this information, Hattie outlines eight ways of thinking that underpin teachers' actions and decisions in a school. These are:

1. seeking feedback on what they need to change, enhance or continue to do as they work with students

2. believing that they can influence student success in school

3. understanding that students learn in multiple ways

4. talking with students to help them crystallise their ideas

5. recognising that assessment of student progress provides valuable feedback to teachers

6. embracing diversity and recognising the challenge this poses

7. developing positive relationships with students and staff

8. teaching parents the language of learning.

It is not hard to see that teachers who do this would also be very confident and assured as teachers, believing they can have a positive effect on students, recognising that students construct learning in many ways, and taking responsibility to help students learn. Teaching, Moreno (2007) argues, is about being close to students and caring about their lives, and about building learning communities capable of responding to the needs of students as citizens who have a right to learn.

Educators and future change

Hargreaves (2012) argues there has been a paradigm shift in the mindset of educational leaders on how they push educational frontiers to achieve change and a more sustainable future. Many now recognise that if change is to be achieved, it requires high quality teachers, positive and powerful professional associations, and lively learning communities; the last two being contexts in which teachers practise their professional craft. In fact, Hargreaves (2012, 13) maintains that 'it is teachers' sense of professionalism that ultimately drives the impetus for change'.

These comments affirm Hattie's (2011) findings about the key role of teachers in effecting and managing change. While some teachers may feel stressed from different reform agendas and respond reactively to change, many others respond proactively by intervening to moderate attitudes towards testing in performative cultures when they believe these cultures badly affect student learning. Given the shifting educational landscapes of recent years, many teachers now recognise the need to develop instructional changes and ways of working that will improve student achievement, share ideas and collaborate with colleagues, and be reflective practitioners who engage in ongoing professional learning. There is no doubt that teachers who respond positively to the challenges of change are more likely to be proactive and innovative, creating new and novel approaches to their work, including building new coalitions with colleagues, parents and the wider community to help define and shape the education agenda.

References

Ball, S (2008) *The education debate*. Policy Press, Bristol.

Clandinin, J, Downey, C and Huber, J (2009) Attending to changing landscapes: shaping the interwoven identities of teachers and teacher educators. *Asia-Pacific Journal of Teacher Education* 37: 141–54.

Day, C, Elliot, B and Kingston, A (2005) Reform, standards and teacher identity: challenges of sustaining commitment. *Teaching and Teacher Education* 21: 563–77.

Department of Education, Employment and Workplace Relations (2011) *Review of funding for schooling: final report*. Australian Government, Canberra.

Dulfer, N, Polesel, J and Rice, S (2012) *The experience of education: the impacts of high stakes testing on school students and their families: an educator's perspective*. Whitlam Institute, University of Western Sydney.

Groundwater-Smith, S, Brennan, M, McFadden, M and Mitchell, J (2001) *Secondary schooling in a changing world*. Harcourt, Sydney.

Hargreaves, A (2005) Educational change takes ages: life, career and generational factors in teachers' emotional responses to educational change. *Teaching and Teacher Education* 21: 967–83.

Hargreaves, A (2012) Singapore: the fourth way in action? *Educational Research Policy and Practice* 11: 7–17.

Hargreaves, A and Shirley, D (2009) *The fourth way: the inspiring future of educational change*. Corwin, Thousand Oaks, California.

Hattie, J (2011) *Visible learning for teachers: maximizing the impact of learning*. Routledge, Hoboken.

Kelchtermans, G (2005) Teachers' emotions in educational reforms: self-understanding, vulnerable commitment and micropolitical literacy. *Teaching and Teacher Education* 21: 995–1006.

Levin, B (2007) Sustainable, large-scale education renewal. *Journal of Educational Change* 8: 323–36.

Mausethagen, S (2013) A research review of the impact of accountability policies on teachers' workplace relations. *Educational Research Review* 9: 16–33.

McCormick, J, Ayres, P and Beechley, B (2005) Teaching self-efficacy, stress and coping in a major curriculum reform. *Journal of Educational Administration* 44: 53–70.

Moreno, J (2007) Do the initial and continuous teachers' professional development sufficiently prepare teachers to understand and cope with the complexities of today and tomorrow's education? *Journal of Educational Change* 8: 169–73.

Priestley, M, Edwards, R and Priestley, A (2012) Teacher agency in curriculum making: agents for change and spaces for manoeuvre. *Curriculum Inquiry* 42: 191–214.

Sahlberg, S (2011) The fourth way of Finland. *Journal of Educational Change* 12: 173–85.

Smeed, J (2010) Accountability through high-stakes testing and curriculum change. *Leading and Managing* 16: 1–15.

Troman, G (2008) Primary teacher identity, commitment and career in performative school cultures. *British Educational Research Journal* 34: 619–33.

14. Ten Lessons from Changing Policing Organisations

Christine Nixon

In this chapter I will share my learnings from the past 40 years working with change in the New South Wales Police Service, Victoria Police and the Victorian Bushfire Reconstruction and Recovery Authority. In 2011 Melbourne University Press published my memoir *Fair cop*, with Jo Chandler. Writing this book allowed me time to contemplate my life and perhaps sharpen my reflections on a range of issues and experiences.

All of us have personal experience of change, or have driven change in our lives, organisations, departments or businesses. These are my lessons.

1. The environment for change is critical

I often start my leadership workshops with a clarification about the way we should treat each other during our time working together. Setting the ground rules or guiding principles helps those involved to focus and hopefully begins to create an environment of trust.

Hugh Mackay (2011), in *What makes us tick*, gives great guidance on the way Australians are driven. Mackay suggests there are ten desires that drive us— desires such as to be taken seriously, to belong, for control, for something to happen, for love, for our place, for something to believe in, to connect and to be useful. Looking at employees through these 10 desires allows a more inclusive view and a recognition and respect for their contributions. If leaders have a framework of seeing all employees as difficult and not interested in change then that sometimes means we misjudge our colleagues and employees and do not give them the opportunity to contribute.

Becoming the 19th Chief Commissioner of Victoria Police in April 2001 gave me the opportunity to draw on all my experience gained in the previous 30 years. I also knew that the most important thing to do was to draw on the long experience of the organisation, on its history, its failures and successes, and the willingness of many people to think about the way the future could be better. I knew there were many people in the organisation who believed we could be much better than we were.

2. Why the reasons for change are important

There are many reasons for organisations to consider change: a new appointment like my own, a major crisis, a push for renewal, budget cutbacks, new research findings, new challenges, change of direction or simply that there are better ways that things could be done.

One of the things to remember is that people need a good reason to get involved in change. They might not like the reason, but by at least articulating it, or better still, by them articulating the need, they will have a base to understand what they might be facing and more importantly why.

Over my time in policing, a number of issues caused change: corruption, budgetary constraints, human resource issues, introduction of new technology, a series of underworld murders, terrorism issues, rising crime rates and a recognition that members of the organisation needed to be better managed and led.

The 2009 Victorian bushfires massively affected many people's lives. They lost loved ones, their homes, businesses, their communities. Many took years to come to terms with their losses, many were unwilling to change, but in this case they had no options available to them to avoid radical changes to their lives.

I remember once trying to convince a group of senior police in New South Wales to consider a new way of working with communities. At the end of the presentation one very senior police officer said that according to what I had just presented, all of his career had been a waste of time. I told him that is not what I said, but his response was, 'That's what I heard'. A lesson learned from this short conversation was to be careful about treading on the past to get to the future. A recognition that we are all of our own time helps both the initiator of change and those involved to understand each other's perspectives.

3. Get to know the people in the organisation and your stakeholders—they must be involved

When you take up a new appointment or move to a new organisation, you need to take time to get to know the people you are working with. When I joined Victoria Police I made arrangements to visit as many members as I could in the first six months. I wanted to meet them for them to get to know me and what I stood for, and for me to understand from them what they saw as the most important issues facing the organisation. By the conclusion I had met over 6,000 members in their workplaces. We met in small one-person police stations, in groups of 300 or 400 people in the crime and traffic departments or in large police stations such as Frankston. More than 500 separate issues were raised during these discussions. I am sure my colleagues and I all wondered how we would meet the expectations of so many people within the organisation. I will say more later about how this task was to be accomplished.

I also needed to meet all of the senior team. They are a powerful group and can make or break a change program. We talked about the challenges facing us, about our organisation's history, what we did well and what we did poorly, the strengths and capacity we should build on, and what they would have done if they had been appointed to the top job. I met with over 40 of the senior team in one-on-one interviews. I learned a lot about the history of the organisation, about many of the team's experiences, goals and aspirations and perhaps on some occasions where bodies were buried, metaphorically speaking.

At the time we also determined that all of us would go out into the workplace, spend time in offices, police stations, police cars and with the specialists and professional support staff. Listen to them, give them a chance to tell us what we needed to do to make Victoria Police the best it could be.

I and my colleagues also accepted many invitations from groups all over Victoria to speak at breakfast, luncheon and tea, so we could hear what the community had to say about Victoria Police and what they wanted from us. We met with many members of local government, religious organisations, disparate service organisations and members of the business community.

All of these discussions and many more went to guiding our directions for the future and to providing Victoria with better policing.

Professor Mark Moore from Harvard University's Kennedy School of Government suggests we need to create public value in the public sector. To do this you need legitimacy or authority from the authorising environment to bring about a change, a clear problem to be solved or a goal to be achieved, a demonstrated capacity and skills from within the organisation or outside it, to be able to achieve the goals. By this stage in the change process I knew we had clear goals to reduce crime, make people safer, reduce the road toll and fix the problems identified by the members. We had legitimacy from the government and the community. Now we had to find the capacity from within and without to achieve our goals.

4. Look for leverage

An opportunity arose when I learned that I would be required to report the previous year's crime statistics to the community and government. Crime rates had been climbing for some years and figures looked pretty appalling. I had found leverage to get the organisation to focus on the issue of crime. I called upon some of my colleagues to take responsibility for a particular issue of concern. They joined me at a press conference the following day when I announced to the media and community that these four senior police officers would be taking responsibility on behalf of Victoria Police for reducing crime and working out how to improve our response. The categories chosen were stolen motor vehicles, breaking into premises, robberies, and family violence.

We amalgamated the other 500 issues raised by the members into 80 key projects; leaders for each were chosen, and people from all the different parts of the organisation volunteered or were assigned to work on them and come back with a viable way forward within three months.

Other opportunities came along that helped or required us to focus: counterterrorism, which occurred as a result of the terrible attacks of 9/11 in the United States; criminal investigation, because of the growing death toll in underworld murders; corruption prevention, resulting from uncovering problems within the drug squad.

5. Understand the signals and culture

Proponents of strategic planning talk about a model sometimes called the 'iceberg model of change'. It suggests that when we are thinking about organisational change, we mostly pay attention to the top 10 per cent of the iceberg—the strategies and structures and systems. The proponents argue that we pay less attention to the remaining 90 per cent. The view held by many is that success or failure depends on whether or not you pay attention to the 90 per cent that is unseen. This portion can be the home of real power structures, the history of successes and failures, the 'this is the way we do things around here' approach, the beliefs and values, the fears and unwritten control mechanisms. It can also be the language and signals that those in the organisation take from what you are trying to do or what you are saying.

In the early stages of my time in Victoria Police I was asked by police members of the gay and lesbian community to march with them in the gay pride march to be held the following year. I accepted without hesitation, given that I knew members needed support, were doing a good job and that they invited me to participate. I did not quite understand the implications of this decision until some time after. I received over 800 emails from members of the organisation, in the main expressing their anger and regret that I had decided to march. Various media outlets were either enraged or baffled. I did march in what turned out to be a relatively small community event which received a significant amount of publicity. A powerful signal was sent that I would support members of Victoria Police no matter their race or sexual preference as long as they were doing a good job. To the community it came to mean that I was my own person and I was a strong supporter of diversity.

The Labor government had committed to an additional 1600 police officers in early 2001. A great advertising campaign was put in place that inspired people from a range of different backgrounds to join Victoria Police. It also became an inspiration to many within Victoria Police. It signalled a new force for a new century and signalled that women and people of minority backgrounds were very capable of carrying out the diverse roles available in policing. It destroyed the myth of a stereotypical police officer. We also commenced plans for a significant number of police stations to be built or revamped. By the time I left Victoria Police, more than 200 police stations had been rebuilt or built. This $300 million program conducted over 10 years made an enormous difference to the environment in which police officers worked and in which the community visits, willingly or not.

6. Set goals and accountabilities

Setting out clear directions, breaking the work into manageable chunks, dealing with simple issues first, can make the change process more efficient. I remember a piece of research done in the 1990s by Telstra that suggested what people want when they go to work is for someone to know where the organisation is going, and to know what their role is, and for there to be good management to help them get the job done. Having people clearly understand the goals and accountabilities requires an enormous amount of communication. Today technology can assist in that process but nothing beats sharing the data, presentations and openness.

Clearly articulated goals such as, in our case, reducing crime and death and serious injury on the road, and holding people accountable for delivering against those goals is very important. Telling people what needed to be done but not micromanaging allows empowered people to try new ways of working.

The 80 task forces that were set problems to solve all reported back with ways to solve or mitigate issues. Some were adopted straight away, others became part of a five-year strategic plan. Of the four key crime areas that were identified, three saw significant reduction in crime rates and in the fourth, a much better response to family violence was implemented across Victoria and across a number of government departments. Crime dropped overall by nearly 30 per cent between 2001 and 2010.

We also introduced a process called Compstat, a model of accountability which had previously been used in New York City and other parts of the United States. Various statistical indicators were adopted to compare the performance of different divisions or departments against previous performance and against each other. This method of accountability took some time to settle in but once we finally agreed on what could be measured and why, it gave us an important tool to drive the reform process. Personal performance review, particularly by people at senior levels, became part of the regular processes of the organisation.

7. Understand the research, what works and what does not

As part of a continuous improvement focus we commissioned a significant amount of research on topics ranging from family violence to organised crime, sexual assault, traffic management, juvenile justice, organisational reform, financial management and a number of other areas. The results of this research and our participation in it meant we were up to date with best practice in policing around the world. At one point we had over 20 different research grants with universities throughout Australia and in some parts of the United States. We tried to ensure that our policy formulation was underpinned by the research, the experience of the members involved and the input from the community. For instance, in working on counterterrorism we formed a multi-faith advisory committee, a broader community advisory group and collaborated with academics involved in writing about terrorism issues to help us formulate the best way forward. When we became aware of the major psychological issues facing members, we trained over 600 civilians and police officers as peer support councillors. The evidence that this was the way forward came from a range of psychologists and from the experience of other police organisations.

8. Good management is critical

I remember asking my then boss in New South Wales, Inspector John Avery, what he thought good management was. He suggested I could go read books or I could think about the good managers that I had worked with, who I would walk over hot coals for. It was a pretty good answer and I remember at that point in my career I could think of two managers I had had who had made an enormous difference to my life.

I have since asked many groups both inside and outside policing the same question. You might be surprised that the number of good managers people remember is not as many as you might think. But Inspector Avery went on to say that I might think about the characteristics of these managers and I might follow their lead in the way that I managed people.

Managers can make an enormous difference in people's lives and bad managers can damage people; I have certainly seen my share of the latter. Although business and government organisations spend an enormous amount of time and money on teaching people how to manage, it is really not that complicated. Simply put, it is how you would like to be treated yourself.

In Victoria Police we developed a range of programs designed to improve managers' skill and leadership capacities. We moved people to various positions to expand their skills and on some occasions took people out of management positions when they were best suited for other, perhaps more technical, roles. We also provided personal mentors so that managers might be assisted in developing their capacities, to reflect on their own behaviour and how they might be affecting those they managed.

9. Resilience

Change is hard and will challenge us all. Once the process of change begins, you might be in for a rough ride. You just have to persevere and remain committed without wavering. I am often asked how I stay so resilient under the various pressures I have faced as a senior manager, involved in so many change projects over so many years. I have undertaken a range of courses and studies over the years and have developed a checklist that helps me when things get tough:

- Have a focus, a goal, something you believe in, and take pleasure and consolation from your achievements.
- Develop a capacity to reflect on your own behaviour and that of others—this will determine whether you are part of the problem or part of the solution.
- Have a network of people you can call on and ask their advice. Know that you do not have all the answers.
- Do not always been in a rush to find the answer. Leave the space open to let an answer evolve.

- Make the group do the work. I am often known for saying 'So what do you think?' I might know the answer but it is far better that people are offered the opportunity to contribute and perhaps come up with a better answer than you may ever have found.

- Ensure the goal you are trying to achieve is worthwhile and worth the risk.

- Live a balanced life and know that you have coped and will again.

- Have a sense of humour and try not to take yourself too seriously.

- Know when it is time to go—we can occasionally go too early, but we can often stay too long. We only have a finite amount of energy. Recognise it might be time to move on.

10. Overcoming fear and finding courage

Both organisations and individuals often limit themselves in what they might achieve. The limits can come from previous experiences, personal and organisational history, fear of failure or of ridicule. Leading change requires recognition of these limits and a belief in people's ability to overcome these barriers.

Challenging the status quo and forcing change carries varying degrees of risk for all involved. People may lose power and influence, may perceive loss of face, may lose confidence and feel their contribution is devalued.

It has been suggested to me that I would have had a much easier time in policing if I had just left things alone and gone with the flow. This was not my way nor do I believe that it is good leadership. Leadership is not about personal popularity, it is about good results.

Organisations and individuals today are in a continuous state of change. Leaders need to take up their responsibility to lead. Professor John Kotter recently suggested in a blog that 'Leadership is about vision, about people buying in, about empowerment and, most of all, about producing useful change'.[1]

For me, if I see the difference in people's lives when crime is reduced, lives are saved on the road, less violence occurs and when people feel happy and rewarded at work, then I am rewarded too.

---

1   blogs.hbr.org/2013/01/management-is-still-not-leadership/ accessed 28 May 2014.

References

Mackay, H (2011) *What makes us tick*. Hatchett, Australia.

Moore, MH (1995) *Creating public value: strategic management in government*. Harvard University Press, Cambridge MA.

Nixon, C with Chandler, J (2011) *Fair cop*. Victory Books, Melbourne.

15. Change Management in Materials Conservation

Ian D MacLeod

Within Australia there are more than 250 practicing conservators who are members of our professional society, the Australian Institute for the Conservation of Cultural Materials (AICCM). Conservators are employed by state and commonwealth archives, art galleries and museums, and 20 per cent of the members of the institute are engaged in private practice (AICCM 2013). For every type of material there is a specialist conservator who knows how to stabilise and preserve elements of our material culture that range from ephemeral art works to plastic furniture and toys to digital media. The world of the conservator is secured by a bastion of rules and regulations that were established in the last 100 years. This chapter draws on my experience during a 35-year museum career, especially in strengthening mutual understanding between practitioners in materials conservation and their senior managers and in meeting modern-day requirements of increased efficiency and public engagement.

Having served eight years as a practising bench conservator and research chemist, I became head of the conservation team at the Western Australian Museum 27 years ago and was able to begin the process of introducing change. The time had come to change perceptions of senior management regarding conservators and their roles in the museum. Initially my role was almost like that of a peacemaker who would share information between conservator and management camps so that trust began to be re-established. Tensions began to dissolve and operational trust came to fruition. In particular, management gave greater credence to reports made by conservators and acted on them. Having demonstrated a commitment to change management, it was perhaps not surprising that a restructure of the museum saw additional management roles added to my responsibilities. This led me to gain a wider view of the operations of the museum.

The year 1993 saw the largest change in the 120-year history of the museum. The Minister for Culture and the Arts made the decision to close the main museum building in Perth and bought a 3.5-hectare site 9 km from the city centre with an existing 9,000-square-metre tilt-slab building on it. There was also a 3,500-square-metre adjoining steel bonded warehouse and a two-storey, 1,200-square-metre administration complex. The greatest change in my working life occurred when I was appointed project manager for the relocation of 3.5 million objects and 60 staff. My task was also to convert the empty warehouse into a state-of-the-art collections research and storage facility and to achieve it in 18 months on an $11 million budget. The process completed my metamorphosis from a research officer studying corrosion of copper on shipwrecks to a museum director. Despite the increased administrative load, my job requires me to continue to conduct research into better conservation and preservation methods for museum collections. The outputs of this work are new and cost-effective methods of stabilising collections which have placed the museum at the front of collections management practice. It is on this basis that my reflections on change management in materials conservation are presented.

Changes in operating environments

The first program for conservators began at the University of Canberra in 1980. Before the introduction of the inaugural program run by Professor Colin Pearson, most conservators in Australian cultural institutions had been European-trained technicians in paintings and objects conservation. Much fine work was done by highly skilled tradespeople who were well versed in working with a wide variety of material types. In the nineteenth century most of the present role of conservators was done by preparators of natural science specimens or by willing bands of seamstresses who worked on textiles. Faithful sacristans have worked in churches for hundreds of years conserving the textiles that form the basis of ecclesiastical garment collections. They used traditional methods of stitching down degraded fibres of sacred and preciously embroidered fabrics onto sympathetic new support structures. From the time of the classic painters in the Renaissance, the restoration of images on canvas was done by assistants in the schools of Rembrandt and other renowned portrait artists.

Interventive conservation went out of fashion, replaced by rigid obedience to traditional 'recipes' found in major works and in the early publications of the International Council of Museums Committee for Conservation. Understanding of the causes of decay that were written up by Plenderleith and Werner in the 1960s and subsequently (Plenderleith and Werner 1971) languished. As a consequence, conservators were periodically confronted with unexpected secondary complications of the treatments. I give the following examples of such interactions to help elucidate the complexities of the operating environment for objects in museum collections, which have particular storage requirements.

Months or years after an apparently successful intervention, the surface of ceramics can become covered with white efflorescences of hydrated calcium acetates as the low-fired earthenware corrodes in an atmosphere containing acetic acid, coming from the decay of old wooden showcases. These storage cabinets were often made of oak, which is one of the worst timbers to use, but it is one that had been traditionally used in institutions in Europe. There are, however, timbers that age to give a neutral pH, such as Queensland hoop pine, and this is now the preferred wood for construction of showcases and pallets in storage areas.

A similar problem occurs in showcases made of particle board used for storing lead and its alloys, for these objects can grow white whiskers of lead acetate and lead formate as the objects corrode in a microenvironment of acetic acid and formic acid fumes. Such reactions can take place in a matter of a few months after installation. They reveal that suppliers have not kept to the design specifications of the museum and have used formaldehyde in the manufacture of the medium-density particle board. The formic acid which leads to the problem comes from the oxidation of that formaldehyde.

These problems are exacerbated as an unexpected consequence of solving another problem. In efforts to minimise exchange of gases from an external uncontrolled environment with delicate objects inside the showcases, high quality seals can have the desired effects of minimising stresses in objects caused by rapid changes in relative humidity. But the adverse consequence stemming from high quality seals is to exacerbate the degradation issues associated with the off-gassing of volatile organic compounds, as described above. Exclusion of these corrosion issues from off-gassing is part of the due diligence which has to be exercised when objects are on loan from another institution, since such uncontrolled events can lead to great tensions between the borrowing and the lending museums and galleries.

Thus one change in the operating environment has been to reintroduce and build on understanding about decay and active intervention. Another has been in workflow and prioritising the order in which objects are treated. In the first decade of its operations the Western Australian Museum conservation laboratories saw a large volume of shipwreck material appearing, as a result of major underwater archaeological excavation. Previous management directions allowed the conservators to pick and choose what objects they wished to treat, using the rationale that ultimately all of the collection had to be treated, so it did not matter which ones were done first. Forty years on, the museum is still treating objects that were raised in the 1970s excavation programs on the wrecks of the Vereenigde Oostindische Compagnie (Dutch East India Company) vessels *Batavia* (1629) and the *Vergulde Draeck* (1656). Staff much prefer to treat more glamorous objects such as pulley blocks and wooden food bowls rather than less than desirable objects, like ordinary pieces of timber that came from the hull planking. One of the changes I introduced was to prioritise by importance rather than glamour.

An ageing workforce and unusual demographics

A long-term challenge is the structure of the workforce, epitomised by a colleague working in archaeological conservation of Egyptian sites, who wrote to me saying:

> I think a lot about the change that should be happening in this field. We need to be part of that change. In my opinion, what needs to change is engaging in more collaboration between the conservation field and allied fields and moving out of the straight jacket that we seem to have put ourselves into. [There needs to be] an end to the oodles of graduates that think single-focus object conservation is what they are going to do for the rest of their lives and that this is real conservation. How to justify what we do in the wider community in better ways is vital and we need a focus on encouraging more diversity in our field. Our field is full of old white ladies, that's right! There are not enough men and not enough non-white people in our field and the lack of diversity is going to be an issue in the future as the population changes.

Conservators in Australia are also strongly represented by women, but there is a more even gender distribution in conservation scientists and in senior management of conservation departments. Nevertheless there were only three Indigenous conservators working in Australia in 2013.

We also need changes in training and engagement. Another colleague wrote:

> Conservation training programs need to be integrated into existing departments within Universities, so that cross-training is ensured. … i.e. archaeological conservators train in archaeology, and archaeologists in conservation. One way is to embed the training programs in already-established departments as some programs are already doing.[1]

When museums and galleries around Australia support flexible training programs that facilitate the training and employment of Indigenous people in the conservation of Aboriginal collections, a new and exciting era will have arrived. We need to develop new training opportunities in-country in order to capitalise on the power of connection of the people with the artefacts, since this will result in an increased capacity to tell of the non-tangible cultural heritage values embodied in the collections.

---

1   C Chemello, senior conservator, Kelsey Museum of Archaeology, University of Michigan, pers comm 12 January 2013.

Tradition, training and tales

Conservators need to have fine motor coordination skills, and keen eyes for detail and the discernment of patterns. Although my experience in museum practice has come through on-the-job training as a conservator, I have the necessary basic skills for the work through training as an experimental scientist. What was an unfamiliar experience to me was finding a team that seemed to be split down the middle into those who had received on-the-job training and those who came from a physical sciences background. Those who had learned their craft of being a conservator through an apprenticeship of working alongside practitioners had not been trained to write up detailed comments about the treatment. Yet from my perspective as a manager detailed analyses of data obtained from a variety of assessments and reporting the conservation outcomes form an essential step in improving outcomes for the organisation. Recourse to an array of comparative analyses is essential for the task of continuous improvement. We shifted the culture by starting a series of internal presentations through which the conservation team gradually built up the courage to share their treatment methods. Gradually treatment reports became more detailed and a sense of pride was engendered when the conservators were able to demonstrate that they knew more than the maritime archaeologists about the objects.

Upon enquiry as to why nobody collected corrosion products from degraded silver coins, the answer 'We have not done that before' was thought to be a sufficient reason why nothing should change. The underlying response appeared to be based on a combination of fear of new processes and puzzlement that there was a new approach to degradation. When it was explained that there were great opportunities to recover important archaeological information and technical data on the manufacture of the coins and of their site history that would show conservators in good light, the outright suspicion diminished. Bringing in new experts to undertake this work made the addition of this new process feasible.

When I joined the museum conservation team it had been in operation for a decade in cramped and poor conditions in a former American World War II laundry at the rear of the Fremantle Arts Centre. My arrival was met with a mixture of curiosity and suspicion. Who the heck was this chemist who had come to join the team as a research officer? After a few months one of the staff said 'Just wait until you have been here for a year or two and you will also lose your enthusiasm'. The reason this did not occur lies perhaps in the nature of the individual parties concerned and the nature of the training received. For team members who had been 'apprenticed', there was greater cynicism, while for those from a more academic background, the opportunities for creating a profile were apparently boundless. Joining the museum at a time when there was public adulation of the work of the shipwreck excavators and conservators was enjoyable, for it seemed that all we touched turned to gold. New challenges of formerly untreatable objects were presented and solutions to complex problems of decay were found—the treated artefacts are still stable more than 30 years later. There was an openness of shared experiences of roughing it on field work in the remote parts of Western Australia and of rapidly finding new solutions to complex stabilisation problems thousands of kilometres from the laboratory in Fremantle. The challenge was to enthuse wider museum staff with the same energy and creativity.

Fortunately for the museum, the laboratory was led by a physical chemist who pioneered new treatment methods for the most problematic of all objects, viz., cast-iron cannonballs. Being spherical in nature they have a high surface area to volume ratio, and are very responsive to changes in their microenvironment when they move out of the sea and into the dry air of the excavation field station. Conservators were happy to embrace the need for the most expeditious movement of the cannonballs from their acidic and chloride-rich solution under the protective marine concretions into caustic solutions, which inhibit corrosion, and begin the conservation of the objects. They knew that this worked since previous experience without recourse to this treatment had caused cannonballs to fall apart in a matter of hours after documentation had taken place. This willingness to accept changed procedures was in part due to changes in practice in the Netherlands on their wooden shipwrecks from the polders, and in Sweden with the work of the *Vasa* (1628) shipwreck in Stockholm (De Jong 1975, Håfors 2010). If a process was discovered, developed and tested overseas then it 'must be OK'.

Preventive conservation rises from the wreckage of intervention challenges

The fashion in materials conservation has changed from intervention to prevention since there were often unwanted secondary effects on objects following treatments by traditional methods. An example of these types of processes is found in the desalination of copper alloy objects in solutions of sodium sesquicarbonate, after initial citric acid stripping. Following many months of soaking, an unattractive blue–green patina would often cover the surface. This artificial patina was remarkably uniform and made the objects look artificially aged or somehow contrived. In some cases the objects were speckled with bright blue crystals of chalconatronite, first seen on Egyptian bronzes recovered from tombs along the Nile. The reaction to such problems was to store the untreated objects in sealed bags containing oxygen scavengers and vapour phase corrosion inhibitors to stop the chloride-induced decay process.

Rather than deal with the underlying cause, this storage approach simply puts off intervention for years and leaves it in the hands of a future generation of conservators.

Analysis of the solution liquids which were free of such problems and those with the undesired patina showed that the build-up of soluble copper ions in the wash solution was the critical issue. There was nothing inherently wrong with the treatment, so long as the solutions were not allowed to turn a deep blue of the copper (II) carbonate complex. Regular changes of the washing solutions would prevent this but the drawback was the time and the chemical costs associated with this approach. An alternative was to use the reactivity of copper ions and aluminium metal to remove copper in solution. Placing crumpled soft-drink cans or aluminium cooking foil in the wash solution removed copper and so prevented the unwanted patina forming on the desalinating objects. There was also new monitoring equipment to check on the progress of the treatment to replace prolonged washing.

Resistance to adopting the new approach was overcome by having a contract conservator do the experiment. Because this new method removed the problem, staff have now accepted the change since it was wrought by an independent overseas colleague and not something introduced by management. This was the catalyst to bring about the change in perception amongst the tenured staff.

Introduction and use of key performance indicators

An underlying belief that it was possible to quantify the work that conservators were doing led to the development of a way of measuring the output of the laboratory. In terms of budget management and demonstration of effectiveness, it was important to find some yardstick to confirm the reasons why the laboratory had to be supported. There was a real need to convert the intangible elements of conservation into some numerical system or deal with the consequences of an externally imposed set of values. The risk with the latter process is that there would be no control over the input parameters. During discussions with many conservators at national council meetings of the Australian Institute for the Conservation of Cultural Materials in Canberra, I discovered that no other institution had developed suitable indicators. My colleagues encouraged me to have a go and wished me luck.

Many conservators seemed to prefer curators to hand them the objects with little or no engagement about the expected outcomes. The next contact would take place months or years later, on return of the artefacts once they had been stabilised and documented. This approach supported the thesis that conservation was part of a mystery of controlled chemical magic that had been wrought upon the objects. However, such approaches were likely to be misinterpreted by senior budget managers within the museum hierarchy.

The solution to the problem of monitoring the output was to establish the degree of complexity of the conservation process and the procedures that were involved in the treatment program, and to use this as one factor in an output matrix. Simple level one tasks would involve photographic documentation and preparation of custom supports and general cleaning. As the scope of the works increased, the level increased up to a maximum of 10, which involved extensive analysis of the object, a series of physical and chemical assessments of the materials before and after treatment, and writing up the observations and conclusions into a publishable paper and presenting them at a conference.

By using this degree of difficulty coefficient, the output of the conservators dealing with complex objects and very intricate procedures with detailed analytical work could be 'weighted' so that one object could gain an output or activity score of 10. In the same vein hundreds of simple objects were ranked as level one tasks, as they were jobs of low complexity. Using such a system showed that the quarterly output of the laboratory was relatively steady when the number of objects completed was corrected by the degree of difficulty. Having been able to demonstrate that the output of the laboratory could be readily quantified, the museum management team relaxed and accepted the simpler output of jobs completed per month as an indicator of productivity. The massive variations in the number of completed works was understood as being a reflection of the varying degrees of complexity of jobs, and was not seen as a slur on the productivity of particular staff.

Change management and tenured staffing

Given the low numbers of trained conservators, there is value in aligning personality with task complexity, as part of good career path management. A metals conservator decided that they wanted a change from the relatively messy work of treating corroded coins in formic acid solutions. One of the reasons was that the outcomes of the treatments were somewhat problematic, especially if there was no residual solid metal in the core of the coins. This lack of control was distressing to the member of staff concerned, who liked positive outcomes. A move into the more managed world of textiles conservation took place and over the years the conservator became quite accomplished at this area of work. The change worked for a decade but tensions within the textile team plus a desire to create a personal niche were the drivers for the next change. Following a staff development opportunity of being trained in paper conservation techniques, the third and final transition was effected. Paper conservation is regarded as having the most controlled set of outcomes when standard methods are applied. The person is now fully content and is very productive.

When I transitioned into management I had to take over a program for the treatment of the *Batavia* and *Vergulde Draeck* timbers mentioned above. This allowed me to develop an applied research program which has resulted in better outcomes for the treated objects and better managed shipwrecks. Having established in situ corrosion measurements on metals on shipwrecks, it seemed logical to apply similar methods for waterlogged wood. Whilst cleaning a 3000 litre tub of iron-stained waterlogged wood from the *Vergulde Draeck* wreck, I assessed the pH and the voltage of the corrosion products. The most surprising result was that, despite having been excavated for more than 30 years, the timber underneath the layer of rust was still in a fresh anaerobic microenvironment, as pristine as the day it was taken from the ocean floor after immersion for more than 300 years. This meant that the massive amounts of iron corrosion products, from cannon and fastenings, would still be able to be extracted in the wet state without damaging the delicate degraded structure of the waterlogged wood. Results from a new research officer had shown that reactive timbers should not be held in tap water but in a weak solution of polyethylene glycol. This approach simultaneously began the extraction of soluble iron (II) corrosion products from the timber and stabilisation of the waterlogged structure. This resulted in objects becoming available for examination by the archaeologists six to eight years ahead of schedule.

Working as a team of an organic chemist research officer and the curator of conservation led to a new approach of quantifying the burial and storage microenvironment. The previously viewed poor cousin of materials began to take its correct place on the treatment stage. Data on the pH and the reduction potential or voltage due to soluble electrochemically active components proved to be an indispensable tool. The method was extended to the in situ assessments of wooden wrecks in a post-excavation microenvironment: this approach has become international best practice. The Western Australian Museum conservation team is now acknowledged as a world leader in this area, with key workers receiving invitations to give plenary lectures at international symposiums. How was this change wrought? It was done through the art of subtle suggestion that if the research officer wanted to try this approach, then they would be able to achieve success and establish a new line of work. As head of the department, I was in a position to determine allocation of budgets and treatment priorities, so the path was made easier and the staff involved ran with it. The change was fundamentally good for the collections.

Conservation and sustainability of large collections

The collections of the Western Australian Museum cover the full spectrum of earth and planetary sciences, terrestrial and aquatic zoology, anthropology, social and maritime history and maritime archaeology. The bulk of the output from the conservation laboratory has been focused on the materials needs of the objects most at risk, and these consist of maritime archaeological materials. This determined the juxtaposition of the museum laboratories with the offices and storage areas of the department of Maritime Archaeology in Fremantle. While the number of shipwreck objects represents only 4.2 per cent of the entire collection, they consume 60 per cent of the conservation time in hands-on treatment and in the areas of research and development.

For all organisations operating in the cultural sector, almost all of the budget is fixed on salaries and utility costs. Fixed costs consume 91.3 per cent of available funds, leaving $92,000 a year for conservation consumables and external services. The fixed costs of gas and electricity to run the central collections and research centre are approximately $1.2 million. This high cost is relatively small on a per artefact basis, since 94.4 per cent of the 4.6 million objects are housed on this site and the cost of services can be seen as a measure of the organisational contribution to preventive conservation through provision of storage in optimal conditions. The combined preventive and interventive conservation costs amount to close to $2 million or roughly 44 cents per object per year. This is in many ways a very small per item cost for preservation of the collection of the people of Western Australia. But high costs and sustainability are an Australia-wide issue, with the Western Australian Museum amongst the worst funded cultural institutions in Australasia. Sustainability of collections is a major topic of conversations amongst museum directors.

Recent escalations in the cost of gas and electricity amounted to more than $200,000 a year, which brought close attention to the continuing cost of storing the objects in standard conditions of $22\pm0.5°C$ and 50 ± 5 per cent relative humidity. By manually resetting the building management system to 23°C in the summer and 21°C in the winter and keeping the relative humidity at the same level, about $85,000 was saved in the first year. The reason why only two adjustments were made is that Perth typically has a hot dry summer and a cool wet winter. In other climates it is advisable to change the temperature set points at the spring and autumn equinox and at the summer and winter solstice. Apart from the benefit of saving the cost of one conservator's salary, there were no consequences of the small changes.

No one noticed the changes until they were documented in a management report. A debate then arose between the importance of rigid adherence to the international standard and a more realistic and pragmatic approach. The basis of the latter was that most collection stores fail to achieve the rigorous standards, which are mere guidelines. The principal issue is that one should avoid rapid swings in temperature and relative humidity as these can cause significant stress to paintings, to some organic specimens and to some fine furniture as well as to Indigenous cultural materials. Owing to the thermal mass of the 9,000-square-metre building and the volume occupied by the millions of items, resetting of the temperature takes 24 hours to be effected throughout the complex and such changes have a negligible impact on collections.

It is not logical to assume that maintenance of environmental conditions is of such great significance that variations cannot be allowed. Recent research by the Canadian Conservation Institute in Ottawa has shown that collections can in fact take a much larger range of temperatures and relative humidity without any significant damage. Typically the relative humidity is allowed to gradually vary by ± 10 per cent and the temperature by $\pm 2.5°C$, and this relaxation can provide significant savings on the running cost of a collection store and laboratories (O'Connell 1996).

In Europe and in the United Kingdom whole museums are now being closed because governments cannot afford to run them and to keep caring for the collections. In such situations the curators and conservators all lose their jobs, so a demand for 'ideal conditions' can result in a pyrrhic victory. Four years ago a collections management working party of the Australian Institute for the Conservation of Cultural Materials began to collect data on storage conditions and the need to find a new set of guidelines (Bickersteth 2011). Once such recommendations have been endorsed on a museum by museum basis, the Council of Australian Museum Directors would be in a position to adopt the Australian standard museum conditions and apply them to specifications for loans within Australia. Currently very large sums of money are spent in trying to attain the European (International) exhibition conditions. When visiting conservators and curators come to check on our conditions at the time of mounting a travelling exhibition, they acknowledge that their museums in the UK do not keep the conditions that they are specifying for their loans.

Conservators by the very nature of their training become experts at noticing fine detail and changes in the conditions of objects under their care. One of their greatest challenges in ensuring continuing relevance of their arguments for specific storage and exhibition conditions is their capacity to think holistically about the organisation that employs them. It is unrealistic to ask for more funds from the government to improve wages, conditions, the storage of collections and proper access to professional development. All organisations have finite budgets, so that managing change and bringing about improved conditions is best done through self-examination. Team leaders need to be champions of change and to have a commitment to bring about the necessary shifts in attitudes. When a dispassionate analysis of the current operating museum environmental conditions is conducted, the black and white rules can be seen to change their hue and become more of a grey colour. Change management is best effected through internal discovery to find the courage needed to take collections and their management into a more sustainable future. Without that leap of faith the chance of the objects speaking to generations of museum visitors as yet unborn is very limited.

References

Australian Institute for the Conservation of Cultural Materials (AICCM) (2013) Membership report of Secretariat to Council, January 8.

Bickersteth, J (2010) Observations on new national standards. *AICCM Newsletter* 115: 9.

De Jong, J (1975) *The conservation of old waterlogged wood from shipwrecks found in the Netherlands.* Development Authority, Lelystad, Netherlands.

Håfors, B (2010) *Conservation of the Swedish warship Vasa from 1628,* 2nd ed. Vasa Museum, Stockholm.

O'Connell, M (1996) The new museum climate: standards and technology. *Society of American Archives, Readings in Preservation, Abbey Newsletter* 20(4–5): 50–60.

Plenderleith, HJ and Werner, AEA (1971) *The conservation of antiquities and works of art: treatment, repair and restoration.* Oxford University Press, London.

16. Change and Continuity in Anthropology: Examples from Christianity and from the situations of contemporary Indigenous Australians

Francesca Merlan

Anthropology and change

My chapter focuses on change in anthropology, with some comparative references to other social sciences. I illustrate what I have to say through two particular areas of ethnographic research and theorisation—the anthropology of Christianity, and of the contemporary situations of indigenous peoples, particularly in Australia. My treatment is focused, rather than comprehensive; I make no claims to completeness. My view is that, despite its importance, change remains relatively under-conceptualised in these areas, and one of my aims is to encourage greater adequacy among all of us practitioners.

We may define change as difference in some field, object or relation over time. That brief, rough and ready definition raises plenty of issues of importance in the social sciences, which is after all about social life and its self-aware and other-aware players, familiar in some version to all of us. Among other questions, how and when do we discern change? Whose discernment of change is at issue? What are seen to be its consequences? Along what dimensions do we notice and conceptualise change?

To position anthropology in relation to change, I am going to begin by claiming there is a kind of schizophrenia in the social sciences. We talk about some phenomena as if they are inevitably associated with great and irreversible change (e.g. economic modernisation, industrialisation, many new technologies, or colonialism). These are areas of 'change-assertiveness'. It is taken almost for granted that their occurrence or operation involves change, often great change, but it always turns out to be complicated to specify what that change amounts to, and how to specify the sorts of processes, relations and dimensions involved.

On the other hand, we talk about other phenomena, such as certain kinds of social relationships, with a great deal more 'change-reluctance'. Consider, for example, the issue of the relation of Indigenous people (for whom one of the accepted 'tribal' terms is Ngunuwal) to Canberra. If talked about in the framework of colonisation, we might think in terms of great change having occurred in Indigenous relationships to the place we now call Canberra, the created national capital, as the form of life of Indigenous people changed drastically. But now that some national land rights scaffolding exists for recognising relationships to places, and recognition is associated with particular social and political values, we are concerned to acknowledge this relationship as continuous— though we might admit some discontinuity in its having been unrecognised or ignored for some period of time. We background 'differences over time' for the Ngunuwal because—despite the obviousness of many questions the assertion may raise that the *Ngunnawal people* (alternatively called *Ngunawal tribe* by a competing group) are the Indigenous Australian inhabitants whose traditional lands encompass much of the area now occupied by the city of Canberra, Australia, and the surrounding Australian Capital Territory—we are concerned to assert, to 'socially construct' (Hacking 1999), as some would say, a relation of continuity between people and place. Perhaps it is very significant that some see this relationship as linked to our common present; it is less a remote historical process that we are talking about because of that. It is also one about which there are strong views and engagements, on the part of anthropologists and others.

It seems we can hardly get much further without mentioning the twin of change: continuity. We could define this as stability in some field, object or relation over time, which perhaps is very likely to have implications for the present. It is often observed that continuity should not be taken for granted: if things seem to remain the same over time, that also requires explanation. Again, there are questions of perspective: what do people themselves, in their various situations, make of change and/or continuity and its implications for them and their lives?

I hope that my examples, though spare, have been sufficient to show that, for both change and continuity, there are questions about modalities of sociohistorical change, people's discernment and experience of it as such, and their evaluation of it. I also have meant to intimate that both change and continuity involve expenditures of energy; both are actively produced in the human world, and discerned in particular circumstances. And especially the above example of continuity is such because it connects directly with the/our present. That also leaves it open to a politics of contemporary position-taking. There are those who would deny the relation of Ngunuwal to Canberra (including rival Indigenous groups), and in that process, would probably take a critical view of continuity of their relation to the area as 'constructed', perhaps even in the negative sense of fabricated.

I next want to locate anthropology historically, relative to its sister disciplines, as having been much more oriented to continuity than change. The most obvious comparison and contrast is with the closely allied social sciences—notably sociology. Anthropology emerges in this context at the high end of a continuity–change spectrum in terms of what anthropologists often assert about their research subjects; but both disciplines, from their beginnings, have been mobilised by concerns about change.

Let us take this back to disciplinary emergences. It is a generalisation—but useful for present purposes—to say that sociology, from around the eighteenth or early nineteenth century, depending on how you trace it, emerged as a recognisable discipline gaining some of its energies from anxieties about the force and inexorability of change in so-called modern or developed societies. Many of its theorists (Comte, Saint-Simon, much more recently Tarde, Durkheim, and many others) were also practitioners concerned with social planning, improvement and remedial activity to mitigate the destructiveness of processes of change. Anthropology, on the other hand, from roughly the nineteenth century onwards, began to be visible as an emergent area of change-reluctance, much more concerned with non-industrial or preindustrial societies, and many of *its* predecessor theorists and earlier and later practitioners (Morgan, Tylor, Leenhardt) with documentation, protection and preservation of native peoples who were undergoing colonisation and missionisation. Thus there has always existed in anthropology an anxiety about loss, alongside concerns for preservation; and a recognition of relatively great power differences between dominant social orders and those colonised or otherwise marginalised peoples with whom anthropologists have tended to do their research. (Present differences between sociology and anthropology can no longer be described in terms of concerns with 'modern' and 'pre-modern' societies, respectively, but I am talking about earlier disciplinary histories and the perspectives of their practitioners, as well as some measure of continuity.) The 'deep structure' and 'deep history' of anthropology become more intelligible when considered as a series of perspectives on social life which arose in a context of world expansion, and with its research concerns focused on peoples who were among the less powerful in those processes.

There are now often aspects of reparations politics—in the case of Indigenous peoples, for instance, land and native title or other similar claims—that ask of them to demonstrate their continuing attachment to lands and traditions as the requirement and justification of those claims. This supports and amplifies concerns for authenticity, traditionality and unchangingness of law and custom among those people which may constitute for them a source of pride, as well as a considerable problem to the extent that they no longer are as they were, and do not live up to such expectations. This demand comes from the wider political society (such as Australia), not explicitly from anthropologists; but it tends to coincide with and support certain kinds of continuity-oriented depictions and forms of theorisation (Austin-Broos 2011).

Continuity thinking and the anthropology of Christianity

A few years back anthropologist Joel Robbins (2007) argued that there had been a failure of an anthropology of Christianity to coalesce (as compared with anthropologies of Islam and Buddhism, for example, which he sees as having greater disciplinary coherence). In considering why that might be, he argued that what he called 'continuity thinking' is in the 'deep structure of anthropological theorizing'. He identified continuity thinking as consisting in tendencies for anthropologists to argue for social persistence (even if some change is admitted); that what people experience as new is perceived through the old or conventional and accommodated to it; and to see change as a kind of 'perpetual process' in time, rather than eventful and discontinuity-producing. Anthropologists give primacy to continuity, he argued.

This might be seen as a matter of degree, or variation, compared with related social sciences like sociology. Anthropology and sociology do share a good amount of DNA, but as I said above, sociology was, from its recognised inception, more about 'us' than 'them', and more impelled by questions and anxieties about change which was nevertheless widely (never universally) accepted and seen as ineluctable, rather than about conservation and anxieties about loss of a diversity of 'others'.

How does his claim about primacy of continuity thinking relate to Robbins' point about the lack of a coherent anthropology of Christianity? Anthropology is at variance with Christianity, he asserts. Christianity is a religion of radical change, both with respect to conversion and eschatology. Its underlying postulates concerning time and change are different from those of anthropology, which emerged in some opposition to Christianity and its practical arm, missionisation.

Robbins also argues that anthropologists have been more concerned with belief as a state of mind, and something that can be stated propositionally ('belief that'), rather than belief as an act ('belief in'), as reflected, for example, in someone's slaughtering a chicken or hanging a stone in the corner of their house. I think a sharp differentiation between these two is problematic, but there is something to a distinction between that which is more and less explicitly articulated. At any rate, Robbins argues that concern with belief as propositional is compatible with continuity thinking, in that belief is seen as something that endures, rather than as an act.[1]

A final facet to his argument has to do with anthropology as a social science of the Other, of difference. Robbins (2007, 16) quotes anthropologist Stephan Palmié (1995, 92): 'Our public identity (as well as our careers) in no small measure hinges upon our ability to represent certain social realities as "authentically different" (and if possible, traditionally so).' In other words, there is an investment in otherness, on the part of anthropologists as well as in others' expectations of them and their subject matter. Anthropologists stereotypically work with people on Pacific Islands or the Amazon, not with Poles or high-energy particle physicists. (There is of course contemporary anthropological work with precisely such people, so I am citing stereotypes that have their roots in earlier and some continuing anthropological practice, not my view of anthropology's range of practice today.) Concern with otherness is linked to a fear of homogenisation and change which might level difference; hence tendencies in anthropology to represent difference as persisting. I think there is some truth to this. But as per my remarks above about the Ngunuwal, such concerns are not limited to anthropology or anthropologists. To an extent they are an expression of concerns widespread within our societies, which get projected upon certain kinds of people in particular, and made part of the weft of disciplinary developments that have a lot of common warp with others. Such concerns need to be subjects of constant critical awareness.

Change and Indigenous Australians

That brings me to a second class of examples. I can speak of this subject from personal experience and conviction, and also cite a number of other colleagues as examples.

Anthropological models of change with respect to Indigenous Australia have changed quite considerably over time, but—this is my plea—not as much as they need to. They continue, in many cases, to be loosely articulated as a matter of change in certain 'domains' of activity or description, such as 'kinship',

---

1   This raises a question about how Robbins would see the relation between Christianity as a religion of radical change, and what he claims to be a basic Western cultural emphasis on belief as propositional; but I leave that aside here as something he does not directly address in this material. I think the proposition that Christianity is a religion of radical change is also a large generalisation: one needs to specify where emphases on radical change may be, and their impacts on people being introduced to varieties of Christianity.

or in sociohistorical accounts of the relations between Indigenous and non-Indigenous people and institutions. All these are important. But alongside these necessary accounts, in what kinds of critical terms may change be understood?

Certain influential early models argued that comprehensive trends of change were linked to seemingly small changes: Sharp (1952) presented a seemingly simple shift from stone axe to steel axe in Cape York as linked to and cascading into a whole series of changes, in overt behaviour, in technology and conduct—relations of kinship and gender, trading partnerships, relations with whites—which effectively radically altered Cape York Indigenous societies over a short span of time. We might call this an instance of 'collapse' theory. Sharp's depiction has both something positive and something not so positive about it. Sharp saw beyond change as simply involving, for example, material repertoire, and proposed that the chain of connections and implications of stone to steel, of technology to social relations, was far-reaching. On the other hand, he had little to say about adaptations by which social relations and the cultural field were reshaped, and different forms of life continue, rather than simply imploding. Other models featured adaptive processes, new negotiations, and interrelations with settlers more fully. To what extent has ethnography and research developed into more adequate evaluation and theorisation of change?

Indigenous Australia and wider societal politics of change

When I first began research in the Northern Territory in 1976, I had come from some similarly remote-feeling Great Plains research venues in North America. I sort of expected Australian Aborigines would be in similar situations to American Indians in agency towns and outlying settlements, and in general I think I had correctly gauged that they were exposed to a considerable range of impacts and influences from Australian settler society. I did not have particular expectations about peoples being 'traditional', culturally pristine or integral. So I was not disappointed. I got to know people in a whole variety of living situations, characterised by greater or lesser degrees of regular contact with versions of Australian society—in towns, on pastoral stations, or further afield.

However, two or three years after I began research, things started to happen that made clear an era of land rights was in preparation, and its operation was going to bring with it a whole series of expectations about the completeness and traditionalism of Indigenous people's connections to country—a phenomenon to which I referred above. This was going to impose upon current research, and upon Indigenous people themselves to varying degrees, a concern about how to respond to emergent possibilities. Claimable country under the *Land Rights Act* was all Crown land, and Crown land tended to be remote and not to have been used for productive settler ventures. Hence in many cases Aboriginal people, as they moved closer in to settler centres over decades and especially with changes in wage structures which caused many pastoralists to toss them off the land, had also become distanced from some of what were notionally their traditional areas, and the fullness and fluency of their knowledge was sometimes less than expected under the *Land Rights Act*.

So I spent a good part of a book I wrote on this subject arguing that the law, though intended to be beneficial, acted as an anti-change machine (Merlan 1998). Its requirements made it very difficult for researchers to treat the situations of these Aboriginal people in historical and experiential terms, as well as in unvarnished terms of cultural difference and increasing influence of dominant societal practices and norms upon them. Rather, in terms of the emerging legal issues one was stuck with arguing about Indigenous connection to land as a matter of ontology—their very being as tied up with landedness. This is, one can see, a way of asserting and producing continuity. Such a view can lead to conclusions that Indigenous people disconnected from land no longer have the qualities and credentials that others expect. Many non-Indigenous detractors of land rights in the Northern Territory had long since come to the conclusion— perhaps many did not need any real evidence about the condition of Indigenous people to do so—that they did not deserve anything at all, any more than any other Territorian battler who has had to work hard for his block, and does not get anything given to him. These kinds of arguments may sound familiar because they have been aired so often.

This is important because it is all about wider societal politics of change, which, as I have said, also becomes part of the subject matter of what anthropologists can and did say about change. My position, simply put, was to argue for the objective reality of considerable change, and the importance of theorising change, as well as describing and accounting for the different understandings people have of it: what people make of themselves, and their situation, and think about change, in their circumstances. Arguments about change needed to be placed in a framework of Indigenous–non-Indigenous relationship, and to eschew nostalgic or accusatory fixation with change in Indigenous social orders as 'loss' (while recognising that both non-Indigenous and Indigenous people may see it that way or, alternatively, may wish for transformation). The complications of describing and theorising change relationally must be recognised, particularly for people between whom and the mainstream there continue to be large gulfs of difference, including power differences of marginalisation and dispossession. I argued (Merlan 1998) for placing the relations of Indigenous and non-Indigenous people, and their consciousness of each other, front and centre in an 'intercultural' framework. I also consider it important to keep in mind the assertion by Robert Tonkinson, whose work is discussed below, that the aims, desires, forms of social action and imagination of many Indigenous people remain quite distinct from that which the Australian majority would conceive of, or wish (Tonkinson 2004, 184).

Let us now consider another anthropologist, Gaynor Macdonald, who has done research for many years with Wiradjuri people in western New South Wales (Macdonald 2004, 2008). Up north, and especially in the land rights context, expectations and stereotypes were held that Indigenous people ought not to change: they were supposed to be traditional, and much criticised if seen not to be so; and, correspondingly, the extent of change was either excoriated by some as disqualifying, or de-emphasised by others seeking to retain a favourable positioning for Aboriginal people, in which traditionality was in focus.

Gaynor encountered stereotypes in the academy and outside it that southern Aboriginal people do not have any culture left. Any differences between them and others were not seen as culturally of value, but as deficits. So Gaynor has spent years doing what she describes as 'reinscribing recognition of the distinctive cultural practices, characterising Aboriginal peoples' lives in southeast Australia'.[2] In other words, she sees much Wiradjuri practice as cultural in being learned and transmitted and taken as normal in a given milieu, as against the contrasting encompassing environment, roughly, of mainstream rural white Australia. She challenges a long-held view that these differences simply reflect failed processes of incorporation of Wiradjuri into the Australian mainstream, and have no consistency and substance of their own. So, in a way, she has been trying to counter thinking that says that everything has changed, and changed for the worse, levelling any worthwhile difference. She cannot, however, be accused of Robbins' 'continuity thinking': she is too aware of sociohistorical change for that. So her position lies in detaching notions of culture and difference from evaluations of authenticity and traditionality, and in arguing that culture (or what we may call cultural, in order to avoid reification and holism) changes, as do the people in specific historical circumstances. In this I agree with her, but we would also agree, I think, that Australian cultural politics, especially those of legitimation and recognition, will not easily be shifted from focusing on authenticity and traditionality.

---

2   Gaynor Macdonald web address, University of Sydney, sydney.edu.au/arts/anthropology/staff/profiles/macdonald.shtml.

Indigenous Australia: two versions of continuity thinking

Now I want to briefly take the case of two anthropological colleagues who, I think, have a different approach to describing and theorising change, and have produced, in my estimation, versions of continuity thinking, combined later (in the second case) with a modified view of societal transformation. They have postulated ontological continuity of Indigenous people and culture as inhering in specific areas of practice and thought, and seen these as relatively impervious to outside influence (partly because some Aborigines explicitly struggle to keep them so). In creating these depictions they produce valuable accounts of aspects of Indigenous sociality and condition, but the emphasis on, or assumption of, fundamental centrality and continuity of certain kinds limits their attention to subjecthood, agency, and internal shifts within immediate Indigenous social domains as well as with institutions which intersect with family, community life, and many aspects of wider Australian life. When change becomes overwhelmingly obvious—as at least one of these anthropologists now concedes—what is happening is seen as being related to particular recent policy changes and management regimes. But were there not forms of change all along?

It is not fortuitous, I think, that both have done research in geographically fairly remote areas of Australia. This not only means that contacts with settler Australia were in fact later than elsewhere and typically involved selected groups of outsiders rather than major settlement; but even more importantly, that these anthropologists see questions of change and continuity through this lens of 'late contact', positing a protracted continuity of separate and distinctive 'Indigenous culture' into the present, or until recently. I would argue instead that the question of what even selective settler–Indigenous interaction produces, and how to theorise it, has long been an issue.

Robert Tonkinson (formerly at The Australian National University, and then at the University of Western Australia until his retirement) has done long-term research both in Vanuatu and with the Mardudjara of Australia's Western Desert. Though at times he has used comparison between them as an instrument of description and exploration, I will concentrate on what he has to say about the latter here. In a recent publication Tonkinson (2012, 20) said of his years of work:

> Initially, my research attention was dominated by the many obvious continuities that linked living Mardu Aborigines, a Western Desert people, to their recent 'pre-European' existence, but over time my research trajectory has shifted inexorably to one that foregrounds transformations in the analysis of Western impacts.

A first matter of importance is the link Tonkinson makes, implicitly and explicitly, between environment, remoteness and cultural conservatism. The Mardu lived in an arid and marginal environment. They might therefore be seen as 'late contacted' and/or shielded for a time, and able to return to the desert at times, but did this mitigate the consequences of their relations with outsiders? This short introduction exemplifies some of the aspects of Tonkinson's argument which foregrounds environment and location:

> Shielded by their forbidding environment, the Mardu were left largely undisturbed until relatively recently. They were attracted from the desert to fringe settlements: mining camps, pastoral properties, small towns, and missions, initially for brief periods. However, inducements offered by Whites who desired their labor (and, in the case of women, sexual services), plus a growing taste for European foodstuffs and other commodities, drew them increasingly into the ambit of the newcomers. Inevitably, they eventually abandoned their Nomadic, hunter-gatherer adaptation for a sedentary life close to Whites. Migration began around the turn of the century and ended as recently as the 1960s. The Mardu remain today among the more tradition-oriented Aborigines in Australia.[3]

The Mardu lived in places that were remote from intensive or large-scale settlement, but were contacted by colonists with a variety of interests. Not only did all sorts of settler enterprises and persons enter into the areas they regularly frequented, but one may not underestimate the significance of their responses. They did not stay put: they walked to places of interest to them, and into contact with whites, and there began the usual, unequal and often exploitative forms of labour, sexual and other relations. The community of Jigalong arose as a rations depot from the 1930s and later served as a maintenance station along the rabbit-proof fence. Missionisation of the Mardu began after World War II. Tonkinson's view is that the disciplinary nature of the mission regime was undoubtedly oppressive with its dormitories, segregation of children, and so on. However, he also sees this as having put a barrier between Indigenous people and their would-be saviours, in a way that contributed to separation, with the Mardu remaining among the 'more tradition-oriented'. We begin to sense the need to closely examine the variety of relations with outsiders, and also resulting internal shifts in Mardu social relations, rather than simply an emphasis upon the maintenance of distance between themselves and whites. The various pieces of the puzzle do not seem to add up to a view of Mardu as culturally unaffected;

---

3   Read more: www.everyculture.com/Oceania/Mardudjara-History-and-Cultural-Relations.html#ixzz2K5jIgCE3.

they obviously had many kinds of relations with various sorts of outsiders, while observably maintaining certain practices (ceremony among others) more strenuously than Aborigines in many other locales.

In everything he has written Tonkinson has, rightly, been concerned to present Mardu as agentive, not mere passive subjects of colonising forces. But internal to this is a kind of emphasis upon continuity. He writes of their agency as having been predominantly directed towards protecting and maintaining Mardu cultural integrity. Everything else that has happened therefore appears as something aberrant, e.g.:

> For the Mardu, access to alcohol and increasing Westernization pressures have led to considerable social problems, which remain unresolved. A recent movement to establish permanent outstations on or near traditional Mardu lands is partly in response to these pressures, particularly the damaging effects of alcohol, but it also relates to the advent of large-scale mining exploration in the desert. The Mardu strongly oppose these activities, and since the formation of a regional land council in the mid-1980s, a major concern has been to protect their lands from desecration and alienation.[4]

In explaining how the Mardu have oriented themselves towards cultural integrity, and also seeing the explanation of cultural persistence among the Mardu as a 'challenge' (Tonkinson 2004, 184) given the 'constancy of change', Tonkinson places considerable importance upon ritual and a presumably associated ideology. Drawing upon some major anthropological epitomes of Aboriginal life and culture (e.g. the work of WEH Stanner), as well as his own experience, he writes of Indigenous 'assent to the terms of life', a kind of quiescence or stoicism; and permanence and fundamental abidingness as permeating their feelings for the country (forms made by Dreamings, remaining for all time), the combination of which discourages questioning, scepticism and self-reflection. Myth, too, is seen as a medium of absorption of what may in some respects be seen as contemporary or new information and understanding into a framework of stable, if not static, understandings. While individuals receive new information via dreams and revelations (Tonkinson 1970) this, too, is seen as largely incorporated into ongoing frames. Ideology and ritual are seen as stabilising domains of life activity, reproducing and sizing contemporary life in familiar frames.

Now this is a fairly common and established picture of Indigenous ideology. It results, for Tonkinson as for some others, in a dichotomous framework of 'two worlds', or two 'domains', Aboriginal and non-Aboriginal, or *ngurra* 'camp'

---

4   Read more: www.everyculture.com/Oceania/Mardudjara-History-and-Cultural-Relations.html#ixzz2K5n6kHSo.

and *maya* 'house', as the Mardu themselves often seem to epitomise this social difference. Aborigines are represented as having actively striven to keep these separate, and particularly in Tonkinson's earlier work (1974), this sometimes was seen as triumphal 'resistance' to the missionaries and their impositions. In this way, a sense of them as culturally integral is presented despite difficulties for them in achieving this. Tonkinson presents the socioculturally most central, as well as most rigorously defended, of Indigenous domains as Law or the ceremonial life.

In recent work, as indicated in the 2012 quote above, the balance of emphases has changed. Tonkinson (2007) presents the Mardu as still concerned to sustain differences of importance to them, and values of kin, country and ceremony as still core to sense of themselves and their way of life, but deliberate separation as no longer a successful strategy. Among other things, 'self-determination' policy and its successors have increasingly focused on making Mardu more directly involved in the administration and management of their communities, thus handing them responsibility for a different kind of 'business' than their Law, and in the process, blurring distinctions between Aboriginal and whitefella domains. He sees Mardu as having been reluctant to deploy their own organisational and logistic skills to management of community affairs (2007, 47); and practice of ceremony is weakened by numerous changes, including access to alcohol and drugs. Another feature of the present is heightened and more pressured mobility (to accomplish life tasks, for example—medical visits, bureaucratic paperwork), and a wider choice of residential locations (not only in remote communities, but in towns)—both realisations of valued autonomy, Tonkinson argues, but—one might also suppose—of social and cultural diversification and reorientation.

There seems little doubt that, in regions like this, remoteness from majority Australian society was relevant in many ways; and that ceremony and Law were highly valued Aboriginal activities, and areas of practice and imagination. But a problem with the presentation of 'domaining' and a core way of life so assertively, is that many things that are actually happening at any given time fall outside this frame, and thus appear as Aborigines failing to live in their own valued terms. These may be terms that Aborigines themselves articulate less clearly than ideal norms, or not at all. But they require some kind of theorisation that does not posit entire areas of activity (including Law) as necessarily or only conservative, but takes even those valued areas as possible arenas of change, or linked to changes in people's experience, sense of themselves, relationship to country, and to other people.

To wind back historically: how to treat Mardu going into places of European occupation, and rapid integration of Mardu into some forms of relationship with outsiders, in terms of its consequences for social relations among themselves and with others? Many explicit forms of Mardu self-presentation and self-understanding do, indeed, emphasise continuity over change (in the words of Indigenous people all over the country, and Mardu too, 'your laws change all the time, our Law never changes'). But at the same time an enormous number of things about Indigenous life and its relation to new people and elements are changing apace, perhaps unremarked or unarticulated, though certainly constituting some good proportion of the everyday. Not without conflict, of course; and not without inequality and the recognition of inequality.

However, Tonkinson says himself that his early work was 'dominated by the many obvious continuities that linked living Mardu Aborigines, a Western Desert people, to their recent "pre-European" existence'. This kind of representation generated a picture of normative Aboriginal subjectivity as continuity-oriented, to kin, place, ceremony. Obviously some parts of that depiction are consonant with Indigenous social practice and ideology; yet, clearly also, many aspects of change—differences in fields, objects and relations—were already afoot; for one, the basic shift from a self-subsistent life to a much more materially dependent one. What were the forms of Mardu self- and other-understanding in and of these situations? What were the patterns of internal relations, activities and movements, in undoubtedly growing awareness of the presence of outsiders? Was the Law always simply a domain of separation between Mardu and whites, or were there possibly changes in Mardu thinking and experience, that also made their way into the practice of Law, however separate it may seem? Do people sometimes continue to do some of the 'same' things, but re-position and relativise them in new ways? For example, when Mardu are exposed to teachings about God and Church but also continue to go to ceremony, do they simply shut those teachings out? Or do they, as others have reportedly done, also make overt amendments to their forms of ceremonial practice, as reported for missionised people further north in the Pilbara (Petri and Petri-Odermann 1970)? How tenable is it to identify particular domains of practice—like Law, or ceremony—as unchanging core to a form of life, and as impervious to outside influence? And to think of changes in social life in terms of such 'domains' of activity, instead of conceptualising some of the modalities of change in more fluid and distributed ways?

I think another example is useful to make more explicit one of the points inherent in the above discussion: that how and whether anthropologists characterise change, and continuity, is influenced by the main focus of their research. In the two cases I am considering these research areas turn out to be precisely those in which the strongest claims for continuity are made.

Howard Morphy has worked with Indigenous 'art' and artists in the Northern Territory since the 1970s, and is an authority on the art and aesthetics of Yolngu people of north-east Arnhem Land. Over the years he has also been involved, together with his wife Frances who did linguistic work on one of the Yolngu dialects, in museology, film, multimedia, as well as native title work.

One of the summary points he and Frances Morphy assert on this research basis is that the Yolngu are encapsulated but not colonised. What should we take this to mean exactly? Is it possible to be 'encapsulated' without consequence for experience, relationship and practice? Is the focus on Yolngu being (and feeling?) enclosed within another, foreign social order? Or having around them an enclosing capsule, which restricts access to them and by them? What does such a view say about the anthropologist's concept of Indigenous awareness? The word 'colonisation' clearly has a negative ring; but what if we were to ask more neutrally about the influences upon Yolngu, which they may incorporate into their lives, both wittingly (as in choosing, say, to watch television or videos, go to church, drink alcohol, go to or not go to school) and unintentionally (as when influences from such sources become part of their concerns and imaginative horizon)?

The Morphys argue that Yolngu retain what they have come to call 'relative autonomy' in two respects: first, with respect to Euro-Australian society; and second, in internal areas of Yolngu life, some of which have retained much more continuity than others (Morphy and Morphy 2013). For instance, patterns of residence and kinship relations have, they say, shown great continuity, while the hunter-gatherer subsistence economy has been transformed into a 'mixed' economy in which hunting and gathering is supplementary. This makes some kinds of (fairly conventional) divisions into 'domains' such as 'the kinship system', 'the system of technology and production' and 'the ideational system', and claims that there has been more change in some areas than others. There may be more change in some areas of activity and social relationship than others; but what would be adequate evidence for this, and what are adequate conceptual and methodological bases for such an argument? I submit that quarantining change in terms of social and technical divisions or domains is more difficult than labelling makes it seem; and that there need to be a variety of levels and resources for conceptualising change. Quarantining is difficult partly because people themselves are active across such notional domains, their experience and action not restricted to one. All notional domains could offer examples of such complexity, but let us take the example of one form of activity.

Morphy sees Yolngu art production as having considerable continuity; or at least some of the content of what is depicted in Yolngu artworks is 'traditional', its matter the travels, locations and interactions of dreaming figures within landscape, and content still largely tied to Indigenous notions of consubstantiality among people, places and dreamings.

However, the very category of 'art', I have previously argued (Merlan 2001), has involved considerable change in some ways, as do the materials and the conditions of wider display of the works. Designs and stories such as these were not, as is also true of central Australia and elsewhere, displayed to an outside public. They are now produced in a quite different time frame and for different audiences, including markets, than was previously the case. Here as elsewhere this has occasioned some internal debate about what may be represented and what not. This indicates that people certainly do recognise identity in what is being shown, and continuities in who may paint which designs, but sometimes differ over how these things are to be transferred into a very different environment, and who has authority over the production of designs, among other matters. Morphy (1991) has argued for various kinds of change in Yolngu painting, so the question is not whether anything has changed, but what has changed, how the people involved see this, and how they articulate ways of understanding change and continuity in their current situation.

Distinguishing between paintings that are mainly geometric, and others that are mainly figurative, Morphy (1991) shows that the former encode the most highly restricted ('inside') and valued meanings and relationships in ways that the latter, relatively more 'outside' figurative paintings and motifs cannot; and that European interest in Yolngu painting has been accompanied by changes in production and the ways and venues in which painting currently figures. Women also have greater access to inside meanings than before. Yet overall, Morphy's argument is that Yolngu painting remains a fundamental underpinning and medium of Yolngu society and knowledge, with change in the forms of knowledge and understanding considered only rather peripherally.

One thing I think Yolngu have managed with success is transfer of some of what they themselves think of as high cultural production—dancing, painting, song and so on—into a number of new, highly constructed environments (involving non-Indigenous partners and collaborators) which are framed in a way that brings respect and admiration for their accomplishments from a wider Australian public. One of the best-known and most innovative offerings has been the music of Yothu Yindi, a group with both Aboriginal and *balanda*[5] (non-Aboriginal) members formed in 1986, and combining Aboriginal music with rock and pop sound and instrumentation.

The emergence of the popular Garma festival—a now annual three-day event organised from Yirrkala which brings together ceremony (*bunggul*), song (*manikay*), art (*miny'tji*) and Yolngu dance for display to outside audiences and locals—is a great example, in a limited time frame and highly constructed environment, of another aspirational presentation of Yolngu culture which has met with great popular acclaim.

Especially if one's interests focus on the art industry and ceremonial practice (however innovatively modified to incorporate contemporary opportunities and constraints, as with Garma) the Yolngu world looks much more ordered than if you look at health (mental and physical), economic dependence, social tensions, alcohol and drug abuse, suicide rates, impoverished educational provision, literacy. Morphy's art study (1991, 304) indeed mentions alcohol issues only briefly, and in conclusion, in the time-honoured manner of anthropological ethnographic closing mentions of change. There is something to be said for different kinds and rates of change and continuity in different areas of social activity, which is one sense the Morphys want to give to 'relative autonomy'. But it is not clear how neatly many of these things can or should be separated from each other as 'domains', nor is it clear that one is justified in beginning in many of these areas from an assumption of autonomy, which in this case would presumably mean Yolngu organisation of activity and context, without (major) influence from others. It is, most of all, not clear how one may evaluate change which takes the kind of course I have described: a certain (increasing?) elaboration of high cultural production for shared (Indigenous and non-Indigenous) consumption, which people may be enormously proud of, and not readily describe in terms of change but assert as evidence of cultural continuity despite the obvious novelty of some fundamental aspects of these arrangements. Such a discussion needs a series of critical concepts which are not simply descriptive of kinds of activity, or meta-political notions (such as 'autonomy'). Ways of expressing directions and trends of change are important, as are description and interpretation of changing relationships and practices.

It is clear that Yolngu leadership is more articulate than in many other parts of Australia about a notion of biculturalism, and in assertions of the equivalence of Yolngu and Balanda cultures. In part, this needs to be understood in terms of the relatively benign history of missionisation, which was the principal form of colonisation of this area until relatively recently.

---

5   *Balanda* is the term used for 'whites' in north-east Arnhem Land, said to be derived from the word 'Hollander' (via Makasar Balanda, Malay Belanda, from Dutch Hollander).

Morphy's view of Yolngu culture, and its vocabulary of 'relative autonomy', is in fact very like that of some articulate Yolngu: of a social order that retains its fundamental distinctive character and brings that to adaptive, creative interaction with outsiders, balancing 'white man's society and Yolngu society'. What presumptions concerning change and continuity underlie that?

I think it is all too easy to see (especially north-east Arnhem Land, and perhaps parts of Australia's deserts, as opposed to more densely and diversely colonised areas of Australia) through a lens of relatively late contact; and to minimise the consequences of mission-led education, occupational and domestic change efforts, as not full-fledged until the postwar 1950s. It certainly is appropriate to recognise great differences between settler and Yolngu social dynamics. But to simply take an integralist view screens us from grasping conditions that Yolngu inhabit today, as well as from adequately conceptualising previous Indigenous–non-Indigenous relations. Today's conditions manifest themselves in diverse ways: dramatically, for one thing, in the emergence of high suicide rates among those who live in, or shuttle between, outlying outstations and larger settlements like Yirrkala; more benignly, for another, in the manifest biculturalism of Yolngu rhetoric directed to an outside audience. Where in Australia is this to be found, and what social conditions have fostered it?

The overt and latent effects of long-term Methodist mission presence (established in 1935)—including transformation of residence patterns, daily routines, joint mission–Indigenous political and land rights activism which became famous throughout Australia in the matter of the Bark Petition of 1963[6]—cannot be understood only in terms of Yolngu cultural integralism asserting itself in adaptive forms (see e.g. Baker 2010). In my view, understanding of the kinds of persons and orientations that resulted from the north-east Arnhem mission period and later events requires theorisation of Indigenous–non-Indigenous relations at many levels and across time. 'Relative autonomy', the label the Morphys apply to the Yolngu situation, defers conceptualisation of fundamental aspects of social process in favour of a culturally integralist 'minimum change' view. Importantly, it sidelines questions of shifts in connections between practice and how and what people think, and the growing sense of awareness of other ways of living in many respects. Yolngu are proud of the culture they are able to present yearly at the Garma festival. But what changes when culture is projected into these constructed environments, before outside audiences, as has long been the case with Indigenous 'art'? Assumptions are being made

---

6   A petition sent to Parliament in Canberra from north-east Arnhem Land in protest of the federal government's acquisition of an area as a mining lease, without consultation with people at Yirrkala. The petition is on permanent display in Parliament House in Canberra. Clearly missionaries and Yolngu collaborated in the production of this document, but celebratory acclaim tends to ignore, perhaps understandably, the participation of the former, and highlight the role of the latter.

concerning continuity here, without that being adequately subjected to analysis of its organisation, the collaborations and intersections of ideas and interests. To even understand the rather considerable extent to which Yolngu are given to objectifying 'society' and 'culture', and the terms in which they do so, requires another view of sociohistorical process which the concept of 'relative autonomy' only glances off.

Conclusions

Some ways of positing research orientations in the social sciences, I said at the beginning, are 'change-accepting'—such is the vocabulary of urbanisation, sedentisation, and colonisation. Some are change-resistant, and I have concurred to an extent with Robbins' general view that anthropology has (often) been so (though I have not considered or accepted all of his generalisations about Christianity). But anthropology, as a social science that prides itself on 'going where the people are' (Hart 2002), ought, I think, once again not only to go there, but also to attempt renewal of its critical theorisation of processes of change and continuity. Such theorisation, I have argued from Australianist examples, cannot be well founded on structural notions of domains of social, economic or technical activity and relationship. Experiential and cognitive processes extend across all kinds of human activity. They require critical and conceptual vocabularies and forms of analysis which appear, still, to only be inchoate in all of the indigenist work I have presented here, including only partially developed in my own. In my view, anthropologists need to be clear that broad characterisations of people as 'tradition-oriented' or otherwise form part of an often emotively laden, public as well as sometimes indigenous, vocabulary of evaluation: what people make of themselves and others in circumstances as they apprehend them. We need to recognise these evaluations as one of the dimensions for critical analysis, rather than as an anthropological position—and focus instead on development of better frameworks for articulating how shifts in kinds of practice and kinds of people relate to each other.

I think that all of us whom I have discussed would be likely to agree that we have to pay attention to regional differences in how settler–Indigenous histories are to be described in different parts of Australia, and the different periodisation of colonisation and power-laden impacts upon Indigenous societies. I have suggested that studies of geographically remote Indigenous social settings are liable to simplify the social consequences of remoteness, seeing it as contributing to separation and cultural conservatism. But recognition of regional differences, however important, is not the main issue. More fundamentally, I think we differ in the ways in which we analyse those histories as involving differences in fields, objects and relations over time, i.e. in the ways we conceptualise change. We differ in conceptualising dynamics of Indigenous–non-Indigenous interaction, and the dispersed effects of social forces that are not directly visible, and are not articulated as such in people's ways of understanding themselves.

I have grouped Macdonald and myself together in that we seem to agree that Indigenous–non-Indigenous social and cultural differences persist in changing ways—and that these differences *are* cultural, that is learned and reproduced; but also, that even what seems (to subjects themselves) to be most fundamental to the way they are is open to history. In the case of long-term colonisation of the Wiradjuri, they have completely discontinued their practice of Law, but they continue to reproduce what they and others see and sense as distinctive familial relationships and social forms. The forms these practices take are certainly shaped, not only by their own preferences, but in relation to exclusionary and power-laden practices of colonial, now postcolonial, Australian state and society with respect to Indigenous people who continue to be seen as 'different'. But even oppressive change cannot be understood only deterministically: it develops along paths people take within circumstances as they encounter them. Not all change is simply repressive, nor is well-intentioned remedial change always liberatory. Most importantly, as Joel Robbins points out, we have not adequately developed critical categories needed to characterise change and people's perception of it. Many social science theorisations of change take it that the 'new' is always perceived through the 'old', but this leaves unexplored cultural constructs of novelty, the very question of what people perceive as new, and how.

I have grouped Tonkinson and Morphy together in that they start/ed from another end of a spectrum: from assumptions that there are certain domains or areas of social practice that are central and relatively impervious to change. While Indigenous Australians no doubt see supreme value in some kinds of activity—like ritual—over others, this does not by itself tell us how they may act to preserve it, or not do so. We also need to be able to account for those reports, and experiences, of Indigenous people who decide that rituals should not be reproduced, that sacra should be given away or given into custody, sold (Batty 2006). Any such explanations must take account of changes in Indigenous people's relations among themselves, and between themselves and outsiders. Recent work by Tonkinson moves much more, as he himself notes, to foreground 'Western impacts', but still requires a conceptual basis for dealing with these observations. In any case it is clear that we cannot, in this field as in others, unproblematically attribute continuity to Indigenous practice and experience without considering the question of repositioning of practices and values posed by Indigenous–non-Indigenous co-presence, mutual awareness, and forms of interaction.

Are changes in kinship and certain kinds of social relations more or less open to change? There often seems to be a supposition that domestic, familial and kin relations are more persistent and less permeable (as the Morphys posit of the Yolngu). Yet there is still a dearth of solid suggestions and evidence about how to critically evaluate what is persistent, and what more fluid, in these relations that clearly, in many places, remain observably different from other patterns.

It is, I have suggested, not fortuitous that Tonkinson's and Morphy's domain-linked claims of centrality have emerged from research grounded in religion, ritual, and art. These, as recent developments have shown, are indeed constituted within Indigenous practice and value as special, high cultural, frames if you will. In fact, much of what we now call Aboriginal 'art' was originally not detachable from the framework of ritual. But I have suggested that in some ways high valuation, in historically particular contexts, has made some of these practices readily transposable into new, constructed frames (of art galleries, museums, performance spaces), where indeed the high valuation that Indigenous people have long attributed to them can be renewed and reshaped—in interaction, often, with outsiders.

In other historically particular settings such as that of the Wiradjuri, comparable practices have waned, and disappeared, and undoubtedly in earlier times were sometimes discouraged or overtly suppressed. The range of newly constructed frames, like the art market and Garma, selectively reach well outside the Yolngu social space to connect particular people with institutions and markets elsewhere. No similar sort of cultural product has emerged from within the interrelation of Wiradjuri and non-Indigenous Australia. In these spatial, material and social shifts of Yolngu art there are dimensions of both continuity and change. This invites further consideration (see Anderson 1995, for instance) of what methodological and theoretical tacks we may take in trying to analyse what happens when something that was formerly Indigenous-internal is brought to an external audience—rather than simply assuming, or idealising, its continuity.

References

Anderson, C (ed.) (1995) *Politics of the secret*. Oceania Monographs, Sydney.

Austin-Broos, D (2011) *A different inequality: the politics of debate about remote Aboriginal Australia*. Allen and Unwin, Sydney.

Baker, G (2010) 'We just cry for our country': the boycott and the Goulburn Islanders. *Australian Historical Studies* 41(3): 302–18.

Batty, P (2006) White redemption rituals: reflections on the repatriation of Aboriginal secret-sacred objects. In T Lea, E Kowal and G Cowlishaw (eds) *Moving anthropology: critical Indigenous studies*. Charles Darwin University Press, Darwin: 55–63.

Hacking, I (1999) *The social construction of what?* Harvard University Press, Cambridge, Mass.

Hart, K (2002) Anthropologists and development. *Norsk Antropologisk Tidsskrift* 13(1–2): 14–21.

Macdonald, G (2004) *Two steps forward, three steps back: a Wiradjuri land rights journey*. LhR Press, Canada Bay.

Macdonald, G (2008) Difference or disappearance: the politics of Indigenous inclusion in the liberal state. *Anthropologica* 50(2): 341–58.

Merlan, F (1998) *Caging the rainbow: places, politics and Aborigines in a north Australian town*. University of Hawai'i Press, Honolulu.

Merlan, F (2001) From cultural production to Aboriginal art. In Thomas, N and Pinney, C (eds) *Beyond aesthetics*. Berg, London: 201–34.

Morphy, H (1991) *Ancestral connections: art and an Aboriginal system of knowledge*. University of Chicago Press, Chicago.

Morphy, F and Morphy, H (2013) The hegemony of the 'mainstream': anthropological theory and government policy in Australia's Northern Territory. *American Anthropologist* 115(2): 174–87.

Palmié, S (1995) Against syncretism: 'Africanizing' and 'Cubanizing' discourses in North American òrìsà worship. In R Fardon (ed.) *Counterworks: managing the diversity of knowledge*. Routledge, London: 73–104.

Petri, H and Petri-Odermann, G (1970) Stability and change: present-day historic aspects among Australian Aborigines. In RM Berndt (ed.) *Australian Aboriginal anthropology*. University of Western Australia, Perth: 248–76.

Robbins, J (2007) Continuity thinking and the problem of Christian culture: belief, time and the anthropology of Christianity. *Current Anthropology* 48(1): 5–38.

Sharp, L (1952) Steel axes for Stone-Age Australians. *Human Organization* 11(2): 17–22.

Tonkinson, R (1970) Aboriginal dream-spirit beliefs in a contact situation: Jigalong, Western Australia. In R Berndt (ed.) *Australian Aboriginal anthropology*. University of Western Australia, Perth: 277–91.

Tonkinson, R (1974) *The Jigalong mob: Aboriginal victors of the desert crusade*. Cummings, Menlo Park.

Tonkinson, R (2004) Spiritual prescription, social reality: reflections on religious dynamism. *Anthropological Forum* 14(2): 183–201.

Tonkinson, R (2007) Aboriginal 'difference' and 'autonomy' then and now: four decades of change in a Western Desert society. *Anthropological Forum* 17(1): 41–60.

Tonkinson, R (2012) Anthropologies of change: theoretical and methodological challenges. In P McGrath and T Bauman (eds) *Anthropological approaches to the study of social change. a workshop for native title anthropologists*. AIATSIS, Canberra: 18–23.

Tonkinson, R and Tonkinson, M (2010) The cultural dynamics of adaptation in remote Aboriginal communities: policy, values and the state's unmet expectations. *Anthropologica* 52(1): 67–75.

17. Learning about Change Through Industrial Open Innovation in the Fast-Moving Consumer Goods Sector

Sarah Pearson

Whilst some of us thrive on change, many people find it threatening. Tension between the Darwinian drive to evolve and our social need to fit in with the *status quo* plays out in industry just as much as in our individual lives. In no situation is this more obvious than the role of innovation within industry, where innovation *is* change and often requires *us* to change just as much as the product or process that is being replaced. Us as employees, and us as consumers. This chapter gives an insight into how industry thinks about change, particularly relating to innovation within the fast-moving consumer goods sector. It also presents two case studies demonstrating how competitive market pressure has driven changes in innovation practice, especially encouraging open innovation. The second case study which stems from my own experience also demonstrates how to overcome the understandable internal inertia that blocks successful change, and how to work with failure.

Innovation as a microcosm of industrial change

When considering change in an industrial setting, one needs to be aware of the tensions that exist: tensions between corporate and individual needs, as well as between the long-term survival of the company and the need to demonstrate short-term success. The process of innovation heightens these tensions, requiring short-term actions to drive long-term commercial success, sometimes requiring change before the need is obvious, and flavoured with the inherent risk of failure and hence threat to individual careers. This is all assuming that consumers are driving the need for change. Throw in consumers who may also need to be encouraged to change if the driver is technological advances, even when the benefits are obvious, and you have a real challenge on your hands.

Innovation

Innovation has many definitions. For the purposes of this chapter I describe it as:

Change that delivers value.

Value could mean the delivery of new products, new services, and new processes that improve profit through increased revenue, or cost reduction.

In spite of these tensions, innovation plays a key role in the long-term survival of a company, with innovative and collaborative companies consistently outperforming their counterparts. Globally governments have recognised this and put numerous programs in place to support innovation. But even with this recognition of its importance, and government support to encourage it, innovation is not a simple activity to embed.

Challenges for industrial change

Whilst industry is often portrayed as an unemotional and logical entity, this is merely a macroscopic view. Our legal system reinforces this through corporations law, where a company is given rights and responsibilities as if it were an individual, with stringent implications when that 'individual' either fails to comply with the law or fails to succeed. The company is assumed to have a long-term future, and its leaders are expected to make decisions in the short-term to secure this long-term success.

However, if a company is no longer able to pay its bills, it is no longer allowed to trade, and effectively ceases to exist. This leads to the sense that a company will do all in its power, in a strategic and logical manner, to survive. It also encourages a culture of risk-aversion, since the consequences of failure can be dire.

Yet companies comprise people: people with fears and ambitions, preconceptions and views of self that have been built up over years of experience, outside the work environment as well as inside it; people without access to the entire information set ideally needed for strategic decision-making. Nor will all of their individual decisions be obviously logical, unemotional or aligned to long-term company survival. Hence when attempting to understand and drive industrial change, one must take into account the individuals, with all their individual strengths, commitment, and foibles.

With this in mind it is fairly simple to identify a number of reasons why industrial change is challenging and is seen as a threat by individuals, including these:

- In the short term, change requires energy. This can be daunting, even if the long-term gains are obvious. Rather like in a chemical reaction, a catalyst is often required to encourage people over the 'activation energy' barrier. People need a reason to put in this energy—what is in it for them?

- Change can also be perceived as a threat to people's jobs and sense of self-worth in the workplace. Change invariably raises the thought that something must be wrong now in order to require this adaptation. When employees base their self-image on success in the workplace, change that implies that they could be doing better is challenging. People need to see how the change will help their self-image.

Next I present two case studies of driving change in industry, outlining ways in which these and a number of other challenges can manifest, and suggesting actions that can be taken to overcome them. Each case study is based on experience working in industrial innovation, where change was necessary to improve productivity and competitive positioning.

Case Study 1: Competition as a driver of open innovation

In the fast moving consumer goods sector of today's world, the rate of product innovation is so rapid that companies have to adopt new approaches to product development in order to remain competitive. The old linear approach, involving the sole use of internal research and development (R&D) teams, no longer delivers new products at a sufficiently rapid pace to keep up with consumer demand or competitor supply.

Consider the frequency of new product launches in the electronics industry, or the personal goods sector. How can a company keep up with this pace using only internal R&D groups, its own ideas? Something has to change in the way organisations develop new products in order to meet this acceleration and stay in the competitive game. This competitive driver is proving a strong catalyst for change.

In order to react to this competitive environment, companies are looking outside their organisational boundaries for new ideas, new products, or solutions to current technical challenges in order to speed up their innovation process. Rather than devoting years to solving technical challenges or developing new products themselves, companies are realising that a more efficient approach is to seek external partners who have either solved the technical challenges, or developed new products already. This speeds up the process to product launch, and helps the company to grow more rapidly. This is termed by most as 'open innovation'.[1]

Open innovation example

Proctor & Gamble employs a connect + develop[SM] program of activity, devoted to sourcing new product ideas from outside the company globally. By looking outside the company Proctor & Gamble are able to launch new products without spending many years on development themselves.

The face cream product Olay[TM] Regenerist, for example, did not come wholly from Proctor & Gamble R&D teams, but involved sourcing technology already developed by a small French company (Sederma). A partnership was formed between Proctor & Gamble and Sederma, and this product is now sold around the world within Proctor & Gamble's broader brand portfolio. The partnership meant that Proctor & Gamble saved years of development work, getting a new product to market fast. For Sederma, it allowed access to global routes to market that would have taken many years to develop themselves.

Large successful companies, such as Proctor & Gamble, General Mills, and Cadbury, have turned to this new model for innovation in order to beat their competition and drive improved corporate growth. Yet whilst open innovation is a logical, efficient and effective method for innovation, without the threat of competition most companies would not consider making the necessary changes for fear of having to deal with their associated challenges.

---

1   Open innovation differs from outsourcing. In outsourcing the organisation looks for another organisation to provide a service that it no longer wants to deliver itself (such as cleaning). In open innovation, the organisation seeks solutions to its challenges, or new product ideas, externally, which may lead to contracting research, collaborative projects, joint ventures or simply purchasing the technology, business or idea.

Proctor & Gamble, considered to be global leaders in open innovation, represent a classic example of how competitive pressure led them to take on the challenges of this change in innovation practice. During the year 2000, Proctor & Gamble reported several profit warnings. Some of their leading brands had weakened and their competitors were making the most of this. The market lost confidence in the company, leading to a severe downturn in the share price: the stock price dropped 50 per cent over the six months from January to June. Something had to be done. The energy for change had to be found.

The company's new Chief Executive Officer, AG Lafley, realised that in order for the company to rise above this challenge it needed to put innovation at the centre of all that it did. Why? Because it needed to return to high growth rates, achieved through the delivery of new products and new markets—fast. When you are an $80 billion+ company, growth rates above a few per cent pose significant challenges in a competitive environment. Hence not only did something have to be done, but something different had to be done. Lafley turned to open innovation.

To speed up their innovation process and hence shorten the time to launch new products and enter new markets, Proctor & Gamble were forced to look outside for new technologies and ideas. The new approach has paid off. Thirteen years on and Proctor & Gamble have developed more than 2000 global partnerships, delivered dozens of global game-changer products to consumers, accelerated innovation development and increased productivity, both for Proctor & Gamble and its partners.

While competition is a key driver of this change, there are other exogenous changes that make it a sensible strategy, such as the change in distribution of R&D spending beyond the traditional concentration in large multinationals to being spread over a large number of small companies; and the connectedness of our society making it so much easier to connect to people and ideas on a global scale, rapidly. So it is not merely a need driven by competition, but an opportunity driven by a growth in ideas being generated in numerous organisations and the ability to connect to them.

Speeding up the innovation process

When looking for new ways to invigorate the Pringles brand, Proctor & Gamble came up with the idea of printing images on potato crisps. They soon realised that they needed to look externally for ideas of how to print edible dye images on potato crisps. Their open innovation team discovered a bakery run by a university professor in Italy that had developed a way of printing edible images on cakes. A few small changes were required to adapt this technology for Pringles, but they were able to launch Pringles Prints in just eight months compared to the usual two years. Within one year, the new product grew Proctor & Gamble's revenues 14 per cent, extraordinary for such a large company.

The new approach has proved incredibly successful, so much so that many companies around the world are implementing it and learning from Proctor & Gamble's experience. However this did not happen overnight and required significant change in behaviour, and the experiences of strong barriers to change, and threats to individual perceptions of self-worth. The next section outlines some of these challenges through a case study of starting up an open innovation approach at Cadbury plc.

Case Study 2: Overcoming internal barriers to open innovation

Cadbury plc started to look to open innovation as a tool to enhance innovation productivity in late 2006. The Chief Technology Officer at Cadbury initially drove the change, drawn to the idea through competition: a number of his colleagues in other companies had started to adopt the strategy, including Cadbury competition.

The company soon came to realise that open innovation could accelerate their innovation process and provide access to new ideas the company would not have dreamed of on its own. Not only did they believe that no one company can own all the world's best scientists, but also that solutions to technical challenges could already exist in non-competing industry sectors.

This challenged the embedded approach, where expert scientists were hired to work on technical aspects of new product development, priding themselves (quite rightly) on their technical expertise and contribution to the company's goals. These experts saw themselves as the best in their field—why would they need to look outside for ideas? What did it mean for their own self-worth? Some had also tried looking outside for ideas in the past and it had failed: 'Well, we tried that once before and it hasn't worked. Why would we bother again?' We needed to be able to say 'How can I help you achieve your goals and make you look good?', and 'Okay, well perhaps that didn't work in the past, but here's something that has worked for you now.'

A pilot project was used to kickstart the new innovation activity. It was so successful that a small UK-based team was set up with a global remit to develop an implementation strategy, grow capacity, develop an open culture, and deliver value through sourcing technology solutions and new product ideas from broad areas outside confectionery. I helped out with the pilot project, and subsequently took on the lead role driving the change across the company globally. I set up a small UK-based group that quickly evolved into a globally linked open innovation team, strongly embedded internally and externally and aligned with global category strategies.

Over an 18-month period a list of global technology needs was agreed with the business; more than 60 searches for different needs were conducted, with licensing, collaboration and co-development projects initiated globally. In addition, numerous patents were granted, non-food technology was identified for a novel product platform, and the development of an open culture led to external partner involvement in half of the long-term research projects. Cadbury received recognition as innovative leaders and external parties began to approach us with ideas.

How was this change in approach driven? What were the keys to this success? There were many well recognised keys, such as strong leadership support (from the Chief Technology Officer initially, and after a short period the Chief Executive Officer too), a dedicated team, and appropriate resources. As the head of open innovation, I was also given the title 'Open Innovation Champion', signalling the importance of this new approach to the rest of the company globally.

In addition we came to understand the following keys to success:

- the critical importance of delivering value in early stages
- the need for ownership and trust
- building cross-functional and integrated support
- working with failure.

Early value delivery

When I took on the role of open innovation champion I looked for literature discussing the mobilisation of change, to help shape how I would go about implementing this challenging new approach at Cadbury. I was pretty unsuccessful in finding what I needed, but I did come across a publication suggesting that successful change is led by results. Promising results before implementing change can work, but starting with results is even better. This was instrumental in my strategy, and I later found that others leading open innovation had experienced the same.

By demonstrating early wins, getting others on board and encouraging them to embrace the change is much easier. People see the reason for change. There are several ways of ensuring this, one being the use of an 'under the radar' pilot project to test out the change. The other (which can be combined with the first) is to start with 'low hanging fruit'—focusing on a challenge for the change process where you are sure an impact can be demonstrated.

At Cadbury, the six-month pilot project was run quietly inside the long-term R&D centre in the UK. A few key supporters outside the centre were involved, but the project was not highlighted around the company. Two technical challenges important to the business were chosen, and broad searches for solutions outside the company sought.

We found several promising solutions for these challenges. A novel technology used for pressure sensors in sails, with the potential to provide a new product platform in all three categories (chewing gum, candy and chocolate) was also discovered fairly quickly. Demonstration of this early success led to buy-in, support and resources from the R&D leadership level within the company.

The next step involved rolling the new process out across Cadbury globally. In order to encourage people to change, to overcome the cultural and energy barrier to looking outside for ideas and the perceived threat to their capability and self-worth, this early win was used as a tool to demonstrate how powerful the new approach could be.

The major lesson in this process was that the early win had to be more than just an idea. People needed to be able to see and touch the new product. It needed to be tangible and its value obvious. Prototype products were made, designs drawn up, and templates outlining the impact on and benefits to the business developed. These were then shared and communicated globally around the business, with leaders and those below them responsible for project delivery.

The key here was to learn and speak the 'language' that helped demonstrate the value. The appropriate language for most was that of a tangible product. For others it related to bottom line impact, such as an indication of market size and likely revenue as well as brand impact.

By showing employees the early win and making sure that they could see how we could help them deliver new products and solve their technological challenges, we got widespread support and involvement. The early win acted as a catalyst for change, giving people the reason, or impetus, to overcome inertia and consider trying out the new approach.

Ownership and trust

The second and most important key to success was the need to demonstrate without a doubt that we were there to help employees and the company achieve their goals—that we were not in competition, not simply a fad, but there to provide support and that we were not a threat to experts, but there to help them achieve their goals. New product development teams had tight deadlines to meet regarding product launch. The open innovation team needed to show that we were there to help them speed up development, so that they could reach their targets effectively and at times more efficiently.

In order to achieve this, part of the strategy for growing the open culture across Cadbury involved ensuring that the open innovation team searched for technology that would directly assist the new product development and R&D teams with their product development plans. I had seen a number of companies failing in their open innovation activity when their external searches were not linked to internal company needs. They would be sent out to 'find something interesting', and like the cat coming home with the mouse, discovered that what they found was not what the company wanted.

In order to avoid that outcome, we asked the new product development and R&D teams to help compile a needs list, a list of technologies that they would like us to access. The open innovation searches were aligned to this list, ensuring that they were owned by the new product development and R&D teams.

This played three important roles:

- involvement and ownership of the open innovation process by the new product development and R&D teams. This helped reduce the threat to their self-worth as they were in the driving seat, with us helping them to find ways to deliver to their targets faster and hence leading to greater success for them

- the knowledge that if technologies were found that met the identified needs, they would be seen as valuable, thereby reinforcing the value of open innovation
- ensuring that when technologies were found they would be brought into Cadbury and used in new products. This helped deliver success through the open innovation process, as well as giving external collaborators the confidence that their technologies would be used.

Ownership of change can also be encouraged through appraisal systems. Whilst the usual incentive systems play to short-term results and rewards, key performance indicators can be devised that help to guide behaviour change for longer term benefits. Companies can assess short-term steps that will support the long-term change, and reward employees for taking these steps.

For instance, each employee at the Cadbury R&D centre was given roles, responsibilities and goals to reach over the course of 12 months. A range of key performance indicators were used to assess achievement of these goals, with bonus payment being related to these. Each member of staff had one indicator related to their open innovation activity in order to help grow the culture and focus, thereby supporting ownership and engagement with the overall strategy as it grew.

Whilst in the early days of this activity some of it would not be successful, the key performance indicators were designed to encourage at least trying this new approach. Before we started the program, only a handful of long-term research projects involved external partners. After a year of applying the key performance indicators, and supporting the open innovation activity, half of the long-term research projects involved collaborations with external partners. Most employees had at least considered whether looking outside would yield productive results.

Another barrier to widespread engagement with open innovation is the issue of confidentiality and trust. How can you safely share information externally with other companies, knowing that your competitors could access the information? In the past, innovation has been kept securely within corporate boundaries as companies are justifiably concerned that their competition will use any information on new product ideas and technologies to inform their own strategic planning. Trust and appropriate processes need to be built with employees before they will be convinced to change their behaviour and start to talk with people outside the company, including in some instances their competitors.

The way that we addressed this was to build trusting relationships with each employee who had a need to seek external technologies, work alongside them to decide whether or not the information was too sensitive to be able to share externally in any form, and then define and agree a non-confidential description of the technology or science that we could share with external parties. We developed a process of sharing the descriptions with them, having them check that we had understood correctly and reinforcing that this was their search, to help them, in a safe way.

By working closely with the new product development and R&D employees, we were able to build confidence that we would act in their best interest and with care to find the external technology that they required, without jeopardising the project. This led to confidence in the open innovation team and process, thereby encouraging greater support and involvement.

Cross-functional, integrated support

When considering change within a company, thought needs to be given to who needs to be drawn into the change process. At an early stage in the Cadbury process it became clear that we needed to reach out to more than just the new product development and R&D teams. Marketing functions tend to drive product launch decisions in the fast-moving consumer goods sector, making it important to reach out to them as well for driving change in the innovation process.

In order to bring them 'onside', I spent considerable time working with the marketing groups, building trust, explaining the new approach, and demonstrating how we could help them achieve their launch goals. Again the quick early wins helped establish the potential of open innovation to help marketing groups reach their goals of launching competitive products.

As with the R&D groups, we asked marketing employees to help us compile a needs list that would be used to guide the open innovation searches. Once this was completed, we had a list of technologies to look for that linked to real needs within the company, from the new product development, R&D and marketing teams.

The efforts of the open innovation team were split approximately 80:20— 80 per cent of our efforts were dedicated to delivering solutions to the known R&D challenges, thereby reducing time to market; and 20 per cent were dedicated to finding new technologies that could meet a consumer need or give Cadbury a dramatic commercial advantage.

We also made sure that we were open to serendipitous finds: we were frequently approached by organisations with good ideas, or we stumbled across interesting technologies during our networking. In order to help filter these ideas we worked closely with the marketing and consumer foresight groups to gain an understanding of consumer trends and commercial strategies. Selling these novel ideas internally would have been very difficult without a good understanding of the marketing strategy and long term consumer needs, and strong relationships with the global marketing teams.

Whilst it was a major advantage to have reached this stage, it soon became clear that it was a piecemeal solution. My vision was to incorporate open innovation into a multifunctional approach, involving employees from a range of groups such as new product development, R&D, marketing, legal and manufacturing areas within Cadbury. We developed a method for identifying and agreeing medium term technology needs with integrated multifunctional involvement, followed by a decision process about whether to make internally, buy from outside, or partner to co-develop the necessary technology. In this way open innovation was integrated into global innovation strategy setting, in a multifunctional process, having managed to deliver change across company functional boundaries.

Working with failure

Whilst I have talked mainly of success so far, it is important to consider how to deal with failure when it occurs, as well as how to mitigate it when designing successful change programs. If there is no failure, then arguably there has been no innovation. How do you accept and work with failure whilst acting to maximise success?

The practical approaches described above were developed in order to mitigate failure, as well as to maximise success. For instance, knowing that siloed R&D activity would not help in terms of taking ideas to market, I involved cross-functional teams and worked closely with the power brokers in marketing. If I came up with ideas on my own, who would listen? Why would they listen? But if I had had people working with me to come up with that idea, there was a much bigger chance that the process was going to be successful.

We also worked on several external searches at a time, running a portfolio of projects so that if one failed, at least we would have other success stories to tell. When an idea failed to be accepted by the company, we kept a record of it in case it was merely a timing issue. Quite often ideas that are rejected one day are accepted another when strategies and markets change. And finally, if an approach did not appear to be working, we stopped doing it quickly and tried to learn from our failure—the 'fast failure' approach.

Conclusion

Change is hard. It requires energy and a compelling reason to jump on board: energy from those leading change, and energy from the followers. In spite of the widespread sense that companies are ruthlessly focused on success, industry is not immune to this challenge, even when the need for change is obvious. However, the drive to remain competitive can provide the energy to help individuals and organisations accept new ways of working and delivering value.

Industrial innovation, a microcosm of change, is itself innovating. Innovation is accelerating. Companies are being forced to adapt and innovate more and more rapidly as their customers demand new products and services with a voracious appetite, and competition finds ways to deliver fast. This is forcing them to learn new ways to energise their employees, to embrace new approaches, new business models, new products and services, new processes.

This chapter has discussed a number of approaches used successfully in industrial change programs, specifically related to industrial innovation. Key insights to consider from this experience include the obvious, such as supporting champions to lead change, and demonstrated support from the top. As well as this, experience has shown that quick wins, a service approach to showing how the change can help employees achieve their own goals, gaining buy-in from a range of stakeholders across institutional boundaries, and working with failure can greatly enhance successful growth of change uptake.

18. Increasing Interest in the Economic Determinants of Structural, Technological and Climate Change

Jim Butler

Perhaps the most succinct definition of economics is that it is the science of scarcity. This is an abbreviation of the fuller definition provided by Lionel Robbins in the 1930s as 'the science which studies human behaviour as a relationship between ends and scarce means which have alternative uses' (Robbins 1932, 15). While these definitions appear to be clear and concise, they belie deeper philosophical issues around the nature of the discipline which have been, and continue to be, debated by scholars. For example, Robbins viewed economics as a positive science that concerns itself with understanding facts and analysing 'what is' as opposed to a science that concerns itself also with normative issues, with the value judgments that underlie economists' policy prescriptions, and with arguments about 'what ought to be'. An example of a more recent contrary view of science in general, and economics in particular, is provided by Boldeman (2007).

Notwithstanding these deeper recurring issues, the succinct definition of economics as the science of scarcity serves the useful purpose of locating it as a science which studies phenomena that involve scarcity—and few would dispute that. In terms of change, then, the changes with which economics concerns itself are those associated with the problem of scarcity. Such changes are manifold and vary considerably through time. In the UK in the first half of the nineteenth century, the introduction of the Corn Laws, which imposed heavy import duties on imported grain (thereby increasing the price of bread), occupied the minds of a number of economists. In numerous countries the twenty-first century presents a different set of challenges, including the development of markets for human tissue, body parts and surrogates for human reproduction, and the problem of rationing scarce geostationary orbit slots for the placement of satellites.[1] But these changes all have, as their underlying bedrock, the common theme of striving to satisfy more wants of humankind with the limited resources at our disposal.

---

[1] A geostationary orbit of a satellite is one that results in the satellite orbiting the Earth above the equator at a speed matching the Earth's rotation, thus appearing to remain stationary. Most communications satellites are in geostationary orbit.

Observing that economics, as the science of scarcity, is interested in change from that point of view is a very broad beginning to a chapter on economics and change. After all—at the risk of being platitudinous—scarcity and change are both ubiquitous, so this starting point could be construed as an argument that economists are interested in everything! So how might this enquiry be narrowed to cast more light on how economics deals with change?

To begin, consider the following question: Of the multitude of changes that have occurred and will continue to occur in society, are there particular *types* of change that are of enduring interest to economists? While it is not the purpose of this chapter to fully develop a typology of change for this purpose, some interesting insights can be gained by considering the broad types of change that have consistently occupied the minds of economists regardless of time and place.

Investigation of these broad types begins by turning to *The new Palgrave dictionary of economics*, a major and authoritative work first published in 1987 with the second edition appearing in 2008.[2] The online version of the dictionary allows both editions to be searched for the word 'change' in article titles across all topics in the dictionary. The results of this search are shown in Table 1. The overlap between the types of change appearing in article titles across the various editions of the dictionary is clear: 'structural change' and 'technical/ technological change' feature in a number of titles in both editions. 'Agricultural growth and population change' has disappeared, and 'climate change' is a new entry, in the 2008+ editions.

Table 1: *New Palgrave dictionary* articles with 'change' in the article title.

1987 edition	2008+ editions[a]
1. Structural change	1. Structural change
2. Technical change	2. Technical change
3. Agricultural growth and population change	3. Skill-based technical change
4. Biased and unbiased technological change	4. Structural change, econometrics of
	5. Climate change, economics of
	6. Biased and unbiased technological change

(a) Includes the 2008 edition plus all new articles included in the dictionary since then.

To illustrate how economics approaches these types of changes, attention in the remainder of this chapter will focus on structural change, technological change, and climate change.

---

2   The first edition comprised four volumes, and the second eight volumes. The original Palgrave's dictionary of political economy comprised three volumes and was first published in 1894. Palgrave was 'a banker and one-time editor of *The Economist* whose avocation was economics' (Stigler 1988, p.1729).

Structural change

Structural change, also sometimes referred to as structural transformation, refers to large-scale changes in the composition of industries in an economy. Traditionally, economics has distinguished between primary industries (such as agriculture, fishing, forestry, mining), secondary industries (manufacturing and construction) and tertiary industries (services). It has been observed over a long period that, as economic development occurs, economies tend to undergo structural change, moving away from a predominant reliance on primary industries as the source of a nation's wealth to secondary and tertiary industries. The industrial revolution which began in Great Britain in the second half of the eighteenth century, and subsequently spread to Western Europe and the US, is testimony to this. The works of Fisher (1939) and Clark (1940) are two examples of this argument concerning economic development and structural change.

Two features of how economics deals with structural change are of interest here. The first, which leads to a theme that recurs in later discussion, relates to how the discipline has changed its approach to understanding structural change. Matsuyama (2008) argues that the earlier literature on this subject 'is mostly descriptive, trying to provide a sweeping overview of the development process, with the emphasis on the multifaceted nature of structural change'. He goes on to argue that 'recent work tends to be more analytical, using formal models designed to focus on a few specific aspects of structural change'. This shift from a descriptive to an analytical focus reflects an attempt to gain a deeper understanding of the causal connection between economic development and structural change. Having observed an association between the two, what is the causal relationship between them—if any? Does economic development cause structural change by creating a major shift in the pattern of demand for goods and services? Does structural change cause economic development to occur because it reflects major increases in productivity brought about by innovation and invention? Or does causality run in both directions, a possibility mentioned by Matsuyama (2008): 'There is also an increasing awareness that the two-way causality between economic growth and structural change can provide possible explanations for development failures.' Finally, it is possible that both occur simultaneously but are not causally connected, being driven by some other underlying causal factor common to both.

The second feature of interest arising out of how economics deals with structural change is the growing realisation that the conventional threefold classification of industries (primary, secondary, tertiary) is itself in need of change in that it needs to be augmented with a fourth category—information-/knowledge-based industries. Spawned by developments in information technology and discoveries in other new fields such as biotechnology, these new industries generate wealth by using information and knowledge to generate further innovation and inventive activity. Drucker (1969, 12), in his book *The age of discontinuity*, argues:

> Technologically, the established 'modern' industries may still enjoy a long period of growth and advance ... But in their ability to provide the thrust for further substantial growth of the developed economies, they are mature, if not stagnant.

This brings us to the second major type of change that warrants discussion—technological change, itself a major contributor to structural change and a new fourth category of industries.

Technological change

The production function is a central concept in economics, showing the relationship between the quantities of inputs used in producing a product (or service) and the maximum output of that product attainable from those quantities of inputs. The production function, so defined, is based upon a given technology for transforming inputs into outputs. Technological change occurs when that transformation process changes. By and large, technological changes are of interest when they enable more output to be achieved with any quantity of inputs—referred to as cost-reducing technological changes because they reduce the cost of producing products. As the science of scarcity, economics is interested in cost-reducing technological change because it enables us to make more efficient use of limited resources.

Technological change is an important determinant of economic growth. It has played a major role in structural change in the economy, and is responsible for many improvements in production processes and consequentially increases in productivity and national income. It stands to reason, therefore, that economists would be interested in the determinants of the rate of technological change. However, for many years, technological change was assumed by economists to be exogenous, that is, it was assumed that its determinants were non-economic in nature, and were therefore outside the economic system and not amenable to economic analysis. This was particularly evident in growth theory, where economists concentrated on the role of physical quantities of inputs in the production function in generating higher output rather than on the nature of the input–output transformation process—the technology—embodied in the production function. Thus, for example, differences in growth rates between countries were seen as being due to differences in their resource endowments—countries with higher growth rates tended to have relatively greater resource endowments. When technology was recognised as playing a role, for example, in the models of economic growth developed by Solow (1956) and Swan (1956) in which technology was the mechanism by which a country could continue growing despite the law of diminishing returns, it was assumed to be exogenous.

The assumption of exogenous technological change was also invoked in an industry-specific context even when the pace of such change was a major feature of the industry. In the healthcare industry, for example, which has experienced rapid technological change, it is only more recently that economists have begun to study the determinants of the rate of technological change in healthcare more seriously. This is notwithstanding the conclusion by Newhouse (1992) that technological change in healthcare was responsible for well over half of the increase in expenditures on medical care over a 50-year period in the US.

In both of these areas—economic growth and health care—more recent work in economics has sought to treat the rate of technological change as endogenous, that is, as being determined by economic factors within the system. Endogenous growth theory makes the determinant of the rate of technological change internal to the economic system by allowing firms to earn monopoly rents from research activities that result in the production of new knowledge. These research activities generate new knowledge because they lead to investment in human capital. The enhancement of a nation's human capital will lead to economic growth by leading to the development of new forms of technology and efficient and effective means of production.[3] In healthcare, researchers have hypothesised that the rate of technological change is endogenous to the health insurance system. With widespread health insurance in many countries, patients face relatively low or even zero out-of-pocket expenses for many healthcare services. Therefore patients, and doctors acting on their behalf, have little incentive to reject new technologies even if their health impact is small because the patient's financial exposure is very limited or zero. Knowing that their products will be sold into heavily insured markets, firms in the healthcare sector have a stronger incentive to invest in research and development relative to firms in other industries. These features were incorporated into a model of insurance and innovation in medical care by Goddeeris (1984) who also showed that insurance results in technological change that is less cost-reducing or more cost-increasing than in other industries.

As seen with structural change, economists working on technological change have made concerted attempts to improve understanding of the causes of such change. This interest in causality reflects a determination not to simply accept

---

3   Aghion and Howitt (2009) provide an overview of growth theory in economics including endogenous growth theory.

and describe change, but to understand its economic determinants. Our third type of change of significance to economics—climate change—also demonstrates this characteristic.

Climate change

As economics is a social science, economists' work on climate change has grown commensurately with the increasing acceptance by climate scientists of the anthropogenic cause theory of climate change. The essence of this theory is that, by generating increasing emissions of greenhouse gases (especially carbon dioxide), human behaviour is causing a long-term increase in global surface temperatures.

Economists' interest in this topic is motivated by what Hardin (1968) referred to, in the title of his famous paper, as the tragedy of the commons. The 'commons' refers to common property resources—resources which do not have defined private property rights but which are owned by society in common. This lack of property rights allows individuals to use such resources without paying any access fee because there is no defined owner of the resource. As a consequence, individuals can overexploit such resources in the sense that they can harvest them beyond the point where the marginal value of the resource to them is equal to the marginal cost imposed upon society at large by their exploitation. This often results in degradation of the quality of the resource and, if utilisation is sufficiently high, can also lead to its disappearance. For example, in the absence of property rights over the fish in the sea, overharvesting can lead to reduction in fish stocks and eventually to their extinction; in the absence of property rights for geostationary orbits in space, overcrowding can result in degradation of service quality in telecommunications because of the proximity of neighbouring satellites; and in the absence of property rights in inner and outer space, gases from humankind's activity can accumulate in the earth's atmosphere to levels that potentially adversely affect life on earth.

In principle, the solution to the tragedy of the commons would seem to be the creation of property rights in common property resources, thus allowing their use to be governed by a functioning market or by some form of regulatory apparatus. For both technical and political reasons, this can be difficult—on the latter, witness the difficulties in arriving at international agreements on the management of climate change.

The remainder of this chapter focuses on two particular facets of economics and climate change. The first, which is not unique to how economics interacts with climate science but is usefully illustrated by it, is how economists deal with uncertainty and debates regarding the validity of scientific hypotheses advanced by other scientists. The economist qua economist has no particular knowledge or expertise in climate science so relies on the state of the art as enunciated by experts in that field. Where consensus or near-consensus has been achieved in that field, the economic assessment of various options for reducing or preventing anthropogenic climate change, mitigating its effects and adapting to its existence can proceed with some confidence. The magnitudes of the costs and benefits associated with these options can be estimated within reasonable bounds and sound policy advice can be formulated.

While there now appears to be a wide consensus on both the existence of, and anthropogenic cause of, global warming, uncertainty continues to exist about the magnitude of the effect of carbon dioxide emissions on global temperatures and the downstream effects on economies. The effect of this uncertainty on the work undertaken by economists was highlighted in earlier work by Nordhaus (1982, 242): 'Depending on the scenario, the effect of a CO_2 doubling ranged from minus 12 percent of global GNP to plus 5 percent. These are clearly very large impacts, but they are also very uncertain.' Narrowing this uncertainty has proved to be a difficult task. A recent article in *The Economist* entitled 'Climate science: a sensitive matter', published on 30 March 2013,[4] states: 'The climate may be heating up less in response to greenhouse-gas emissions than was once thought.' This assessment is based on work by climate scientists who found 'surface temperatures since 2005 are already at the low end of the range of projections derived from 20 climate models'.

The second facet of economics and climate change of interest in this chapter is the parallel development of thinking with respect to causes of change in the two sciences. The economist's growing interest in endogenous causes of technological change has already been discussed above. In their entry on climate change in *The new Palgrave dictionary of economics*, Goulder and Pizer (2008) refer to this in the context of climate change: 'Climate change is an inherently long-term problem and assumptions about technological change are particularly important. The modelling of technological change has advanced significantly beyond the early tradition that treated technological change as exogenous.'

How does this parallel the development of thinking in climate science with respect to the causes of climate change? For many years, society has regarded weather and climate-related events as being acts of God—changes that were outside the control of humans. The concept of an event being an act of God also plays an important role in the law of contracts where a defendant can invoke act of God as a defence against an action for breach of contract, and in the insurance industry where ideally the event to be insured against (such as damage to crops)

---

4   www.economist.com/news/science-and-technology/21574461-climate-may-be-heating-up-less-response-greenhouse-gas-emissions (accessed 2 June 2014).

is outside the control of the insured individual or organisation. While the language of climate science does not express the anthropogenic cause theory of climate change as being a search for endogenous causes of climate change, the concept underlying that theory parallels the economists' search for what this discipline labels endogenous causes. At this level of discourse, economists' increasing interest in endogenous causes of change shares the climate scientists' view of climate change as being endogenous to human behaviour and not entirely an act of God.

Conclusion

As with other sciences, both natural and social, economics is concerned with the causes and consequences of change. Of particular interest in this discipline are changes that impinge upon the problem of scarcity and human ability to address that problem with limited resources. The main theme of this chapter is that, over the last half century, economists have become increasingly interested in understanding the causes of change. For too long, the intellectual convenience of assuming causes of change to be exogenous to the economic system and to humankind itself have held sway. The growing interest in endogenous causes of change holds the promise of deepening our understanding of how to improve the welfare of society by broadening the array of possible instruments available to achieve that goal. This development in economics is argued to parallel a similar development in climate science which itself has become heavily involved in research on endogenous causes of climate change. Perhaps this trend reflects a growing interest in human behaviour as an important cause of changes in nature and society—maybe humankind causes change, thereby influencing our own destiny, more than we previously thought?

References

Aghion, P and Howitt, PW (2009) *The economics of growth*. MIT Press, Cambridge MA.

Boldeman, L (2007) *The cult of the market: economic fundamentalism and its discontents*. ANU E Press, Canberra.

Clark, C (1940) *The conditions of economic progress*. Macmillan, London.

Drucker, PF (1969) *The age of discontinuity: guidelines to our changing society*. Harper and Row, New York.

Fisher, A (1939) Production, primary, secondary and tertiary. *Economic Record* 15(1): 24–38.

Goddeeris, JH (1984) Insurance and incentives for innovation in medical care. *Southern Economic Journal* 51(2): 530–9.

Goulder H and Pizer, WA (2008) Climate change, economics of. In Durlauf, SN and Blume, LE (eds) *The new Palgrave dictionary of economics.* 2nd ed. Palgrave Macmillan, London, www.palgravemacmillan.com.au/palgrave/onix/isbn/9780333786765 (online version used).

Hardin, C (1968) The tragedy of the commons. *Science* (New Series), 162(3859): 1243–8.

Matsuyama, K (2008) Structural change. In Durlauf SN and Blume LE (eds) *The new Palgrave dictionary of economics.* 2nd ed. Palgrave Macmillan, London, www.palgravemacmillan.com.au/palgrave/onix/isbn/9780333786765 (online version used).

Newhouse, JP (1992) Medical care costs: how much welfare loss? *Journal of Economic Perspectives* 6(3): 3–21.

Nordhaus, W (1982) How fast should we graze the global commons? *American Economic Review* 72(2): 242–6.

Robbins, L (1932) *An essay on the nature and significance of economic science.* Macmillan, London.

Solow, RM (1956) A contribution to the theory of economic growth. *Quarterly Journal of Economics* 70(1): 65–94.

Stigler, GJ (1988) Palgrave's dictionary of economics. *Journal of Economic Literature* 26(4): 1729–36.

Swan, TW (1956) Economic growth and capital accumulation. *Economic Record* 32(2): 334–61.

19. Visual Fine Art: Documenting change, influencing change, and subjected to change

John Reid

Preamble to four propositions

I begin with a selective chronology with pictures, mainly photographs. Every moment accounts for the state of things in the universe. A photograph is a sample of sequential moments. Photographs that are symptomatic of the times, emblematic of place, or foreshadow historical significance are notable markers in the universal ledger. Photographs, like memories, assist in the comprehension of time and with the perception of change.

Mid-2012

The Australian National University (ANU) radically changed its approach to music education. More than 30 positions at the University's School of Music were declared vacant in an unprecedented act of academic cleansing. A collective shiver like the feathering of kettledrums spread through the rest of the university community, to resonate most acutely in the School of Art as yet another exercise in the transformational change of creative art education in Australia (Figure 1). At the end of the previous decade, the Victorian College of the Arts had fought a sustained assault on its constitution. More recently, the technical and further education sector in New South Wales had written off its heritage in art education and thrown its programs into the jaws of the open market.

Figure 1 Protest jam, ANU, 14 May 2012.

A composite photograph of members of the Canberra community who have joined a rally called by the ANU Student Association and the ANU School of Music students and staff to protest a planned restructure of the ANU School of Music and associated staff redundancies.

Source: John Reid, 2012.

Late 2012

A group of climate scientists and visual artists prepares a submission to a city council on Australia's eastern seaboard to develop collaborative procedures for addressing climate change impacts with communities within the council's shire. Climate change scientists (as knowledge generators), artists (as aesthetic communicators) and community leaders (enthused with local wisdom) were part of the shire constituency. They were all keen to act as agents to encourage changes in behaviour that affects climate and that will enable us to cope with anticipated future climatic conditions (Figure 2). A comprehensive council strategic plan on climate change already existed, providing a framework for genuine engagement between all parties. An election and a change of councillors changed all of that—for the worse!

Figure 2 Queensland's Gold Coast, March 2013.

(iPhone panorama.)

The Gold Coast on Australia's eastern seaboard is, and will continue to be, a hot spot of change from sea-level rise and coincident severe climatic events.

Source: John Reid, 2013.

February 2013

During a table-stop conversation in a campus cafe, an old friend and professor of history recalled that 25 years ago the university's department of history had 25 tenured members of academic staff. This was a heartfelt lament compounded by the difficulty in making a direct comparison with how the discipline is now positioned in the university. Historians bed the dreams of visual artists (Figure 3).

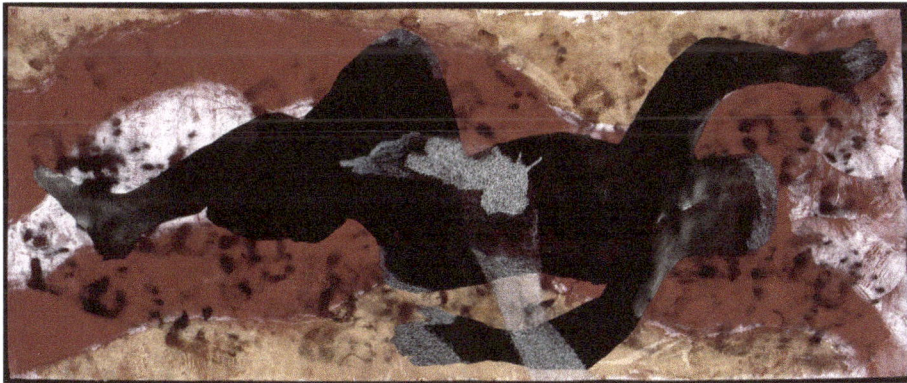

Figure 3 *Deep in blood*.

(Mixed media on card.)

Australian and Persian historical narratives informed this artwork.

Source: Nazanin Moradi, 2004.

March 2013

David Mabberley, executive director of the Royal Botanic Garden in Sydney (the oldest science institution in Australia), remarked on ABC Radio National that the discipline of botany—'the plant voice'—had been lost altogether in some universities through its amalgamation with other lines of scholarly inquiry. This is a loss for the visual arts. The aesthetic visualisation of plants, that present themselves patiently for the eternal artist gaze, is enhanced by knowledge about their being and their role in the complex ecological systems of the Earth (Figure 4). Botanists, where are you?

Figure 4 Bundock Creek—lowland chain of ponds.

(Digital print from colour transparency.)

The plant life in this picture is typical of an ecologically healthy Australian creek known as a lowland chain of ponds.

Source: Carolyn Young, 2004.

April 2013

My email server signals (in one of its last gestures before it changes to 'The Cloud') that a few seconds ago I had been contacted by Change.org. The contact informed me that an initiative harnessing the support of 41 000 online signatures had delivered honour roll recognition for fallen peacekeepers by the Australian War Memorial Council. I was invited to click on green underlined text at the end of the email to start my own petition for change. As with practitioners in any other discipline (except, I suspect, information technology), artists can be found at every point on the spectrum of human response to electronic information technologies—from Luddite to early adopter. Almost all visual artists have now joined the digital revolution. Here is evidence. I still have an office pigeonhole (mailbox) down the corridor that now receives mail by snails. On my way to my office, to open my computer and read the email to which I have previously referred, I collected from my snailhole a printed invitation. On slender, glossy card the Australian National Capital Artists Inc (ANCA), a Canberra-run artist initiative, announced its most recent exhibition, *ANCA NOW!* (27 March —

21 April 2013) showcasing the work of 27 of its current artists, amid a blaze of coloured pixels (Figure 5). The pixel motif also happens to be the graphic emblem on the organisation's logo.

Figure 5 Invitation to *ANCA NOW!* (Australian National Capital Artists showcase exhibition, Canberra ACT), 27 March – 21 April 2013.

Source: Australian National Capital Artists, 2013.

First proposition: Artists have changed into good collaborators

This selective 18-month chronology of change in the discipline of the visual fine arts comes from the perspective of my individual practice as a fine artist, researcher and teacher. It is intended as a curtain raiser for my first proposition: that despite political and fiscal constraints, the subject matter of visual art inquiry is pervasive, more so than ever, and that there is an associated emergent inclination for visual artists to interact with other scholars. Essentially, the proposition is that artists are positioning themselves as good collaborators. This is substantiated by a number of cross-disciplinary research programs, emanating from within educational institutions of art themselves, and their positive reception within universities at large—especially from disciplines where research results have an immediate bearing on public policy. Developments manifest in many scholarly disciplines are now, as a matter of course, contenders for aesthetic visual registration.

Artists have not always been renowned for entertaining a comprehensive outlook or for being keen collaborators, as the clichéd notion of a solitary figure marooned in a garret in dialogue with art materials, alcohol and other drugs shows. Artists blessed with intuition, insight and active imaginations have always drawn content from experience as their life unfolds—and artists continue to do so today. But as schools of art changed from single purpose institutions to take their place in universities, artists found themselves at a table set as a smorgasbord of contemporary ideas. Added enthusiasm to make the most of this opportunity derives from the fact that subject matter is not taught as part of the curriculum in tertiary schools of art. There are some exceptions, where the medium is its own subject. But realistically, it is not possible to teach subject matter, not at the level of tertiary scholarship, to hundreds of students addressing as many different topics. In the teaching of a language, the focus is on vocabulary, grammar, pronunciation, idiom, writing and conversational skill—not on what the student might ultimately articulate with their new proficiency. The visual artists are taught likewise with an emphasis on how to express ideas visually and aesthetically—whatever the ideas might happen to be.

Field Studies, a program at the ANU School of Art, took full advantage of this expanded intellectual landscape. Developed in conjunction with the university's (then) Centre for Educational Development and Academic Methods in 1995, the School of Art Field Studies program provides for the input of expert knowledge into the creative process. This is achieved not only by tapping into disciplines across the campus but through a well-established procedure for canvassing a broad spectrum of wisdom and understandings residing in the community at large. More than 40 programs have been convened, resulting in a considerable audit of change with hundreds of aesthetic assessments (that is what works of art are) created for the cultural record throughout the eastern states of the country. During the last 15 years the program has changed too. In 2007 the program became the focus of the School of Art's first Australian Research Council Linkage project with the Murray–Darling Basin Commission (now Authority) as the collaborating organisation. Now, Field Studies is configured as a generic procedure with wide scope and application. Through the Field Studies program visual artists have engaged proactively with a considerable range of scholarly disciplines.

Collaboration with music

Music, from a visual art perspective, is highly valued; especially contemporary music composed and played in response to place. In this respect, currency between music and visual art develops when a place, and the forms of life it supports, is jointly investigated as a source of inspiration.

In Figure 6, the ANU School of Music Contemporary Music Ensemble directed by Tor Frømyhr, Head of Strings in 2009, prepares for a public concert of impromptu performances inspired by field research around Benalla, Victoria. The venue was the Benalla Art Gallery where an exhibition referencing the

Benalla region by artists from the ANU School of Art was exhibited. A highlight of the evening concert was an impromptu performance by the ensemble, inspired by the artwork on the gallery walls. Figure 7 is an artwork that was played as a graphic score by the ensemble at that performance.

The music and the visual art were intentionally pitched to encourage the community to reflect on the attributes of (their) place as a prerequisite for shaping public policy. As the world inexorably changes, formulation of public policy never ends.

Figure 6 ANU School of Music Contemporary Music Ensemble in rehearsal, Benalla Art Gallery, Victoria (Tor Frømyhr third from left).

Source: John Reid, 2009.

Figure 7 Night photograph of emissions around Benalla (detail).

(Digital photograph.)

Source: Marzena Wasikowska, 2009.

Collaboration with history

Historians, and in particular oral historians, provide visual artists with narrative content that can significantly charge their imaginings. In the past, field research programs have commissioned oral histories from writers recruited from … anywhere. Dick Aitken, a Canberra writer pictured on the Goulburn River floodplain, Shepparton, Victoria, is taking notes in conversation with Aboriginal Yorta Yorta Elder Ella Anselmi on an ANU School of Art Field Studies program in 2006 (Figure 8).

Figure 8 Canberra writer Dick Aitken records knowledge of place from Yorta Yorta Elder Ella Anselmi (right), Shepparton, Victoria.

Source: John Reid, 2006.

Dick's oral history interviews provided valuable references for artists. The emotionally moving Indigenous narratives such as the ones that Ella told inspired the artwork reproduced here as Figure 9.

Now, ANU offers a graduate course in oral history, life stories and memory. That's a change! Let's bring these students and visual artists together.

Figure 9 *Floodplain*, series 1–4 no. 1 (detail).

(Ink and wash on rag paper.)

Source: Antonia Aitken, 2006.

Collaboration with cultural relations

A collaboration between visual artist Dr Frank Thirion of Canberra and Indigenous Elder John Williams Nubbarow of the Iwaidja people, Northern Territory, during fieldwork in 2011 at Calperum Station near Renmark, South Australia, generated a painting titled *Shadowland* and a sculpture titled *Guuldok* by Thirion, who was inspired by Nubbarow's recounting of the Iwaidja 'lightning spirit' story (Figure 10). Regrettably a joint undertaking such as this one is a rare component of the Field Study program. For this to happen more often the scheduling of the program's field trips would need to be open-ended.

Figure 10a *Shadowland*.

After John Williams Nubbarow, Iwaidja people's 'lightning spirit' story.

(Natural pigments on wood.)

Source: Frank Thirion, 2011.

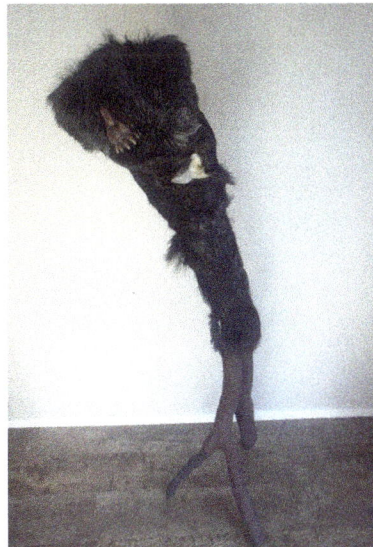

Figure 10b *Guuldok*.

After John Williams Nubbarow, Iwaidja people's 'lightning spirit' story.

(Natural pigments, feral goat pelt on wood.)

Source: Frank Thirion, 2011.

Collaboration with biological and earth sciences

Knowledge from botany, zoology, soil science and landscape ecology combines with art sensibilities at a gathering of landscape ecologists and visual artists in a contested forest near Braidwood, New South Wales, in 1996 (see Figures 11 and 12).

Figure 11 Professor Brendan Mackey (right of centre, wearing a white hat), formerly of the ANU Fenner School of Environment and Society, with his Landscape Ecology class and artists from the ANU School of Art Field Study program, in a patch of forest dominated by plumwood (*Eucryphia moorei*) and tree ferns (*Dicksonia antarctica*), Monga State Forest, NSW.

Source: John Reid, 1996.

Figure 12 *Untitled*.

(Eucalypt branches, twigs and bark). Monga State Forest, NSW.

Source: Dan Maginnity, 1996. Photograph by John Reid, 1996.

There in Monga, the scientists mesmerised the artists with their discerning investigations of the physical and biological relationships of the forest—with their analytical approach, descriptive terminology and narratives of symbiotic relationships. The artists reciprocated with beguiling, opinionated imagery that drew heavily on the intellectual input from the scientists' ecological assessments, as well as on a sustained, personal immersion in the quality sensory environments of the forest. Supported by accounts from both the arts and the sciences, a resilient local community changed the fate of the forest from becoming a chipped commercial commodity to a national park that celebrated Monga's forests as an irreplaceable asset of natural heritage. The forests of Monga flourish today as a wonderful resource available to the educational institutions of the national capital not far away.

Collaboration with the environmental sciences

Commensurate with the contests over the fate of Monga forests was a temporary change in ANU's structure that facilitated a widening of perspectives in the visual arts within the university. In August 2001, a suite of 12 national institutes was superimposed over the entire university. Academics were invited to elect membership to the institute with which they identified in terms of their research and teaching interests. Many disciplines within ANU were represented in the membership of the National Institute for Environment. There was a quirk in funding arrangements for this Institute and extra money fell into its coffers. Cash is a very effective agent for the acceleration and realisation of simmering attitudinal change. Idealism was dealt a budget line. Artists from the School of Art began working in earnest with scientists of all complexions through the Institute for Environment. As shown in Figure 13, sculptor, Wendy Teakel, ANU School of Art, produced a sculptural work informed by consultations with human ecologist David Dumaresq, ANU Fenner School of Environment and Society.

Figure 13 Artist Wendy Teakel (far right), ANU School of Art, at a public floor talk with her sculptural work in the exhibition *Factor of Ten: A Future Worth Having*, in 2002.

David Dumaresq (third from right), ANU Fenner School for Environment and Society, discusses the work that he helped inform.

Source: Marzena Wasikowska, 2002.

With the 'Factor of Ten' event, the prevailing paradigm of artists tinkering with scientific equipment in a laboratory to the bemusement of all gave way to formalised, genuine collaborations. Artists began to create works that were informed by scientists through one-on-one consultations, that were instructive as well as being aesthetically and emotionally powerful, and that were publicly exhibited in conjunction with conceptually related scholarly events such as conferences and seminar programs. The public was engaged in a program of gallery floor talks where it was difficult to distinguish the presenting artists from the scientists. There was no shortage of spirited, knowledgeable discussion. There was time for genuine contemplation by all concerned. This was the collaborative agenda that laid an enduring foundation still influential today. Visual aesthetic imagery informed by science brings a human, high-fidelity, emotional dimension to science communication.

Second proposition: Artists are good archivists of change

My second proposition is that artists are good archivists of change. In fact, I would argue that the fine arts deliver artefacts from which come the most eloquent, manifestly human punctuations of time. A fine artwork, primarily consisting of exquisitely related forms, subsequently evokes (exquisitely again) the conceptualisation of other relationships. In this respect the production of artwork entails a creative commitment without compromise within the gambit of human capability. The perception of fine artwork literally electrifies the brain. One is irrevocably changed. Think of Picasso's *Guernica* (1937), as it is perceived now, and Peter Dombrovskis' *Morning mist, Rock Island Bend, Franklin River, Tasmania, 1979* (1979), as it may have been perceived in 1983, when the (ultimately successful) campaign to stop a dam project was at its height.

Third proposition: Fine artworks can be potent agents for or against change

To further complicate the matter, fine artworks are not just calibrations of change; they can be potent agents for or against it—proposition three. Famous Australian examples are Russell Drysdale's austere outback paintings commissioned in the late 1940s to underscore the public acceptance of the Snowy Mountains Scheme (a Federal imperative to irrigate), and Dombrovskis' Franklin River photograph mentioned above, which was commandeered into the 1983 election campaign to politically undermine the damming of a river (a state imperative to generate hydroelectricity). Drysdale's paintings promoted change; Dombrovskis' photograph arguably prevented it.

Fourth proposition: A prediction that artists will expand their competence in research methods and project management

My fourth proposition about change in the visual arts is a prediction: artists will become proficient in a broad range of research methods, and competent (perhaps reluctantly) in the finer points of project management. Although visual artists will continue to collaborate with scholars in disciplines as outlined above, other aesthetic operatives will dominate the creative arts scene. People who have postgraduate qualifications in both the visual arts and other fields of expertise are emerging in increasing numbers. It is not uncommon to find artists combining well-developed aesthetic sensibilities with the scholarly exercise of scientific or historical methods of inquiry. Research-focused schools of art will induct artists into the investigative methods of the social sciences and develop more rigorous action research procedures for creative production. Traditional methods for the confident exercise of intuition and the imagination for the formulation of concepts from quality sensory encounters with the world will still hold their ground. Schools of art will persist as enclaves where proof is not pre-eminent. But the dollar will rule. Collaborative research of social consequence usually involves considerable amounts of publicly accountable money. Aesthetically astute, visually literate researchers who are also competent project managers will score the prize.

Conclusion

Change will undoubtedly peg my four propositions to the early part of the twenty-first century. Collectively they assert that visual fine artists are influential in the dynamics of change, as immersed scholarly collaborators and discerning archivists; and that they are set to play more equitable roles in publicly funded research in the social sciences. In the course of any settlement in which I am held to account for these views, I will simply appeal to a fifth proposition: that the medium in which visual artists are most eloquent is a visual one and reliant, if at all, on a mere title of text. As a pre-emptive strike, see my ace card (Figure 14) in the case for change from a visual art perspective.

Figure 14 *Walking the solar system, Shepparton Vic.*

(Digital photograph.)

John Reid, 2012. Walk duration: one minute. Distance travelled: approximately 1,800 kilometres relative to the sun. Walk adviser and camera operator: Marzena Wasikowska.

Source: John Reid, 2012.

Part 3
Synthesis

20. Improving Research Impact by Better Understanding Change: A case study of multidisciplinary synthesis

Gabriele Bammer

The requirement to demonstrate research impact is growing in prominence. It is no longer sufficient for research to provide greater understanding of a problem or issue. Researchers and those who fund them want to see findings used to bring about an improvement. Evaluation of research, and of research organisations, is therefore increasingly focused on measurement of outcomes in terms of policy change, improvement in professional practice, changes in community behaviours and attitudes, and patents and other indicators of commercialisation. This chapter examines research impact and the ability to improve it through the lens of better understanding change.

The focus of this chapter is on a key insight which has been largely neglected in considerations about research impact, but which is highlighted by the 18 disciplinary and practice perspectives on change in this book. This is that research findings enter a dynamic world, where everything is changing all the time. As researchers we sometimes operate as if the world is static, just waiting for our findings in order to decide where to head next. Instead, for research to have impact, researchers must negotiate a constantly changing environment.

The first part of this chapter draws together threads from the preceding chapters and the symposium discussion to describe the inevitability of change, as well as to examine continuity and conservation, inertia and resistance to change, and the propositions that change does not necessarily lead to improvement, that success is in the eye of the beholder, and that any attempt to influence change can have unpredictable outcomes.

The second part of this chapter examines three topics thrown into sharp relief when research impact is seen as involving a process of negotiating a dynamic change environment. It deals first with the challenges of managing opportunity costs, transaction costs and potential compromises to integrity. These require diverse levels and forms of research impact to be validated, which is the second topic considered. An additional requirement is a reward system that can encompass the complexity of research impact in a dynamic change environment. This is addressed in the third topic: a new publication culture as the primary assessment structure.

Finally, an appendix to the chapter provides a brief description of multidisciplinary research and the synthesis of multidisciplinary perspectives, as well as of the emerging discipline which underpins this project, Integration and Implementation Sciences (I2S). As explained in the appendix, a multidisciplinary approach invites experts from different disciplines and practice areas to tackle the issue under consideration (in this case, change) as they see fit, which provides an array of rich perspectives. One or more syntheses are then tailor-made around topics of interest to the synthesisers (in this case there is one synthesis focused on research impact). As demonstrated in this chapter, not all of the perspectives are drawn on equally in the synthesis, and there are many valuable insights on change provided by the disciplinary and practice experts that are not used (because they are not directly relevant to the synthesis topic). A synthesis does not therefore absorb or replace the multidisciplinary perspectives; instead it draws on them selectively to illuminate a particular topic.

The dynamic change environment

Lindell Bromham's chapter on evolutionary biology is a potent reminder that we live in an environment of constant change and that everything is connected, as demonstrated by bringing together the following three quotations:

> Evolutionary change is continuous and inevitable: nothing stands still in the biological world ...

> The world around us is the product of evolution: not just the actual biological organisms such as the trees, birds and insects, but also many features of the environment such as the soil, atmosphere and buildings, which have been constructed by the actions of organisms over time. This life-built environment is in a constant state of change, as are all the biological lineages that inhabit it ...

> No species exists in isolation ... Species both create and respond to changing environments, creating a tangled web of interactions in space and time.

At the human scale, Peter McDonald's chapter on demography also focused on the inevitability of change in that discipline's concentration on 'childbearing, death, disease, disability, migration, entry to and exit from relationships; education and employment; and housing types or tenures'.

A similar point about the dynamics of change was made by Kate Carnell (personal communication, 2013[1]), reflecting on life as a politician:

> What we are dealing with now isn't what we were dealing with five years ago or 10 years ago … So change is inevitable. So politics is, I suppose, about attempting to ensure that your part of the world is anticipating that change, ahead of that change, and maximising the potential of that change. And also, why would you go into politics if you didn't want to change anything? It's not a great lifestyle. I mean you wouldn't do it for the lifestyle or for the money.

As Michael Wesley commented on Kate Carnell's chapter, 'It's a bit like the old John Howard line, reform is the ever receding finish line' (personal communication, 2013).[2]

The dynamics of change in business were described in Sarah Pearson's chapter, which highlighted competition as the driver of change, as in the following quotations:

> Without the threat of competition most companies would not consider making the necessary changes for fear of having to deal with their associated challenges …

> Change is hard. It requires energy and a compelling reason to jump on board: energy from those leading change, and energy from the followers …

> The drive to remain competitive can provide the energy to help individuals and organisations accept new ways of working and delivering value.

Change is not, of course, uniform. Mark Stafford Smith pointed out the importance of 'the tempo and scale of change … that's about a rate of change as opposed to a direction or degree of change' (personal communication, 2013). In terms of tempo, Lindell Bromham highlighted that 'no one, including Darwin, ever expected that the pace of morphological evolutionary change would be uniform over time' (personal communication, 2013). Grant Wardlaw's chapter on security-based intelligence adds further complexity by demonstrating that there

---

1 Quotations labelled 'personal communication, 2013' are taken from the transcript of the two-day symposium which brought together most of the chapter authors (see Chapter 1 for a description of the process).
2 John Howard was the Australian Prime Minister from 1996–2007. In 2005 he is reported to have said, 'Economic reform in this country, and the challenge of economic reform, is like participating in a race towards an ever receding finishing line' (*The Age*, 27 August 2005; www.theage.com.au/news/national/howard-vows-to-stand-firm-over-labour-reforms/2005/08/27/1124563060427.html), and 'Economic reform is like participating in a race towards an ever-receding finishing line' (*The Sydney Morning Herald*, 15 October 2005; www.smh.com.au/news/national/the-real-deal/2005/10/14/1128796703087.html).

can be major discontinuities, making the new situation 'almost unrecognisable'. Until fairly recently this field was characterised by slow-moving 'intelligence puzzles', now replaced by fast-moving 'intelligence mysteries—questions whose answers are inherently unknowable in detail (often because even the targets do not know precisely what they are going to do until they do it)'.

Scale of change can be illustrated by required responses. Some responses, for example, are constrained to an individual, or community, or a geographical region. Others, like global environmental change, have to be 'responded to at every level from households through to international UN [United Nations] level. So there's no way you can think about this problem without thinking about the multi-scale nature of it. And that's true in time as well as space, as well as organisational scale' (Mark Stafford Smith, personal communication, 2013). Beverley Raphael (personal communication, 2013) added another dimension, contrasting 'change that we can impact on' with 'change which is out of control', and likening the latter to a tsunami.

Finally, embracing the inevitability of change is not universal, as Francesca Merlan (personal communication, 2013[3]) noted in her comments on Lindell Bromham's chapter: 'One of the useful things in this account for the social sciences is the easy acceptance of the inevitability of change. It's going to happen and … [is] inherent in the very process of reproduction itself … This may … help social scientists feel easy about the same thing.'

The rest of this section describes different dimensions of the dynamic change environment:

- continuity and conservation—i.e. stopping change from happening— require work
- there is often inbuilt inertia or resistance to change, so that once something exists it can be hard to get rid of
- even though change happens all the time, it does not necessarily lead to improvement
- success is in the eye of the beholder
- any attempt to influence change can have unpredictable outcomes.

---

3 Francesca Merlan was unable to attend the symposium, but provided written comments which are used here and elsewhere in this chapter.

Continuity and conservation require work

A corollary to the inevitability of change is that stopping change from happening requires effort, whether this is conservation of artefacts or environments, or continuity in social affairs and behaviour.

Ian MacLeod's chapter on materials conservation illustrates the inevitability of change in the form of decay and provides some insight into the range of techniques available to prevent and inhibit decay:

> For every type of material there is a specialist conservator who knows how to stabilise and preserve elements of our material culture that range from ephemeral art works to plastic furniture and toys to digital media.

For example,

> Willing bands of seamstresses ... worked on textiles. Faithful sacristans have worked in churches for hundreds of years conserving the textiles that form the basis of ecclesiastical garment collections. They used traditional methods of stitching down degraded fibres of sacred and preciously embroidered fabrics onto sympathetic new support structures.

Nevertheless, as he pointed out in the symposium discussion, 'There gets to a point of diminishing returns, and you've got to make the hard decision of what do you preserve and what do you let go, and let decay take its natural course' (Ian MacLeod, personal communication, 2013).

When it comes to environments, Lindell Bromham (personal communication, 2013) pointed out that 'we automatically think of conservation as, 'put a fence around it, keep it as it is'. That's not possible. You can't do it.'

Conservation is similarly challenging in social affairs, as Francesca Merlan described in her chapter on anthropology: 'Both change and continuity involve expenditures of energy; both are actively produced in the human world, and discerned in particular circumstances.'

Lindell Bromham (personal communication, 2013), reflecting on Francesca Merlan's chapter, embellished this point:

> Genetic change is inevitable, mutations are always arising; if you see sequences staying the same in the genome, it's not because nothing's happening, it's because something very active is happening, which is the removal of any changes that arise. So you could think of the same thing perhaps in ritual, that if you see it staying the same, it's not because it's failed to move, but because people have actively kept it the same.

We see therefore that keeping artefacts, environments and social practices the same requires energy. There are also additional dimensions in the social realm, where power and legitimacy can be connected to continuity.

In highlighting insights provided by the discipline of sociology in his chapter, Craig Browne pointed out:

> It is probably a banal, though nevertheless true, insight that individuals towards the top of a field or social hierarchy generally argue for either the preservation of the existing order or for managed change.

Furthermore he alerts us to the fact that:

> Sociologists often think about change in a comparative and constructionist manner, since they seek to demonstrate that what is assumed to be natural and permanent is actually a product of historical processes and culturally specific practices.

He drew on theorist Pierre Bourdieu to elucidate the disguising of the effort that goes into maintaining continuity:

> The denial or veiling of effort is part of the logic of reproduction, because social legitimacy is regularly achieved by the perception of a person and practice as given, natural and normal.

Francesca Merlan used her work with Indigenous Australians to highlight political pressure to demonstrate continuity in order to achieve land and other rights:

> There are now often aspects of reparations politics—in the case of indigenous peoples, for instance, land and native title or other similar claims—that ask of them to demonstrate their continuing attachment to lands and traditions as the requirement and justification of those claims. This supports and amplifies concerns for authenticity, traditionality and unchangingness of law and custom among those people which may constitute for them a source of pride, as well as a considerable problem to the extent that they no longer are as they were, and do not live up to such expectations.

In her chapter she went on to argue that these expectations are unrealistic and that anthropologists have not gone far enough in exploring this challenge.

There is often inbuilt inertia or resistance to change, so that once something exists it can be hard to get rid of

The effort that goes into producing continuity can also lead to structural inertia or resistance to directed change. Michael Wesley's chapter on international relations shines a powerful light on this topic. He argued that contemporary international relations 'tends towards routines and stasis, accreting over time structures and forces of inertia that are periodically overwhelmed by underlying change'. Inertia results from 'the increasing routinisation of international life', where international institutions, for example,

> preserve the power structures and expectations that existed at the time of their establishment. This makes them extremely hard to adapt to the evolution of international relations, and equally hard to abolish, given the reputation capital and hopes that have been invested in them over the years. The solution to the declining relevance of existing institutions is rather to simply establish new ones—which turn out to be equally inflexible and of declining relevance over time.

He drew on other work to add:

> Inertia is the result of the difficulty and cost of change and the investment of the powerful in current ways of doing things. Several factors play interlocking roles in supporting inertia and routinisation. Institutions and relationships often embody *high start-up and sunk costs*. Often they were negotiated at an opportune time that is unlikely to recur; inevitably they are seen, for all of their defects, as being better than no institution, agreement or relationship at all. Existing institutions exert strong *learning effects*, by favouring those who adapt their strategies and expectations to the existing rules. These are buttressed by *adaptive expectations* that favour existing ways of doing things over innovation. Bureaucratic objectives tend to be moulded by institutional possibilities, rather than vice versa. *Routinisation incentives* tend to multiply activities that comply with existing structures and crowd out opportunities for innovation. *Competency traps* breed familiarity with existing rules and bureaucratic training becomes oriented to most effectively using those rules.

In his chapter Grant Wardlaw drew on the work of others to highlight an additional cause of inertia, namely that at least some agencies 'are built to be reliable, consistent and predictable—not adaptive'. He argues, 'the intelligence system as a whole is not designed to cope well with change ... Particular parts of the system have, in effect, been designed not to adapt.'

Inertia highlights the point that while change is inevitable, the speed of change is far from uniform and may be glacial in some areas. As Craig Browne pointed out in his chapter, inertia is also a prime concern in sociology:

> Sociological research has regularly demonstrated that change has been limited in major areas of social relations, especially those to do with longstanding inequalities. Sociologists quite often find discrepancies between the widespread social perceptions of changes in the circumstances of subordinated social groups and their actual conditions. For example, the overall remuneration of female labour compared to male labour has not changed as much as might be presumed from the enacting of equal pay legislation in Australia several decades ago. These kinds of discrepancies highlight the complexity of explaining change and the constraints upon changing enduring dimensions of society.

Drawing again on Pierre Bourdieu, he added another explanation for inertia:

> Many embodied social practices may be quite resistant to conscious modification, yet represent the unrecognised components of social assessment … Social actors have an intuitive understanding of probability in social life. Consequently, they are always making implicit assessments about what they can achieve and the amount of effort that would be involved in significant change.

In her chapter, Kate Carnell described how the system in which politics is embedded leads to inertia and resistance to change, as well as the frustration that this causes:

> Politicians want to make their electorate, state and country a better place. Most start wide-eyed and optimistic. The mechanisms of government and the sheer difficulty of bringing about change often produce disenchantment and cynicism. The impediments to delivering real change start with your own party and supporters. Then there is the media, our relatively short political cycle, the bureaucracy, and intolerance to any political leader's policy failure.

As she pointed out in her chapter, in addition to inertia, change fatigue is a potent factor:

> With new policy and change come some great successes, some average outcomes and a few failures. And the failures are seized on by both the opposition and the media. The media say that good news does not sell, so a feeding frenzy over a government initiative that has not worked is great copy … The longer politicians are in power, the more things there will be that have not gone quite right … Change fatigue is a real

thing in politics. With change comes risk and with risk comes the very real possibility of failure (or at least lack of success). I believe this is the reason many governments become increasingly risk-averse the longer they spend in office.

Finally, Sarah Pearson (personal communication, 2013) described how inertia is also a problem in business, and gave one example of a mechanism which businesses are developing to prevent inertia from setting in:

> It's the same in innovation. It's actually very easy to start something, or relatively easy to start something new, a change or something new, actually stopping something, the change that stops something is really, really hard and in innovation you call it fast failure. So companies are really trying to learn how to fail fast ... they want to know when they know they've failed.

This is achieved using 'stage gate processes. So you have your projects managed and they have specific timelines where they have to meet certain criteria and if they don't—dead.'

Change does not necessarily lead to improvement

Evolutionary biology is again very helpful here, demonstrating that much change is self-generating and often negative and maladaptive. Lindell Bromham (personal communication, 2013) pointed out:

> We often think of both evolution and other kinds of change, for example institutional changes, being driven by a need to improve but actually there [are] an awful lot of trends in change that are just driven by underlying generation of change and may not actually be positive.

The point that change does not necessarily lead to improvement is also fundamental to Mark Stafford Smith's chapter on global environmental change, where he cited ideas about nine planetary boundaries and the necessity to keep change within a 'safe operating space ... to have confidence that the planet will continue to function in the relatively benign state that it has during the past 8000 years. In this time, modern civilisation, agriculture, cities and technologies have developed.' (There is evidence that three of the planetary boundaries have already been transgressed.)

Debate about change and improvement is highlighted in Michael Wesley's chapter which describes three competing views about the direction of change, one which sees change as improvement and two which do not. They are:

- teleology, which sees change as 'progressive and unidirectional' to a future that is 'safer, more prosperous, more just, and more sustainable'
- cyclicality, which argues that 'periods of peace and prosperity … usually come to an end in a catastrophic conflict that resets the basic ordering of power in the world'
- episodism, which views change as 'episodic and unpredictable in its timing, extent, and direction'.

Sociology has also grappled with this issue, specifically in terms of change and progress, as Craig Browne noted in his chapter. In particular, 'sociologists are now more reluctant than their predecessors to equate change with progress'. This is particularly evident in interpretations of modernity:

> It had previously been presumed that modernisation would lead all societies or nation states to share a common pattern of institutions and cultural values. In effect, change would lead to a convergence in the form of modern societies and underpinning this assumption was the equating of modernising change with other notions, especially those of progress, rationalisation and development.

But as he also pointed out,

> Assumptions about the overall development of society and social evolution are probably still implicit in sociological analyses that are addressed to other topics, like gender and education, sexuality and consumption.

The point here is that any underlying assumption that change equates to improvement or progress should be questioned, rather than assumed to be correct. Other considerations about the direction of change—perceptions of success and unpredictability—are dealt with in the following sections.

Success is in the eye of the beholder

Change is 'not value neutral. It depends on who you ask' (Simon Chapman, personal communication, 2013). The point was illustrated by the following exchange at the symposium. Michael Wesley (personal communication, 2013) to Kate Carnell: 'I think that quite often change is in the eye of the beholder, and it made me start to think that someone who disagreed with you politically might look at your period as Chief Minister and say, "Well they did nothing, they were a do-nothing government"'. Kate Carnell (personal communication, 2013): 'I agree with that. I think that probably the people who perceive that about my time would say not that I didn't do anything but I did a lot of bad stuff.'

At the symposium Mark Stafford Smith (personal communication, 2013) raised the issue of: 'whether you can predict whether it's going to be good or bad which is a different challenge'. Craig Browne (personal communication, 2013) added:

> The problem isn't so much knowing that retrospectively, we can know retrospectively what is good or bad change … I think the difficulty is more practical in a sense. Should we initiate change on the assumption that it will lead to a good? … How we decide on that of course is a contested issue.

While this issue was not explored in more detail, it is significant for research impact.

Any attempt to influence change can have unpredictable outcomes

The inevitability of change, the interconnectedness of what is changed and the various aspects of change dynamics discussed above mean that attempts to influence change can have outcomes which are unpredictable. As Jim Butler (personal communication, 2013) noted, 'by the very fact that we're talking about change, we're going to talk about uncertainty'. Even when, as Lindell Bromham described in her chapter, the mechanism for change is 'breathtakingly simple', as for evolution, the outcome can be 'devilishly complex'. The reason is that 'species both create and respond to changing environments, creating a tangled web of interactions in space and time'. This interconnectedness and ever-changing environment and context hold true for the social aspects of life as well.

One aspect of this is 'the arms races between predators and prey, plants and herbivores, pathogens and hosts' described by Lindell Bromham in her chapter. This has a direct parallel in intelligence, as described by Grant Wardlaw in his chapter: 'Adaptation is a two-way street. As intelligence gets better at finding and understanding its targets, the smarter targets also adapt to evade intelligence.'

Unintended consequences are a key dimension of unpredictability. Craig Browne drew on the work of Michel Foucault to demonstrate that outcomes can be the opposite of those intended:

> The notion of unintended consequences is a feature of many sociological conceptions of change, but Foucault's historical genealogies show how movements for humane punishment, sexual liberation and liberties were themselves implicated in the extension of power and resulted in the more intensive disciplining of prisoners, the regulation of sexual identities, and the consolidation of governmentality.

Unintended consequences can also feature even in relatively straight-forward circumstances, such as materials conservation, as described in Ian MacLeod's chapter. For example,

> Months or years after an apparently successful intervention, the surface of ceramics can become covered with white effloresences of hydrated calcium acetates as the low-fired earthenware corrodes in an atmosphere containing acetic acid, coming from the decay of old wooden showcases. These storage cabinets were often made of oak, which is one of the worst timbers to use, but it is one that had been traditionally used in institutions in Europe.

While these are easier to manage than major unexpected social changes, unintended consequences at all scales can be important for research impact.

Another dimension of unpredictability is unexpected events. Peter McDonald demonstrated the challenges of prediction, citing two demographic projections for Australia's future population in his chapter which 'do not even overlap with each other, despite just a three-year difference in the publication of their results'. As he explained, 'These two projections differed dramatically from each other because, between the two projections, Australia's international migration level rose very considerably.'

In discussing demographic predictions at the symposium, Lindell Bromham (personal communication, 2013) added:

> Of course there will always be completely unexpected changes ... Consider the HIV. No one could have predicted HIV bursting onto the world stage in the late 70s and early 80s and yet HIV has reversed life expectancy trends in Africa. So anyone who was projecting forward on life expectancies in Africa in the 1970s got it completely wrong because they are going backwards now.

Another aspect is knowing that change is required, but not knowing if it will happen, as Mark Stafford Smith pointed out in his chapter for global environmental change:

> It is certain that there is major change occurring on a decadal to centennial timeframe, but there is considerable uncertainty about where that change will end up and what impacts it will have. A large part of this uncertainty is a result of not knowing whether humanity will choose to respond to mitigate the changes.

Overall, there was little consideration of the importance of context as a factor underpinning unpredictability, except in how it limits what is possible. This was highlighted in the quotation from Karl Marx (1977, 301; first published 1852) cited by Craig Browne in his chapter:

> 'Men make their own history, but they do not make it just as they please; they do not make it under circumstances chosen by themselves, but under circumstances directly encountered, given and transmitted from the past.'

Mark Stafford Smith (personal communication, 2013) made a very similar point in referring to 'path contingency', where decisions made today limit options available in future.

There are other aspects of unpredictability that were not covered or teased out in the chapters or the symposium discussion:

- change depends on interactions between people, who have their own values and interests and may therefore behave in unexpected ways
- serendipity can be a key factor
- impact may not be in proportion to the quality, veracity or importance of the data
- decisions often have to be made without a solid evidence base.

All of these are important in considering research impact.

Research impact as a process of negotiating a dynamic change environment: Issues and consequences

Laying out the complexities of the dynamic change environment highlights the challenges of achieving and assessing research impact. Researchers seeking to influence change are buffeted by a range of forces—some supportive, some hostile, some neutral—and even in the best circumstances unpredictable outcomes may occur. There is no sure way to negotiate a path through those forces and there are no guarantees of success. No consequences at all or adverse unintended consequences are always real possibilities. Those assessing research impact must be sensitive to the realities of the vortex of change—for example, that hard work and skill are not always rewarded, that luck may play a large hand, and that good intentions may be punished with bad outcomes.

Focusing on change and its complexities highlights three topics relevant to research impact which warrant particular consideration. The first is the challenges that must be recognised and managed—opportunity costs, transaction costs and potential compromises to integrity. These in turn demonstrate that there can be no one size fits all for researchers seeking to achieve impact. The second topic therefore explores the requirement for diverse levels and forms of research impact to be validated and presents three frameworks which provide a systematic way to document the diversity. Finally, the process of rewarding research impact must be able to encompass this diversity, as well as the complexities of achieving change. This is addressed in the third topic, which proposes a new publication culture as the primary assessment structure. While these issues were not addressed specifically in the chapters or symposium discussion, both provide a range of illustrations for the points made.

Costs and compromises: Three challenges to recognise and manage

As research impact moves from being a relatively minor add-on to the main business of discovery and becomes a more significant aspect of the work of researchers, the vagaries and difficulties of achieving research impact are thrown into greater prominence. These lead to three particular challenges—at both individual and institutional levels—which are teased out here. The first is opportunity costs, especially the trade-off between achieving new insights or discoveries and achieving impact. The second is grappling with the negative sides of achieving research impact, what may be called the transaction costs. Third is reputational risk; the challenges to integrity that can result from engagements and actions to achieve research impact.

Opportunity costs

Opportunity costs for individual researchers are centred on three limited resources: time, energy and expertise. Researchers need to allocate how much time they will spend on improving understanding and how much on achieving impact. Each requires not just hours, but also commitment, which can be thought of as the level of energy devoted to them. Finally the expertise required for achieving research impact is quite different from that required for improved understanding (discovery). And expertise not only has to be acquired, but also maintained, by staying on top of new and improved methods and processes as they are developed.

A simple example is the academic papers which researchers are trained to write. Writing to reach the media, policymakers, business or civil society actors requires different styles from that of the academic world. The necessary skills have to be learnt, which demands time and energy. With social media providing new outlets, researchers also have to stay up to date, assessing when and what social media outlets may have the best reach into the audience of interest, and learning how to use them.

Furthermore, written evidence is not necessarily the most effective form of communication to these groups. At least sometimes, images and prototypes may be more useful. Dee Madigan and John Reid both highlighted the power of images in their chapters, with John Reid stating: 'Visual aesthetic imagery informed by science brings a human, high-fidelity, emotional dimension to science communication'. Influencing change in commercial products is likely to be most successful when there is a prototype, as Sarah Pearson (personal communication, 2013) described:

> To get the company [Cadbury] to change I had to show them something tangible. I started with pictures: didn't work. I started with something they could just touch: didn't work. They had to be able to eat it. So I think when you are trying to bring about change some tangible way of explaining what the change is about really helps.

Again, developing effective images and prototypes requires time, energy and skill.

Further illustration of opportunity costs, along with the broad range of skills required, is provided by the intense engagements with change described by Simon Chapman. He provided insights into two ways in which researchers contributed to tobacco control efforts: by helping prepare the ground and by helping ensure success.

Let us start with helping prepare the ground. Reflecting on an interview he undertook with former Australian federal government health minister, the Hon. Nicola Roxon, about her decision to introduce plain packaging legislation for tobacco products, Simon Chapman (personal communication, 2013) said:

> The point that she made repeatedly is that it doesn't just happen. You don't sit bolt upright in bed one night and go: 'Someone has given me an idea—let's do it'. And she talked about the notion that there was a confluence of big shoulders to stand on that had come through historically, which had conditioned both her colleagues and the community that this was something which would be a no-brainer and they could do.

One way researchers can help prepare the ground is by developing a high, credible public profile through publicising their research and its relevance to the issues. Again Simon Chapman from his chapter:

> I 'meet' these people [politicians and senior policymakers] many times each month, often at times when they are most relaxed and receptive. I had never met Nicola Roxon until invited to her 2008 prevention forum. As we met, she said 'I feel I have known you most of my life', referring to my long involvement in news media. So while I had never previously had the opportunity to put proposals to her directly, it was immediately clear that I had done so on innumerable occasions as she awoke to radio news and commentary, in her car as she drove to work or around on weekends, via her newspapers, through television news and via any online feeds she may have followed. Her cabinet colleagues would also all need to be voracious news consumers, so when health portfolio items arose, they too would be acquainted with the public narratives about these issues that have been circulating in news media.

Simon Chapman (personal communication, 2013) enlarged on the need for long-term involvement:

> Debates obviously evolve. The start of a debate is seldom where a debate ends up, and I think those of us who are involved in pushing for social change recognise the natural history of a debate and that there are times when you go out and advocate for change and you know that you are going to be treated like a lunatic, but that if you are just a bit

patient, in ... five to 10 years ... you start seeing conservatives alluding to the same things that you were arguing for as a radical and it becomes mainstream and before you know it it's legislation.

In terms of helping ensure success, in his chapter Simon Chapman described what happened when the introduction of plain packaging was announced: 'From that moment, those working in population-focused tobacco control in Australia did little else for the next two years than concentrate our efforts to ensure the announced bill would be passed.' This included helping 1) develop new effective packaging, 2) meet national and international legal challenges, 3) draft legislation, and 4) get cross-party political support.

It is clear that such activities require time and energy as well as skills in communication, including effective framing of issues and lobbying. These in turn require an understanding of the targets for these activities. Simon Chapman was seeking to influence a section of government, but for other research the potential end-users may be in business or civil society. Understanding the end-users is a time-consuming task and can be daunting. For example, it is a substantial undertaking to identify the relevant departments, committees and individuals (in government, for instance), as well as existing policies and likely positions that will affect how the research findings are received, and then to figure out when and how best to provide the research evidence and what follow-up is desirable, especially to achieve action and to counter opposition.

In addition to understanding where and how to target their efforts, researchers also need to appreciate the context which guides what is possible at that particular time. These were described in different ways by Craig Browne and Christine Nixon. In his chapter, Craig Browne pointed out that 'major changes in social structures are conditioned by the strains, conflicts and contradictions of a social order'. Christine Nixon made this more concrete in her chapter, highlighting the need to deal with 'the home of real power structures, the history of successes and failures, the "this is the way we do things around here" approach, the beliefs and values, the fears and unwritten control mechanisms'. Understanding and negotiating these can be critical in achieving change, including research impact. A particular relevant skill is recognising and using leverage. In Christine Nixon's case these were events and opportunities 'that helped or required us to focus'. She described, for example, how she used problems within the drug squad to focus on her goal of corruption prevention and concern about large numbers of underworld murders to strengthen criminal investigation.

Seeking to achieve research impact therefore requires time, energy and expertise, with a trade-off for individual researchers between conducting research to improve understanding and seeking to achieve change based on their research findings. Individual researchers will differ in how they prefer to make this trade-off and, as I argue in a subsequent section, such diversity must be accommodated.

Let us now move to opportunity costs at the institutional level, where the primary limited resources are funding and reputation. Only funding will be dealt with here. Universities and other research organisations have to decide what proportion of resources to dedicate to supporting research focused on discovery and how much to supporting impact.

In research organisations, supporting impact commonly occurs through the media offices, offices for commercialisation and academic centres on science communication. While such facilities provide important assistance to researchers seeking to achieve research impact, they cover only a small part of the terrain. Researchers who want to influence the government policy process, for example, are often left to their own devices in figuring out how the process works, who to target, how best to engage, and how to navigate the circumstances of the time, as outlined earlier. There is little opportunity for them to systematically learn from others or to contribute the knowledge and expertise they gain to others. This leads to considerable and wasteful reinventing of the wheel.

In my book *Disciplining interdisciplinarity* (Bammer, 2013), I argue for the establishment of a new discipline (Integration and Implementation Sciences or I2S), as a repository for the expert knowledge required to strive for research impact.[4] Academics trained in I2S would specialise in the implementation process and be involved as collaborators on projects that aim to have research impact (just as statisticians are included on projects that involve quantitative analysis). These specialists would bring to the partnership the best current understandings of how to achieve impact, including effective ways of framing issues, identifying targets, and interacting with them. Establishing such a discipline provides a mechanism for capturing a range of pertinent experience and for building a body of relevant theory and practice. I2S provides an answer to the opportunity cost dilemma for individuals by focusing on effective collaborations. Just as individual researchers generally do not have all the skills for improving understanding in their area of expertise and overcome this through team work, they could also find collaborators for some or all aspects of research impact by partnering with I2S specialists.

---

4   I argue that research integration is also essential for effective implementation or impact. This is particularly relevant for teams tackling complex problems. In these case I2S specialists would contribute skills in, for example, effective ways of combining different disciplinary insights, bringing to bear relevant stakeholder perspectives, dealing with the system as a whole and minimising adverse unintended consequences.

While this could solve the opportunity cost for individuals, it highlights the opportunity cost at the institutional level. Establishing such a discipline requires funding, which has to come from somewhere. And leaving the establishment of a new discipline to one side, institutions face the same issues if they try to improve support by expanding their current activities in media liaison, commercialisation or science communication. Indeed individual researchers often ignore this institutional trade-off when they lobby for more support.

Managing opportunity costs on either the individual or institutional level is not straightforward, and there are no easy answers. But if effective research impact is to become a norm, the issues must be brought into the light and sorted out.

Transaction costs

This section explores costs incurred when researchers seek to have impact, picking up on the comment made by Christine Nixon in her chapter: 'You might be in for a rough ride'. There is often resistance from those with interests in maintaining the status quo, who can use a range of tactics. Peter McDonald (personal communication, 2013) described one such tactic: 'If you are sticking your head up and you are sticking your head up often ... you quite often get labelled ... It's a kind of way to prevent change'.

Criticism can also come from academic colleagues, as Simon Chapman described in his chapter. Some researchers he interviewed

> had encountered colleagues who questioned the motivation of media-engaged researchers, seeing their promotion of research as an unseemly, 'ego-driven, empire-building' activity. These critical colleagues dismissed those who engaged with the media as 'self-promoting' or 'show ponies', terms 'designed to circulate the view that proper science is science which does not seek to promote or publicize its findings'.

Attacks can also be extreme, although these were not discussed in the chapters or at the symposium. For example, when a recommendation to trial heroin prescription based on research that I led achieved government support (subsequently withdrawn), the editor of a prominent newspaper accused me of being a drug dealer. Similarly, government uptake of Bruce Chapman's research on an income-contingent loans scheme to fund higher education (described further below) led to highly personal attacks, especially from university students. These included a 'wanted' poster, accusing him of 'crimes against education' (Chapman, personal communication, 2009).

By and large, researchers are poorly prepared for these kinds of attacks, especially in coping with the stress they can cause or in knowing how to effectively respond. Research institutions can also come under attack, which can range from pressure to sack the academics involved, to threats, or actual cuts, to funding.

There is little documentation or analysis of either individual or institutional attacks. There are advantages in closing down such attacks as soon as possible, by denying them the 'oxygen' of discussion. But the downside is that individuals and institutional leaders are largely on their own when such attacks occur and cannot easily draw on the wealth of previous experience—successful and unsuccessful—in handling attacks. As with managing opportunity costs, managing transaction costs is not straightforward. But again the issues must be brought into the open, so that they can be carefully considered and acted on.

Potential compromises to integrity

Integrity is the cornerstone of the research enterprise. Attacks on individuals and institutions discussed above are almost always based on impugning their integrity. Often the parties involved have acted with the utmost propriety, but not always. Indeed in seeking to achieve change there can be temptations to let 'the ends justify the means' that can destroy the trustworthiness of both individuals and institutions. This is probably the biggest challenge that needs to be addressed in relation to achieving research impact. Here I am not going to reflect on deliberate misconduct, but I am going to briefly discuss two ways of 'crossing the line' to illustrate the kinds of issues that need to be considered and dealt with.

The first is errors of judgment. Let us take an example from Kate Carnell's chapter on politics, where she described her regret at compromising her values to get her government's budget passed:

> At one stage in my time as ACT Chief Minister, two of the three independent members whose support I needed to pass the government's budget refused to pass it unless I agreed to amendments to abortion laws … I finally agreed to their demands but have regretted it ever since … I was publicly committed to pro-choice, so what was I doing supporting these changes to the abortion laws? I should not have compromised on the issue.

Putting oneself in Kate Carnell's shoes, it is easy to understand how an unwillingness to lose power (the consequence of the budget not being passed) combined with fatigue can lead to an error of judgment. Indeed we all make errors of judgment, often without as good an excuse as intense pressure or fatigue. This is pertinent to the issue of research impact, because errors of judgment are more visible (and fair game for opponents) when there is public engagement. Researchers and research institutions need to consider how errors of judgment will be handled.

A second way of crossing the line is losing sight of, and respect for, other people's values. There are many complex threads in this argument. I present one here as an illustration. While it is now commonly accepted that researchers, like everyone else, are influenced by their values, it can be argued that there is still a fundamental role for researchers to respectfully take other values into account in their work. This may often be incompatible with seeking to achieve impact. Take for example, the following insight from Simon Chapman's chapter:

> It has long been banal to note that policy adoption is not simply a matter of presenting the best facts and evidence to policymakers and sitting back to watch evidence triumph over other considerations. With rare exceptions, policy entrepreneurs and advocates need to engage in serious, extended and highly strategic efforts to ensure that evidence is communicated in ways that make it publicly and politically compelling, so that inaction is not an option. Policy solutions need to be framed in ways that make their rejection problematic.'

Effective framing may involve ignoring and even denigrating other values. It is easy to get caught up in such processes. This leads on to a range of other issues, including when it is appropriate, and indeed essential, for researchers to take sides.

There is a potent interplay between transaction costs, potential compromises to integrity and the realities of political engagement, where even when researchers act with integrity, there is no guarantee that opponents will 'play fair'. These issues stem directly from understanding the complexities of achieving change which must be grappled with if research impact is to be more effectively achieved. Again there are no easy answers here, but the issues need to be recognised, discussed and managed.

Recognising diverse levels and forms of research impact

As outlined above, negotiating a dynamic change environment requires time, energy and different skills from those needed to undertake excellent research. There may also be unpleasant interactions with opponents, threats to funding and reputational traps. Add to this the vagaries of the process outlined earlier, including the unpredictability of outcomes and the subjectivity of success. Not surprisingly, while some researchers revel in the hurly-burly of a highly political engagement to drive change, for others this is anathema. It seems unreasonable, therefore, to require all researchers to conform to particular ways of achieving impact, and more sensible to validate a range of possibilities. The challenge then becomes how to document and assess numerous options in ways that acknowledge different inputs of time, energy, expertise and what might be called political capital.

As a starting point, three frameworks are presented to tease out key aspects of research impact and to illuminate its diverse levels and forms. They address:

- how research can have impact
- kinds of change
- where the research is targeted.

The frameworks were developed by combining insights from the preceding chapters and the symposium discussion with my previous work (Bammer, 2013). The aim is to give researchers and those assessing research impact a systematic way to describe what is being attempted and what has been achieved. An agreed systematic description is essential for effective evaluation, which is described in the next section. If the systematic approach looks useful, the next step will be to flesh out the frameworks, for instance, by testing them against a number of case examples.

How research can have impact

Research can have impact by informing, triggering or driving change (Figure 1). These require different skills and practices and also differ in terms of opportunity costs, transaction costs and potential challenges to integrity.

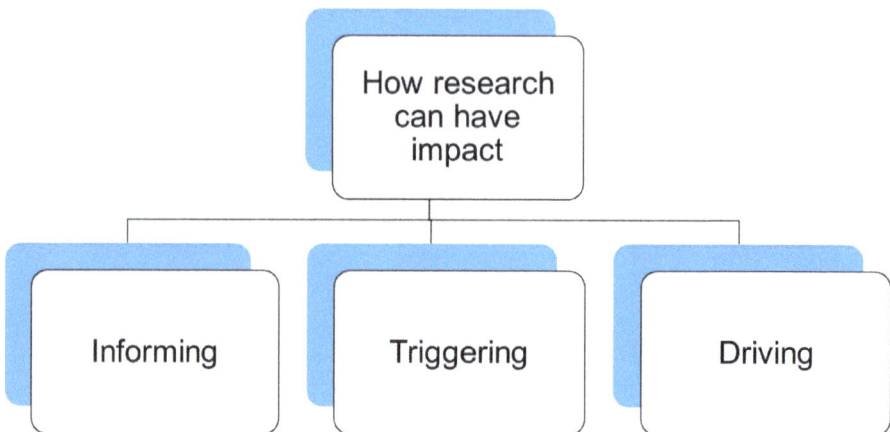

Figure 1 A framework for understanding and assessing how research can have impact.

Source: Author's illustration.

Informing change involves providing all or part of the evidence base for change, including illuminating options for change. To use a piece of the quotation from Simon Chapman presented earlier, this is largely 'a matter of presenting the best facts and evidence' and is probably the most common way in which researchers seek to achieve impact, although there is significant diversity in the sophistication of the framing used. An example is Robyn Gillies' chapter which makes a case for altering Australian government policy using, among other things, a review of evidence from overseas experience.

Triggering change occurs when the research provides a catalyst for change. Common forms of triggering are producing a breakthrough finding or idea, and agenda setting. A breakthrough finding is often the solution to an essential missing piece of a research puzzle that allows a body of evidence to be employed in real-world change. The work of John O'Sullivan and colleagues which contributed to the development of wi-fi is an example. They discovered the critical technology that allowed information to be sent over many different frequencies and recombined at the receiver.[5] A breakthrough idea generally provides an effective way forward on a recognised policy or practice issue. An illustration is Bruce Chapman's work on a loans scheme to fund higher education, where the breakthrough idea was that repayments would be contingent on income.[6] Agenda-setting usually involves concerted action to promote a neglected issue to bring it to the attention of those responsible for making change happen. The reports of the Intergovernmental Panel on Climate Change[7] provide an example.

Driving change results from investigation usually combined with direct liaison with those responsible for change, or actively concerned about it, including policymakers, business entrepreneurs or activists. The researchers may take an activist role themselves to promote implementation of their research findings. Often, research not only continues to accumulate evidence related to the change, but also evaluates changes which take place, investigates how to counter opposition and studies how to accommodate evolving circumstances. For example, research producing a new product such as a pharmaceutical or a machine is in itself generally not enough for commercial implementation. This may require ongoing negotiations with entrepreneurs or companies to demonstrate the potential of the product, overcoming vested interests who stand to lose market share if the product is introduced, and investigating tweaks to the product as problems emerge. Simon Chapman's chapter also provides an example of driving change, illustrating the research, interactions and actions involved

---

5 en.wikipedia.org/wiki/John_O%27Sullivan_%28engineer%29.
6 The original idea and other potential applications are briefly described in Bruce Chapman (2014) 'Financing the future', in the online magazine *Advance*: crawford.anu.edu.au/files/uploads/crawford01_cap_anu_edu_au/2014-12/summer_2014_advance_for_web.pdf.
7 www.ipcc.ch/.

in the introduction of plain packaging of tobacco products. That chapter also provides insight into how this activity fits into a longer term research and activism campaign for tobacco control. Driving change is most likely to have significant opportunity and transaction costs, as well as reputational risks.

Kinds of change

Different kinds of change may also have different costs and risks, as well as requiring different skills and techniques for achieving them. This framework aims to tease out the main categories of change relevant for thinking about research impact, which may be useful both in describing research impact and also in assessing it. Let us start by categorising two primary types of impact:

- making change happen
- responding to particular proposed or ongoing change.

Within each of these there are subcategories (see Figure 2).

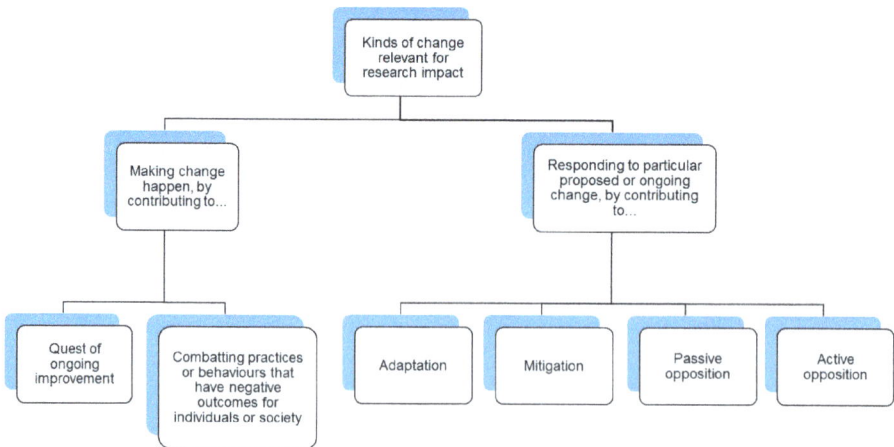

Figure 2 A framework for understanding and assessing kinds of change relevant for research impact.

Source: Author's illustration.

Two ways of making change happen that are important for research impact are 1) contributing to the ongoing quest for improvement and 2) combating practices or behaviours that have negative outcomes for individuals or society. Examples of contributing to the ongoing quest for improvement include technological research such as the development of wi-fi, and social research such as the development of an income-contingent loans scheme which aimed to provide accessibility to higher education in an environment where government provision of free higher education was no longer seen as sustainable.[8] Tobacco control research is an example of combating practices or behaviours with negative outcomes for individuals and society.

Responding to change involves reacting to change that is proposed (such as the introduction of a new tax or the construction of a new dam) or that is already ongoing (such as global environmental change or the spread of an infectious disease). It can be useful to tease out four types of response along with how these are relevant to understanding research impact.

First, adaptation involves adjusting to the consequences of proposed or ongoing change, and is illustrated by demographic research on population ageing which highlights the need for altered housing, transport and infrastructure that is suited to the elderly (as suggested in Peter McDonald's chapter).

Second, mitigation involves influencing the path of proposed or ongoing change to lessen likely negative outcomes. This can be exemplified by a different kind of demographic research, such as examining the potential effects of increasing migration or measures to increase the birthrate as strategies for a country concerned about low population growth (as suggested in Peter McDonald's chapter). Adaptation tends to be less controversial than mitigation.

Third, passive opposition[9] involves not complying with proposed or ongoing change. A hypothetical example would be research on how to avoid paying a new tax and its likely consequences for citizens and the government.

Finally, active opposition involves working to halt proposed or ongoing change. Examples include materials conservation research on ways to stop decay in museum artefacts (as suggested in Ian MacLeod's chapter) or anthropological research demonstrating the cultural value of a place scheduled to be destroyed by mining or other development (as suggested in Francesca Merlan's chapter).

Change can also be incremental, adaptive or transformational. Incremental change can be thought of as the tweaking of policies and practices over time in order, for example, to accommodate altered circumstances or respond to unintended consequences. Adaptive change or adaptive management, as described in Mark Stafford Smith's chapter, differs from incremental change in that it involves regular reassessment and retargeting in order to avoid triggering a change that cannot be recovered from. At the symposium Paul Griffiths (personal communication, 2013) provided a useful analogy likening incremental change to artillery fire, where each shot is followed by adjustments, depending on how close it got to the target.

---

8   See references to the work of John O'Sullivan and Bruce Chapman above.
9   Mitigation is differentiated from passive and active opposition here, but opposition could also be seen as a form of mitigation.

By contrast, adaptive management is like a game of pinball, where the aim is not only to strike targets but also to avoid falling into the drain, which ends the game. Transformational change involves a radical reformulation of policy or practice. Each of the six types of change presented in Figure 2 could be incremental or transformational, whereas adaptive management applies to responses to ongoing change—such as global environmental change—where moving outside a safe operating space is a real possibility.

Where the research is targeted

The arena which is the target for change will influence the skills and techniques required, as well as the costs and risks to be negotiated. Further, any effective description and assessment of change is predicated on understanding the target(s). First, as shown in Figure 3, the primary target may be one or more of government, business or civil society.[10] Second, the aim may be to affect policy, which can be usefully thought of as general guidelines and incentives influencing change, or it may be to affect practice, which is the actual implementation of measures to affect change. An example of research influencing government policy change is where demographic researchers advise governments to earmark funding to build more aged-care accommodation and help them figure out the proportions of different kinds of accommodation (e.g. independent living, assisted living and nursing care) to be funded. An example of research influencing civil society practice change is where public health researchers provide an online self-help program that citizens can use to tackle depression and anxiety.

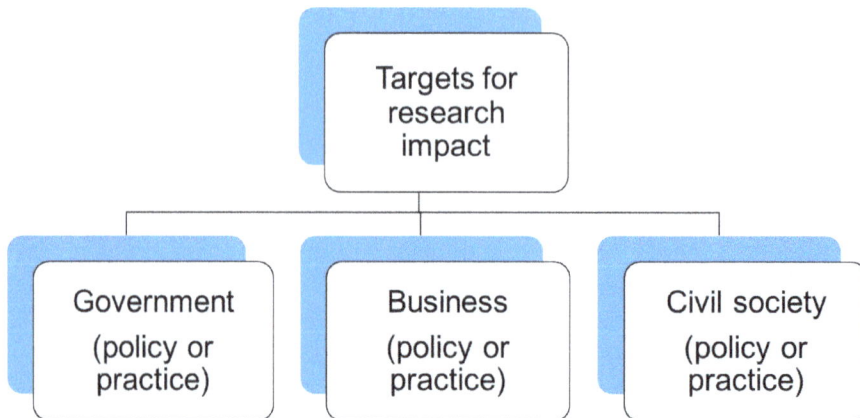

Figure 3 A framework for understanding and assessing targets for research impact.

Source: Author's illustration.

---

10   Civil society refers to non-government organisations including universities, as well as unorganised community groups such as residents of a particular area (such as a suburb affected by a toxic hazard) or sufferers of a specific disease (such as mesothelioma).

A new publication culture as the primary assessment structure

If researchers are to be validated in taking an array of stances in relation to research impact, from relatively little involvement to being highly active, this must also be reflected in the reward system. Here I am not going to review the substantial literature on the requirement for new reward structures, or existing and proposed schemes. Instead the focus is on one way of assessing impact which does not seem to have been given much formal consideration, namely developing a peer-reviewed publication culture (Bammer 2014). I argue that having assessment structured around publications can potentially encompass both diverse kinds of researcher engagement with impact and also the complexities of the dynamic change environment.

There are three additional advantages of using peer-reviewed publication as the cornerstone of describing and assessing research impact:

- Publication is already the main accepted way for researchers to report on their findings, allowing the findings to be distributed, shared and built on.
- Peer-review is already the main accepted way for research findings to be assessed.
- In the longer term, peer-reviewed publication could allow for the development of effective metrics for assessing research impact.

Currently, coming to grips with how researchers can effectively negotiate the complexities of the dynamic change environment is hampered by lack of reporting and analysis. Much experience—both successful and unsuccessful—goes undocumented and does not contribute to an overall fund of knowledge about achieving research impact. Instead, informal anecdotes are the main way researchers learn from each other about how to achieve and assess research impact. Only the most obvious successes are celebrated. A publication culture provides a platform for lessons to be shared.

In such publications, researchers engaged in driving change, for example, would describe what they set out to achieve, how they went about it, the context in which they operated along with the forces they encountered, what the outcomes were and, most importantly, the lessons learnt for the further development of theory and practice about attaining research impact. One consequence of the dynamic change environment is that what the researchers set out to achieve may be quite different from what they actually accomplished, so that highlighting both is an important aspect of publication.

A critical outcome of a publication culture is to build a body of theory and practice about attaining research impact. The aim is not to identify foolproof formulae, but rather general principles and transferable processes that can be adapted to specific contexts. The aim is for such a body of theory and practice to encompass and build on not only the diversity of ways of achieving research impact described in the previous section, but also the complexities of the dynamic change environment.

As is the case now, journals and books would be the key publication formats, but it is also worth thinking about how a publication culture could embrace effective use of social media. Encouraging documentation and publication and assisting this by providing useful and agreed frameworks for writing about research impact will make more readily available a rich picture of what researchers undertake and how they handle the complexities of the dynamic change environment.

If we focus on journals, it is possible to imagine eclectic generalist journals and focused specialised ones. In fact examples of the latter already exist and are growing in numbers. They include *Implementation Science* and *Science Translational Medicine*, to mention two in the health domain. Established journals are increasingly including papers about implementation. It is also possible to imagine journals specialising in various aspects of research impact, with one journal focusing on research communication, another on driving change, and yet another on informing government policy change. Such journals would be particularly useful in sharing lessons across areas, for example, by enabling population health researchers to trade lessons with environmental and security researchers on effective problem-framing or engagement with social media.

A publication culture also provides scope for innovation in how implementation is reported. It is possible to imagine, for example, an impact on policy being analysed not only through the eyes of the researchers involved, but also through those of the policymakers they targeted. Even more ambitiously, all the involved parties (lobbyists, opponents, special interest groups, and so on) could be invited to contribute, providing a 360 degree view. Better than anything else this would illustrate the complexities and competing interests involved.

Peer-review would be the main assessment tool, because those who have realised or attempted to achieve impact themselves are in the best position to assess the efforts of others. Peer-review can accommodate existing discipline and area differences, because like will assess like. For example, economists have a privileged place in affecting government policy, as there is a tradition of economic research being called on by government policymakers. Economists would therefore assess each other, but not those from other disciplines whose history of influence is different. Similarly, some areas, such as tobacco control, have a longer history of engagement with policy and practice change than others, such as obesity reduction. The standards by which tobacco control efforts are assessed would therefore be different from those for assessing obesity reduction efforts, with different kinds of peers involved in the assessment. For peer-review to work, appropriate colleges of peers must be established.

Peer-reviewed publications can not only accommodate different forms and levels of research impact, but can also allow more complex attempts at research impact to be recognised and rewarded. For example, extra kudos may be given to those who achieve or seek to achieve impact on problems which require engagement with several targets, who tackle complex problems with no clear solutions, or who work with problems embedded in a highly volatile context.

The kind of metrics that work for assessing research *findings* through publication should also work for assessing research *impact* through publication. However, because the publication culture for research impact is still in its infancy, it will take some time for these metrics to become established and effective. Importantly, if metrics for both findings and impact count, it should be possible to accommodate the diversity of researcher enthusiasm for engaging with research impact, by allowing publications on findings to be traded off against publications on impact. This would allow some researchers to be assessed primarily by their publications on findings, while others are assessed primarily by their publications on impact; and there are, of course, a range of options in between. Researchers can therefore be judged against their choices in terms of engaging with research impact, in other words, how effective they are for the choices they have made, not by some arbitrary gold standard.

Finally, let us review the challenges of establishing a peer-reviewed publication culture for assessing research impact. First, keeping on top of the literature is already a major challenge for most researchers and this proposal will only add to that burden. It may, however, give added impetus to the work of information scientists in improving cataloguing and search strategies. Second, the peer-review system is far from perfect. But (to adapt Winston Churchill's assessment of democracy), I suggest that 'no one pretends that peer-review is perfect or all-wise. Indeed … peer-review is the worst form of assessment except for all those other forms that have been tried from time to time'[11]. Certainly there is work to be done in developing effective—and realistic—criteria for peer review of research impact.

---

11   In a speech to the House of Commons on 11 November 1947, Churchill described democracy thus: 'Many forms of Government have been tried, and will be tried in this world of sin and woe. No one pretends that democracy is perfect or all-wise. Indeed, it has been said that democracy is the worst form of Government except for all those other forms that have been tried from time to time.' From *Churchill speaks: collected speeches in peace and war, 1897–1963*, Chelsea House, London (1983), source www.goodreads.com/work/quotes/1716637-churchill-speaks-1897-1963-collected-speeches-in-peace-war, accessed 28 February 2015.

There are several other challenges relevant not just to establishing a peer-reviewed publication culture, but for all ways of assessing research impact. Recognising and documenting them is a first step to developing effective ways of dealing with them.

The first is allocation of credit. As we have seen in some of the chapters and in the analysis of the dynamic change environment, researchers play one role among many. In a change to government policy, for example, critical roles may also be played by the relevant minister and other politicians; various public servants; specific reporters, editors and owners in the media; and particular members of lobby groups. Teasing out the relative value of each of these contributions is impossible because their effects are neither additive nor independent.

A second challenge is that at least some change is most effective when no public credit is taken. Ian MacLeod (personal communication, 2013) provided an example in the symposium discussion [identifiers have been removed]:

> My work on [Indigenous] rock art showed there was massive acidification. I was concerned about it. I got a briefing with the minister. When the minister heard about it she was alarmed and she said, 'Well, are you going to leak it to the media?' and I said, 'No minister, of course not,' and she said, 'I'll organise a briefing with [company]'. So I briefed [company], they didn't like what I said. They analysed the data and then they spent four and a half million dollars rapidly introducing different types of burners, and they reduced their NO_x[12] emissions by a factor of six times and then nothing was said. It didn't come out in the media, only you around here know it and the ministers involved, but see there are other ways of bringing about change, because all I was concerned was with the fate of the rock art. I didn't mind how I got the change done, but the change was managed that way and so it was hair-raising but good.

A third challenge is assessing partial success and failure. How should we evaluate a good process that produced no outcomes, for example because political circumstances changed? What about research that produced successful change but also led to major unintended adverse consequences? What credit should be given to impact primarily produced by luck rather than a good process or good research findings? What about the successful uptake of research findings that result from poorly designed studies or that have been incorrectly interpreted? A way through such dilemmas needs to be found, so that rewards are appropriate and researchers are not dissuaded from attempting to achieve research impact.

---

12 NO_x is a generic term for the mono-nitrogen oxides NO (nitric oxide) and NO_2 (nitrogen dioxide).

In this section I have laid out a specific proposal that would allow research impact to be more effectively described and assessed. It builds on the dominant peer-reviewed publication culture for describing, distributing and evaluating research findings, as well as existing trends evidenced by the growth of journals specialised on impact in particular areas. There are major challenges. No system to measure research impact will be problem-free and this applies to existing and mooted schemes. A peer-reviewed publication culture will also not provide a perfect solution, but it may be good enough.

Conclusion

This chapter seeks to provide fresh thinking about research impact by approaching it through a new consideration, namely that research impact involves a process of negotiating a dynamic change environment. The multidisciplinary author perspectives in this book's chapters and the symposium discussion illustrate the complexities encompassed by change. In turn, the complexities underpin three topics that have been largely neglected to date, each of which is also illustrated by the chapters and discussion. For achievement and assessment of research impact to become core research activities, effective ways must be found to address the associated opportunity and transaction costs, as well as potential challenges to research integrity.

It must be possible for researchers to choose greater or lesser involvement with achieving research impact. Reward systems need to be flexible enough to accommodate and validate this range of choices. An essential requirement is effective ways to describe different kinds of research impact and a start is made here by proposing frameworks for three primary ways that research can have impact, for different kinds of change and for different targets. A proposal is also made for how a peer-reviewed publication culture about research impact could provide an effective basis for assessment.

To round this chapter off, it is worth asking some big questions. There is no doubt that change should be informed by research evidence. But how much should the whole research enterprise move beyond discovery to implementation? Political engagement which is fundamental to much of the achievement of research impact is at odds with the rational detachment required of researchers (see also Gadlin and Bennett, 2013). If researchers are not to be the main players in achieving research impact, then who? If (some) researchers are to be the main players, how can they best be supported and rewarded?

References

Bammer, G (2013) *Disciplining interdisciplinarity: integration and implementation sciences for researching complex real-world problems*. ANU E Press, Canberra. http://press.anu.edu.au?p=222171.

Bammer, G (2014) Studying the effects of studies. *Australian Financial Review* (Education Section), 17 February: 35.

Gadlin, H and Bennett, LM (2013) Interdisciplinarity without borders. Commentary in Bammer, G *Disciplining interdisciplinarity: integration and implementation sciences for researching complex real-world problems*. ANU E Press, Canberra. http://press.anu.edu.au?p=222171.

Marx, K (1977, originally published in 1852) The eighteenth Brumaire of Louis Napoleon. In D McLellan, ed. *Karl Marx: selected writings*. Oxford University Press, Oxford: 300–25.

Appendix: Multidisciplinary research and Integration and Implementation Sciences

This chapter has provided an example of how multidisciplinary research can be synthesised. In this appendix I review the strengths and weaknesses of multidisciplinary research and provide a brief overview of Integration and Implementation Sciences (I2S), which has underpinned my approach to organising this project.

Multidisciplinary research and its synthesis

As described in Chapter 1, the approach used in this book is multidisciplinary. Every contributor tackled the issue of change as they saw fit. There was no attempt to start with a shared framework or a common specific aspect of change. A multidisciplinary approach therefore allows the richness of different perspectives to be demonstrated.

Another strength of a multidisciplinary approach is that these perspectives can be combined in many different ways. Anyone can tailor-make their own synthesis by selecting the points that are meaningful and useful to deepen their understanding of change-related issues that concern them. In this chapter I have tailor-made a synthesis around my interest in research impact. In Chapter 1 I also flagged a longer term interest in using the perspectives in this book to start a process for providing general principles to guide thinking about change, and a roadmap to the specific approaches to change of different disciplines and practice areas. Others could use the same material for different syntheses, such as developing a toolbox of novel strategies for responding to escalating health care costs or examining similarities and differences in leading change at international, national and local levels.

A multidisciplinary approach is most useful in two situations. One is in dealing with projects that are broad and relatively unconstrained, rather than those which have a specific focus. Two of the earlier examples are relevant: developing general principles to guide thinking about change and a roadmap to specific disciplinary and practice interests, as well as examining change at international, national and local levels. The second is when attempting to move thinking on a topic away from conventional lines, and to generate fresh approaches. This is the purpose in this chapter on research impact and would, for example, also be the case when developing a toolbox of novel strategies for responding to escalating health care costs.

There are diverse ways in which synthesis can be undertaken. As mentioned in the examples above, individuals who are readers of the contributed perspectives can do the synthesis, or it can be a group process. Synthesis can also be undertaken by the contributors themselves: the whole group, a subgroup, or an individual contributor. As in this project, the synthesis can also be undertaken by the organiser, with the written contributions embellished by a gathering of the authors in a symposium. Individual synthesisers will generally build on pre-existing expertise or interest. Group synthesisers will usually add to this by using dialogue to draw together and build on their members' expertise and reflections on the contributed perspectives; this can involve formal dialogue methods, informal processes, or a combination of these.

The strengths of a multidisciplinary approach also contain the seeds of its weaknesses. The main challenge with multidisciplinary research comes in synthesising the contributions, as it is not certain what the points of intersection will be with the interests of the person undertaking the synthesis, or even if there will be any. Synthesis requires considerable, time-consuming sifting of the material. Care must also be taken in interpretation, especially when points of interest to the synthesiser are relevant in a different context from that in which they were presented by the contributor.

Other challenges in multidisciplinary research are common to all research involving multiple perspectives. In particular, the value of the disciplinary and practice perspectives is greatly dependent on the expertise of the contributors. And the choice of contributors relies on the skills of the project leader or organiser.

To round off this discussion, let us briefly compare multidisciplinary research with interdisciplinary and transdisciplinary research (I will not differentiate between the latter two here). In interdisciplinary and transdisciplinary research, the project commences by establishing a shared focus, and often also a common framework, for working together. This necessarily and deliberately limits which perspectives are brought to bear and the approach they take. Rather than the wide-ranging treatments of a topic found in multidisciplinary research, the disciplinary and practice perspectives in interdisciplinary and transdisciplinary research are directed to the agreed shared focus of the overall project. Synthesis of these perspectives is then much more straightforward, because the focus for it is established when the project commences. Each approach—multidisciplinary, interdisciplinary and transdisciplinary—therefore has advantages and disadvantages. It is important to choose the approach most suitable for the project at hand.

This appendix concludes with a brief introduction to I2S, which has motivated my interest in change. I2S supports multidisciplinary, interdisciplinary and transdisciplinary research.

Introducing Integration and Implementation Sciences

My role in the project is as a specialist in the emerging discipline of I2S. The primary focus of I2S is to improve research contributions to tackling complex problems like global environmental change, organised crime and escalating health care costs. To this end, I2S is developing a repository of methods and concepts, along with illustrative case examples, that researchers can draw on.

A core component of I2S is to provide (and continue to develop) tools that researchers can use to contribute to policy and practice improvements in how complex problems are responded to. These include understanding how relevant policy and practice arenas operate and where research inputs fit, as well as practical ways of communicating and engaging with policymakers and practitioners.

I2S also recognises that the strength of the evidence is critical. For complex real world problems this requires synthesis of knowledge from all the relevant disciplines and practice areas. I2S tools include methods for determining which perspectives are most useful, as well as for synthesising them. But implementing research based only on the best available evidence is not enough; due consideration must also be given to what is not known. Ignoring unknowns can lead to unpleasant surprises and unintended adverse consequences, and I2S provides tools for mitigating these problems.

Providing research support for policy and practice change, synthesising knowledge, and understanding and managing diverse unknowns are the three domains of I2S. Each domain is structured around a five question framework which provides a systematic approach to organising the repository of methods, concepts and case studies. A detailed description of I2S can be found in Bammer (2013).

The novel aspects of I2S are:

1. the three domains and five-question framework, which aim to provide an effective and efficient way of gathering and organising widely dispersed concepts and methods relevant to tackling complex real-world problems

2. thinking of integration as bringing together both what is known and what is not known about the problem of interest (rather than only synthesising knowledge) to support policy and practice change

3. taking on the job which is currently no one's business, that of drawing together knowledge about change, so that it is better understood and managed, particularly by researchers contributing to tackling complex problems

4. arguing for a new discipline and for including this disciplinary expertise in teams seeking to have research impact on complex real-world problems.

I2S therefore aims to contribute to strengthening research impact in multiple ways: by providing a one-stop shop for methods and concepts for achieving research impact, as well as illustrative case studies; by providing ways to deal with unknowns, especially as triggers to unintended consequences; and by highlighting the importance of understanding change and, in the longer term, providing general principles to guide thinking about change, and a roadmap to the specific issues covered by different disciplines and practice areas.

Integration of the change symposium participants.

Source: Frank Thirion, 2013, amalgamating individual photographs taken by John Reid, 2013.

Contributors

Gabriele Bammer

Gabriele Bammer is developing the new discipline of Integration and Implementation Sciences to improve research strengths for tackling complex real-world problems through synthesis of disciplinary and stakeholder knowledge, understanding and managing diverse unknowns and providing integrated research support for policy and practice change (see i2s.anu.edu.au). This is described in *Disciplining interdisciplinarity: Integration and Implementation Sciences for researching complex real-world problems* (ANU E Press 2013). Between 2011 and 2013 she was Director of the Research School of Population Health, Director of the National Centre for Epidemiology and Population Health and co-Director and then Director of the Australian Primary Health Care Research Institute at The Australian National University (ANU). She is an ANU Public Policy Fellow, an inaugural Fulbright New Century Scholar alumna and has held visiting appointments at Harvard University's John F. Kennedy School of Government (2002–2014), ETH-Zurich and the Universitaet fuer Bodenkultur in Vienna. From 2007–2013 she was the convenor of the Australian Research Council Centre of Excellence in Policing and Security's Integration and Implementation research program.

Lindell Bromham

Lindell Bromham is a professor in the Centre for Macroevolution and Macroecology, Research School of Biology at The Australian National University. She is an evolutionary biologist whose research primarily focuses on the way that we can use analysis of DNA sequence data to understand evolutionary past and processes. She applies comparative analyses to processes of evolutionary change spanning timescales from the beginnings of the animal kingdom half a billion years ago to the emergence of new viral diseases. She established the ANU cross-disciplinary research network Tempo and Mode to bring together disparate perspectives on large-scale evolutionary patterns and processes (tempoandmode.com), and is the author of *Reading the story in DNA: A beginner's guide to molecular evolution* (2008) and *An introduction to molecular evolution and phylogenetics* (forthcoming, 2016), both with Oxford University Press..

Craig Browne

Craig Browne is a senior lecturer in the Department of Sociology and Social Policy, University of Sydney. He is currently co-editor of *Theory*, the newsletter of the International Sociological Association Research Committee on Sociological Theory RC 16, and a Vice-President of the

International Sociological Association Research Committee on Concepts and Terminology RC 35. His recent publications include the book *Violence in France and Australia—Disorder in the postcolonial welfare state* and (in the journal *Revue de Internationale Philosophie*) Postmodernism, ideology and rationality. The perspective that he is developing on social change is related to his book projects, which include *Critical social theory* (Sage) and *Habermas and Giddens on modernity: A constructive comparison* (Anthem Press).

Jim Butler

Jim Butler has a PhD in economics from the University of Queensland and more than 35 years research and consulting experience in health economics. Until recently he was Director of the now defunct Australian Centre for Economic Research on Health. He has been a Wiener Fellow at Harvard University and Visiting Associate Professor at the University of Pennsylvania. His consulting experience includes projects for numerous public and private sector organisations in Australia and overseas, including the World Bank, AusAid, the Asia-Pacific Economic Cooperation (APEC) Business Advisory Council, and the Office of Health Economics (London UK). He has also been a member of advisory boards for global pharmaceutical companies. His research interests include health insurance, health care financing, hospitals costs and health technology assessment/economic evaluation. He has been a member of the Australian Government's Medical Services Advisory Committee (MSAC), which advises the Minister for Health and Ageing on evidence relating to the safety, effectiveness and cost-effectiveness of new medical technologies and procedures. This advice informs Australian Government decisions about public funding of these services. He was also Chair of MSAC's Evaluation Sub-Committee. From 2012 to 2015 he was Chair of the Australian Government's Advisory Council on Intellectual Property.

Kate Carnell

Kate Carnell AO was appointed Chief Executive Officer (CEO) at the Australian Chamber of Commerce and Industry in 2014. Before that she was CEO of beyondblue, a national, independent, not-for-profit organisation working to address issues associated with depression and anxiety. Previously, she was CEO of the Australian Food and Grocery Council and of the Australian General Practice Network and is a pharmacist by profession. She was elected to the ACT Legislative Assembly in 1992 and was elected Chief Minister in March 1995 and re-elected in 1998, serving until 2000. Kate was appointed an Officer of the Order of Australia in 2006 for her services to community through contributions to economic development and the medical sector.

Simon Chapman

Simon Chapman AO PhD FASSA is a professor in the School of Public Health, University of Sydney. He has published 500 articles in peer reviewed journals and 19 books and reports. His h-index is 51 (lifetime citations 9,400). His *Public health advocacy and tobacco control: Making smoking history* was published by Blackwell (Oxford) in 2007 and his co-authored *Let sleeping dogs lie: What men should know before being tested for prostate cancer* by Sydney University Press in 2010. In 1997 he won the World Health Organization's World No Tobacco Day Medal and in 2003 he was voted by his international peers to be awarded the American Cancer Society's Luther Terry Award for outstanding individual leadership in tobacco control. In 2008 he won the NSW Premier's Cancer Researcher of the Year medal; the Public Health Association of Australia's Sidney Sax medal; and was a NSW finalist in Australian of the Year. He was deputy editor (1992–1997), then editor (1998–2008) of the British Medical Journal's *Tobacco Control* and is now its editor emeritus. His current research involves examining how health issues are covered in news media; characteristics of public health research (and its dissemination) which impact on public health policy; and the natural history of unassisted smoking cessation.

Robyn M Gillies

Robyn Gillies is a professor of education at the University of Queensland. She has worked extensively in primary and secondary schools on a number of Australian Research Council projects designed to help teachers embed student-centred pedagogical practices into their classroom curricula to promote student engagement, problem-solving, and learning. Her research interests include inquiry learning in science and mathematics, supporting teachers to improve children's reading achievements in rural communities, student-centred pedagogical practices in the learning sciences, and improving school engagement for socially disengaged youth. She is the author of five books and over 150 journal articles and book chapters. In 2006 she was the recipient of an Outstanding Contribution Award presented by the American Educational Research Association and in 2010 she received an Achievement Award for Outstanding Contributions to Research from the International Association for the Study of Cooperation in Education, United States.

Paul Griffiths

A philosopher of science with a focus on biology and psychology, Paul Griffiths was educated at the University of Cambridge and The Australian National University, receiving his doctorate from ANU in 1989. After teaching in Australia and New Zealand, he moved to the University of Pittsburgh in 2000, returning to Australia in 2004 as an Australian Research Council Federation Fellow. Currently he is based at the University of Sydney where he is University

Professorial Research Fellow in the Department of Philosophy and Associate Academic Director for Humanities and Social Sciences at the Charles Perkins Centre, a multidisciplinary research institute of University of Sydney focused on obesity, diabetes and cardiovascular disease. He is also a visiting professor in the Economic and Social Research Council Centre for Genomics in Society at the University of Exeter, UK. He is a Fellow of the American Association for the Advancement of Science, Fellow of the Australian Academy of the Humanities, President of the International Society for History, Philosophy and Social Studies of Biology, and from 2006–2012 was a member of the Australian Health Ethics Committee of the National Health and Medical Research Council. His latest book, with Karola Stotz, is *Genetics and philosophy: An introduction*.

Ian D MacLeod

Ian MacLeod is Executive Director of Fremantle Museums and Collections at the Western Australian Museum. He is a corrosion chemist and materials conservator with a passion for decay. He studied at the University of Melbourne for his PhD; then research positions at the University of Glasgow and Murdoch University in Perth, Australia prepared him for the transition to studying decay of metals on historic shipwrecks with the Western Australian Museum. Applied electrochemistry has helped him develop new techniques for conserving museum collections including the use of in-situ corrosion measurements on historic shipwrecks, with particular emphasis on the use of sacrificial anodes to preserve materials on the seabed. His studies on the Japanese shipwrecks from World War II in Chuuk (Truk) lagoon in the Federated States of Micronesia have provided the government with data on the decay rates of the wrecks. At the Getty Conservation Institute he worked on preparing detailed notes for a book on the *Conservation of shipwrecks: Sites and artefacts*.

Dee Madigan

Dee Madigan is an advertising Creative Director with over 20 years' experience working in the industry. As well as campaigns for some of the world's biggest brands including HSBC, Diet Coke, J&J and Rexona and Nestle, Dee is a social marketing expert and was Creative Director for the Australian Labor Party for the 2013 Federal election and for the 2015 Queensland State election. She is a political commentator on both Sky and the ABC and is author of *The Hard Sell*, a book on political advertising. She runs her own ad agency, Campaign Edge.

Peter McDonald

Peter McDonald AM is a professor at the Crawford School of Public Policy at The Australian National University. He was President of the International Union for the Scientific Study of Population for the years 2010–2013 and is a Member of the Council of Advisers of Population Europe. He is frequently consulted on the issue of population futures (causes, consequences and policies) by governments around the world, especially in Australia, Europe and East Asia. In 2008, he was appointed as a Member in the Order of Australia. He is Deputy Director of the Australian Research Council Centre of Excellence in Population Ageing Research. He was appointed as an inaugural ANU Public Policy Fellow. He has worked previously at the Australian Institute of Family Studies, the World Fertility Survey and the University of Indonesia. In 2015, he was awarded the prestigious Irene B Taeuber Award by the Population Association of America.

Francesca Merlan

Francesca Merlan, previously at Sydney University, has been Professor of Anthropology in the School of Archaeology and Anthropology at The Australian National University since late 1995. She has conducted field research, essentially on questions of change and articulations across fields of social and cultural difference, in northern Australia, in Papua New Guinea, and in southern Germany—in all three places, with a focus on transformations in people's lives associated with shifts in their relationships to place and place-based livelihood. She is currently working on a book on the topic of encounters between Indigenous and non-Indigenous people at different points in time from early colonial arrival to the present of her field research in northern Australia.

Christine Nixon

Christine Nixon APM was Chair of the Victorian Bushfire Reconstruction and Recovery Authority from February 2009 to September 2010. Prior to joining the Authority, Christine was the 19th Chief Commissioner of Victoria Police leading 14 000 staff. She joined Victoria Police in April 2001, after serving with the New South Wales Police from 1972 and attaining the rank of Assistant Commissioner. Christine is a Fellow of the Australian and New Zealand School of Government, the Australian Institute of Police Management, the Australian Institute of Management and the Institute of Public Administration Australia. She is also a member of the Monash University Council, Chair of Good Shepherd Microfinance and Monash College Pty Ltd. Currently she lectures with the Australian and New Zealand School of Government in various courses including leading a workshop on Women in Leadership—Achieving and Flourishing. She also runs her own Women Leading Change workshops (christinenixon. com.au). She mentors and advises various organisations on leadership and organisational reform.

Sarah Pearson

Sarah Pearson is an internationally experienced Open Innovation practitioner and advocate for collaborative innovation in Australia. She drives innovation strategy and practice in both corporate and government arenas, and is passionate about helping Australia benefit from this effective and efficient approach in both industrial and social innovation applications. She is currently Chief Executive Officer of the CBR Innovation Network, an entity set up to transform the Australian Capital Territory economy through innovation and entrepreneurship. She is also a Board Director on seven boards covering manufacturing, industry peak bodies, social innovation, angel investment and STEM (science, technology, engineering and mathematics) support. Sarah's eclectic career has spanned industrial innovation, academia, management consulting, government, and science communication, from the University of Oxford, to McKinsey, Cadbury and The Australian National University. Sarah has also published extensively through the media of TV, radio, books, academic journals, magazines and newspapers, and is an author on eight international patents for cancer diagnosis and novel confectionery.

Beverley Raphael

Beverley Raphael AM, MBBS, MD (Syd), FRANZCP, FRCPsych, Hon MD (Newc), FASSA is Emeritus Professor of Psychiatry at the University of Queensland, Professor of Psychological & Addiction Medicine at The Australian National University and Professor of Population Mental Health and Disasters at the University of Western Sydney. She has had extensive experience in the development of disaster mental health in Australia and internationally. She has also been involved in research, policy and program development for children's mental health including promotion, prevention and early intervention, as well as mental health research and policy more broadly. She is Chair of the Australian Child and Adolescent Trauma and Loss Grief Network (funded by the Australian Government). She has extensive research experience in children's mental health and has research programs in this field at ANU and the University of Western Sydney. She provides consultation and advice to the Australian Government Child Mental Health Forum, KidsMatter, and other bodies. She is the author of numerous publications relevant to this field.

John Reid

John Reid is an Emeritus Fellow of The Australian National University and a Visiting Fellow in both the School of Art and the Fenner School of Environment and Society at ANU. He is a visual artist, teacher and pedagogic researcher. As an artist he works with the media of photography, collage and performance. The environment and human rights are the enduring themes of his artwork. As a teacher, he is a convenor of the School of Art Environment Studio Field

Study program that provides students with field research opportunities for fine art production. His research is concerned with procedures for artist engagement with scientists and community leaders to create aesthetic visual material that enhances community deliberation of values that are fundamental to the development of public policy.

Mark Stafford Smith

Mark Stafford Smith coordinates climate adaptation research in CSIRO in Australia; in this role he has been oversighting a highly interdisciplinary program of research on many aspects of adapting to climate change, as well as regularly interacting with national and international policy issues. He has over 30 years' experience in drylands systems ecology, management and policy, including senior roles such as Chief Executive Officer of the Desert Knowledge Cooperative Research Centre in the early 2000s, and Program Leader of the CSIRO Centre for Arid Zone Research in Alice Springs in the late 1990s. His significant international roles include being past vice-chair of the International Geosphere-Biosphere Programme's Scientific Committee, and co-chair of the Planet Under Pressure: New Knowledge towards Solutions international global change conference in London in 2012 in the lead-up to Rio+20. In 2013 he was appointed chair of the inaugural Science Committee of the Future Earth platform for coordinating research on global environmental change. He continues to actively publish, adding to over 160 peer-reviewed contributions to science, as well as many presentations and publications for less specialised audiences.

Grant Wardlaw

Grant Wardlaw RFD has held senior executive positions in crime intelligence, research and policy organisations, including being Senior Fellow, Australian Research Council Centre of Excellence in Policing and Security, National Manager Intelligence in the Australian Federal Police, National Director Criminal Intelligence in the Australian Crime Commission, Executive Director of the Australian Bureau of Criminal Intelligence, Director of the Commonwealth Government's Office of Strategic Crime Assessments and Acting Director of the Australian Institute of Criminology. He is currently a visiting fellow at The Australian National University. Grant has postgraduate qualifications in psychology, international relations and international law and is a Fellow of the Australian Institute of Management. He has consulted internationally and published widely in the fields of terrorism, illicit drug policy and law enforcement intelligence and is the author of *Political terrorism: Theory, tactics and countermeasures* (Cambridge University Press).

Michael Wesley

Michael Wesley is Director of the Coral Bell School of Asia Pacific Affairs and Professor of International Affairs at The Australian National University. His career has spanned academia, with previous appointments at the University of New South Wales, Griffith University, the University of Hong Kong, Sun Yat-sen University and the University of Sydney; government, where he worked as Assistant Director General for Transnational Issues at the Office of National Assessments; and think tanks, in which he was Executive Director of the Lowy Institute for International Policy and a Non-Resident Senior Fellow at the Brookings Institution. Michael has also served as the Editor in Chief of the *Australian Journal of International Affairs*, a Trustee of the Queensland Art Gallery and a Board Member of the Australia Television Network. His most recent book, *There goes the neighbourhood: Australia and the rise of Asia*, won the 2011 John Button Prize for the best writing on Australian public policy.

www.ingramcontent.com/pod-product-compliance
Lightning Source LLC
Chambersburg PA
CBHW061242270326
41928CB00041B/3368